WITHDRAWN

# Critical Essays on
# Margaret Fuller

# Critical Essays on
# Margaret Fuller

## Joel Myerson

G. K. Hall & Co. • Boston, Massachusetts

Copyright © 1980 by Joel Myerson

---

*Library of Congress Cataloging in Publication Data*
Main entry under title:

Critical essays on Margaret Fuller.

  (Critical essays on American literature)
  Bibliography:
  Includes index.
  1. Ossoli, Sarah Margaret Fuller, marchesa d',1810–1850—Criticism and interpretation—Addresses, essays, lectures.  I. Myerson, Joel.  II. Series.
PS2507.C7    818'.3'09    79-17244
ISBN 0-8161-8283-3

---

*This publication is printed on permanent/durable acid-free paper*
MANUFACTURED IN THE UNITED STATES OF AMERICA

# CRITICAL ESSAYS ON AMERICAN LITERATURE

This series seeks to publish the most important reprinted criticism on writers and topics in American literature along with, in various volumes, original essays, interviews, bibliographies, letters, manuscript sections, and other materials brought to public attention for the first time. Joel Myerson's volume on Margaret Fuller represents the most substantial collection of scholarship on this writer ever published. In addition to reprinted reviews and essays, it contains an important overview of scholarship by Myerson and an important new essay on Fuller's *Woman in the Nineteenth Century* by Marie Oleson Urbanski. We are confident that this collection will make a permanent and significant contribution to American literary scholarship.

JAMES NAGEL, GENERAL EDITOR

*Northeastern University*

# CONTENTS

| | |
|---|---|
| Introduction | vii |
| William J. Pabodie, "The Dial" | 1 |
| James Freeman Clarke, [*Summer on the Lakes*] | 2 |
| Caleb Stetson, [*Summer on the Lakes*] | 3 |
| Orestes A. Brownson, [*Summer on the Lakes*] | 5 |
| Lydia Maria Child, "Woman in the Nineteenth Century" | 7 |
| Charles F. Briggs, [*Woman in the Nineteenth Century*] | 8 |
| Anonymous, [*Woman in the Nineteenth Century*] | 16 |
| Orestes A. Brownson, "Miss Fuller and Reformers" | 19 |
| Frederic Dan Huntington, [*Woman in the Nineteenth Century*] | 26 |
| Charles Lane, [*Woman in the Nineteenth Century*] | 28 |
| Rufus Wilmot Griswold, [Margaret Fuller] | 32 |
| Edgar Allan Poe, "Sarah Margaret Fuller" | 35 |
| Anonymous, "*Miss Fuller's Papers on Literature and Art*" | 40 |
| Anonymous, "Modern English Poets" | 46 |
| Anonymous, [*Papers on Literature and Art*] | 53 |
| Anonymous, [*Papers on Literature and Art*] | 56 |
| Anonymous, [*Papers on Literature and Art*] | 57 |
| Frederic Henry Hedge, [*Papers on Literature and Art*] | 62 |
| Rufus Wilmot Griswold, [Margaret Fuller] | 63 |
| James Russell Lowell, ["Miranda"] | 64 |
| James Russell Lowell, "Studies for Two Heads. I." | 66 |
| Charles Mayo Ellis, [*Memoirs of Margaret Fuller Ossoli*] | 68 |
| Anonymous, "Memoirs of Margaret Fuller" | 70 |
| Anonymous, "Memoirs of Margaret Fuller Ossoli" | 73 |
| Anonymous, "Memoirs of Sarah Margaret Fuller" | 81 |
| Anonymous, "Vanity *versus* Philosophy. Margaret Fuller Ossoli" | 89 |
| Émile Montégut, "Margaret Fuller Ossoli" | 92 |
| Matthew Arnold, [Margaret Fuller] | 96 |
| Anonymous, [*Memoirs of Margaret Fuller Ossoli*] | 97 |
| Caroline Healey Dall, "Margaret Fuller Ossoli" | 102 |
| A. Bronson Alcott, "Margaret Fuller" | 110 |
| Harriet Martineau, [Margaret Fuller] | 112 |

| | |
|---|---|
| Julian Hawthorne, [Margaret Fuller and Hawthorne] | 114 |
| Frederick T. Fuller, "Hawthorne and Margaret Fuller Ossoli" | 117 |
| Julian Hawthorne, "Mr. Hawthorne and His Critics" | 129 |
| Henry James, [Margaret Fuller] | 131 |
| Anonymous, "The Real Margaret Fuller" | 133 |
| Harriet Hall Johnson, "Margaret Fuller as Known by her Scholars" | 134 |
| O. W. Firkins, [Margaret Fuller and Emerson] | 141 |
| Vernon Louis Parrington, "Margaret Fuller, Rebel" | 143 |
| Granville Hicks, "A Conversation in Boston" | 150 |
| Harry R. Warfel, "Margaret Fuller and Ralph Waldo Emerson" | 161 |
| Oscar Cargill, "Nemesis and Nathaniel Hawthorne" | 178 |
| Austin Warren, "Hawthorne, Margaret Fuller, and 'Nemesis'" | 192 |
| Arthur R. Schultz, "Margaret Fuller—Transcendentalist Interpreter of German Literature" | 195 |
| Roland Crozier Burton, "Margaret Fuller's Criticism of the Fine Arts" | 209 |
| Wilma R. Ebbitt, "Margaret Fuller's Ideas on Criticism" | 216 |
| Henry A. Pochmann, [Margaret Fuller and Germany] | 228 |
| Francis E. Kearns, "Margaret Fuller and the Abolition Movement" | 247 |
| Martin Duberman, [Fuller and Lowell's *A Fable for Critics*] | 255 |
| Margaret V. Allen, "'This Impassioned Yankee': Margaret Fuller's Writing Revisited" | 257 |
| Madeleine B. Stern, "A Biographer's View of Margaret Fuller" | 264 |
| Marie Olesen Urbanski, "The Genesis, Form, Tone, and Rhetorical Devices of *Woman in the Nineteenth Century*" | 268 |
| Index | 281 |

# INTRODUCTION

Critical commentary on Margaret Fuller has always been marked by a degree of personalism, for few writers have been able to judge Fuller's works without bringing in her personality as well. In contemporary reviews of her works she is portrayed as a perceptive and astringent critic of American life and letters, while at the same time she is criticized for arguing feminism and being a Transcendentalist. Recent criticism, too, seems unable to avoid bringing in biography and the opportunity to discuss her admittedly colorful life.

Realizing that her position in life would have been different and much higher had she been a man, Fuller from youth concentrated on cultivating her mental powers and competing with men on purely intellectual terms. The pattern of her life—from prodigy to author to revolutionary—is not only intrinsically interesting, but also influenced the lives of those who knew her. Horace Greeley, Nathaniel Hawthorne, Henry David Thoreau, and especially Ralph Waldo Emerson, whose usually defensive reserves she tried to break down, were all affected by her during important phases of their lives. Fuller's personality and what happened when she came in conflict with the restraints of the time are of interest to all students of American literature and the history of women in America. This interest is reflected in the large body of criticism written about Fuller.

Early studies of Fuller examined the woman, not the writer. The 1852 *Memoirs of Margaret Fuller Ossoli* portrayed Fuller as a self-centered and aloof person, a picture that Thomas Wentworth Higginson tried to balance in his 1884 biography. In this reaction to her life by contemporaries and later writers, one can trace the history of woman's position in America: as woman's role became less confining, the less traditional aspects of Fuller's life—her individualism, her agressive intellectuality, her romantic liason with her future husband Ossoli—became more acceptable. More recent studies have centered on her feminist positions, her interest in continental—and especially German—literatures, and her critical writings.

In choosing the contents for *Critical Essays on Margaret Fuller*, I have tried to select a series of works that would accurately reflect criticism on Fuller from 1840 to the present. Because every book-length study of Fuller is in print and readily available in libraries, I have decided not to reprint sections from these books, preferring instead to make available less accessible works of equal quality. I have also avoided the "standard" works, such as Higginson's biography or the *Memoirs*, because they are easily found and because they have already been quoted at length in other books on Fuller. This volume, then, complements the book-length publications on Fuller already available with essays that have not been, in nearly every case, reprinted.

William J. Pabodie's review of the first number of the *Dial* in July 1840 shows that, from the start, critics reviewed Fuller more often than they did her works. The three reviews of *Summer on the Lakes, in 1843* show the varied reactions of men who knew her: James Freeman Clarke, a friend, praises the book; Caleb Stetson, an acquaintance, writes a mixed review; and Orestes A. Brownson, who disliked Fuller, slashes the book.

The six reviews of *Woman in the Nineteenth Century* also reflect the personalism involved in Fuller's contemporary reception. Lydia Maria Child and Charles Lane, both reformers sympathetic to the Transcendentalists, praise the work, while Brownson, who was not impressed by Transcendentalism, pans it. Both Charles F. Briggs and the *Ladies' National Magazine* are put off by claims for female equality, and this is reflected in the reviews. Brownson and Briggs, as well as Frederic Dan Huntington are all disturbed by the "peculiarities of style and manner" they see among the Transcendentalists, including Fuller, and this colors their reviews. The six reviews of *Papers on Literature and Art* show a more balanced approach, as they mostly avoid personal comments. But, again, Fuller's "Transcendental" style is attacked, even as her judgments are, for the most part, upheld. Not surprisingly, the seven reviews of the *Memoirs of Margaret Fuller Ossoli*, the biographical work put together by Emerson, William Henry Channing, and Clarke, reflect a great deal of personal criticism of Fuller's life and personality.

The other essays reprinted here fall into two groups: personal comments by her contemporaries (and the controversies over them) and general critical assessments of her work.

The personal comments on Fuller by Rufus W. Griswold, Edgar Allan Poe, Matthew Arnold, Caroline Healey Dall, A. Bronson Alcott, Harriet Martineau, and Henry James also show how Fuller's personality influenced their response to her writings. James Russell Lowell's poetic attacks on Fuller, the result of her negative comments on his poetry, should be read in conjunction with Martin Duberman's summary of the events. Harry R. Warfel's piece on Emerson points out many of the problems in that relationship, as does the selection from O. W. Firkins. The essays by Julian Hawthorne, Frederick T. Fuller, Oscar Cargill, and Austin Warren all comment on Fuller and Hawthorne. The anonymous article on "The Real Margaret Fuller" reinforces the problem Fuller had in gaining critical acceptance because of her personality. More positively, the essays by Harriet Hall Johnson and Granville Hicks show Fuller as, respectively, a dedicated teacher and a gifted conversationalist. Madeleine B. Stern's description of the challenges presented by studying Fuller's life is an excellent summary statement for this group of essays.

The twentieth-century essays here reprinted all deal with Fuller's writings. Arthur R. Schultz and Henry A. Pochmann both evaluate Fuller's works on German literature. Roland Crozier Burton and Wilma R. Ebbitt discuss Fuller's critical powers. Francis E. Kearns examines Fuller and abolitionism, while Vernon Louis Parrington and Margaret V. Allen present an overview of Fuller's life and writings. Marie Olesen Urbanski's essay, written especially for this volume, concludes the selections with a detailed study of one work, *Woman in the Nineteenth Century*.

The standard bibliography of writings by Fuller is Joel Myerson, *Margaret Fuller: A Descriptive Bibliography* (Pittsburgh: University of Pittsburgh Press, 1978). Of the nearly 350 articles, essays, and poems Fuller contributed to newspapers and periodicals, most remain uncollected. Fuller published five books during her life: *Conversations with Goethe in the Last Years of His Life* (Boston: Hilliard, Gray, 1839); *Günderode* (Boston: Elizabeth Peabody, 1842); *Summer on the Lakes, in 1843* (Boston: Charles C. Little and James Brown, 1844): *Woman in the Nineteenth Century* (New York: Greeley & McElrath, 1845); and *Papers on Literature and Art*, 2 vols. (New York: Wiley & Putnam, 1846). The first two, translations from the German, have not been reprinted since 1852 and 1861, respectively. However, a new facsimile reprinting of *Conversations with Goethe* will be published in 1979 by Brunner/Mazel of Larchmont, New York, with an introduction by Joel Myerson. The University of South Carolina Press will publish, also in 1979, a facsimile of the 1845 *Woman in the Nineteenth Century*, with an introduction by Madeleine B. Stern and a textual afterward by Joel Myerson.

Arthur B. Fuller took up the task of editing his sister's writings after her death: his edited text of *Woman in the Nineteenth Century*, a few dozen uncollected *New York Tribune* essays, and many previously unpublished extracts from letters and journals appeared as *Woman in the Nineteenth Century, and Kindred Papers* (Boston: John P. Jewett, 1855); his edited texts of *Summer on the Lakes* and the travel letters from Europe to the *Tribune* were published as *At Home and Abroad* (Boston: Crosby, Nichols, 1856); reviews and miscellaneous writings from the *Western Messenger*, *Dial*, and *Tribune*, along with a generous selection of poetry, were collected as *Life Without and Life Within* (Boston: Brown, Taggard, and Chase, 1860). Fuller's translation of *Tasso* was added to the contents of *Papers on Literature and Art* to form *Art, Literature, and the Drama* (Boston: Brown, Taggard, and Chase, 1860). None of Arthur Fuller's texts are faithful to his sister's original intentions, since he attempted to polish her style and eliminate matter he believed unnecessary. An unrecovered and abortive work by Fuller is discussed in Alexander E. Jones, "Margaret Fuller's Attempt to Write Fiction," *Boston Public Library Quarterly*, 6 (April 1954), 67–73. There are three modern anthologies of Fuller's writings: *The Writings of Margaret Fuller*, ed. Mason Wade (New York: Viking, 1941); *Margaret Fuller: American Romantic*, ed. Perry Miller (Garden City, N.Y.: Doubleday, 1963); and *Margaret Fuller: Essays on American Life and Letters*, ed. Joel Myerson (New Haven: College and University Press, 1978). Only the last one is edited according to modern textual standards and is fully annotated.

An edition of Fuller's letters—nearly 1,000—is being done by Robert N. Hudspeth, and when completed it will provide a much-needed single and reliable text. An annotated list of the letters Hudspeth has located, as well as a list of known but unlocated letters, has been published: "A Calendar of the Letters of Margaret Fuller," *Studies in the American Renaissance 1977*, ed. Joel Myerson (Boston: Twayne, 1978), pp. 49–143. At present, most of Fuller's manuscript letters are at the Boston Public Library and the Houghton Library at Harvard University. A glimpse of the Boston Public Library's holdings is given in Margaret Munsterberg, "Margaret Fuller Centenary," *Boston Public Library Quarterly*, 2 (July 1950), 245–268. Published texts are generally untrustworthy. Many letters are printed in the *Memoirs of Margaret Fuller Ossoli*, 2 vols. (Boston: Phillips, Sampson, 1852); but the editors—Emerson, William Henry Channing, and James Freeman Clarke—took great liberties in transcription and lost many of the manuscripts as well. Most of Fuller's letters to Emerson are printed accurately in *The Letters of Ralph Waldo Emerson*, ed. Ralph L. Rusk, 6 vols. (New York: Columbia University Press, 1939); those to James Nathan, with whom she was romantically involved in New York, are printed with less accuracy in *Love-Letters of Margaret Fuller* (New York: D. Appleton, 1903). Three important collections of letters to Fuller are: *The Letters of James Freeman Clarke to Margaret Fuller*, ed. John Wesley Thomas (Hamburg: Cram, de Gruyter, 1957); Leona Rostenberg, "Mazzini to Margaret Fuller, 1847–1849," *American Historical Review*, 47 (October 1941), 73–80; and Leopold Willisz, *The Friendship of Margaret Fuller D'Ossoli and Adam Mickiewicz* (New York: Polish Book Importing Company, 1947). Extensive selections from Fuller's European correspondence are given in Emma Detti, *Margaret Fuller Ossoli E I Suoi Corrispondenti* (Firenze: Félice Le Monnier, 1942 [Italian and English]).

There is no edition of Fuller's journals. Sections of them are printed inaccurately and at random in the *Memoirs*. Two journals have been edited with care: Joel Myerson, "Margaret Fuller's 1842 Journal: At Concord with the Emersons," *Harvard Library Bulletin*, 21 (July 1973), 320–340; and Leona Rostenberg, "Margaret Fuller's Roman Diary," *Journal of Modern History*, 12 (June 1940), 209–220.

The standard bibliography of writings about Fuller is Joel Myerson, *Margaret Fuller: An Annotated Secondary Bibliography* (New York: Burt Franklin, 1977). The bibliography in Madeleine B. Stern, *The Life of Margaret Fuller* (New York: Dutton, 1942), is excellent for material published through 1942 on the people and events surrounding Fuller.

Biographical information on Fuller is available in the many accounts of the Fuller family. Of general interest are [Arthur B. Fuller], "Historical Notices and Genealogy of the Fuller Family," *New England Historic and Genealogical Register*, 13 (October 1859), 351–363, revised and expanded as *Historical Notices of Thomas Fuller and His Descendants, with a Genealogy of the Fuller Family, 1638–1902* (Cambridge, Mass.: n. p., 1902); and Arthur B. Nichols, "Thomas Fuller and His Descendants," *Publications of the Cambridge Historical Society*, 28 (1943), 11–28. Fuller's father is the subject of Leona Rostenberg, "The Diary of Timothy Fuller in Congress, January 12–March 15, 1818," *New England Quarterly*, 12 (September 1939), 521–529. For information on Arthur B. Fuller, see "Arthur Buckminster Fuller," *Heralds of a Liberal Faith*, ed. Samuel A. Eliot (Boston: American Unitarian Association, 1910), III, 128–31; Richard F. Fuller, *Chaplain Fuller* (Boston: Walker, Wise, 1864); and [Thomas Wentworth Higginson], "Arthur Buckminster Fuller," *Harvard Me-*

*morial Biographies*, [ed. Higginson] (Cambridge, Mass.: Sever and Francis, 1866), I, 79–94. Richard Fuller's impressions of his sister and their contemporaries are given in *Recollections of Richard F. Fuller* (Boston: Privately printed, 1936) and in "The Younger Generation in 1840 from the Diary of a New England Boy," *Atlantic Monthly*, 136 (August 1925), 216–224; see also Walter Harding, "Visit to the Wachusett, July 1842 by Richard Fuller," *Thoreau Society Bulletin*, no. 121 (Fall 1972), 1–4. The Fuller Family Papers are in the Houghton Library of Harvard University.

There are a number of full-length biographies of Fuller. The *Memoirs* greatly influenced the public's picture of her for years to come: a picture of an egotistic, intellectually aloof person. An overly sympathetic portrait of Fuller by one who knew her is Julia Ward Howe, *Margaret Fuller (Marchesa Ossoli)* (Boston: Roberts, 1883). The best nineteenth-century biography is Thomas Wentworth Higginson, *Margaret Fuller Ossoli* (Boston: Houghton, Mifflin, 1884), which quotes extensively from her journals and letters in an attempt to correct the picture of Fuller as "a little too much in the clouds," the impression given in the *Memoirs*. The narrow focus of Katherine Anthony, *Margaret Fuller. A Psychological Biography* (New York: Harcourt, Brace and Howe, 1920), and the semi-fictional approach of Margaret Bell, *Margaret Fuller* (New York: Charles Boni, 1930), limit their usefulness today. Mason Wade, *Margaret Fuller: Whetstone of Genius* (New York: Viking, 1940), is a good general biography but lacks annotation, as does Faith Chipperfield, *In Quest of Love: The Life and Death of Margaret Fuller* (New York: Coward-McCann, 1957), a thesis-ridden book of little scholarly use. Paula Blanchard, *Margaret Fuller: From Transcendentalism to Revolution* (New York: Delacorte Press, 1978), is a good overview of Fuller's life. Fuller's last years are discussed in detail by Joseph Jay Deiss, *The Roman Years of Margaret Fuller* (New York: Thomas Y. Crowell, 1969), which quotes extensively from her writings during this period. The best introductory book on Fuller is Arthur W. Brown, *Margaret Fuller* (New York: Twayne, 1964), a conscientiously researched and concisely stated study of Fuller's life and writings. Bell Gale Chevigny, *The Woman and the Myth: Margaret Fuller's Life and Writings* (Old Westbury: Feminist Press, 1976), is an interesting collection of Fuller's writings and comments on her by contemporaries, tied together with a good running discussion of Fuller's life and thought. Good brief biographies, both by Joel Myerson, are the "Introduction" to Myerson's edition of *Margaret Fuller: Essays on American Life and Letters*, pp. 7–30, and the Fuller entry in *The American Renaissance in New England*, ed. Joel Myerson (Detroit: Gale Research, 1978), pp. 66–72. Stern's *The Life of Margaret Fuller* remains today as the most valuable biography. It is the most detailed and best researched life, and it is especially strong in describing Fuller's environment.

Certain aspects of Fuller's life have attracted scholars more than others. Her stay in Providence is the subject of Charles R. Crowe, "Transcendentalism and the Providence Literati," *Rhode Island History*, 14 (July 1955), 65–78; Henry L. Green, "The Greene-St. School of Providence, and Its Teachers,"

*Publications of the Rhode Island Historical Society,* n.s. 6 (January 1899), 199–219; Edward A. Hoyt and Loriman S. Brigham, "Glimpses of Margaret Fuller: The Green Street School and Florence," *New England Quarterly,* 29 (March 1956), 87–98; °Harriet Hall Johnson, "Margaret Fuller as Known by her Scholars," *Christian Register,* 21 April 1910, pp. 426–429;[1] and Annie Russell Marble, "Margaret Fuller as Teacher," *Critic,* 43 (October 1903), 334–345. Manuscript journals kept by students in Fuller's school at Providence are located at the American Antiquarian Society, Brown University, and the University of South Carolina.

Fuller was best known for her conversational powers; unfortunately, the only extended account of her Conversations is in Caroline Healey Dall, *Margaret and Her Friends* (Boston: Roberts, 1895), discussed in Joel Myerson, "Mrs. Dall Edits Miss Fuller: The Story of *Margaret and Her Friends*," *Papers of the Bibliographical Society of America,* 72 (II Quarter 1978), 187–200. °Granville Hicks, "A Conversation in Boston," *Sewanee Review,* 39 (April–June 1931), 129–143, writes an imaginative reconstruction of a Conversation by Fuller in November 1840.

Fuller's role as editor of the *Dial* can be traced in George Willis Cooke, *An Historical and Biographical Introduction to Accompany THE DIAL,* 2 vols. (Cleveland: Rowfant Club, 1902); Joel Myerson, *The New England Transcendentalists and the Dial: A History of the Magazine and Its Contributors* (Madison, N.J.: Fairleigh Dickinson University Press, 1979); and Myerson, "An Annotated List of Contributions to the Boston *Dial*," *Studies in Bibliography,* 26 (1973), 133–166. Her critical principles as editor are discussed in Helen Hennessy, "The *Dial*: Its Poetry and Poetic Criticism," *New England Quarterly,* 31 (March 1958), 66–87; and Donald F. Warders, " 'The Progress of the Hour and the Day': A Critical Study of *The Dial*," Ph.D. dissertation, University of Kansas, 1973. A more general view of Fuller's periodical career is provided in Clarence L. F. Gohdes, *The Periodicals of American Transcendentalism* (Durham: Duke University Press, 1931).

A general account of Fuller's relations with Brook Farm is Karl Knortz, *Brook Farm und Margaret Fuller* (New York: Druck von Hermann Bartsch, 1886 [German]). Comments on Fuller at Brook Farm are listed in Joel Myerson, *Brook Farm: An Annotated Bibliography and Resources Guide* (New York: Garland, 1978). An excellent picture of her life at New York is in Constance Penta, "Fuller's Folly: The Eccentric World of Margaret Fuller and the Greeleys," M.A. thesis, Columbia University, 1960.

Much of Fuller's reputation lies not with her writings but rather with the effect she had upon those who knew her. Martha Ann Tull, "Contemporary Portraiture of Margaret Fuller," M.A. thesis, George Peabody College, 1929, presents a general survey of published comments by Fuller's contemporaries. Her relationship with Emerson—with Fuller unsuccessfully attempting to force him from his usually aloof position—has always fascinated scholars. Most of their correspondence is printed in *The Letters of Ralph Waldo Emerson,* ed.

---

[1] Items preceded by an asterisk are reprinted in the present volume.

Rusk. Fuller's comments in Joel Myerson, "Margaret Fuller's 1842 Journal: At Concord with the Emersons," are valuable, as are Emerson's comments on her in *The Correspondence of Emerson and Carlyle,* ed. Joseph Slater (New York: Columbia University Press, 1964), and *The Journals and Miscellaneous Notebooks of Ralph Waldo Emerson,* ed. William H. Gilman et al., 14 vols. to date (Cambridge: Harvard University Press, 1960– ). Interesting studies of their friendship are John Bard McNulty, "Emerson's Friends and the Essay on Friendship," *New England Quarterly,* 19 (September 1946), 390–394; Ralph L. Rusk, *The Life of Ralph Waldo Emerson* (New York: Scribners, 1949); Marie Olesen Urbanski, "The Ambivalence of Ralph Waldo Emerson Towards Margaret Fuller," *Thoreau Journal Quarterly,* 10 (July 1978), 26–36; and °Harry R. Warfel, "Margaret Fuller and Ralph Waldo Emerson," *PMLA,* 50 (June 1935), 576–594.

No less intriguing is Fuller's relationship with Hawthorne, whose possible use of her in his writings is discussed by Francis E. Kearns, "Margaret Fuller as a Model for Hester Prynne," *Jahrbuch für Amerikastudien,* 10 (1965), 191–97; and Kelly Thurman, "Margaret Fuller in Two American Novels: *The Blithedale Romance* and *Elsie Venner,*" M.A. thesis, University of Kentucky, 1945. Hawthorne's comments in *The American Notebooks,* ed. Claude M. Simpson (Columbus: Ohio State University Press, 1972), are important. General studies of the two are °Oscar Cargill, "Nemesis and Nathaniel Hawthorne," *PMLA,* 52 (September 1937), 848–862; Paul John Eakin, "Margaret Fuller, Hawthorne, James, and Sexual Politics," *South Atlantic Quarterly,* 75 (Summer 1976), 323–338; William Peirce Randel, "Hawthorne, Channing, and Margaret Fuller," *American Literature,* 10 (January 1939), 472–476; and °Austin Warren, "Hawthorne, Margaret Fuller, and 'Nemesis,'" *PMLA,* 54 (June 1939), 615–618.

Information concerning Fuller and Alcott can be found in *The Journals of Bronson Alcott,* ed. Odell Shepard (Boston: Little, Brown, 1938); *The Letters of A. Bronson Alcott,* ed. Richard L. Herrnstadt (Ames: Iowa State University Press, 1969); F. B. Sanborn and William T. Harris, *A. Bronson Alcott: His Life and Philosophy,* 2 vols. (Boston: Roberts, 1893); and Odell Shepard, *Pedlar's Progress: The Life of Bronson Alcott* (Boston: Little, Brown, 1937). Thoreau's relationship with Fuller can be followed in *The Correspondence of Henry David Thoreau,* ed. Walter Harding and Carl Bode (New York: New York University Press, 1958); Walter Harding, *The Days of Henry Thoreau* (New York: Alfred A. Knopf, 1965); Marie Olesen Urbanski, "Henry David Thoreau and Margaret Fuller," *Thoreau Journal Quarterly,* 8 (October 1976), 24–30; and Charles Thomas Waller, "A Contrast of the Religious Thought of Henry David Thoreau and Margaret Fuller," M.A. thesis, University of Georgia, 1959.

Studies of other figures of the time who knew Fuller well are also informative. Among the most useful are Helene G. Baer, "Mrs. Child and Miss Fuller," *New England Quarterly,* 26 (June 1953), 249–255; Charles E. Blackburn, "James Freeman Clarke: An Interpretation of the Western Years (1833–40)," Ph.D. dissertation, Yale University, 1952; Arthur S. Bolster, *James Freeman Clarke: Disciple to Advancing Truth* (Boston: Beacon, 1954); George Willis

Cooke, *John Sullivan Dwight: Brook-Farmer, Editor, and Critic of Music* (Boston: Small, Maynard, 1898); Charles Crowe, *George Ripley: Transcendentalist and Utopian Socialist* (Athens: University of Georgia Press, 1967); Jane Ball Davidson, "Margaret Fuller and Edgar Allan Poe: A Relationship Between Literati," M.A. thesis, American University, 1968; Edwin Gittleman, *Jones Very: The Effective Years 1833-1840* (New York: Columbia University Press, 1967); Horace Greeley, "Margaret Fuller," *Recollections of a Busy Life* (New York: J. B. Ford, 1868), pp. 169-191; William Harlan Hale, *Horace Greeley: Voice of the People* (New York: Harpers, 1950); Robert N. Hudspeth, *Ellery Channing* (New York: Twayne, 1973); Georgiana Bruce Kirby, *Years of Experience: An Autobiographical Narrative* (New York: Putnams, 1887); Frederick T. McGill, Jr., *Channing of Concord: A Life of William Ellery Channing II* (New Brunswick, N.J.: Rutgers University Press, 1967); Joel Myerson, "Caroline Dall's Reminiscences of Margaret Fuller," *Harvard Library Bulletin*, 22 (October 1974), 414-428; *The Journals of Charles King Newcomb*, ed. Judith Kennedy Johnson (Providence: Brown University Press, 1946); F. B. Sanborn, *Recollections of Seventy Years*, 2 vols. (Boston: Richard G. Badger, 1909); John Wesley Thomas, *James Freeman Clarke: Apostle of German Culture to America* (Boston: John W. Luce, 1949); and David Alec Wilson, "Margaret Fuller Has to Listen (1846)," *Carlyle on Cromwell and Others (1837-1848)* (London: Kegan Paul, Trench, Trubner, 1925), pp. 346-351. The background to Lowell's devastating satire on Fuller in *A Fable for Critics* can be pieced together from *Letters of James Russell Lowell*, ed. Charles Eliot Norton, 2 vols. (New York: Harpers, 1894); °Martin Duberman, *James Russell Lowell* (Boston: Houghton Mifflin, 1966); and Leon Howard, *Victorian Knight-Errant: A Study of the Early Literary Career of James Russell Lowell* (Berkeley: University of California Press, 1952). A possible influence on Fuller is discussed in Fordyce Richard Bennett, "Margaret Fuller, Greaves, and the Sexes," *American Transcendental Quarterly*, No. 21 (Summer 1976), 35.

Critical studies of Fuller's writings have centered either on her comments on foreign literature or on her criticism in general. The most inclusive study of Fuller and foreign literature is Russell E. Durning, *Margaret Fuller, Citizen of the World. An Intermediary Between European and American Literatures* (Heidelberg: Carl Winter, 1969). Particular areas of her interest are discussed in Lucy Gregory, "The Influence of George Sand on Margaret Fuller," M.A. thesis, Columbia University, 1918: Ursula Kearns, "The Translations of Margaret Fuller," M.A. thesis, Columbia University, 1949; Mary Ruth Miller, "Margaret Fuller's Part in the Language Interests of American Transcendentalism," M.A. thesis, University of North Carolina, 1946; Maud Cannell Quayle, "Margaret Fuller's Attitude Toward France," M.A. thesis, University of California, 1913; and William Silas Vance, "Margaret Fuller," "Carlyle and the American Transcendentalists," Ph.D. dissertation, University of Chicago, 1941, pp. 329-355.

German literature exerted the greatest influence on Fuller; good general studies in this area are °Henry A. Pochmann, *German Culture in America: Philosophical and Literary Influences 1600-1900* (Madison: University of

Wisconsin Press, 1957); °Arthur R. Schultz, "Margaret Fuller—Transcendentalist Interpreter of German Literature," *Monatshefte für Deütschen Untericht*, 34 (April 1942), 169–182; and Stanley M. Vogel, *German Literary Influences on the American Transcendentalists* (New Haven: Yale University Press, 1955). Probably the author who exerted the most influence on Fuller was Goethe, and not surprisingly much has been published on this subject: Frederick Augustus Braun, *Margaret Fuller and Goethe* (New York: Henry Holt, 1910); Braun, "Margaret Fuller's Translation and Criticism of Goethe's *Tasso*," *Journal of English and Germanic Philology*, 13 (April 1914), 202–213; Russell E. Durning, "Margaret Fuller's Translation of Goethe's 'Prometheus,'" *Jahrbuch für Amerikastudien*, 12 (1967), 240–245: Harry Slochower, "Margaret Fuller and Goethe," *Germanic Review*, 7 (April 1932), 130–144; and J. Wesley Thomas, "New Light on Margaret Fuller's Projected 'Life of Goethe,'" *Germanic Review*, 24 (October 1949), 216–223.

The most worked-over area of Fuller scholarship is that of her published criticism. Her theoretical ideas are examined in Roland Crozier Burton, "Margaret Fuller's Criticism: Theory and Practice," Ph.D. dissertation, University of Iowa, 1941: and °Wilma R. Ebbitt, "Margaret Fuller's Ideas on Criticism," *Boston Public Library Quarterly*, 3 (July 1951), 171–187. Fuller's literary criticism is discussed by Patrick Frederick Berger, "Margaret Fuller: Critical Realist as Seen in Her Works," Ph.D. dissertation, St. Louis University, 1972; Wilma R. Ebbitt, "The Critical Essays of Margaret Fuller from the New York *Tribune*," Ph.D. dissertation, Brown University, 1943; Josephine J. Fay, "Margaret Fuller, Literary Critic," Ph.D. dissertation, St. John's University, 1951; Sharon Kaye George, "Margaret Fuller: American Literary and Social Critic," Ph.D. dissertation, University of Texas, 1975; Henry Lawrence Golemba, "The Balanced View in Margaret Fuller's Literary Criticism," Ph.D. dissertation, University of Washington, 1971; Vivian C. Hopkins, "Margaret Fuller: American Nationalist Critic," *Emerson Society Quarterly*, No. 55 (II Quarter 1969), 24–41; Helen Neill McMaster, "Margaret Fuller as a Literary Critic," *University of Buffalo Studies*, 7 (December 1928), 35–100; and Margaret Wallace, "Margaret Fuller: Critic," *Bookman*, 69 (March 1929), 60–67. Specific areas of Fuller's criticism are covered in °Roland Crozier Burton, "Margaret Fuller's Criticism of the Fine Arts," *College English*, 6 (October 1944), 18–23; and Elizabeth F. Shore, "Margaret Fuller and Welfare Journalism," M.S.W. thesis, University of California, 1956.

Other aspects of Fuller's thoughts and writings are discussed by Margaret V. Allen, "The Political and Social Criticism of Margaret Fuller," *South Atlantic Quarterly*, 72 (Autumn 1973), 560–573; °Allen, "'This Impassioned Yankee': Margaret Fuller's Writing Revisited," *Southwest Review*, 58 (Spring 1973), 162–171; Elsie Furbush Brickett, "Studies in the Poets and Poetry of New England Transcendentalism," Ph.D. dissertation, Yale University, 1937; Lawrence Buell, *Literary Transcendentalism: Style and Vision in the American Renaissance* (Ithaca: Cornell University Press, 1973); Susan P. Conrad, *Perish the Thought: Intellectual Women in Romantic America 1830–1860* (New York: Oxford University Press, 1976); Ann Douglas, *The Feminization of*

*American Culture* (New York: Alfred A. Knopf, 1977); Kathleen Deidre Guerin, S.N.D., "Margaret Fuller d'Ossoli: Modern American Humanist," Ph.D. dissertation, University of Minnesota, 1975; Vivian C. Hopkins, "Margaret Fuller: Pioneer Women's Liberationist," *American Transcendental Quarterly*, No. 18 (Spring 1973), 29–35; °Francis E. Kearns,"Margaret Fuller and the Abolition Movement,"*Journal of the History of Ideas*, 25 (January–March 1964), 120–127; Kearns, "Margaret Fuller's Social Criticism," Ph.D. dissertation, University of North Carolina, 1960; Mary Maxine, "Margaret Fuller: From Liberal to Radical, a Foreshadowing of the Feminist Movement," Ph.D. dissertation, University of New Mexico, 1973; °Vernon Louis Parrington, "Margaret Fuller: Rebel," *The Romantic Revolution in America 1800–1860* (New York: Harcourt, Brace, 1927), pp. 426–434; Kathryn A. Pippin, "Margaret Fuller's Views on Education," M.A. thesis, University of North Carolina, 1972; Daniel Edgar Rider, "The Musical Thought and Activities of the New England Transcendentalists," Ph.D. dissertation, University of Minnesota, 1964; and Barbara Welter, *Dimity Convictions: The American Woman in the Nineteenth Century* (Athens: Ohio University Press, 1976).

Only two of Fuller's books have been studied in detail. *Summer on the Lakes* is the subject of Richard V. Carpenter, "Margaret Fuller in Northern Illinois," *Journal of the Illinois State Historical Society*, 2 (January 1910), 7–22; Madeleine B. Stern in her introduction to the B. De Graff facsimile reprinting of *Summer* (Nieuwkoop, The Netherlands, 1972). An able study of Fuller's feminist book is Marie Olesen Urbanski, "Margaret Fuller's *Woman in the Nineteenth Century*," Ph.D. dissertation, University of Kentucky, 1973. Fuller's reception in Britain is incompletely surveyed in Frances M. Barbour, "Margaret Fuller and the British Reviewers," *New England Quarterly*, 9 (December 1936), 618–625. For a more complete listing of contemporary reviews of Fuller's writings, consult Joel Myerson, *Margaret Fuller: An Annotated Secondary Bibliography*.

Despite the amount of material published on Fuller, much good scholarship needs to be done: an accurate and complete edition of her writings; a new and comprehensive biography built upon the large amount of material made available since Madeleine B. Stern's book in 1942; studies of Fuller and her contemporaries; and more detailed examinations of *Summer on the Lakes* and *Woman in the Nineteenth Century*. An instructive article in this respect is °Madeleine B. Stern, "A Biographer's View of Margaret Fuller," *AB Bookman's Weekly*, 53 (4 February 1974), 427–428, 430.

I am grateful to James and Gwen Nagel for editorial assistance and reading the manuscript; to Janice Gandy for typing; and to Robert E. Burkholder and Stephen and Carrie Garrison for much assistance. And to Greta, of course, many thanks and much gratitude—it is not easy to share a house with what James called the "Margaret-ghost."

J.M.

Columbia, South Carolina
22 November 1978

# "The Dial"

### William J. Pabodie[*]

Miss Fuller is a woman of extraordinary application and industry, and is of consequence in possession of rich stores of varied learning. Her command of expression is wonderful, so that she finds no difficulty in putting forth her information in the best possible manner. Nothing is allowed to rest in dust-gathering obscurity on the loaded shelves of her store house; but all her rich wares, whether of domestic manufacture or foreign importation, (and 'tis in the latter she most largely deals) are brought forward, as occasion requires, and displayed to the admiring gaze of her astonished auditors. 'Tis with open eyed wonder and admiration that we have listened to her rich and eloquent conversation. She has exquisite humor and satirical acerbity, great tact, has somewhat tho' not much of the speculative reason, surpassing memory, is quick in her perceptions, voluble. But in the higher powers of the soul, in those powers which constitute genius, we think her sadly deficient. She has little or no intuitive perception of either truth or beauty, and with all her application, no genuine love of knowledge, it seems to us, for its own sake, but for the eclat with which it is attended. And yet to a superficial, an undiscriminating observer she might appear to be a woman of extraordinary genius—so replete is her memory with the ideas of the best writers. But for her opinions, in so far as they are her own, we regret to say that we have no respect. She is deficient in that faculty which the transcentalist would term the spontaneous of pure reason, wanting insight. Her mind is chiefly valuable as a repository—admirable arranged, 'tis true, as well kept. She is a great woman in her way, but her course lies not among the stars.

[*]From W[illiam]. J. P[abodie], "The Dial," *Providence Daily Journal*, 27 July 1840, p. 2.

# [*Summer on the Lakes*]

### James Freeman Clarke[*]

The West is our American Romance, our unwritten Poetry, our Eldorado, our Utopia, our Atlantis. It is so changeable in its features that the description of yesterday will not do for to-day; the picture, which a year ago was considered a good portrait, cannot be recognized as a likeness now. Hence the charm and the necessity of new books about the West.

Miss Fuller has given us a charming little volume, full of description of scenery and manners, in a graceful form. She has done wisely in not making a guide book, which, as we said above, would have become useless in another year; she has not given us a volume of maps, but a portfolio of sketches, some in outline, some filled out and carefully finished. The book is a very interesting one, and we recommend it to all who wish to see our every day life made interesting by the power which belongs to a mind, possessing at once, faculties of keen perception, profound reflection and constructive imagination.

But we should do great injustice to this book in representing it merely as a pleasant book of travels. It belongs to a class of which we can rarely find a specimen. It is full of suggestion, rich in matter, to be read and read again, and to appear new with each new reading. It comes to us with the stores of a mind which has thought much and seen much and experienced much, and which can, therefore, touch no subject without conveying a thousand suggestions and incitements to thought by every word. This is a book for study as well as for entertainment, and we hope that the sale of it will be such as to encourage its author to give the public more of those rich results of genius and study, which her friends have so long known and prized, but which belong, by their nature, to a wider circle than even that which has the privilege of regarding this lady as its light and ornament.

---

[*]J[ames]. F[reeman]. C[larke]., [Review of *Summer on the Lakes*], *Christian World*, 2 (6 July 1844).

# [*Summer on the Lakes*]

### Caleb Stetson[*]

We took up this work with eager expectation. Knowing the extraordinary endowments of its author, we looked for an uncommon book, and we were not disappointed. It is indeed an uncommon book, not at all like an ordinary journal of travel. It is impossible to give an analysis of its contents, and we shall attempt nothing more than to record the impression which a careful reading of the work left on our minds.

It is a work of varied interest, rich in fine observation; profound reflection and striking anecdote. It breathes throughout a spirit of perfect benignity and love—generous, humane, and free from prejudices of every kind. In regard to all things and persons that come under her notice—especially the character of the native Indians, of whom she has collected many fine stories before unknown to us,—it would be difficult to find a writer so liberal, just and discriminating. To a class of readers who can sympathize with her in feeling and taste, and appreciate her philosophic and poetic insight, she has furnished a rare intellectual entertainment. She has imparted a new and classic interest to the uncultivated regions which surround our Northwestern waters.

Miss Fuller's book is in a high degree subjective. It is not so much a description of the beautiful lake scenery in the midst of which she passed the summer months, looking upon all things with the eye of a poet and artist, as a record of her own impressions and of the recollections they called up. Accordingly, amidst scenes so novel and striking she writes not from without, but from within. It is not that she overlooks the nature which smiles or frowns around her. She often gives us descriptions of such beauty as to show that she has an eye and a heart for everything lovely or grand in the external creation. But evidently she is much more occupied with what is passing in her own soul, than with the objective realities which present themselves to the senses.

We do not make these remarks by way of complaint. We like to have travellers, as all others, give free expression to what presses upon their own minds and hearts. In that way we get sincere and earnest books. We notice this subjective tendency of the writer as a peculiar excellence. It gives to her work its most remarkable characteristic. We can never anticipate what she will say, from knowing her point of view and the objects which surround her. She throws

---

*[Caleb Stetson], "Notice of Recent Publications," *Christian Examiner*, 37 (September 1844), 274–76.

her own being into the outward world and gives it a new character. Niagara, Superior, the log cabin, the savage chief, are not to her what they are to another person. Forest, lake, prairie, the beauty and fragrance of flowers, the music of birds, have all a significance and a language to which the mood of her own mind gives a peculiar interpretation. It is always interesting to observe the workings of such a mind in unwonted scenes. And this writer gives full utterance, if not to the natural impressions which external objects produce, at least to the secondary results of the reflection they excite.

This reflective tendency often draws into her journal things quite unlooked for and most remote from her field of observation—things connected by no apparent link of association with the objects which seem to fill her eye and mind. These underground associations, unintelligible to those who are not in the secret of her thoughts, sometimes give an air of pedantry to her remarks. We are persuaded that she has a mind too noble to wish to display her rich stores of knowledge for the sake of display, and therefore we find it difficult to account for the introduction of so many allusions to classic antiquity, to Europe and its arts, manners and literature. It appears often strained, unnatural, out of place. Tales also unexpectedly appear—such, for instance, as the German story of the "Seeress of Prevorst"—which have no connexion with the scenes she visited, except the accidental fact that they occurred in the course of her reading or were called up from the depths of her memory by some mysterious association. Such portions of her work might have been written as well at Boston, Rome, or Constantinople, as on the shores of our Western waters.

There is often a certain stiffness, an unnaturalness, in the style of the work. We are unable to suppose that it proceeds from defective taste in a person of so fine a culture. It results perhaps from over-carefulness and severity in a mind unwilling to trust to natural and simple impressions, and allow them to utter themselves in their own way. She does not let her thought or emotion write itself out. We cannot help feeling that the intellect is too predominant—that she is too conscious of style—that she writes under the constraint of an artistic view, in conformity with some ideal that is not congenial with her nature and does not allow it free action. She seems to be afraid of the simple utterance of a first impression or thought, as if it had not weight or firmness enough to go out of her hands without elaborate refining and re-coinage. Accordingly we find something cold, stately, almost *statuesque*, in her language. It has not the warmth of life which her heart would give it, if she would yield herself trustingly to its impulses with less of intellectual criticism. It reminds us sometimes of Coleridge, sometimes of Walter Savage Landor; yet we see no marks of imitation. It seems to us rather, that in aiming to be classical she loses sight of nature, or too sternly represses its genuine instincts in obedience to some law which she has prescribed to herself. The beautiful flower must not bloom out spontaneously with its own shape and hue; it must be fashioned into some preordained form and its colors be retouched, before it is fit for exhibition. We make these remarks with diffidence, for we mistrust our taste and judgment when we find ourselves presuming to criticise a writer whose mind is so full of manifold forms of beauty and grace.

# [*Summer on the Lakes*]

**Orestes A. Brownson**[*]

The publishers tell us that this book has had a very respectable sale, which we are glad to learn, for the writer's sake. Miss Fuller is a woman of more than ordinary abilities, and, we are told, of rare attainments. She is said to possess remarkable conversational powers, and her conversations, which she has been in the habit of holding, we believe, as a means of meeting her expenses, are represented by her friends to be in the highest degree brilliant, instructive, and inspiring. This we can partly believe, though we have never had the honor of listening to her in her happiest moments. Her writings we do not like. We dislike them exceedingly. They are sent out in a slipshod style, and have a certain toss of the head about them which offends us. Miss Fuller seems to us to be wholly deficient in a pure, correct taste, and especially in that tidiness we always look for in woman. Then, we detest her doctrines. We know nothing more abominable. She is a heathen priestess, though of what god or goddess we will not pretend to say. She is German, heart and soul, save so far as Germany may retain traditionally somewhat of Christianity. We believe no person has appeared among us whose conversation and writings have done more to corrupt the minds and hearts of our Boston community. For religion she substitutes Art; for the Divinity who has made us, and whom we should worship she would give us merely the Beautiful; and for the stern morality of the Gospel, such principles as we may collect from the *Wahlverwandtschaften*, and Goethe's *Correspondence with a Child*. She is, in fact, the high-priestess of American Transcendentalism, and, happily, ministers now at an almost deserted fane.

We admit that she has read much and variously; but her notions are crude, and the materials she has collected lie fermenting in her intellectual stomach, and generate all manner of strange and diseased fancies. She is ill at ease. She has no quiet, no repose. She has no faith, no hope. She now reminds us of the old heathen Euripides, now of the modern skeptic, Byron, and finally, of the cold indifferentism of Goethe dashed on the warm woman's heart of Bettina Brentano. We see in her a melancholy instance of the fate which awaits a gifted woman in an age of infidelity. All she needs, to be the ornament of her sex, and a crown of blessing to her country, to be at peace with herself and the world, is the firm, old-fashioned Catholic faith in the Gospel. Her soul would then burst its fetters, all her powers would find free scope, and her heart the rest after which it yearns.

---

[*][Orestes A. Brownson], [Review of *Summer on the Lakes*], *Brownson's Quarterly Review*, 6 (October 1844), 546–547.

The book before us is characteristic. It is marked by flashes of a rare genius, by uncommon and versatile powers, by sentiments at times almost devout; but after all it is a sad book, and one which we dare not commend. Alas! it is melancholy to contemplate the noble victims sacrificed to the Moloch, Doubt; still more sad, when the sacrifice is made by priests aping the forms of Faith, and the vestments of Piety! God grant the ages of Faith may return, that our sons and daughters may return and come to Zion, obtain joy and gladness, and sorrow and sighing flee away!

# "Woman in the Nineteenth Century"

Lydia Maria Child[°]

  This is the title of a book now in press in this city, which will be likely to excite a good deal of remark, for and against. It is from the pen of Margaret Fuller, a woman of more powerful intellect, comprehensive thought, and thorough education, than any other American authoress, with whose productions I am acquainted. Her style is vigorous and significant, abounding with eloquent passages, and affluent in illustration; but it is sometimes rough in construction, and its meaning is not always sufficiently clear. This does not arise from affectation, or pedantic elaboration; it is the defect of a mind that has too many thoughts for its words; an excess by no means common, either in men or women. She is a contralto voice in literature: deep, rich, and strong, rather than mellifluous and clear.

  The book in question is written in a free energetic spirit. It contains a few passages that will offend the fastidiousness of some readers; for they allude to subjects which men do not wish to have discussed, and which women dare not approach. But the clean-minded will not sneer; for they will see that the motive is pure, and the object is to ennoble human nature.

  There is a great deal of unuttered thought and suppressed feeling, concerning the terrible discords of society, as it now exists. The passion of love, divorced from the pure and elevating sentiment, is felt to be unsatisfactory, as well as degrading. More and more earnestly rise the questions, "Is love a mockery, and marriage a sham? What is woman's true mission? What is the harmonious relation of the sexes?"

  This extending murmur of the human heart, this increasing conviction that woman should be the friend, the companion, the real partner of man in all his pursuits, rather than the mere ornament of his parlor, or the servant of his senses, cannot be silenced.

  The author of "Woman in the Nineteenth Century," has uttered noble aspirations on this subject, rather than definite theories. She is wise enough to see, that to purify the atmosphere will gradually affect all forms of life.

  I quote a few passages at random, to give some idea of the import and tendencies of the book. . . .

---

[°]L[ydia]. M[aria]. C[hild]., "Woman in the Nineteenth Century," *Broadway Journal*, 1 (15 February 1845), 97.

# [Woman in the Nineteenth Century]

Charles F. Briggs*

## [PART ONE]

It will be a happy time for the world, but especially happy for the reading part of it, when people shall be content to accomplish, in the shortest time possible, whatever they may feel themselves called to do. TIME FLIES, should be inscribed on the door-posts of every author's dwelling. An emblematic figure, like that in the Hall of our National Legislature, does not appear to be sufficiently striking, though it tells the hours as they fly. The author who writes to amuse, may write as long as he can amuse, even though he should write tales longer than the Grand Cyrus, or Sir Charles Grandison; but the author who writes to instruct, cannot write too briefly, for we have much to learn, and but little time to learn in; one third must be given to sleep, another third, at least, to labor, and the rest to study, to amusements, to writing, and talking, and sight-seeing. The time that the best of us can devote to reading, is but short, and therefore, we cannot afford to read books which lack method, or which contain more words than are necessary to convey the author's meaning, provided he have any. That Miss Fuller is justly chargeable with wasting the time of her readers, her most devout admirer cannot deny. Her book consists of two hundred pages, but all that it contains of her own suggesting, might be fairly compressed into a third of the space. The title is a misnomer to begin with; the one under which the essay was once published, "The great Law-suit, Man *vs.* Men: Woman *vs.* Women," was much better, because, having no particular meaning, it created no improper expectations. Miss Fuller informs us that she changed it because it was not understood; she will have to change the present one, for an opposite reason. We keep looking for woman of the nineteenth century, but we only find a roster of female names from Panthea to Amelia Norman. The propriety of the title is the more doubtful from the following passage in her preface.

> "By man, I mean both man and woman. I lay no especial stress on the welfare of either. I believe the welfare of the one cannot be effected without that of the other.

*[Charles F. Briggs], [Review of *Woman in the Nineteenth Century*], *Broadway Journal*, 1 (1, 8, 22 March 1845), 130–131, 145–146, 182–183.

> My highest wish is that this truth should be distinctly and rationally apprehended; and the conditions of life and freedom recognised as the same for the daughters and the sons of time."

The style is somewhat stilted, but the thought is just and philosophical, and proves Miss Fuller to be a thinking, right-judging person. Why could she not, then, since she thinks so correctly, call her book, Man, or Society in the Nineteenth century, and so plead in a straight forward manner in behalf of man, without any specialities about woman's rights or woman's wrongs, as though she had either rights or wrongs, which are not also the rights and wrongs of men. We certainly did not expect from a woman of Miss Fuller's natural and acquired powers, the wretched cant which we hear so often from men, who, having no claim upon man, seek for the sympathies of women, and from women, who, having as little claim upon the sympathies of men, try for it by speaking in the name of their sex, about woman's mission, woman's influence, and woman's rights; and we have not been disappointed; she seems to entertain a wholesome horror of the whole tribe of shallow canters. But then, if we do not misapprehend her, which we are not sure of, she has errors of her own which are more dangerous, because not so shallow as the others. She forgets, or rather seems to forget, that God created man male and female, notwithstanding the declaration in her preface, which we suspect, contains, like the postscript of a woman's letter, the face which she intended to put into the body of her work. She is dissatisfied that women are not men, and takes offence at the term "women and children"; words which to us sound sweeter for being spoken together. She is offended that women should esteem it a compliment to be called masculine, while men consider it a reproach to be called feminine. "Early I perceived," she says, "that men, in no extremity of distress, ever wished themselves women." Of course not. It is the law that woman shall reverence her husband, and that he shall be her head. We may love those whom we protect, but we can never wish ourselves in their place, although we naturally wish to be like those from whom we receive protection. The wish of Desdemona that Heaven had made her like Othello, is the sweetest touch of nature in Shakspeare. Some have doubted what she meant, but they have only to read her wish by the light of revelation, and her meaning is clear. Miss Fuller says:

> "I have urged on woman, independence of man, not that I do not think the sexes mutually needed by one another, but because in woman, this fact has led to an excessive devotion, which has cooled love, degraded marriage, and prevented either sex from being what it should be to itself or the other. . . . That her hand may be given with dignity, she must be able to stand alone."

This, we conceive to be the radical error of Miss Fuller's reasoning, and directly opposed to the law of nature, of experience and revelation. She says,

> "A profound thinker has said, that no married woman can represent the female world, for she belongs to her husband. The idea of woman must be represented by a virgin."

He was a very shallow thinker, or a joker. It would be as reasonable to say that none but a deaf man could give a true idea of music. Woman is nothing but as a wife. How, then, can she truly represent the female character who has never filled it? No woman can be a true woman, who has not been a wife and a mother. These are not accidental characters like those of mistress and servant, which may be thoroughly understood without being acted; but they are the natural destiny of woman, and if she is kept from them, her nature is distorted and unnatural; and she sees things through a false medium. Her report, therefore, of a character which she never filled, must be received with distrust.

It is not easy to discover from Miss Fuller's essay what her precise ideas of the true relation of man and woman are; although on some points she is sufficiently distinct. Mrs. Jamieson, with true womanly feeling, said that she would prefer being Mary of Scotland to Elizabeth of England; but Miss Fuller would prefer being the termagant Queen and swearing by "God's teeth." Colonel Emily Plater and Madame George Sand sound pleasantly in her ears. "If you ask me what offices women may fill," says Miss Fuller, "I reply any; let them be sea captains if you will." Very good, let them. We have a queen of England, and England claims to be mistress of the seas; let us have a woman Admiral. But we take sides with Spinoza, and answer that woman cannot command. She lacks the chief qualities of a commander. She cannot invent. She is an apt imitator, but she cannot originate; and therefore we have no fears that we shall ever see woman in our halls of legislature, or in command of our ships or armies. "A party of travellers lately visited a lonely hut on a mountain. There they found an old woman that told them she and her husband had lived there forty years; why, they said, did you chose so barren a spot? She did not know, it was the man's notion. And during forty years she had been content to act, without knowing why, upon the man's notion. I would not have it so"; says Miss Fuller. In the name of all that is monstrous, what would she have? Would she have the woman to leave her husband, or would she have the husband abandon what he believed to be for his interest to do, to satisfy a whim of his wife? She is not bound to provide for him, but he is bound to provide for her, and therefore he must be allowed the privilege of following his own business in his own way, unless she can advise him better; but he must be the judge of the advice. The old woman was a true woman and a good wife, who had no thought but to please her husband. Women who have any other thoughts have no business with a husband. If there is anything clear in revealed and natural law, it is that man is the head of the woman. All the beauty, all the harmony, all the happiness of life is centred in this truth. The most perfect woman that the world has ever known, one who was tried as no other woman was ever tried, who was endowed by nature as few women have ever been endowed, the sweetest, purest being that ever bore the name of woman, counted herself nothing but the wife of her husband, would know no law but his will, no happiness but his love; and when his love grew cold, and he became dead to her, though living, she still remained true to him. The world has abounded in Ephesian widows, but there has been only one Eloisa. Yet Eloisa is the true type of perfect woman. But Eloisa is not the type of Miss Fuller's ideal wife: she is better pleased with such a wife as Madame Roland, whose equality with her husband, and congeniality of tastes and employments, made her his companion and friend. She was, in truth, no wife at all, at least, to him, and she fully exemplified the truth which Miss Fuller denies, that love is a necessity with woman.

"This is one of the best instances (the marriage of Madame Roland) of a marriage of friendship. It was only friendship, whose basis was esteem; probably neither party knew love, except by name;" says Miss Fuller. But Thiers says; "Elle respectait et chérissait son époux comme un père: elle éprouvait pour l'un des Girondins proscrits une passion profonde, qu'elle avait toujours contenue."

### [PART TWO]

The great defect of Miss Fuller's book is a want of distinctness. We can easily discover that her chief concern is to help remove the evils which afflict society; but we cannot discover any hints of the means by which they may be removed. She is sufficiently learned, sufficiently vigorous, and sufficiently earnest, but not sufficiently plain and direct. We have too much of the Scandinavian mythology and the Greek tragedy, and too little of what the book professes to deal with—woman in the nineteenth century. The most direct writing is on a topic that no virtuous woman can treat justly, because she must of necessity be imperfectly informed; it is exceedingly painful to read a portion of her work, which we feel must have been painfully produced; and though we cannot but respect her for her courage in printing it, we regret that she should have felt herself bound to do so, since no good can possibly result from it. There are a thousand existing evils in society which a woman may freely censure, and a thousand topics of pervading interest which she may freely discuss, with profit to her sex, without verging towards those that the innocent had better not know the existence of. We wish that Miss Fuller had loosened the fibula of her arrows, and let them fly at the practices which are, indeed, the direct causes of the lewdness which she deplores, instead of treating of the lewdness itself, which she can only know by hearsay, and of course but imperfectly comprehend.

The only way in which any good can be rendered to society, is by making woman more womanly and man more manly. To make sailors of women and milliners of men, is to have imperfect sailors and imperfect milliners. The advocates of woman's rights who are for putting men and women on a level, point to France as a proof that women are capable of performing all the duties of men; but they would hardly be willing to accept of the morals or the politics of France, which they must do if they adopt her practices. The difference between the sexes in this country is all in favor of the women: the law of courtesy grants them every thing, and the law of the land gives them more than they could ask. The privilege of voting is one which they could not exercise if it were granted, and it is the only privilege that is withheld from them. No change can bring them any good, or at least no greater privileges than what they enjoy at present. Men labor for little else than to make women happy; the cream of every enjoyment is skimmed for their express use, while the sour milk is drank by their lords; the instincts of the mass can be trusted more safely than the speculations of any individual. Men and women fall naturally into their proper spheres when let alone, and there can be no need of any violent revolutions to displace them from their true positions. The restraints which Miss Fuller complains of as hindering women from becoming blacksmiths, sailors, and soldiers, are the restraints which Nature has imposed, and which can never be overcome. As we have already said, the mind of woman is not endowed with the elements of command, because she cannot originate. There are no other restraints to her doing so, but her own weaknesses. Miss Fuller glories in the "triumphs of female authorship"; but we know of no woman who can claim the merit of originality. And we have no peculiar "signs of the times" in any work which has appeared from a woman's hand. In the Arts, where the creative faculties are tested, women have done nothing. Drawing and painting are considered a necessary part of every woman's education, but the world has produced no famous woman-artist of any kind; yet their way of life peculiarly fits them for artistic employment. There are no restraints upon woman in any civilised country, to prevent her becoming an architect; yet we have never heard of but one architectural work, and that a very recent one, produced by a female. All women are instructed in the rudiments of music, yet we have no female composers.

The employments of women are distinct from those of men, and the more perfect that society becomes, the more distinct they will grow. Therefore, instead of its being a cause of complaint that women are compelled to be women, it should be hailed as a sign, indeed, of the incoming of better times. . . .

It is a most favorable sign indeed, and the next generation of men will be all the better for it. But we should be glad to see the candy saloons and worsted warehouses of Broadway disappear along with the corset stores.

Miss Fuller has a great passion for heroines. Among all the females that she has selected for emulation, not one has been taken from the pure feminine creations of Walter Scott. To combat a postulate of Spinoza, she has extracted a long poem from W. E. Channing, a character of a woman from the tragedy of Festus, and a monstrosity—Mother Perpetua, from Eugene Sue. We see no need of a resort to fiction, while there are Catherines, Elizabeths, and Isabellas in abundance.

There are many admirable little episodes in the book, which ever and anon appear, like springs of sweet water bubbling out of a sterile soil, and charm us by their sparkles and music. . . .

These passages are of greater import than Miss Fuller seems to be aware of, or she would dwell longer upon them, and draw more profitable reflections from them than she has done. The well-being of the body is the great end of all moral teaching, and if this truth were most distinctly comprehended, the moral preacher would not so often preach to so little purpose. It is the too frequent way with moral philosophers and religious teachers, to exalt the dignity of the soul, by treating its habitation, the body, with contemptuous neglect, and it is a very rare thing to find a healthy soul shrined in a gaudy tabernacle. God has affixed the several penalties against any abuse of the body, not only in the natural laws, but in his revealed laws; yet in the days of ignorance and superstition, as well as in these days of knowledge and refinement, men have thought they were doing God a service by mortifying and lacerating the form which He had created in his own image. The most pale, unhealthy, decrepit, and consumptive men in the country, are the denizens of theological seminaries, who waste their vital energies in the vain illusion of studying God's will. They should be, if they rightly interpreted His will, the rosiest, healthiest, happiest men in the world. Man's first offence, which brought death into the world, was a wrong done to his own body; he ate forbidden fruit. Whether the Mosaic cause of the fall be typical or literal, the lesson which it teaches is the same. It was a violence done to his own body that brought suffering upon man and caused his expulsion from Eden. If we are to be restored to Paradise, the body must be restored to its pristine dignity and beauty, by abstaining from the forbidden fruit which destroys it. Shall we neglect the study of God's law, then, for the laws of health? By no means: the law of God is the law of health. Paul preached nothing to Agrippa, but righteousness, temperance, and judgment.

There are some things in Miss Fuller's book, which startle us by their strange sound, and set us a-thinking what they can possibly mean; for instance: "if there were more Marys there would be more virgin mothers;" and some others, equally enigmatical. Miss Fuller is of opinion that the ideal of woman is expressed to a greater height and depth in German literature, than elsewhere, and gives the themes of three ballads, as instances. . . .

We have marked several passages for quotation, which our limits will not allow us to make. Miss Fuller writes vigorously, but womanly; she has gathered together the materials for a very profitable book; but they are so loosely arranged, and so pervaded with threads of error, that as a whole we doubt whether the work will be productive of much either of good or of evil. It will, however, have one good effect. It will cause her to be more generally known than she has been; for although the reading public have been familiar with her name since the first appearance of the "Dial," they have had but an imperfect conception of the exact quality of her mind.

## [PART THREE]

We have encountered, during the past week, some half a dozen notices of our review of Miss Fuller's book, which strangely misrepresent the opinions we expressed of that lady. A writer in the Charleston Mercury, says that we snub Miss Fuller because she is neither a wife nor a mother, and has, therefore, no right to say what a woman should be, "forgetting that nature has so arranged it, that many women cannot be mothers, and that others prefer a single life." We have the best reasons in the world for not forgetting either of these facts. But we spoke of woman, not women. Man, in the same way, is nothing, but as a husband and a father. But there may be good citizens who are neither; who yet, as Lord Bacon says, "in affection and means have married and endowed the public." Miss Fuller's theme is "woman," not any particular classes of women, and she argues that woman may, and should fill any of the duties which properly belong to man, and which are wholly incompatible with the duties of a wife and mother. Miss Fuller suggests nothing, proposes nothing, hints at nothing, for bettering the condition of those of her own sex, who by accident may be placed in the unnatural condition of laborers for their own, or even their husband's bread. There are thousands of women in this city, married and unmarried, mothers and childless, who are compelled to assume the duties of man, and who do, with feminine patience, manfully contend with their destiny, and rule, where they should serve; and protect those who should protect them. But these are unfortunate, not privileged women, who would, like Zenobia, resign the sceptre of power, and gladly become matrons, rather than remain monarchs. The true position of woman is not a disputable point; the universal sentiment of mankind has determined it; God himself has said "her desire shall be unto her husband, and he shall rule over her." Miss Fuller says "no," in very plain terms, "let the desire and rule be the other way," and she instances the case of the woman, who contentedly resided on a mountain with her husband, because he found it for his interest to do so,—and with sufficient distinctness, declares, "I would not have it so." We did not snub Miss Fuller for this, as the writer in the Charleston Mercury asserts, but we are sorry for not doing so, and we repair our neglect, by telling Miss Fuller that no unmarried woman has any right to say any thing on the subject. Let any wife, if one can be found to say it, declare that she would not have it so. But Miss Fuller is not a competent oracle. The writer in the Charleston Courier is not correct in saying that Mrs. Sigourney has no children. She has a son and a daughter.

There is an immense deal of nonsense afloat on the subject of "femality," which can never do any harm to society at large, because the instincts of nature and imperative necessity will keep men and women in their true spheres; but it may, and we have no doubt does produce a good deal of harm in particular cases, by creating improper desires, and unsettling the quiet and content of many a well ordered family. It is not denied that there are Abby Kellys and Lucretia Motts, who have preached with seemingly good effect, to quiet audiences, but it is by no means certain that these women could not have done greater good by an unobtrusive observance of their duties in a different manner. We remember hearing one of them speak at a public meeting once, where the greater part of the assembly was composed of rather rude men, and once or twice while she was speaking, her face and neck blushed scarlet red; it was nature that spoke eloquently in her blood, and should have urged her to desist.

Miss Fuller names Mrs. Siddons as an instance of what a woman may effect in public; but Mrs. Siddons came before the public only as a woman, representing always a woman, either as a wife, a mother, or a betrothed wife.

During the past week, a meeting of young women was held in the Superior Court room of the City Hall, at which a Miss Gray presided, and a Miss Graham acted as Secretary. The object of the meeting appears to have been the consideration of the means by which women may be enabled to earn their bread. We doubt the propriety of such meetings, but they are certainly excusable, and reflect disgrace upon the society which makes it necessary that woman should have to resort to such means to secure an honest support.

There is one kind of employment, particularly adapted to the habits of women, which we hope to see introduced among them—wood engraving. It has already been done in England and France, and we have now before us some specimens of wood-cutting by a young woman, which would not only compare favorably with the best specimens of this kind of art that we have seen, but which possesses a peculiar character of freedom, which we have never seen in the work of any man. A class of young women should be immediately formed, for instruction in elementary drawing, with a view to their becoming wood engravers. It might easily be done at a trifling expense, and we can hardly fear that the city authorities would hesitate to lend their countenance to such an undertaking. Many women, who now support themselves with difficulty by their needle, might earn a handsome competence as wood engravers. It is an art which is daily growing in importance among us, and would be employed to a much greater extent, if we had a greater number of good artists.

# [*Woman in the Nineteenth Century*]

Anonymous*

Whatever may be thought of the opinions advocated in this volume, every candid reader will acknowledge the author's ability. Miss Fuller, indeed, is no common woman. She is a scholar and thinker, is earnest and high-souled, and longs, with almost a poet's yearning, for the amelioration of mankind. Her publication is a discussion of woman's present position and future destiny in society. As such it deserves a notice.

Miss Fuller has traced the history of woman through all ages and in all conditions, and has elucidated her subject lavishly with illustrations from ancient and modern literature. In the course of her remarks she advances some bold opinions. She doubts whether Christianity has elevated the position of the sex. She asserts that our present social system retards, instead of assisting the development of the intellect and heart of females. She thinks that woman is by no means on terms of equality with man—that she has power indeed, but not legitimate influence—that marriage, as at present viewed, makes the wife belong to the husband, instead of forming a whole with him. She denounces as a vulgar error the opinion that love is the whole existence of woman. She seems to consider that sex ought not necessarily to make any difference in avocation, and claims for woman the right, as well as the capacity, to plead at the bar, consult in the senate and thunder at the head of armies. With more truth she wages war against the present system of education.

In some things we find no fault with Miss Fuller. That, in very many cases, woman fills a subordinate position, or is often little more than the favorite slave of a brutal husband, no one can deny. Neither will we assert that the female mind is inferior to that of the male, either in kind or in power. We believe that a girl may be educated so as very nearly to resemble the boy in intellect, just as we know that her physical system may be made as capable of enduring fatigue. We admit that it is quite possible to make good sea-captains instead of indifferent musicians out of girls deficient in tune; to turn young ladies into knavish pettifoggers instead of cunning old maids; to teach a bad woman to lie and cheat in the game of politics as well as in the game of cards; and to transmute with no great trouble, a scolding hoyden into a swearing captain of hussars. In the same

---

*Anonymous, [Review of *Woman in the Nineteenth Century*], *Ladies' National Magazine*, 7 (April 1845), 143–144.

way nervous men might be changed to seamstresses and meek boys into housekeepers. But we doubt whether society or human nature would be the better for it. We are willing to grant that many abuses toward woman exist in the social system, but we are yet to be convinced that the whole system should, therefore, be overthrown, as it would be if the changes which Miss Fuller calls for were to occur. As well might you destroy Christianity for the sins of its professors. Nor does it follow that woman, because her occupations differ from those of man, is necessarily in a subordinate position. To our mind it is as important a work to mould the character of the rising generation as it is to rule that which is on the stage. No mission can be more holy than that of a mother. As a wife, too, woman holds an exalted position. She is, wherever matrimony is not abused, the confidant, the adviser, the helpmate, often the guardian angel of the man; and not rarely do her words and example sustain the husband in disasters that would otherwise overwhelm his soul and consign his fortunes to irremediable ruin. God has given to her a clearer sense of religion than to man and whether this arises from sex or education, the result is still the same: it keeps alive, within the sacred penetralia of home, a reverance for things not of this earth, a longing for supernal happiness, and a treasure of comfort in the darkest hours of sorrow, which would be unknown, if woman, as well as man, mingled promiscuously in the world, and lost, in its hard wear and tear, its knavery, its deceit, its meanness, the heavenly purity of character which now forms her brightest gem. As society is constituted in Christian countries woman is the priest who watches the sacred altar, man is but the Levite who draws the water and waits without. Would you change her situation?

Nor is her influence less than that of the other sex. On the contrary it is even greater, and often more direct. If her throne is the fireside, her empire is the world; if she rules by affection it is better than governing by fear. To make home happy with the light of her smiles, as if an angel had come down and filled the room with radiance, is no unworthy task; to cheer the bed of sickness, to smooth the pillow of remorse, to win the erring back to virtue, surely these reflect no disgrace on woman, surely these do not make her a slave. And we doubt very much whether the law which gives the husband the property of the wife, does not create a community of interest more powerful than could any other means which human wisdom has divined. In a thousand ways she exercises influence. The very character of her ministrations enables her to obtain it when all others, no matter of what sex, would fail. There is scarcely an event that transpires with which the influence of woman has not had something to do: in the choice of a vocation for the child, in the destiny of an empire, in the artist's *chef d'ouvre*, her influence is felt. She inspired Raphael's Madonna, she roused Europe against Napoleon's despotism. And to all time she will continue to exercise influence.

It is not in the social system, but in the abuses of that system where the evil lies: and against these, therefore, the argument should be directed. Marriage is a holy and sacred thing, yet it is far better that when improperly contracted it should continue, than be lightly broken, as in the case of Shelley, which Miss

Fuller seems to favor. It is a choice of evils, and we believe the present doctrine of divorce less injurious than the more loose one of licentious France. But great care should be taken, in forming a matrimonial relation, that the parties to it are congenial in nature; for compatability is of far more importance than splendor of fortune. And when joined in the connubial tie there should be a perfect confidence between husband and wife, a mutual yielding to each others wishes, a love that should raise no questions as to which should be superior, but, in its self-sacrificing nature, ensure a perfect equality.

Modesty is, perhaps, the greatest charm of woman. It is to her like the halo around the Madonna's head, and more than everything else causes that holy reverence with which the first love of man regards his future wife. To send woman out into the arena, where she may declaim, as we have seen her, before a yelling mob, destroys this sentiment and injures her influence. You may call this prejudice on the part of man, but would not women despise him, in turn, if he took up the distaff? Each sex has its vocation, and any departure from it destroys the harmony of life.

It is too often the case that persons, like Miss Fuller, take slight abuses for radical defects, and would overthrow a system when they should rather reform it.

# "Miss Fuller and Reformers"

**Orestes A. Brownson**\*

Miss Fuller belongs to the class described in the preceding article under the name of *Transcendentalists*, of which sect she is the chieftainess. She has a broader and richer nature than Mr. Parker, greater logical ability, and deeper poetic feeling; more boldness, sincerity, and frankness, and perhaps equal literary attainments. But at bottom they are brother and sister, children of the same father, belong to the same school, and in general harmonize in their views, aims, and tendencies. Their differences are, that he is more of the theologian, she more of the poet; he more of the German in his taste, she more of the Grecian; he the more popular in his style of writing, she the more brilliant and fascinating in her conversation. In the Saint-Simonian classification of the race, he would belong to the class of *savans*, she to that of *artistes*.

But Miss Fuller is an *artiste* only in her admiration of art, for she has little artistic skill. Nothing is or can be less artistic than the book before us, which, properly speaking, is no book, but a long talk on matters and things in general, and men and women in particular. It has neither beginning, middle, nor end, and may be read backwards as well as forwards, and from the centre outwards each way, without affecting the continuity of the thought or the succession of ideas. We see no reason why it should stop where it does, or why the lady might not keep on talking in the same strain till doomsday, unless prevented by want of breath.

The title gives no clew to the character of the work; for it is no part of its design to sketch, as one would suppose, the condition of woman in the nineteenth century. Indeed, we do not know what is its design. We cannot make out what thesis or what theses it does or does not maintain. All is profoundly obscure, and thrown together in "glorious confusion." We can attempt no analysis of its contents. As talk, it is very well, and proves that the lady has great talkative powers, and that, in this respect at least, she is a genuine woman.

As we read along in the book, we keep constantly asking, What is the lady driving at? What does she want? But no answer comes. She does not know, herself, what she wants. She has an ugly feeling of uneasiness, that matters do not go right with her; and she firmly believes that if she had—I know not what—all would go better. She is feverish, and turns from one side of the bed to

---

\*[Orestes A. Brownson], "Miss Fuller and Reformers," *Brownson's Quarterly Review*, 7 (April 1845), 249-257.

the other, but finds no relief. The evil she finds, and which all her class find, is in her, in them, and is removed by no turning or change of posture, and can be. She and they are, no doubt, to be compassionated, to be tenderly nursed and borne with, as are all sick people. It is no use attempting to reason them out of their crotchets; but well people should take care not to heed what they say, and especially not to receive the ravings of their delirium as divine inspirations.

Seriously, Miss Fuller does not know what she wants, any more than does many a fine lady, whom silks, laces, shawls, dogs, parrots, balls, routs, jams, watering-places, and despair of lover or husband and friends have ceased to satisfy. She even confesses her inability to formula her complaint. She has a strange gnawing within, an indefinable craving for what she has not, does not know how to get, where to find,—a very unpleasant condition, no doubt, but not an uncommon one. Poor girl! hers is but the common lot of all her Protestant and infidel sisters, and brothers too; for her brothers are hardly less subject to the vapors than her sisters. They are all seeking they know not what, craving what they have not, find not,—now seizing on this bawble, now on that,—a bonnet, ribbon, shawl, cravat, coat, minister, sect, association; but all to no purpose. The craving remains; nothing satisfies; the aching heart nothing fills. Cook the vegetable oyster as they will, serve it up with what condiments, flanked by what sauces, they please, it is never the genuine oyster.

"O, give us something to love!" exclaim a bevy of dear, sweet, enchanting creatures. "Give us something to love; we were made to love"; and round they look with fond eyes and loving hearts, but as ever there is the gnawing, the aching void within. Love is the be-all, the cure-all, the end-all; but, alas, there is nothing to love; no one knows how to love; no one knows how to respond to the true, fond, loving heart. Try again,—again,—another,—another, and still another;—'t is vain. The heart is not met; is not filled; is emptier than ever. Surely there is some mistake. The Creator committed a blunder when he made the world, especially when he made man and woman. Man and woman, it is true, as says our authoress, are but "two halves of one thought"; but the right halves do not come together, or do not match. They get mismatched. Mrs. Jones has got my other half, and I have got Mrs. Peter Smith's,—or am cheated out of it altogether. All this is very provoking, no doubt. To be made capable of loving, to have this free, pure, rich heart, full to overflowing with love, containing a whole ocean of love, large as the Atlantic, nay, as the five oceans together, and warm enough to thaw out either pole, and no one I can love,—nobody but Jim Jones or Peter Smith,—'t is intolerable.

The terrible evil here set forth Miss Fuller thinks is confined exclusively to her own sex. Men have the advantage; with them it is not so bad. There she is wrong. There are those who have beards on their faces, as well as those who have none, who have these cravings, these hearts full of love, such as it is, and an aching void in these same full hearts, because there is no one for them to love. They cannot love Bridget or Sukey, and all but the Bridgets and Sukeys are— not for them. Men are not much more easily satisfied than women; and if women are forced to take to tea, scandal, philanthropy, evening-meetings, and smelling-bottles, men are forced to take to trade, infidelity, sometimes the pistol, and even to turn *reformers*, the most desperate resort of all. All this is sad enough, and really under all this is a grievous evil, of which no serious-minded man will make light. But what is the remedy?

Miss Fuller, so far as we collect her thought from her interminable prattle, seems to think this evil is to be remedied by having it understood that woman has an immortal soul, and by securing her free scope to develope herself. But what change this implies, or would introduce, Yankee as we are, we are unable to guess. Understand that woman has an immortal soul! Why, we are far beyond that already. Read our poets, listen to our philanthropists, abolitionists, Fourierists, Saint-Simonians, dietetic reformers, and other reformers of all sorts and sizes, of all manner of things in the universe, and some others, and you shall find that she is already a divinity, and adored as such. Who has not heard of the "divine Fanny," or not been eager to adore as she made his heart jump by her capers and pirouettes? Not her soul only, but woman's body, is held to be divine, divine from head to foot, and we go into ecstacy of devotion at sight of a "divine ankle." In our ordinary prosaic language, is not woman an "angel," "an angel of purity," of "loveliness," and "too holy for earth"? and they who scorn to bend the knee before their Maker, are they not ready to prostrate themselves at her feet, and kiss the very ground on which she stands?

"The more fools they. But this is not what we want. This is sickening, disgusting." And yet there are comparatively few women seriously offended at it, if they themselves are its object, even though offered by those they have good reasons for believing are double-distilled villains. But enough of this. There are evils, great evils, no doubt, to which both men and women are subject. Neither sex is what it should be, or finds always the fair weather and smooth sea the heart may crave; but we have yet to be convinced that woman's lot, compared with that of man's, is one of peculiar hardship. She is not always the victim, and examples of suffering virtue may be found amongst men as well as amongst women. No doubt, there are evils enough to redress, but we do not think the insane clamor for "woman's rights," for "woman's equality," "woman's liberation," and all this, will do much to redress them. Woman is no more deprived of her rights than man is of his, and no more enslaved. Woman as to her moral and spiritual nature has always been emancipated by Christianity, and placed as a human being on the same platform with man. She is treated, and always has been treated, by Christianity as having an immortal soul, and as personally accountable to her Maker. In this respect man has no claims, and is allowed no preëminence, over her; and what more can she ask?

In the distribution of the several spheres of social and domestic action, woman has assigned to her one sphere, and man another; both equally important, equally honorable. This therefore is no cause of complaint.—But who assigned her this sphere? Has she given her consent to be confined to it? Has she ever been consulted? her assent asked?—And what if not? Who assigned man his sphere? was his assent asked or obtained? Their appropriate spheres are allotted to man and woman by their Creator, and all they have to do is to submit, as quietly, and with as good a grace, as they can. Miss Fuller thinks it is man who has crowded woman one side, and refused her full scope for self-development; and although the sphere in which she moves may really be that most appropriate to her, yet man has no right to confine her to it, and forbid her to take another if she prefer it. She should be as free to decide her own destiny as man is his. All very plausible. But God, and not man, has assigned her the appropriate sphere; and, moreover, we must be ungallant enough to question Miss Fuller's leading doctrine of the perfect social and political equality of the sexes. She says man is not the head of the woman. We, on the authority of the Holy Ghost, say he is. The dominion was not given to woman, nor to man and woman conjointly, but to the man. Therefore the inspired Apostle, while he commands husbands to love and cherish their wives, commands wives to love and *obey* their husbands; and, even setting aside all considerations of divine inspiration, St. Paul's authority is, to say the least, equal to that of Miss Fuller.

Miss Fuller would have all offices, professions, callings, pursuits thrown open to woman as to man; and seems to think that the lost Eden will not be recovered till the petticoat carries it over the breeches. She is quite sure the ancient heathens understood this matter better than we do. They had a juster appreciation of the dignity of woman. Their principal divinities were goddesses, and women ministered in the fane, and gave the responses of the oracles. She is greatly taken with Isis, Sita, Egyptian Sphinx, Ceres, Proserpine. Would she recall these ancient heathen deities, their ancient worship, filled with obscene rites and frightful orgies? Would she restore the Isiac worship? revive that of Syrian Astarte? reëstablish the old custom which prevailed at Babylon, according to which every woman, on a certain festival, must prostitute herself to the first comer in honor of the goddess? readopt the old Phoenician method of obtaining marriage portions for dowerless daughters? have carried again in public procession certain pleasant images which Roman dames were eager to crown with wreaths of flowers? or reproduce the wild Bacchantes with loosened tresses and loosened robes, and lascivious satyrs? These and far worse obtained in the worship of those female divinities, and where woman served the fane, and gave the responses of the gods. Has it never occurred to our learned and philosophic lady to ask, if there was not some relation of cause and effect between the part women took in these ancient religions, and these filthy rites and shameful practices?

We ask not this last question because we would imply that women are less pure, or more easily corrupted, than men. We are not likely to fall into the common herd of libellers of women, and sneerers at female virtue. We have lived too long, or been too fortunate in our acquaintances, to think lightly of woman's worth, or woman's virtues. We remember too vividly the many kind offices we have received from her hand, the firmness with which she has clung to us in adversity, when all the world had deserted us, and also the aid which her rapid intuitions and far-glancing sense has afforded us in our mental and moral progress, if we have made any, to be in danger of this. It has been our good fortune to have experienced all woman's tenderness, all her sympathy when we were in sorrow and destitution, her joy when the world brightened to us, her generous self-forgetfulness and self-sacrifices for the beloved of her heart, and the sweet and gentle companionship in intellectual pursuits and in moral duties which seems to double man's power and to make virtue thrice more amiable; and we do not feel, that, so long as we retain our memory, we can be in danger of speaking lightly of woman, or of doing her injustice. But though we say all this, and could say much more, we still say the two sexes cannot mingle in certain spheres, and on the terms Miss Fuller proposes, without the mutual corruption of both. The fault is not woman's more than man's, perhaps not so much; but the fact is no less certain. While we live in the flesh, restraint and mortification are our law,—whether for men or for women. The things which look to us so enchanting, which even are not bad within certain limits, the glowing pictures of our innocent imaginations, the bright ideals of our youth,— alas! human nature is rotten, trust it not. They who imposed the restraints against which Miss Fuller protests, who separated the sphere of the sexes, and assigned to each as far as possible a separate line of duty, if they were men, must have known all too well what they were about. They may have been men who had lost their innocency; but if so, they had gained—experience.

The first mistake which Miss Fuller commits is the mistake committed by all reformers,—from him who undertook in the Garden to reform God's commandment to our first parents, down to the author of the "Orphic Sayings,"— that the true moral and social state is to be introduced and secured by the free, full, and harmonious development of human nature. This mistake is committed everywhere. Go where we will, out of the Catholic world, we meet it. We find it with Deists and Atheists, with German Rationalists and American Transcendentalists, in the fanciful theories of Gall and Spurzheim, in the dreams of Charles Fourier and Saint-Simon. It is the settled doctrine, and only settled doctrine, of modern philosophy, and apparently the fixed creed of the whole Protestant and infidel worlds,—exception to be made, perhaps, in favor of the Puseyites, and the few remnants of the old Calvinistic sects. It is embraced and hotly defended by hundreds and thousands who have no suspicion of its direct and glaring hostility to experience and revelation. Nothing can be falser or more dangerous than this delusion. Nature does not suffice. Nature cannot be trusted. Away with your wretched cant about "faith in man, in man's nature," his "lofty capacities," "glorious affinities," and "Godlike tendencies." Nature, we repeat, is rotten; trust it not. The fairest, sweetest, purest, dearest affections nature ever knows lead us most wofully astray, and will do so, if not restrained, whatever your moral codes or social arrangements. There is no such thing as a harmonious development of nature. Cultivate nature as you will, observe the nicest balance between all its tendencies, and, before you know it, before you can dream of it, one rascally passion has suddenly gained the mastery, and all is confusion and anarchy within. Nature is cursed. For six thousand years you have cultivated it, and it has yielded you only briers and thorns; cultivate it as you will for six thousand years to come, and it will yield you nothing else. "He that soweth to the flesh shall of the flesh reap corruption."

Another mistake, not less fatal, is also committed by our reformers. They see there are evils, that men and women suffer, and suffer horribly. Their sympathies are awakened, and they seek if relief cannot be found. All this is well, commendable even. But they assume that relief is to come here, and the good craved, but found not, is to be realized in this world, in this probationary life. "The highest ideal man can form of his own powers," says Miss Fuller, "that he is destined to attain." And this ideal is to be attained here. But Eden, the terrestrial paradise, is lost, never to be regained. Man forfeited it, and has been driven forth from it, never to repose again in its fragrant bowers, or beneath its refreshing shades. The earth is cursed; do what you will, rebel as you please, the curse is irrevocable. This world is a prison-house, and escape you cannot till death sets you free. The sooner you come to this conclusion, the better for you, the better for all. This life is and must be a discipline, a probation, a warfare. You must stand on your guard, always in arms, sleepless, and fight, fight for your life, with enemies from all quarters, and of all sorts and sizes, till you are called home to enjoy the victory and the triumph.

We know this is an unpalatable truth to our zealous philantropists, and we know the scorn and derision with which they will treat it. But the realization of a heaven on earth is not the end for which the Gospel was given us. Our Maker has not abandoned us; far from it. He has prepared something far better for us than a terrestrial paradise. He has prepared heaven and its eternal beatitude for us. But we can enjoy that here only through faith and hope. It is ours here only by promise. It is set before us as a glorious prize, as an exceeding rich reward; but it is not to be gained without the dust and heat of the race; nor will it be bestowed till the race is run, till the battle is fought, till the victory is won. Consolations we may have, consolations which the world knows not, cannot give, cannot take away. Angels will minister unto us and revive our fainting strength; but happiness, the full freedom and joy of the soul, are tasted not till the songs and harps of angels welcome us home to our Father's house.

True wisdom consists in fixing our eyes on this heavenly reward, and throwing off all that we may win it. We must count the sufferings of this present life not worthy to be compared with the glory hereafter to be revealed; we must despise the joys of this life, and trample the world under our feet. *Beati pauperes spiritu.* We must despise riches and honors, we must joy in poverty and destitution, and count all things as mere dross for the sake of Christ. This is the law imposed upon us, and no reforms which come not from obedience to this law will avail us aught. Here the struggle, the warfare; there the triumph, the joy.

But we have no room to proceed. As much as we dislike Miss Fuller's book, as pernicious as we regard the doctrines or notions it contains, as utterly as we are forced to condemn the whole race of modern reformers,—all who are seeking to recover the lost Eden on earth, from the harmonious development of nature alone,—we can still believe, without difficulty, that she may be a pure-minded woman, honestly and earnestly struggling to obtain a greater good for suffering humanity. Taking her starting-point, we should arrive at her conclusion. Believing a terrestrial paradise possible, we should strive for it; believing the free, full, and harmonious development of human nature the means and condition of obtaining it, we should protest against whatever restrains nature in woman as well as in man. We believe Miss Fuller wholly in the wrong, but we see no occasion for the kind of animadversions on her or her book, which we have noticed in some newspaper criticisms. She has done or said nothing which should be regarded as a sin by her Protestant brethen. In our remarks we have designed nothing personal against her. We are able, we trust, to distinguish between persons and doctrines. For persons, however far gone they may be in error, or even in sin, we trust we have the charity our holy religion commands, and which the recollection of our own errors and sins, equal to any we may have to deplore in others, requires us to exercise. But for erroneous doctrines we have no charity, no tolerance. Error is never harmless, and in no instance to be countenanced.

# [Woman in the Nineteenth Century]

### Frederic Dan Huntington*

On the whole, we have been disappointed in this book as we like to be disappointed. A woman here vindicates the cause of her own sex without a very large infusion of special pleading—an achievement not slightly meritorious, and deserving no small praise. We took up the volume,—we are willing to confess it candidly,—expecting to find in it a considerable amount of mannerism, affectation, eccentricity and pedantry. It gives us all the more pleasure therefore, to acknowledge that our suspicions were, to a great extent, unjust. The number of inverted sentences, *outré* ideas, far-fetched comparisons and foreign idioms, is more limited than we had feared. Of pedantry, indeed, perhaps there is not an entire absence. Classical characters, and references to mythological fables, are introduced with a frequency which the best taste would hardly sanction; but the error is often committed with a gracefulness and appositeness which partially redeem it. We just notice these faults the more readily, because we believe Miss Fuller might easily be rid of them, and would gain greatly by the change. We observe that exactly in proportion as she becomes thoroughly in earnest, her style becomes straightforward and natural. An honest thinker, who occasionally wields the good Anglo-Saxon phrase so energetically, and with so much directness as she, ought to abandon at once all seeking after the novel, the strange and the startling. Like the class of writers to which she belongs, much read in the authors of another nation, and much delighted with them, she sometimes puts herself under a yoke, while she longs above all things to be free; adopts a constrained air, while particularly ambitious of unrestraint; and while aiming at a healthful exercise of the faculties, falls into a habit of thought that is morbid, inharmonious, without symmetry, and so, of course, unattractive, if not disgusting. Moreover,—to finish cleanly this ungrateful work of censure,—the book lacks method sadly, and should have been relieved to the reader by the kindly intervention, here and there, of a sectional or capital division. It is rather a collection of clever sayings and bright intimations, than a logical treatise, or a profound examination of the subject it discusses.

Whether Miss Fuller's ethical code would correspond precisely with our

*[Frederic Dan] H[untington], [Review of *Woman in the Nineteenth Century*], *Christian Examiner*, 38 (May 1845), 416-417.

own, we should be able to declare with more confidence if she had made it perfectly clear to us what that code is. The same may be said of her standard of manners. But of the general spirit of the essay we can, and we must, speak with sincere and hearty approbation. There is a noble and stirring eloquence in many of the passages, that no susceptible person can fail to be affected by. Great, lustrous thoughts break out from the pages, finely uttered. The pervading sentiment is humane, gentle, sympathetic. Miss Fuller says in one place, "I wish woman to live, first, for God's sake;" and she seems to be possessed by the reverential, devout feeling indicated by this remark. She casts a deserved contempt on the miserable trifling so often exhibited by men in their conversation and deportment with woman, a custom that depreciates and openly insults their character. For our own part, we have often wondered at their patient toleration of the indignity, implied so palpably in this sort of bearing. Mean topics and flippant discourse are perpetually introduced in society for their entertainment, as if they were capable of comprehending nothing else. She urges in respectful terms their rights, both in property, and, as mothers, to their children, suggesting some worthy thoughts for law-makers. She would have woman respectably employed. She would elevate the purposes of their lives, and by dignifying their position and character, restore the ancient chivalrous respect paid them by every manly heart. Her notions do not seem *ultra* nor extravagant. She does not ask that woman may be thrust into man's sphere, but that she may have a right and honorable sphere of her own, whether as sister, daughter, mother, or "old maid." And, for ourselves, we admire the noble appeals, near the close of the work, in which she rebukes vice, and entreats for it a wise but prompt consideration. She has discussed a delicate topic delicately and fearlessly; without prudish folly, without timidity, as a true woman should. No tongue will dare to cavil at her. She is too evidently above all small criticism in this quarter, far up out of its reach. What she has said needed to be said, and, if the age has any necessity, needs, we firmly believe, to be repeated, felt and acted upon. The "nineteenth century" has a mission to woman, as well as she to the nineteenth century.

# [Woman in the Nineteenth Century]

### Charles Lane*

The misfortune in almost every endeavor for Woman's enfranchisment and elevation is the sentiment, that she is to attain them somehow by the gift, or at least the sufferance of Man. Is it not sufficiently felt, that this presumption is the very evil to be cured, the very wrong to be righted; that this assumption is the root of the whole mistake. A mistake so deeply rooted that to eradicate the weed, serious fears will be excited lest the true plant suffer. We now always stand in the presence of sexual men and women, and we are to be brought to the consciousness of associate human souls. It is clear that such a state of mind involves an overthrow of the present civil system as completely as the Christian superseded the Mosaic. And in the self-same spirit too, that is too say, the law is at once fulfilled and destroyed by the gospel.

Antecedent to the Christian era, woman was the hand-maid, the vassal of man. Christ proclaimed her emancipation; at the sound of his voice, the chains should fall from her limbs. But in the sluggish convervatism of human nature, the old law still inheres in our system, and woman, though a little more, perhaps much more, decently treated, does not yet adorn creation by being in her true place. Nor can she, while she looks to man to bestow it, or even to concede it. There needs from him neither gift nor concession. All that is demanded is that he should not take away, should not assume, should not exclude. Woman should have her right place, not by a parade of man's pretended generosity, not with the idea of his permission, but she should be in it, unhindered, unquestioned. It should be an unmarvellous fact, like the relation of the seasons, for the growth of plants. It should happen.

Such a state of human relation, we have said would change the whole social order. It is evident that whatever touches this vital element must ramify throughout every limb of the social body. The modern family of pairs, and their offspring has not set aside ancient polgamy more certainly than the full accomplishment of the Christ life would repeal, yet do justice to, the present order. The time was ripe for *that* exchange. Happiness no more belonged to it— Solomon, the monarch in all his glory of wives and concubines attained not to that consolation which the outcast Hebrew youth of Nazareth found in celibate

---

*C[harles]. L[ane]., [Review of *Woman in the Nineteenth Century*], *Herald of Freedom*, 11 (5 September 1845), 1.

reservation. Through him it was revealed that Woman is man's sister, not his slave; a spirit equal in moral beauty and religious value, not a soulless mortal, excommunicated by her very nature. He declared his kingdom is not of this world; it is not of this order; this plan of governing by force and cunning, by the strong arm and the quick wit; but it is the kingdom of patient labor, quiet understanding of unfailing love. Which is now most a citizen in that kingdom. Woman or Man? Let either world answer.

It is not by inviting Woman more into the male world, to take place at elections, in political meetings, in commercial enterprizes, to become active in civil rights, now pertaining solely to men, that she can arrive at her true position.—She instinctively shrinks from all such externalities, which indeed bring more trouble than advantage to those who now interfere in them, as well as more detriment than progress to the human race. Men who would be the most unwilling to aid woman's restoration, will probably be found encouraging so mistaken a notion as this. It is not by playing more into the outer world's kingdom that her place will be found. But by passing more into the inner kingdom and living carefully a life in conformity to its laws, will she be enabled to become and to remain free and most truly to help man's freedom.

Woman's rectitude can never be dated from that ground, that nature, that system, wherein man's moral nature lies prostrate. Man, a fallen, an erring, a corrupt creature, as he confesses, is proposed to be the instrument of woman's elevation, the donor to her of goodness and purity. Monstrous absurdity. He who is so lost a being; he who enslaves black women in the field, and white women in the factory, for whom the royal palace and the peasant's cottage are alike scenes for the gratification of his lowest lust, is to bestow on woman her just rights. Cruel delusion! Rather is it to be hoped that woman, fleeing from the mockeries, tyrannies and vices of the present order, shall take her firm stand on that holy ground, where souls and not bodies are considered, and woman no longer treated as a chattel to be given away or bargained for, is 'neither married nor given in marriage.'

At all events it is probable, that woman's [responsibilities] . . . must be clearly her own act. That is to say not man's act, but woman's so far as it belongs to humanity to act. And as in this case, the act is but negative, it is quite in accordance with the idea of a spiritual, redeeming and saving operation on the soul by the supreme power.

Whatever opinions may be entertained regarding the ultimate destiny of the human race on the earth, there can be no doubt that for immediate as well as future happiness in this life it is needful there should be no more marriages than are sanctioned by celestial necessity. The purity, we might almost say the existence of the species, depends more on continence, than on marriage. When put on the truest and most serious grounds, how few are there, of either sex, who can declare their fitness for this relation. And unless we place it on the most serious grounds, what do we but permit the world to be transformed into a vast licensed harem?

Freedom, peace, salvation, cannot be expected for woman while she permits herself to be the instrument of man's lowest gratifications, and tolerates a degree of unchastity in him, which in her he would utterly condemn. It is for woman to bar the door against licentiousness, and thereby both herself and man will cease to be its victims. Self denial is the only hopeful means for any improvement, whether moral or physiological, and woman must not expect so great a work as her salvation to be wrought by any easier process. The talking of her redemption, the gilding of her chains by encircling marriage with new prettinesses will but prolong her suffering days and deepen her anguish and pains. This is the point where we are now to look for woman's relief, religious, social, moral, physical. Each sex must bear its own burdens, each must work out its own salvation with fear and trembling. Man cannot restore woman, though he may degrade and destroy her. He can withhold himself from further mischief and restraint is his first duty, but upon woman for woman, it mainly depends to effect her e-man-cipation.

There was a period when the present relation of the sexes, both in marriage, and out of it, afforded a life comparatively happy, but it is the common remark how that time has passed away. The waves of intellect come dashing over the shores of nature, and not a stone, nor a sand grain is left unturned. These waves can only be quelled by another air, by the astral spirit.—The wind that bloweth where it listeth, is even now veering to a milder point, and this volume is a signal proof of the change.

Margaret Fuller has done the state—the moral state—no small service, by her courageous adventure into a field, esteemed so swampy and pathless as this of Woman's condition. The book is strengthening to candid minds, and must be formidable to the nervous conservative of old notions and hereditary lusts from its well selected array of pure and unquestionable evidence. A book on this unexcelled point of humanity, of more liberal scope or truer emphasis has rarely been presented to the public. It is chaste and honorable, cheerful, and faithful.

Authors have ere now infused such life and energy, into their writings as to quicken the reader's soul for immediate action. The Book is laid down in the idea that we can go and grasp the author by the hand, and join him in the enterprise. For the moment we would that this were such an instance. We want to see THE WOMAN. The woman who sits enthroned in the celestial garment of virgin purity, to whom all inferior and less pure spirits bow. The Queen of that world which Christ, the virgin son of a virgin mother, revealed to mankind and of which he is King. But perchance it is better as it is. Outer leadership is never so certain and so steadfast as inward growth, and submission to the universal leader. "Call no man master." Call no woman mistress. There is in this world somewhat too much of this miserable submission to the outward, and too little happy submission to the inward.

How frequently are we told to leave the subject alone, for that woman has her influence through her husband, her brother, her son. This is the very evil under which she suffers, namely that the influence on her and the influence from her must always be transmitted through man, strained through the narrow sieve of his prejudiced mind, mingled with the impurities of his spirit. It is true (and pity 'tis, 'tis true) a solitary woman can play wantonly with the interests of a whole nation as the hired companion of an absolute monarch, or become a mischievous puppet on a corrupt throne; but are these spheres for woman? are these legitimate modes for extension of her true influences, the establishment of her holy rights?

Our authoress is sufficiently possessed by the true idea of the ground of woman's freedom to have diffused it throughout her book. . . .

When the authoress observes, 'The spiritual tendency is towards the elevation of woman, but the intellectual by itself is not so,' (p. 90) she expresses that fact which if followed through its deepest foldings would seriously aid the salvation of so intellectual a female community as that she immediately addresses. Of the worth or worthlessness of intellectual acquisition, few females can speak more profoundly or experimentally than Margaret Fuller. And we hear her verdict. A verdict which no mere observer will gainsay, much less the soul which has sought and in its seeking found. The best element currently acknowledged in the outer world, that world where woman is allowed scarcely any place, is the intellect. And this is surely not a world desirable to draw woman deeper into. There are but three grand lines in the soul, the spiritual, the intellectual, the natural. Neither nature nor intellect can yield to woman what she needs. Nature, by affliction, has not made her more effectively the family slave. Intellect, by all its erudition, sister Margaret says, tends not in itself to woman's elevation. How should it? Human happiness, human growth, depends on the spirit. An active and commanding intellect, no more bestows moral or spiritual life than a large body ensures a large and brilliant intellect; through true spirit growth involves bright intelligence.

Here then are joyful news for woman. The customs of the world will have chained her to so much from which man has been free, have at the same time bestowed on her important immunities denied to man. Among the wealthier classes, she has been exempt from the weights of useless learning and absolute scholastics so direfully imposed on man. In war, the very summit and totality of national vice, she has seldom actually mingled. From drunkeness, theft, and other *social* crimes, she has been comparatively free. And the only vice peculiar to her sex is, without man's more guilty aid, impossible. Had woman, then, a deeper spirit reliance, the hour of her emancipation were not so distant.

'The electrical, the magnetic element in woman has not been fairly brought out at any period. Every thing might be expected of it; she has far more of it than man.' (p. 91.) 'The especial genius of woman I believe to be electrical in movement, intuitive in function, spiritual in tendency.' (p. 102.)

The catholic spirit in which this book is penned, the warm enlightened affection, the practical piety, which breathe in every page, may alarm the narrow, affront the selfish, disappoint the lustful; but the true Woman-Heart will rejoice that such a word has been seasonably spoken. It comes from the word which is in the begining, and to the beginning or primary or inmost love in all hearts it cannot unsuccessfully be spoken.

# [Margaret Fuller]

### Rufus Wilmot Griswold\*

Miss S. Margaret Fuller is a daughter of the late Mr. Timothy Fuller, who from 1817 to 1825 was a representative in Congress from Massachusetts. She exhibited at an early age extraordinary facility in acquiring languages, so that her father was accustomed to speak of her, more than twenty years ago, as one "better skilled in Greek and Latin than half of the professors;" and alluding in one of her essays to her attachment to foreign literature, she herself observes that in childhood she had well-nigh forgotten her English while constantly reading in other tongues.

She made her first appearance as an author, I believe, in a translation of Eckerman's Conversations with Goethe, published in Boston in 1839. When Mr. Emerson, in the following year, established The Dial, she became one of the principal contributors to that remarkable periodical, in which she wrote many of the most striking papers on literature, art, and society. In the summer of 1843 she made a journey to the Sault St. Marie, and in the next spring published in Boston reminiscences of her tour, under the title of Summer on the Lakes. The Dial having been discontinued she went to reside in New York, where she had charge of the literary department of the New York Tribune, which acquired a great accession of reputation from her critical essays. Here in 1845 she published Woman in the Nineteenth Century, an eloquent expression of her discontent at having been created female; and in 1846, Papers on Literature and Art, in two volumes, consisting of essays and reviews, reprinted, with one exception, from periodicals.

Woman in the Nineteenth Century is one of the most brilliant of the many books on the intellectual and social position of woman that has been published. It is difficult however to understand what is its real import, further than to the extent that the author is ill satisfied that there should be difference in the rank and opportunity of the sexes. That there should be some difference in their sphere she seems not unwilling to allow. Like the rest of that diverting company of women who have contemplated a nullification of certain of the statutes of nature, she would but have choice of places and vocations.

Summer on the Lakes evinces considerable descriptive power, and contains some good verses. Her remarks in this work upon the Indians, and that part

---

\*From Rufus Wilmot Griswold, *The Prose Writers of America* (Philadelphia: Carey and Hart, 1846), pp. 537-538.

of our ethnological literature which relates to them, are very superficial, and incautious because this is so apparent. She says of Mr. Schoolcraft's Algic Researches that "a worse book could hardly have been made of such fine materials," that "had the mythological or hunting stories of the Indians been written down exactly as they were received from the lips of the narrators, the collection could not have been surpassed in interest," but that, as it is, "the phraseology in which they were expressed has been entirely set aside, and the flimsy graces common to the style of the annuals and souvenirs substituted for the Spartan brevity and sinewy grasp of Indian speech." Nothing can be more ridiculous than this whole sentence, but it is very characteristic. The phraseology of the tales has of course been "set aside" in translating them into a language radically different, but the antique simplicity of the originals has been as well preserved as the genius of the English tongue permitted. The wife of the amiable and learned author who is thus assailed, herself of the aboriginal race, and distinguished for whatever is peculiar in their character, wrote down and translated many of these myths and traditions, and it is amusing to see even her part of the work ranked on the score of fidelity below the few stories written out by Mrs. Jameson, who, however excellent as a critic of art, was here quite out of her depth—almost as ignorant as Miss Fuller herself, who when this was composed had been about one week west of Buffalo, and had seen perhaps a dozen vagabond Indians across the streets of Detroit and Chicago.

She is fond of epigram, and shows everywhere a willingness to advance any opinion for the sake of making a point. Thus, in a review of Mr. Poe's writings, she makes the observation that "no form of literary activity has so terribly degenerated among us as the tale," because it gave opportunity to remark "that everybody who wants a new hat or bonnet takes this way to earn one from the magazines or annuals." This display of wit was too dearly purchased by so large a sacrifice of integrity. No fact is more generally understood by those who have paid any attention to the advancement and condition of letters here, than that the exact reverse of this is true. Did one who had written with such a positive dogmatism of American literature, know nothing of the genial and indigenous humor of the tales of Irving? the extraordinary exhibitions of passion and sentiment in those of Dana? the fine painting and delicate ideality in those of Willis? the metaphysical subtlety and sombre beauty in those of Poe? the imagination, simplicity, refinement, and tenderness in those of Hawthorne? or of the various qualities which mark the contributions of Mrs. Child, Mrs. Kirkland, Mr. Simms, Mr. Hoffman, and others, to this class of our imaginative writings?

Miss Fuller rarely attempts particular or analytical criticism, but commends or censures every thing with about an equal degree of earnestness. She seems to think that books, like brown stout, are improved by the motion of a ship, and therefore generally eulogizes those which have been imported, and is very severe upon those of home production, excepting a few by personal friends, of the reading of some of which she enjoys a monopoly. These she could praise with safety, but for an incautious habit she has of giving extracts, which belie her commentaries, as in the case of a wretched drama called Witchcraft, which in spite of its quick damnation in the theatre, might have survived creditably enough in her pages, but for the verbiage she quotes from it in an appendix.

    The first volume of the Papers on Literature and Art contains a short essay on Critics, in which she gives a brief exposition of her views of criticism. It is followed by a dialogue between a Poet and a Critic; an imaginary conversation between the Two Herberts, remarks on the Prose Works of Milton, the Life of Sir James Mackintosh, the Modern British Poets, and the Modern Drama, and a dialogue containing sundry Glosses on Poetic Texts. The second volume contains remarks on the Poems of Thom, Prince, Mrs. Norton, Miss Barrett, Robert Browning, and the Lives of Haydn, Mozart, Handel, Bach, and Beethoven; a Record of Impressions produced by the Exhibition of Mr. Allston's Pictures; eulogies on Swedenborg and Wesley, and an essay on American Literature, followed by particular notices of Brockden Brown, Hawthorne, and Longfellow. Some of these papers are admirable, in their way. They are all forcible, and brilliant in a degree. But the greater number are pointed with pique or prejudice. They are not profound, nor are they catholic.

    Miss Fuller has remarkable quickness but not much subtlety of apprehension; general, but not solid acquirements; and an astonishing facility in the use of her intellectual furniture, which has secured her the reputation of being one of the best talkers of the present age. Her written style is generally excellent,—various, forcible, and picturesque,—though sometimes pedantic and careless,—very much like that of her conversation, and probably a result of but the same degree of labour.

    Miss Fuller's latest writings are a series of letters commenced in the Tribune in the fall of 1846, under the title of Scenes and Thoughts in Europe.

# "Sarah Margaret Fuller"

Edgar Allan Poe[*]

*Miss Fuller* was at one time editor, or one of the editors of "The Dial," to which she contributed many of the most forcible, and certainly some of the most peculiar papers. She is known, too, by "Summer on the Lakes," a remarkable assemblage of sketches, issued in 1844 by Little & Brown, of Boston. More lately she has published "Woman in the Nineteenth Century," a work which has occasioned much discussion, having had the good fortune to be warmly abused and chivalrously defended. At present, she is assistant editor of "The New York Tribune," or rather a salaried contributor to that journal, for which she has furnished a great variety of matter, chiefly critical notices of new books, etc. etc., her articles being designated by an asterisk. Two of the best of them were a review of Professor Longfellow's late magnificent edition of his own works, (with a portrait,) and an appeal to the public in behalf of her friend Harro Harring. The review did her infinite credit; it was frank, candid, independent—in even ludicrous contrast to the usual mere glorifications of the day, giving honor *only* where honor was due, yet evincing the most thorough capacity to appreciate and the most sincere intention to place in the fairest light the real and idiosyncratic merits of the poet.

In my opinion it is one of the very few reviews of Longfellow's poems, ever published in America, of which the critics have not had abundant reason to be ashamed. Mr. Longfellow is entitled to a certain and very distinguished rank among the poets of his country, but that country is disgraced by the evident toadyism which would award to his social position and influence, to his fine paper and large type, to his morocco binding and gilt edges, to his flattering portrait of himself, and to the illustrations of his poems by Huntingdon, that amount of indiscriminate approbation which neither could nor would have been given to the poems themselves.

The defence of Harro Harring, or rather the Philippic against those who were doing him wrong, was one of the most eloquent and well-*put* articles I have ever yet seen in a newspaper.

"Woman in the Nineteenth Century" is a book which few women in the country could have written, and no woman in the country would have published, with the exception of Miss Fuller. In the way of independence, of unmitigated radicalism, it is one of the "Curiosities of American Literature,"

[*]Edgar A. Poe, "The Literati of New York City.—No. IV. Sarah Margaret Fuller," *Godey's Magazine and Lady's Book*, 33 (August 1846), 72-75.

and Doctor Griswold should include it in his book. I need scarcely say that the essay is nervous, forcible, thoughtful, suggestive, brilliant, and to a certain extent scholar-like—for all that Miss Fuller produces is entitled to these epithets—but I must say that the conclusions reached are only in part my own. Not that they are too bold, by any means—too novel, too startling, or too dangerous in their consequences, but that in their attainment too many premises have been distorted and too many analogical inferences left altogether out of sight. I mean to say that the intention of the Deity as regards sexual differences—an intention which can be distinctly comprehended only by throwing the exterior (more sensitive) portions of the mental retina *casually* over the wide field of universal *analogy*—I mean to say that this *intention* has not been sufficiently considered. Miss Fuller has erred, too, through her own excessive objectiveness. She judges *woman* by the heart and intellect of Miss Fuller, but there are not more than one or two dozen Miss Fullers on the whole face of the earth. Holding these opinions in regard to "Woman in the Nineteenth Century," I still feel myself called upon to disavow the silly, condemnatory criticism of the work which appeared in one of the earlier numbers of "The Broadway Journal." That article was *not* written by myself, and *was* written by my associate Mr. Briggs.

The most favorable estimate of Miss Fuller's genius (for high genius she unquestionably possesses) is to be obtained, perhaps, from her contributions to "The Dial," and from her "Summer on the Lakes." Many of the *descriptions* in this volume are unrivaled for *graphicality*, (why is there not such a word?) for the force with which they convey the true by the novel or unexpected, by the introduction of touches which other artists would be sure to omit as irrelevant to the subject. This faculty, too, springs from her subjectiveness, which leads her to paint a scene less by its features than by its effects.

Here, for example, is a portion of her account of Niagara:—. . . .

The truthfulness of the passages italicized will be felt by all; the feelings described are, perhaps, experienced by every (imaginative) person who visits the fall; but most persons, through predominant subjectiveness, would scarcely be conscious of the feelings, or, at best, would never think of employing them in an attempt to convey to others an impression of the scene. Hence so many desperate failures to convey it on the part of ordinary tourists. Mr. William W. Lord, to be sure, in his poem "Niagara," is sufficiently objective; he describes not the fall, but very properly the effect of the fall upon *him*. He says that it made him think of his *own* greatness, of his *own* superiority, and so forth, and so forth; and it is only when we come to think that the thought of Mr. Lord's greatness is quite idiosyncratic, confined exclusively to Mr. Lord, that we are in condition to understand how, in despite of his objectiveness, he has failed to convey an idea of anything beyond one Mr. William W. Lord.

From the essay entitled "Philip Van Artevelde," I copy a paragraph which will serve at once to exemplify Miss Fuller's more earnest (declamatory) style, and to show the tenor of her prospective speculations:—. . . .

From what I have quoted a *general* conception of the prose style of the authoress may be gathered. Her manner, however, is infinitely varied. It is always forcible—but I am not sure that it is always anything else, unless I say picturesque. It rather indicates than evinces scholarship. Perhaps only the scholastic, or, more properly, those accustomed to look narrowly at the structure of phrases, would be willing to acquit her of ignorance of grammar—would be willing to attribute her slovenliness to disregard of the shell in anxiety for the kernel; or to waywardness, or to affectation, or to blind reverence for Carlyle—would be able to detect, in her strange and continual inaccuracies, a capacity for the accurate.

> "I cannot sympathize with such an apprehension: the spectacle is *capable to* swallow *up* all such objects."
> 
> "It is fearful, too, to know, as you look, that whatever has been swallowed by the cataract, is *like* to rise suddenly to light."
> 
> "I took our *mutual* friends to see her."
> 
> "It was always obvious that they had nothing in common *between them*."
> 
> "The Indian cannot be looked at truly *except* by a poetic eye."
> 
> "McKenney's Tour to the Lakes gives some facts not to be met *with* elsewhere."
> 
> "There is that mixture of culture and rudeness in the aspect of things *as* gives a feeling of freedom," etc. etc. etc.

These are merely a few, a very few instances, taken at random from among a multitude of *wilful* murders committed by Miss Fuller on the American of President Polk. She uses, too, the word "ignore," a vulgarity adopted only of late days (and to no good purpose, since there is no necessity for it) from the barbarisms of the law, and makes no scruple of giving the Yankee interpretation to the verbs "witness" and "realize," to say nothing of "use," as in the sentence, "I used to read a short time at night." It will not do to say, in defence of such words, that in such senses they may be found in certain dictionaries—in that of Bolles', for instance;—*some* kind of "authority" may be found for any kind of vulgarity under the sun.

In spite of these things, however, and of her frequent unjustifiable Carlyleisms, (such as that of writing sentences which are no sentences, since, to be parsed, reference must be had to sentences preceding,) the style of Miss Fuller is one of the very best with which I am acquainted. In general effect, I know no style which surpasses it. It is singularly piquant, vivid, terse, bold, luminous—leaving details out of sight, it is everything that a style need be.

I believe that Miss Fuller has written much poetry, although she has published little. That little is tainted with the affectation of the *transcendentalists*, (I use this term, of course, in the sense which the public of late days seem resolved to give it,) but is brimful of the poetic *sentiment*. Here, for example, is something in Coleridge's manner, of which the author of "Genevieve" might have had no reason to be ashamed:—

> "A maiden sat beneath a tree;
> Tear-bedewed her pale cheeks be,
> And she sigheth heavily.
> 
> "From forth the wood into the *light*
> A hunter strides with carol *light,*
> And a glance so bold and bright.

"He careless stopped and eyed the maid:
'Why weepest thou?' he gently said;
'I love thee well, be not afraid.'

"He takes her hand and leads her on—
She should have waited there alone,
For he was not her chosen one.

"He *leans* her head upon his breast—
She knew 'twas not her home of rest,
But, ah, she had been sore distrest.

"The sacred stars looked sadly down;
The parting moon appeared to frown,
To see thus dimmed the diamond crown.

"Then from the thicket starts a deer—
The huntsman, seizing on his spear
Cries, 'Maiden, wait thou for me here.

"She sees him vanish into night—
She starts from sleep in deep affright,
For it was not her own true knight.

"Though but in dream Gunhilda failed—
Though but a fancied ill assailed—
Though she but fancied fault bewailed—

"Yet thought of day makes dream of night;
She is not worthy of the knight;
The inmost altar burns not bright.

"If loneliness thou canst not bear—
Cannot the dragon's venom dare—
Of the pure meed thou shoulds't despair.

"Now sadder that lone maiden sighs;
Far bitterer tears profane her eyes;
Crushed in the dust her heart's flower lies."

To show the evident carelessness with which this poem was constructed, I have italicized an identical rhyme (of about the same force in versification as an identical proposition in logic) and two grammatical improprieties. *To lean* is a neuter verb, and "seizing *on*" is not properly to be called a pleonasm, merely because it is—nothing at all. The concluding line is difficult of pronunciation through excess of consonants. I should have preferred, indeed, the ante-penultimate tristich as the *finale* of the poem.

The supposition that the book of an author is a thing apart from the author's self, is, I think, ill-founded. The soul is a cypher, in the sense of a cryptograph; and the shorter a cryptograph is, the more difficulty there is in its comprehension—at a certain point of brevity it would bid defiance to an army of Champollions. And thus he who has written very little, may in that little either conceal his spirit or convey quite an erroneous idea of it—of his acquirements, talents, temper, manner, tenor and depth (or shallowness) of thought—in a word, of his character, of himself. But this is impossible with him who has written much. Of such a person we get, from his books, not merely a just, but the most just representation. Bulwer, the individual, personal man, in a green velvet waistcoat and amber gloves, is not by any means the veritable Sir Edward Lytton, who is discoverable only in "Ernest Maltravers," where his soul is deliberately and nakedly set forth. And who would ever know Dickens by looking at him or talking with him, or doing anything with him except reading his "Curiosity Shop?" What poet, in especial, but must feel at least the better portion of himself more fairly represented in even his commonest sonnet (earnestly written) than in his most elaborate or most intimate personalities?

I put all this as a general proposition, to which Miss Fuller affords a marked exception—to this extent, that her personal character and her printed book are merely one and the same thing. We get access to her soul as directly from the one as from the other—no *more* readily from this than from that—easily from either. Her acts are bookish, and her books are less thoughts than acts. Her literary and her conversational manner are identical. Here is a passage from her "Summer on the Lakes:"—

> "The rapids enchanted me far beyond what I expected; they are so swift that they cease to *seem* so—you can think only of their *beauty*. The fountain beyond the Moss islands I discovered for myself, and thought it for some time an *accidental* beauty which it would not do to *leave*, lest I might never see it again. After I found it *permanent*, I returned many times to watch the play of its crest. In the little waterfall beyond, Nature seems, as she often does, to have made a *study* for some larger design. She delights in this—a sketch within a sketch—a dream within a *dream*. Wherever we see it, the lines of the great buttress in the fragment of stone, the hues of the waterfall, copied in the flowers that *star* its bordering mosses, we are *delighted*; for all the lineaments become *fluent*, and we mould the scene in congenial thought with its *genius*."

Now all this is precisely as Miss Fuller would *speak* it. She is perpetually saying just such things in just such words. To get the *conversational* woman in the mind's eye, all that is needed is to imagine her reciting the paragraph just quoted: but first let us have the *personal* woman. She is of the medium height; nothing remarkable about the figure; a profusion of lustrous light hair; eyes a bluish gray, full of fire; capacious forehead; the mouth when in repose indicates profound sensibility, capacity for affection, for love—when moved by a slight smile, it becomes even beautiful in the intensity of this expression; but the upper lip, as if impelled by the action of involuntary muscles, habitually uplifts itself, conveying the impression of a sneer. Imagine, now, a person of this description looking you at one moment earnestly in the face, at the next seeming to look only within her own spirit or at the wall; moving nervously every now and then in her chair; speaking in a high key, but musically, deliberately, (not hurriedly or loudly,) with a delicious distinctness of enunciation—speaking, I say, the paragraph in question, and emphasizing the words which I have italicized, not by impulsion of the breath, (as is usual,) but by drawing them out as long as possible, nearly closing her eyes the while—imagine all this, and we have both the woman and the authoress before us.

# "Miss Fuller's Papers on Literature and Art"

Anonymous*

Among the recent brilliant and soundly-written articles which have begun to appear with greater frequency than formerly in the columns of the daily press, and which give earnest of the rapid advancement in interest and character of this most important department of literature, few of our readers can have overlooked the belles-lettres contributions to the Tribune. They have been remarkable for high and cultivated thought, and for a sincere and faithfully-pursued moral aim. It is needless to say that they have been characterized by their honesty and independence, and have been very unlike the displays of ignorance, indifference, or hired puffery which have too generally marked our newspaper criticisms. The peculiarity of these papers has been their representation of the individual life of the author; the expression of her sympathies—of the necessities of her intellectual nature; and being such in proportion as that author was educated and in earnest, they have been the standards by which other minds have been directed and governed.—There may have been points of disagreement—fair room for difference of opinion on alleged religious and social tendencies; but apart from this, there was a broad, common ground on which all cultivated readers might meet—where all who had "a jot of heart or hope" for the cause of American Literature, might gather new courage as its sure instincts and future prospects, no less than its present deficiencies, were commented upon with an intense hatred of cant, and an eager reverence for truth.

These papers were written by Miss S. Margaret Fuller, to whose pen the Dial, during the four years of its existence, was indebted for many of its finest and most elaborate articles; the author, too, of the much commented upon "Woman in the Nineteenth Century," and of a unique tour to the Western Lakes, remarkable for its intelligent spirit of observation and a rare beauty of thought.

The volume before us contains a portion of the articles from the Tribune, several papers of great interest from the Dial, others of equal value which have not been at all known to the public, and an original essay on American Litera-

---

*Anonymous, "Miss Fuller's Papers on Literature and Art," *United States Magazine and Democratic Review*, 19 (September 1846), 198-202; concluded in the October number with "Modern English Poets," reprinted immediately below.

ture, the perusal of which we recommend to the candidates for the liberal prize on this text offered by Mr. Graham, of Philadelphia. It formally opens a new era of candor and plain speaking on a subject which has certainly had more than its fair share of nonsense and impertinence.

It will be impossible to follow our author through the various topics treated of in a miscellaneous volume on "Literature and Art." In despair of presenting the author's views as exhibited in each of the articles, we must confine ourselves to a survey of one or two of the leading "papers," merely indicating the subjects of the remainder.

The volume opens with an introductory essay—a prelude, as it were, "On Critics," in which the different varieties of the race are accurately discriminated, and in which, in especial, there are some just remarks upon the numerous branch of the fraternity who make their own petty position and narrow horizon the sphere to which all others must conform. The relation between the "Poet and Critic" is the subject of the succeeding article, in the form of a Dialogue. We then fairly enter upon the book—commencing with the section of English Literature, which contains a variety of detached papers following a general chronological arrangement. There is a study of character in a sketch of the "Two Herberts"—George Herbert, of Bemerton, the poet and saint, and his brother, the finished man of the world and philosopher, Lord Herbert, of Cherbury. Miss Fuller does justice to the temperaments of both these literary heroes—reconciling differences, showing like results under different names, and that God's world is wide enough for both. The sketch of George Herbert's character is derived from a reverent study of his sacred poems, which would do honor to the cloisters of Oxford itself; the local scenery, the description of the lane being, probably, derived from the narrative of the pastoral Izaak Walton. The scene as described, in the neighborhood of Salisbury, bears a singular resemblance to the actual region.

"The Prose Works of Milton" is a fruitful hint to the young readers of America to study the "Areopagiticas" of the great poet. The Life of Mackintosh is a study of character, with a motto from "Sartor Resartus," which of itself, with Miss Fuller for interpreter, is evidence of care and mature feeling. The English Modern Drama, the plays of Marston, Sterling, the tragedy of Athelwolf, Philip Von Artevelde; the Poets of the People, the hand-loom weaver Thom, Prince, the Hon. Mrs. Norton, &c., are severally discussed. An article on Miss Barrett joins in the tributes to this foremost of English poetesses; and another on Browning, is the first American recognition of a new poet, whose vigor and originality, in spite of great eccentricity and harshness, have directed to him the hopes of the new London generation. The Lives of the Great Composers, Haydn, Mozart, Handel, Bach, Beethoven, and a paper on Washington Allston, (a companion to the essay by Mrs. Jameson,) must be left with the philosophical studies of character in the articles upon Swedenborg and Wesley, with a recommendation to the reader's most cherished hours. They will reward a careful and faithful study.

The subject of American literature is certainly no new one, at least so far as the title goes. We remember to have seen essays on American literature and lives of "our authors," so long as we can remember to have seen anything. There was Samuel L. Knapp, who used to write notices of American authors, just as Mr. Poe and Mr. Griswold are doing now-a-days. Every new magazine that was started, and on an average we suppose we may reckon one a month, had its deliberate presidential message on this fruitful theme. Washington Irving gave it an early position in his Sketch-Book; John Neal hammered away upon it, (not forgetting himself,) in Blackwood's Magazine, across the water; Mr. Cooper probably included it in his Notions of a Travelling Bachelor; Mr. Simms, in his last published volume of Views and Reviews, has handled the topic; a cart-load of college addresses have been delivered on it. There has been no want of nursing-fathers and nursing-mothers. In spite of this evidence to the contrary, it is an extraordinary circumstance, that there are here and there found persons of a skeptical turn of mind, who doubt, if after all, any such thing exists as American literature worthy the name. It must be admitted that the forms, the collections, biographies, &c., have been kept up with exemplary diligence. How has it come to pass, that while so much has been written, so much asserted, that so little has been believed. Are all the biographies to go for nothing, the puffs and "first-rate notices?" Yea, verily; posterity will not honor the drafts of the critics; they are good only for oysters and champagne in the present time! "Say something of me that will stick, in heaven's name!" was the language of a distinguished litterateur, whose biography has been written several times, though the gentleman is still in the hey-day of his powers, whose portrait has been engraved, of whom a thousand fine things have been written, and not one believed. Unfortunately, they wont stick; the article reputation can, it seems, be counterfeited by the false imitation notoriety, in all but the essential quality, that, namely, of adhesiveness—the Atalantean strengthening-plaster, as the quack advertisements call it, will never raise the world till it adheres.

Any one who comes before the public in future, with anything more on his lips about American literature, who is talking for oysters and champagne, and not for truth and candor, should be made to feel the peculiarity of his position. He should be gently led by the ears, and instructed to procure the oysters and champagne on some other tack. Such impudent balderdash as has been written on this theme, is disgraceful to the country.

Now, Miss Fuller, be it known at the outset, to prevent all further alarm of an ungallant prologue, does *not* bring before us the old story on American literature. As all America should know, she is no follower of little petty conveniences; she is incapable of the lap-dog school of complaisances, is conscious that her country is great and powerful enough to hear the truth; that its atmosphere is republican, and that there are no ill manners, (which might be accounted such in an old decrepid system of royalty,) in uttering that truth. Whether it will make friends or foes, our authoress is conscious of one guide only; her honest independent convictions,—convictions based on all due knowledge of the literature of the world, and inspired by a generous ardor and a true instinct. Miss Fuller gives a chapter to a summary of the case. It is apparently fragmentary, but will be found upon examination sufficiently comprehensive.

It tests the current literary coin of the country; and it must be admitted, in many cases, finds it of a low per centage of the precious metal; of much of a lower rate; and of all that is counterfeit, our authoress says nothing.

By American literature is meant something more than the mechanical products of paper and type, consumed in the preparations of books by American manufacturers. We suppose if all the sermons preached in the country in a year were to be printed, they would make a very respectable bulk, and fill the shelves of historical societies, as well as Falstaff's ragged regiment filled trenches—"food for powder"—but would they constitute an American literature? They certainly would, according to the standard of dry measure or avoirdupois—whatever it is by which collections of American poetry are made up, and so would equally well a series of bound volumes of the papers filed in chancery, or the complete set of the New-York Directory, which Mr. Putnam bears with him to England for the British Museum. This is not literature, in Miss Fuller's use of the word. By American literature, she understands a literature which shall be an expression of the original, naturally developed life of the country, in such high and elevated forms, as to rank with the literature of the world. *It must be genuine, and it must be elevated.* This, we take it, is what Miss Fuller intends to convey, though in other words; it is what we have always understood to be meant by the phrase,—the standard by which we have measured what has been already attained. Let us see what this standard designs, and how much there is to measure by it. It is an obvious truism when stated, that a literature cannot be called a national literature, unless it is the original spontaneous growth of the country, reflecting the life of the country. Yet simple as this assertion is, it has been anything but followed or lived up to by the so-called American authors. Their chief characteristic has been, that they were imitators and reproducers of foreign models, particularly the numerous school of New-England authors. We have had feeble echoes of the school of Pope, of the school of Addison, the obscurity of Shelley, without the mystic genius which first gave it birth; little imitations of this man's humor and that man's sentiment; American reflexes without end—"very American" Coleridges and Scotts, and Bulwers, and Mrs. Hemanses. We have had European topics and an English handling of them. If models were necessary, if our language was not new, and some reproduction was inevitable, it might have been of the spirit rather than the letter, and the imitation might have been of an age and school of British letters, more in harmony with the true life of our age and people than the comparatively effeminate, enfeebled productions of the days of Addison. The country has yet to profit in faith, simplicity and honesty, by the vigorous, sincere, though unpolished literature of the age of Elizabeth. The established charge of imitation is fatal to the claims of much of our so-called literature, to be considered American literature. There is, of course, much too that is genuine. There are many pure-minded men and women working intelligently in the good cause, to whom all honor is due!

Granted that a literature must be genuine, it must also be elevated. Our newspapers are genuine exponents of the lives of the people in their daily intercourse; in their buying and selling, joke-making and President-making;

but they are not a literature for the country, though they may be creating authors, and may contain a great deal of the raw material. Literature exhibits itself in various forms. Let us call the roll and see what American names are put in. We begin with poetry, and first for the epic. Will Joel Barlow's Columbiad be brought forward, or Dwight's production, "whose christian name was Timothy?"—that era of provincial patriotism has gone by which would have supported such laughable pretensions. No living writer, we believe, has attempted an epic. Well, there is the dramatic. We have hope and expectation only, though Miss Fuller whets that expectation by her good word for a new play, which we trust, with her, may be the harbinger of a new dramatic era for America. Still the dramatic temple is yet to be built. Is Metamora the cornerstone of a national dramatic literature, or Spartacus, or —?—the list is blank. Take the lyric then. There are, undoubtedly, some good song writers, clever versifiers for an occasional sentiment; but where are the Burns, Beranger, or Moore, as these authors represent the life of Scotland, or France, or Ireland? We have no national minstrel. In didactic and descriptive poetry we have Bryant, true to the soil; Dana of just and noble sentiment, though but a very fractional part of Coleridge and Wordsworth in poetic power; Longfellow, enthusiastic, elegant, but looking abroad rather than at home; Mathews, in his Poems on Man, national in his choice of his subject, bold and original in invention, felicitous in imagery; yet, in this work at least, the reformer and critic, rather than the "simple, passionate, sensuous" poet. We will not go on lest we should seem to disparage merit that does actually exist, by bringing it to a standard where it will be found wanting. Yet that standard must be reached before we can claim from the world respect for a worthy national literature.

Does Miss Fuller write at random, then, when she commences her essay? "some thinkers may object that we are about to write of that which has, as yet, no existence."

It will be a more agreeable duty to follow her in her generous estimate of what has been done, than to busy ourselves with what has been left undone.

To Brockden Brown, Nathaniel Hawthorne, and Longfellow, separate papers are devoted. The latter is the least complimentary; it contains, perhaps the passages of the greatest severity in the book. Yet justice is done to what is praiseworthy in the poet's writings. Our authoress has lived in "the Modern Athens," and become tired of hearing Aristides always called the just. The following estimate of his claims is impartial:—"Longfellow is artificial and imitative. He borrows incessantly, and mixes what he borrows, so that it does not appear to the best advantage. He is very faulty in using broken or mixed metaphors. The ethical part of his writing has a hollow, second-hand sound. He has, however, elegance, a love of the beautiful, and a fancy for what is large and manly, if not a full sympathy with it. His verse breathes at times much sweetness; and, if not allowed to supersede what is better, may promote a taste for good poetry. Though imitative, he is not mechanical." Justice is done to the "industry and power of clear and elegant arrangement" of Mr. Prescott. His choice of picturesque subjects, of great interest in themselves, is noticed; and the absence of "leading views and discernment as to the motives of action and the spirit of an era." The common admiration of the merits of Bryant, Bancroft, Dr. Channing, Emerson, Irving, and Cooper, is cordially reiterated—of the poems of William Ellery Channing, Cornelius Mathews, and of the new romance of Margaret, generous mention is made. In connection with the last we have an account of the unpublished play of Witchcraft, which confirms what has been already said of its merit in the daily press; and some supplementary extracts in the appendix, which present still more direct and authentic evidence of its value.

Of the important suggestions relating to the Press we have hardly left ourselves room to speak. Miss Fuller looks to the periodical literature of the country with hope and anxiety; she sees in it a field for the exercise of the most important intellectual and moral services. The Press, honorably directed by educated men of invincible truth and integrity, appears to her, as it is in this country, a station of infinite worth and happiness. May her remarks be cherished.

Here we might leave our subject; but the possible danger of being misunderstood, and of conveying a false impression of the book before us, compels us to add yet a few words. It is usual, when a writer approaches the consideration of "our authors," with any other language than that of undiscriminating eulogy, to raise the cry of Americanism, to talk of foreign criticism and subservience to the English press and British opinions. Now, the writers who usually resort to this stale outcry of Wolf, Wolf! should be the last in the world to say anything of deference to foreign writers, since the source of their weakness, and of the very evil complained of, is the imitation of these very transatlantic monsters. It is not, be assured, most intelligent public, out of any lack of patriotism, or want of reverence for the country, that such authors as Miss Fuller take up the critical lash, or raise the warning voice against the quack and pretender: A true, genuine, invincible AMERICANISM is what is insisted upon,—what is sought out, encouraged, and for which a confident hope is expressed. Nor does a censure of the hitherto prevalent schools of writing imply any censure of the American mind or capacity; it may imply that the age for a national literature has not yet arrived; that the ground has yet to be opened, and the quarries worked, for the very foundations of the temple; but it does not say that there will be no temple, or that the American race will lack genius to build it. Those convinced most deeply of the false and the unreal have the surest faith, in the true. In this they believe, and for this they will strive. The material wants of a vast country, bound by two great oceans, once provided for, actual men and women, youth and old age, friends and lovers, occupying the mountains and valleys, the plains and river-sides, the spiritual interests of man will find a voice. His existence will not pass away unsung. From that bright fervid look which the American wears, will break forth sparks of celestial intelligence. Poesy, the precious power, nourished in the dark soil of material life, shall grow and expand, and shed its precious sweetness on the air. We shall not always be pressing to our lips the faded herbarium of a foreign clime. We shall not always be mocked with the feeble words, the toothless utterances, the withering embrace of age, but shall welcome youth and beauty in our homes.

# "Modern English Poets"

**Anonymous**\*

We resume our comments on the new work of Miss Fuller, the "Papers on Literature and Art." One of the soundest, most clearly written of them all, is the one devoted to the chief of the great bards of England, who have illustrated the nineteenth century. The few present active writers, the Brownings, Tennysons, Miss Barretts, are disposed of in other articles. This is occupied with the preceding generation, the picked men of an illustrious era; and for convenience of grouping, and for the benefit of a classical device, our authoress has chosen the exact number of the Muses. We may find some matter of magazine gossip, in following her footsteps.

First of the sacred nine is Campbell, the author of the "Pleasures of Hope," a title which the poet having had dinned into his ears for half a century, got tired of at last. It would cause him to fume at any time to be thus spoken of, says a wag in one of the magazines, who took a melancholy pleasure in reading the jest for the last time, inscribed on his coffin-plate in Westminster Abbey. Miss Fuller, had she been fortunate enough to have visited England in his life-time, would have been sure of a welcome. In all that she says of Campbell, she does not even mention the palled Pleasures of Hope! To the grace and spirit of Gertrude, she does all due honor, for it touches her sentiment on the side of her sex, and for a similar reason springing out of that mine of poetry and philosophy, which dictated "Woman in the Nineteenth Century;" she thinks nobly, too, of the matronly Constance, in the poem of Theodoric. But the glory of Campbell is in his lyrics, and our authoress sounds the clarion note once more of the "Address to Kemble," which all will agree with her, in ranking among the finest productions of the poet. Macready, it is well known, is in the habit of ekeing out his theatrical speeches with mottos from this poem, and well he may; for the words spoken in behalf of actors, have neither been so frequent or so eloquent, that this could be omitted,

> "His was the spell o'er hearts
> Which only acting lends.—
> The youngest of the sister arts,
> Where all their beauty blends:

---

\*Anonymous, "Modern English Poets," *United States Magazine and Democratic Review*, 19 (October 1846), 316-320; concluded from "Miss Fuller's Papers on Literature and Art" in the September number, reprinted immediately above.

> For ill can poetry express
> > Full many a tone of thought sublime,
> And painting, mute and motionless,
> > Steals but a glance of time.
> But by the mighty actor brought.
> > Illusions' perfect triumphs come—
> Verse ceases to be airy thought,
> > And sculpture to be dumb."

Miss Fuller notices the want of continuous power, the flow of which in the genius of Collins, Shelley, or Coleridge, may be said to resemble the fulness of the fountain; while Campbell's inspiration may be compared to the single flight of the arrow. Campbell, she says, has no purpose; his best effusions read like occasional snatches. True, there was this limitation, but it was a limitation of the man's genius itself, and could not well have been otherwise. No purpose or determination could have altered the matter. Decision of character would only have made it worse. Upon certain conditions Campbell might have become more voluminous; he might have left his mark on more booksellers, but he would not have been greater. There was a certain amount of poetic oil in him to be expended, and when this had blazed out in his few great odes, the flame was extinct. To what purpose to burn artificial tapers, after the heaven-lighting volcano was extinct? Yet this and similar complaints are often enough made, to be worth answering. If Campbell had always written with a purpose, he would have been a comparatively dull poet; little read and speedily forgotten. Why is Miss Fuller forgetful of the "Pleasures," and mindful of the odes? The former was done with a purpose, the latter were not. Akenside is a case in point. He has left a few short poems that may be read, and a long one that no one attempts. He had a purpose, nevertheless, a most invincible purpose; he went to work like a sage with a bust of Plato, probably, before him; he remodelled his poem carefully. he published two different versions at different periods of his life, (making bad worse as usual in such cases, where the sobriety of age corrects the energy though with the license of youth) and the fate of the learned Doctor's "Toils" rather than "Pleasures of the Imagination," has been that nobody reads his book as many times as he wrote it. If Campbell had set to work with a purpose, he would have been duller than Akenside. His genius was a rare plant, not destined to blossom every day. There were probably long level passages, extensive table lands in his life, in which Campbell was dull, perhaps occasionally lashing himself into a little spurious vitality by his spleen—his conversation for the most part being bigoted and malevolent, not seldom profane and indecorous, at some glorious moments the "splendid bile" overflowing in some rich ode, some note of inspiration like "Ye Mariners of England." There was another poem that Campbell should have written with the "Soldier's Dream,"—the "Burial of Sir John Moore." That too was the one "bright consummate flower" of the author's poetical life. Take that away from the published remains of Charles Wolfe, and nothing remains. Campbell should never have written much, not so much even as he did. His strength, like that of the ancient tribe of Israel, after he had done several things which could be counted on the fingers, should have been to sit still. Never was a pension, the temptation to learned indolence, more wisely bestowed, than upon Campbell, if we except the much cavilled at liberality of the little pittance bestowed upon Tennyson. Even with the pension, Campbell would occasionally drivel. Without it, the fate of Haydon might have been his, a lifelong struggle between mediocrity and the public. The claims of the Punch Bowl, the time destroying inventions of company or society, editing magazines, travels to Algiers, could not fill up the vaccuum. He must stuff Time's Wallet with "Pilgrims to Glencoe."

Maudlin magazinists in this favored land, in like manner bawl out lachrymatory howlings in the newspapers, periodically, on the sad fate of Halleck, condemned to the "drudgery of the desk's dead wood," and prophecy the Epics and Don Juans were it otherwise. No one believes this to be gammon, the effusions of vaporous sophomores, or ladies begging stanzas for albums, more than the much honored poet himself. The good sense which has ruled over his verses has inspired him to leave them alone in their glory. If Halleck were to forget himself, read essays on decision of character, or take the prefatory advice of friends to get at our volume every now and then, he would bury his reputation alive. His friends, instead of calling upon him to commit this literary suicide, should pray for the life of John Jacob Astor, and for the perpetuity of the little Temple of Mammon and the weighty ledgers in Prince-street. The immeasurable Propontic fulness which "ne'er feels retiring ebb," belongs only to the great poets of inexhaustible vitality. There is a limit to the exuberance of even their powers. Call not then upon poets of the Campbell school for more.

Second of the nine commemorated by the gentle Margaret, is Moore; but what can a lady know of Anacreon? Yet of that universal classic joy which springs up the symbol of youth and happiness, whether symbolized by the juice of the grape or "the hour when fond lovers meet," she is a participant, cherishing all the wealth of the bounteous Pan. This paper, with the universal, the cosmopolitan love of letters, bears a tinge of personality which, in the name of the fair critic, we would repudiate. She thinks the charm of Moore will fade as he grows old. Gray hairs on Anacreon, the old rogue himself, in his prodigal generosity of sentiment, gave this stick to his critics, are destructive of all sentiment. We cannot see the sequitur. If poets grow old, their works do not. There is no old age, save such as mellows old wine in Love's Young Dream, 'Wreathe the bowl with flowers of soul,' or 'to ladies a round boy.' There may be something in this to the coteries of May Fair who have stiffened over the piano, and grown tremulous singing, "When Love was a Child;" they may sigh for the era of Little, and the raven locks of those early days, the "quaffing, laughing, and unthinking time," and be quite willing to have them back again in place of the polished baldness and "silver wires" on the brow of the Laureat. But what has this new generation in America to do with the decay of Tom Moore? There is no decrepitude in type or old age in sentiment. The virgins and youths, the Horatian audience he wrote for, of the past race, live again, and will live in ever renewing cycles. The case is not so bad, my fair critic. What say you to Anacreon himself; he grew old, lived till towards ninety, and died with a phthisical affection, or as it is poetically apologued, choked to death with a grape stone; he was a venerable fellow, and moreover he is dead and buried long since, with twenty or thirty centuries on the back of him. If there was any outlawry for youth and wine, any statute of limitations in the title deeds of poetry, it might be pleaded here; but Anacreon yet lives, and Miss Fuller, like the Margarets of other days great in history, the Queens and Princesses, we will venture to say, reads him in the original. Still is the Athenian cicada musical to her ear. With an ocean between us, we do not care for Thomas Little's Old Age: it is Anacreon Moore we care for; and when the corpse is interred and the biography written, it will be Thomas Moore, Esq., who shall be dead and buried, and not he who sung the Melodies.

Walter Scott succeeds. It has got to be the fashion—one of those fashions of literature which perpetually pass and repass in society, like the wear of a garment or the cut of a beard, to undervalue his poetry, perhaps because it was once overvalued. Its effects will be remembered while the youth of this generation is remembered, for Marmion and Fitz James were names which stirred the young soul like the sound of a trumpet. They will not die, notwithstanding the persevering efforts of a school of imitators, who have of late years been endeavoring to bring them into disrepute. They are filled with the stirring strains of the old ballad age, called once more into existence, like echoes from a horn suddenly sounded in the exulting highlands. Miss Fuller sees Sir Walter (stout Sir Walter, bless him, God!) reflected in some of these poems more directly, we cannot think completely, than in the novels. Her appreciative remarks will lead many to study these poems, and even by the side of Wordsworth and Shelley. "Good and great man! More and more imposing as nearer seen; thou art like that product of a superhuman intellect, that stately temple, which rears its head in the clouds, yet must be studied through and through, for months and years, to be appreciated in all its grandeur."

Crabbe, we fear our authoress has loved little; she adopts the common criticism, or rather stumbles over it. She would have been better and more characteristically employed in removing the impediment. He is with her the cold man of science, the harsh justiciary of the poor, and nothing more. Now, the very intensity of Crabbe's painstaking in the midst of these novels should lead the critic to suspect something else, since there can be no such self-sacrifice without love. Crabbe was a lover of his kind, a participant during youth and poverty, of the sorrows of the humblest; in better days, when he was the friend of Burke, and inmate of a ducal castle, moderate still, laboriously securing a good name, yet insensible to the noisy harlotry of fame, passing twenty years of his literary life unheard, unseen by the public—in his life, in his writings, he impresses us deeply as the profound humanitarian, not the skin-deep sentimentalist. It is an error that Crabbe's writings are all gloom. Among his tales are the most genial, quaint, benevolent pictures in the language, and hence the admiration for him expressed by such men, representing the manly character in all its moods, as Charles James Fox and Sir Walter Scott. The latter was delighted with the stories of Quaker Courtships and Lovers' Journeyings. Call over the list of English poetical story-tellers, and see if Crabbe can be spared.

There is a world of meaning in the next remark upon Shelley—"I turn to one whom I love still more than I admire; the gentle, the gifted, the ill-fated Shelley." Miss Fuller has elsewhere recorded her early obligation to the wind-harp of Shelley. His ethereal tones and unearthly melodies came to our Pythoness full of the inspiration of the woods and fields, the undefined but mighty harmonies of the spirit land. So should Shelley be read in the luxuriance of midsummer, amidst the bounteous prodigality of nature, the throbbing pulsations of plants and trees, the soft sighing of the celestial ocean of air. Read in the lecture room, turned into a subject of didactic essay, submitted to the scalpel of reviewers, or made a parlor book of, under the glare of Argand burners, would be a cruel and unhappy torturing of the genius of Shelley. He is to be loved, not talked of. Heaven forbid that he should be discussed in a literary *soiree*. We first made the acquaintance of "Alastor: or the Spirit of Solitude," in a scene,—a well wooded mountain, which, though thousands of miles from any spot ever trodden by the feet of Shelley, might have inspired his most literal descriptions in the poem. Neither rock, nor cliff, slumbering trees, or veiled sunny water, were wanting. The insect life fluttered responsive to the verse; the wind swept wildly, how impotently against the rock, the image of human will contending with fate, a passing cloud would temper all earth's joy with momentary gloom. . . .

We are no enthusiasts for the vague, so called transcendental school of poetry—there is no race of impertinents more intolerable than the bastard imitators of Shelley. Their impotent endeavors to span some intellectual void with their slender filaments of thought, remind us of Nat. Lee's vision in Bedlam,

> "I saw an unscrewed spider spin a thought
> And walk away upon the wings of angels."

Poor Nat. Lee, for talking of such things, he found himself in Bedlam; for actually doing them, bardlings in Boston and elsewhere, are encouraged to go at large, breaking loose even from the pinafore, their maternal parent unconscious that they are out.

But Shelley stands alone, and when all which we cannot admire in him, as suggested by our authoress, the infidelity, the war with the world, the unwholesome shadows of private calamity are blotted out, yet something remains for love. With men, or society, or himself, he may be at war—who is at peace? but of Nature, Shelley is an acknowledged interpreter, one of the Druidical priesthood of the Poets. In a genuine tone, says our authoress, "The rush, the flow, the delicacy of vibration in Shelley's verse, can only be paralleled by the waterfall, the rivulet, the notes of the bird and of the insect world.—While reading Shelley, we must surrender ourselves without reserve to the magnetic power of genius; we must not expect to be satisfied, but rest content with being stimulated. He alone who can resign his soul in unquestioning simplicity to the descant of the nightingale, or the absorption of the sea-side, may hope to receive from the mind of a Shelley the suggestions which, to those who know how to receive, he can so liberally impart."

In none of these Papers on Literature and Art, is a calmer, more philosophical spirit of judgment, the characteristic of the volume, exhibited, than in the estimate of Byron as a man, and Coleridge as a poet. Writing of the latter in connexion with Southey and Wordsworth, she is not dismayed by the unsatisfactory form of his writings, their obvious incompleteness in form, but obeying a true poetic instinct, she pronounces him "far more suggestive, more filled with the divine magnetism of intuition than they." Byron's personalities and misanthropy go for little with our authoress; his literary merits are summed up in a comprehensive sentence. "There are many beautiful pictures; infinite wit, but too local and temporary in its range, to be greatly prized beyond his own time; little originality; but much vigor both of thought and expression; with a deep, even a passionate love of the beautiful and grand." When these remarks on Byron were first published, they were accompanied in the magazine with an apologetic note from the editor, as if they had been strange heresies—and they will be read like truisms. We trust this suggestion will not be lost upon the critics who will doubtless be disposed to cavil at the hard opinions expressed in the chapter of the present volume on American Literature. If any one doubts now, a few years hence may correct his judgment. Miss Fuller looks upon books from a high standard, to which the public has not yet travelled, a height indeed to which few of an author's contemporary critics reach.

Southey, Coleridge, and Wordsworth, conclude the nine. They are written of worthily and with admiration. Of Southey, more and more warmly is written, than is commonly written. "Never has Christianity," (says Miss Fuller, of Roderic) "spoken in accents of more penetrating tenderness, since the promise was given to them that be weary and heavy-laden." There is enough in this paper alone, on the Modern British Poets, of which we have given an imperfect summary, to improve the taste and educate the heart of the new generation. It is a guide to profound wealth in the mine of English poetry. The purity of the style, the greatness of the thought, entitle it to be carefully studied; and as a further tribute to its originality we should remember, that it was first published some ten years since, in which time the popular judgment of the authors enumerated, has not a little cleared up.

Books like this of Miss Fuller's, are of eminent service to the country at this time, when its mind begins fairly to waken to the new task in literature which lies before it. Never has there been so fair a field to be reaped. Europe and the old world lie exhausted; America is fresh, new in the resources of her unpainted scenery, her institutions, her developments of individual life and character. But as yet, America is distrustful of her powers, lacks reverence for the true ideal of the country, has not yet been led "to take unto the height the measure of herself." She looks wistfully to the shores of Europe, is more familiar with Alps than Alleghanies, more at home in London than New-York; sends her painters to Germany, her sculptors to Italy, and her actors to England. This will, however, end. A sensitive, intellectual, prosperous people, cannot be content long to live the life of Absentees on their own soil. They will throw off these old ties and associations, with the first movements of the new generation, on the stage of active life. Already the ideal begins to be dimly seen, and its realization to be craved for. The authors of the country begin to point the way. Emerson has sown seed in the soil, which will start up and expand to glorious fruitage. In the addresses of Mathews, there is a sagacious instinct of the true demands of Nationality, an unshrinking conviction, an inevitable truth, which will be acknowledged in the familiar watchwords of the time. Miss Fuller always brings words of faith and life on this theme. "Truth," says she, "is the nursing mother of genius. No man can be absolutely true to himself, eschewing cant, compromise, servile imitation and complaisance, without becoming original, for there is in every creature a fountain of life which, if not choked back by stones and other dead rubbish, will create a fresh atmosphere, and bring to life fresh beauty. And it is the same with the nation as with the individual." Worthily said, TRUTH, THE MOTHER OF GENIUS.

# [Papers on Literature and Art]

Anonymous*

Miss Fuller is a lady of large acquirements, fine powers, and earnest, honest purpose. No one can read her papers without doing justice to her talents and intentions. But with all her merits she has one fault which essentially mars the pleasure of reading her writings, especially her critiques. We allude to a certain dogmatism of tone in enunciating her judgments, a dogmatism often supported by nothing more than "the lady's reason," as it is ungallantly called. This is most evident in her essay on American literature. Her decisions in this essay are pronounced in a style half petulant, half oracular, often inexpressibly amusing rather than particularly edifying. She announces trite truths as though they were new thoughts, and debatable paradoxes as though they were admitted facts. The criticism, too, is the criticism of a *clique*—a kind which is calculated to do more injury to our "infant" literature than the universal puff or universal libel system. A few authors are selected, who happen to be greater favorites in "our set" than with the public, and they are studiously cried up as the true prophets of the land, and their unpopularity ascribed to their original merit. All the rest are imitators or echoers, and however stamped with public approbation are placed on a low round of the ladder of precedence. These decisions are supported with a host of canting expressions, hateful to gods and men; and are calculated to rouse in the public an antagonist feeling, which, in the end, will depress the unjustly exalted below their real merit. Such is ever the effect of an attempt on the part of a clique to manufacture public opinion. As our literary cliques are numerous, and as almost every person who writes belongs to some one of them, and as they all despise each other heartily, criticism becomes a mere game of laudation and depreciation. The Solons of one city are voted dunces by the Solons of another; and the idol of Boston is the target of Charleston. All raise the cry of American literature; each desires that the works of himself and friends should constitute it. The public meanwhile buys and reads what is readable, regardless whether it be puffed or condemned by either clique. We sincerely wish that a few of Miss Fuller's favorites were as popular as some of those she dislikes. But we do not wish to see them march into popularity over the bodies of their equals or superiors.

In this essay R. W. Emerson is called "the sage of Concord." Now it

---

*Anonymous, [Review of *Papers on Literature and Art*], *Graham's Magazine*, 29 (October 1846), 262.

happens that Mr. Emerson not only possesses one of the subtlest of human intellects, but a sense of the ridiculous exquisitely acute. What must be his sensation on reading his new title? Mr. Prescott must feel a fearful chagrin, notwithstanding his American and foreign reputation, at being told that though his materials are rich and fresh he has none of the higher powers of the historian. Mr. Lowell's volumes, we believe, have passed through more than one edition, and he enjoys no small portion of public favor, but how awful must be his depression when he learns from Miss Fuller, that "to the grief of some of his friends, and the disgust of more, he is absolutely wanting in the true spirit and tone of poesy;" that his verse is "stereotyped;" (by the type and stereotype foundry?) that his "thought sounds no depth." We do not see why a man should grieve or disgust his *friends*, because he wants the true tone or spirit of poesy, as friendship has been known to exist toward persons lacking even the power of versification. The attack on Lowell is sufficiently authoritative, insulting, and unsustained by fact or principle; but the criticism on Longfellow is even spiteful. It is the ugliest looking thing in Miss Fuller's volume. It is as inconclusive as it is petulant. The real fault in Longfellow is, that his poetry has passed through many editions, that his genius has been fully acknowledged by his countrymen; that his poems are in the memories of thousands who never read or heard of young William Ellery Channing. We agree with Miss Fuller that the latter has many fine and deep touches of genius; but is it Longfellow's fault that he is not read?

The essay on American literature, therefore, we, in imitation of Miss Fuller's own oracular method, pronounce a piece of adulterated humbug: adulterated, because, with a great deal which will never be believed beyond her own literary circle, it contains a little which has never been doubted by anybody, and is in fact the merest commonplace of the newspapers. All who are praised therein we warn not to be unduly elated; all who are condemned need not commit suicide or profane language. All Mutual Admiration and Mutual Assurance Societies are strictly forbidden to retort upon Miss Fuller and her "worthies" the wrongs they have received in her essay; remembering, in the words of a pious poet, that their "little hands were never made to tear each other's eyes;" or if they desire to have their wrath quenched by a more powerful reason than good old Doctor Watts could give, let them know that

> "To avenge misdeed
> On the misdoer, is misery to feed
> With her own broken heart."

But the value of the present book does not rest on the Essay on American Literature. It contains some dozen other papers, which we cheerfully admit to be valuable contributions to the literature of the day, and to be well worthy of being printed in their present elegant form. We have not space to mention any with particular regard. They well entitle Miss Fuller to a high rank among cotemporary authors, as a good writer, an independent thinker, and diligent student. We trust her present publication will be sufficiently successful to induce her to collect another series of her miscellaneous writings, and thus redeem the promise she makes in her preface. In case, however, her future volumes are devoted, like the present, almost exclusively to foreign writers, and present their claims to attention with as much warmth, we hope that she will dispense with another essay on cotemporaries, berating them for not being more American in feeling. Her own mind has been so completely bathed in foreign literatures, that she appears much better as an appreciating critic of them, than as a depreciating satirist of the literary efforts of American authors.

# [*Papers on Literature and Art*]

**Anonymous**°

Though Miss Fuller has written books ere these, her effulgence as a ° was not much apparent until her connection with the New York Tribune. In the columns of that paper most of the articles in the present volumes appeared, and, partly from their style, and partly from the popularity and wide circulation of that paper, attracted considerable notice. They are principally essays and criticisms, sometimes very ably and justly written, at others weak and partial. Her style, however, is what we do not particularly affect: it borders too much on what we have complained of in a preceding notice—an imitation of the Carlyle style; we think, too, that "this man Carlyle" is one of "this woman Fuller's" Heroes; and mingling with this is a sprinkling of the Emersonian. Why don't these people write naturally, and just as they think? instead of affecting a style as stilty and disagreeable as any conceivable thing. Still Miss Fuller's writings evince a rare talent, and they will be read and admired by thousands who have not yet heard of her. She is certainly a very close student with the Poets, and many of her papers are really charming—we could instance those on the poems of Browning, Miss Barrett, and some others. They are very social books as companions at a winter's fireside, and we dare say their publication will be profitable to both author and publishers.

°Anonymous, [Review of *Papers on Literature and Art*], *New York Illustrated Magazine of Literature and Art*, 2 (November 1846), 432. Fuller signed her contributions to the *Tribune* with an asterisk, as mentioned in the first sentence of the review.

# [*Papers on Literature and Art*]

Anonymous\*

Popular analytics as applied to literature and art occupy a considerable space in the library of the day. They express those trains of speculative meditation which, falling short of what the severity of science demands, yet lifted considerably above the level of ordinary thinking, engage at present so many of those student minds that are begotten of German literature. To the higher class of such minds that of the author of these volumes unquestionably belongs. It is true, the vices of the school in which she has matriculated appear profusely throughout her pages; yet it is but justice to admit that the intrinsic merits which they disclose—and these are of no common order—predominate, on the whole. When the balance is struck, a large surplus of gratification remains to the reader.

Not that perhaps the author tells us any new truth, or sounds the limited depths over which she holds her course as fully as she might. It is the spirit in which her mission is accomplished—the free yet reverential and elevated tone which, with slight interruption, reigns throughout,—the original mood, if not the original thought—that constitute her merits. Nor are these light claims. Raphael has been called Divine for pourtraying such qualities. The writer who paints them shall have his apotheosis too—varying in dignity according to his place in the Pantheon of Genius. There is a "touch of divinity" about Margaret Fuller.

Having, however, thus far rendered our acknowledgments to the author of these papers, we must turn even thus early to the less grateful task of remonstrating with her on those waywardnesses and perversities which the *Dii minores* of literature will sometimes practise upon us mortals, and for which she also must be held largely responsible. The condemnation of these misdemeanours is yet more important than the diffusion of the knowledge of Margaret Fuller's good deeds. Wherefore, at the risk of being placed by her in the ranks of what she stigmatizes as "subjective" critics—a perversion, by the way, of that term, for it is not meant by the Germans to convey reproach, but, on the contrary, to designate the next best thing to the "objective"—we proceed to note and condemn those offences. Were they peculiar to this author only, we should probably dismiss them with a passing remark; but being, as they are, the

---

\*Anonymous, [Review of *Papers on Literature and Art*], *Athenaeum*, no. 999 (19 December 1846), 1287-1289.

sins also of that corporation of writers who seek to Teutonize and stultify the English tongue, we feel it to be a duty to denounce them as far as in us lies. This forced amalgamation of foreign modes of thought and expression,—or rather the parody of those modes—with our own, is in fact the sum and abstract of those offences. From this source they all flow; whether in the shape of mysticism, pedantry, paradox, or bombast,—throughout the whole gamut of affectation.

Doubtless, the introduction of German literature into this country through the labours of Coleridge, Carlyle and others—names which it is hardly necessary to say are individual, not corporate, except as belonging to the chosen guild of master minds—has been on the whole of signal advantage. It shook the tyranny of the positive school,—and weaned us from the superstition of the sensuous to the worship of the spiritual. It is, however, equally certain that these advantages have not been gained without their concomitant evils; namely, the fanaticism that ever follows in the wake of literary revolution—the exaggerated spirit of the reaction. Thus the practical and positive, exposed to the fiery breath of enthusiasts, was not merely softened to its due consistency, but rarefied into the unreal,—until both thought and language evaporated at last into a cloudy incense to the vanity and spiritual pride which transmuted them. Young men began to see visions and old men to dream dreams. An extreme contempt of the lucid arose. Common intelligibility was held as backsliding, and perspicuity as filthy rags. A rhapsodical outpouring of sublime nonsense became the order of the day; and the beggarly elements of sense and purpose were so thoroughly repudiated by these fifth-monarchy men of letters, that their ravings might have been read backwards or forwards, occidentally or orientally, by Anglo-Saxon or by Arab. These fanatics, in fact, conceived that they had nothing to do but string together at random texts taken from Mr. Carlyle's works—and generally the most exceptionable—in order to be themselves Carlyles. They only forgot the one thing needful—the informing spirit of the master. Now this nuisance exists up to the present hour. It has increased, is increasing, and ought to be diminished. Were it confined to the zealots alone, it might be laughed at,—or, for that matter fostered as supplying the compost which manures the field of Hudibrastic satire. But it has created a pestilential atmosphere which occasionally infects even able writers; whilst amongst inferior pens it serves to abet that laxity of construction and careless obscurity which the high-pressure speed of mercenary authorship had already pushed to excess in this our commercial community of letters.

This plague must be stayed. Not, however, by prescribing what would promote its opposite—the shallow-clear. That despotic purism which seeks to restrain the infinite progress of thought within fixed *formulae* of expression is, if possible, a still grosser violation of the prerogative of mind than the licentiousness to which we have been alluding. Language is a science of notation as indefinitely expansive as is trigonometry or the differential calculus,—only still more subtle, as being symbolical of moral ideas instead of the far less complex ones of magnitude and numbers. Transcendentalism is the scope and consummation of all;—but inasmuch as the algebraist best verifies his powers by the symmetry and simplicity with which he expresses the most profound truths, so also is it with the moral analyst. Superfluous notation in either is a weakness,—wrong notation a defect; and when gratuitously wrong,—whether through redundancy or affectation, or any other cause, obscuring or falsifying the idea—a fatuity as well as a failure. This latter is a case which can hardly occur in the exact sciences; but the more complicated processes of moral investigation open a wide door to it,—and accordingly many there be who go by this broad way which leads to literary perdition. A common delusion under which even the least extravagant of the mystic school seem to labour, is the belief, half unconsciously entertained by them, that obscurity is *essential* to transcendentalism. Hence, it is adscititiously employed. But no species of literary supererogation is more vicious, or delusion more delusive. Transcendentalism is not height and obscurity,—but height and clearness. The loftier the thought, therefore, the more imperative the obligation to pursue it with the keenest falcon eye and the most disciplined falcon wing of language. Hood the eye with obscurity, and encumber the pinion with gewgaws, and the mind flutters idly amid the clouds, whilst its fugitive quarry escapes back again into its native wilderness of as yet unexplored speculation. Moreover, even the simplest enunciation of recondite truth is ever likely to be more or less abstruse, owing, as we have already stated, to the complexity of moral ideas and the natural imperfection of language as a calculus to convey them. Hence, any excess of obscurity beyond what is inevitable, impairing its clearness detracts also from its transcendentalism.

In fine, the real antidote for all this is what the mystics themselves are ever prescribing, but never acting on,—namely, sincerity and truthfulness, heart-capacity as well as head;—in a word, the will and the ability to be in earnest. These specifics are commended to us *usque ad nauseam* in every second page of their lucubrations; but, with a singular infatuation wrapped up meanwhile in thick integuments of insincerity, fiction, brain-pride, and pretence. The faith which the mystics preach they possess not themselves; and accordingly, their works belie them.

Now, it is for the occasional indulgence in these vices,—the sins of a wavering faith, one not yet thoroughly sincere or earnestly in earnest, much as she may deem it to be so,—that we must hold the author of these 'Papers' responsible. She is naturally too genuine and healthy-minded to make them the rule; but is just enough tainted by the pestilential contagion described above, to make them the exceptions. For example, the following rhapsody which appears in the first Dialogue of the first volume between the Poet and the Critic:—. . . .

And "very bad," this most assuredly is. Not, however, worse than what follows to the end of the dialogue,—to no one single line of which can we say "very good," or even indifferently good. But we have neither space nor inclination to quote offences at any length. We should not have undertaken the ungrateful task of extracting even so much as we have done, but that we feel it incumbent on us, in strict justice, to furnish a sample of the thing that we, and all equitable criticism as we conceive, must condemn. We do so likewise because it would seem as if the author regarded such passages as these as her best credentials. Their being placed in the van of her array—a preliminary paper—leads to that inference. We think, however, that long before "ten years"—the period which, when alluding to the "crudities" of earlier pieces which she had "outgrown," she assigns to herself for hereafter outgrowing those that may blemish what she writes at this day—she will have put away the childish things contained in the above extract, and along with them several others of the same class which appear in these volumes. To a mind so inherently honest and earnest as hers we would not pay the ill compliment of allotting more than a tithe of that time, for that consummation. She will also, we think, perceive within that interval that the ambitious and affected style—the euphuism of the mystics—has led her into other faults as well as those of obscurity, and caused her to lay down wrong doctrine and misinterpret true. When we would walk on stilts, we are prone to stumble and fall. We cannot pass the sinews and muscles of our motivity through our wooden legs. Consequently, they stump and straddle and totter and trip. Hence the *naïve* fallacy which the author puts into the mouth of the Poet in the extract above. "Well! if you were content with saying it is very good; but you are always crying it is very bad." So that if we are content with saying it is "very good" and do not cry very bad, all is well! In our humble opinion, both cries are false criticism when used thus as shibboleths. Indiscriminate praise is as gross injustice as indiscriminate censure. Nay, further, even praise justly accorded as far as regards the merit to which it is specifically assigned, may yet be as vicious as indiscriminate praise if the peccant portions of the thing judged be left unreproved, thus detracting from the value of the commendation—a principle equally applicable, *mutatis mutandis,* to specific censure. True, there are works of which "it is very good" or "it is very bad" may be predicated on the whole, or partially, without specifying exceptions. But in the great majority of cases these general or partial decisions are either utterly inapplicable or inadequate. Things may be both good and bad and throughout a variety of modifications of each; and here critical equity is distributive, and does not make its awards worthless by decreeing either a promiscuous ovation or a promiscuous penalty. Of this the author herself is at times unconsciously sensible,—unwarily illustrating it by her own practice when she occupies the critic's tribunal. It must, however, be admitted that she is generally on her guard in this respect; and, by the profuse application of the "very good" principle alone, commits much injustice, straining "the quality of Mercy" in defiance of the Bard, until she makes *it* the substance and Equity the accident. Indeed, in the Dialogue under consideration, being a special pleader from the first and not a judge, she makes an *ex parte* statement for her client the Poet throughout; and a wish to indulge in the affectedly familiar vein—a favourite with fanatics, whether puritan divines or Germanized mystics—combining with that bias this "very bad" kind of thing which we have extracted, is the result. Had it not been for these influences, the maxim which the author would have laid down would, we conceive, have been simply expressed after this manner,—viz., that genuine criticism, when pronouncing on meritorious works, has in the generality of cases the tendency to note the excellencies and to overpass the defects. But this unaffected way of stating the case would have expunged the mystic metaphors of the Incarnation and the Creation—consummations that, perhaps, some might think devoutly to be wished—would have caused the supposed essential of obscurity to evanesce, and eliminated the "very bad" portion:—and hence, it was not adopted.

The false doctrine enunciated in the paragraph which we have just been examining is again repeated a few lines further on. Here the "dogmatic replaces the familiar" as the vehicle of expression. The Poet issues his ukase after this fashion,—"If one object does not satisfy you, pass on to another, and say nothing,"—unless the critic can cry "very good," we suppose. We do not, however, find the author following her own advice. With her, it is "Mind what I say, but not what I do:" for when, in the second volume, she reviews Mr. Alston's pictures,—which, on the whole, she very much admires,—and finds amongst them several that do not satisfy her, she does not pass on and say nothing, but very properly stops at each and says something, very much to the purpose, and pretty tolerably severe too. She is, in fact, again off her guard here; and acts instinctively on the true principle, instead of her own false canon. As to the Critic in this Dialogue—who sure enough is a very poor creature, not a giant made by the author to be slain, but a puppet set up to be demolished—he is bullied by the Poet from beginning to end. To the "pass on, say nothing" command, he merely falters out, in euphuistic accents, the following commonplaces of his craft:—"It is not so that it would be well with me, &c.; I must examine, compare, sift, and winnow, &c., until I find the gold," &c. It is not "well with him,"—as the sequel proves. In a word, the Poet smothers him. Like the Duke of Clarence who was drowned in a butt of Malmsey, the wine he so dearly loved—so, the unfortunate penny-a-liner is cruelly lured on to display a voluminous banner of "pearly gray satin" in which he seems to take as much pride as might Norroy King-at-Arms in the royal scutcheon of England—and lo, and behold, "the heavy folds thereof, falling back round the poor man, stifled him probably!" Peace to his *manes*. . . .

# [*Papers on Literature and Art*]

### Frederic Henry Hedge°

These volumes, consisting mostly of selections from Miss Fuller's writings, including, as she informs us in her Preface, some of her earliest, as well as latest, productions, form part of "Wiley and Putnam's Library of American Books." They bear marks throughout of a vigorous mind, discriminating thought, varied and ever ready power, with candid and fearless expression. In the use of language—freedom, copiousness, richness, and precision of words—Miss Fuller has few superiors. By this alone one is repaid for reading these pages, differ as he may from the opinions he finds there. And besides this there is a fulness of meaning, and a kindness as well as boldness of utterance, which make us forget differences, or care not for them. Indeed, in regard to this writer, extravagant as have seemed to us some of her views and words (much less so, however, in this publication, than in the others referred to in the title-page), we are inclined to use the generous language in which she herself has summed up her remarks on the modern British poets:—"For myself, I think that where there is such beauty and strength, we can afford to be silent about slight defects; and that we refine our taste more effectually by venerating the grand and lovely, than by detecting the little and mean." The last epithets have no application here; but the others are strictly appropriate.

We therefore do not stop to point out defects, or consider objections frequently heard. We have run through this collection of pieces with pleasure and profit. That which pleases us least, and the only one, perhaps, that will give much offence, is the view of "American Literature." That she does that literature injustice, most will feel; that she is greatly unjust to one of our living historians, and several of our poets, many will earnestly say. And none, we think, will fail to notice an oracular air and magisterial decision, hardly indicative of meekness, nor helping to inspire in those ignorant of the writer entire confidence in the soundness of her judgment. But for perspicuity of style, for which she has not always been noted, for freedom and freshness of thought, for delicacy and affluence of imagination, with evident truthfulness of heart, these publications deserve to be known and read.

---

°[Frederic Henry] H[edge], [Review of *Papers on Literature and Art*], *Christian Examiner*, 42 (January 1847), 140-141.

# [Margaret Fuller]

### Rufus Wilmot Griswold[*]

Miss Margaret Fuller is best known as a prose writer. Her Woman in the Nineteenth Century, Papers on Literature and Art, Summer on the Lakes, etc., entitle her undoubtedly to be ranked among the first authors of her sex. I have recently re-read these works, incited to do so by the apparent candor and decided sagacity displayed in the Letters she has written to The Tribune during her residence in Europe; and I confess some change of opinion in her favor since writing the article upon her in The Prose Writers of America. Few can boast so wide a range of literary culture; perhaps none write so well with as much facility; and there is marked individuality in all her productions. As a poet, we have few illustrations of her abilities; but what we have are equal to her reputation. She is said to have written much more poetry than she has published.

[*]From Rufus Wilmot Griswold, *The Female Poets of America* (Philadelphia: Carey and Hart, 1848), p. 251.

# ["Miranda"]

### James Russell Lowell°

But there comes Miranda, Zeus! where shall I flee to?
She has such a penchant for bothering me too!
She always keeps asking if I don't observe a
Particular likeness 'twixt her and Minerva;
She tells me my efforts in verse are quite clever;—
She's been travelling now, and will be worse than ever;
One would think, though, a sharp-sighted noter she'd be
Of all that's worth mentioning over the sea,
For a woman must surely see well, if she try,
The whole of whose being's a capital **I**:
She will take an old notion, and make it her own,
By saying it o'er in her Sybilline tone,
Or persuade you 'tis something tremendously deep,
By repeating it so as to put you to sleep;
And she well may defy any mortal to see through it,
When once she has mixed up her infinite *me* through it.
There is one thing she owns in her own single right,
It is native and genuine—namely, her spite:
Though, when acting as censor, she privately blows
A censor of vanity 'neath her own nose."

  Here Miranda came up, and said, "Phoebus! you know
That the infinite Soul has its infinite woe,
As I ought to know, having lived cheek by jowl,
Since the day I was born, with the Infinite Soul;
I myself introduced, I myself, I alone,
To my Land's better life authors solely my own,
Who the sad heart of earth on their shoulders have taken,
Whose works sound a depth by Life's quiet unshaken,
Such as Shakspeare, for instance, the Bible, and Bacon,
Not to mention my own works; Time's nadir is fleet,
And, as for myself, I'm quite out of conceit,"—

°From [James Russell Lowell], *A Fable for Critics* (New York: G. P. Putnam, 1848), pp. 53-57.

"Quite out of conceit! I'm enchanted to hear it,"
Cried Appollo aside, "Who'd have thought she was near it?
To be sure one is apt to exhaust those commodities
He uses too fast, yet in this case as odd it is
As if Neptune should say to his turbots and whitings;
'I'm as much out of salt as Miranda's own writings,'
(Which, as she in her own happy manner has said,
Sound a depth, for 'tis one of the functions of lead.)
She often has asked me if I could not find
A place somewhere near me that suited her mind;
I know but a single one vacant, which she,
With her rare talent that way, would fit to a T.
And it would not imply any pause or cessation
In the work she esteems her peculiar vocation,—
She may enter on duty to-day, if she chooses,
And remain Tiring-woman for life to the Muses."

(Miranda meanwhile has succeeded in driving
Up into a corner, in spite of their striving,
A small flock of terrified victims, and there,
With an I-turn-the-crank-of-the-Universe air
And a tone which, at least to *my* fancy, appears
Not so much to be entering as boxing your ears,
Is unfolding a tale (of herself, I surmise,)
For 'tis dotted as thick as a peacock's with I's.)
*Apropos* of Miranda, I'll rest on my oars
And drift through a trifling digression on bores,
For, though not wearing ear-rings *in more majorum*,
Our ears are kept bored just as if we still wore 'em.

## "Studies for Two Heads. I."

### James Russell Lowell[*]

Some sort of heart I know is hers,—
    I chanced to feel her pulse one night;
A brain she has that never errs,
    And yet is never nobly right;
It does not leap to great results,
    But, in some corner out of sight,
    Suspects a spot of latent blight,
    And, o'er the impatient infinite,
She bargains, haggles, and consults.

Her eye,—it seems a chemic test,
    And drops upon you like an acid;
It bites you with unconscious zest,
    So clear and bright, so coldly placid;
It holds you quietly aloof,
    It holds,—and yet it does not win you;
It merely puts you to the proof
    And sorts what qualities are in you;
It smiles, but never brings you nearer,
    It lights,—her nature draws not nigh;
'T is but that yours is growing clearer
    To her assays;—yes, try and try,
    You'll get no deeper than her eye.

There, you are classified: she's gone
    Far, far away into herself;
Each with its Latin label on,
Your poor components, one by one,
    Are laid upon their proper shelf
In her compact and ordered mind,
And what of you is left behind
Is no more to her than the wind;
In that clear brain, which, day and night,
    No movement of the heart e'er jostles,
Her friends are ranged on left and right,—
Here, silex, hornblende, sienite,
    There, animal remains and fossils.

[*]From James Russell Lowell, *Poems, Second Series* (Cambridge: George Nichols; Boston: B. B. Mussey, 1848), pp. 135–137.

And yet, O subtile analyst,
    That canst each property detect
Of mood or grain, that canst untwist
    Each tangled skein of intellect,
And with thy scalpel eyes lay bare
Each mental nerve more fine than air,—
    O brain exact, that in thy scales
Canst weigh the sun and never err,
    For once thy patient science fails,
    One problem still defies thy art;—
Thou never canst compute for her
The distance and diameter
    Of any simple human heart.

[*Memoirs of Margaret Fuller Ossoli*]

Charles Mayo Ellis*

There is a large circle of readers in our immediate neighborhood whose tender remembrances of a remarkably endowed woman, or whose own affinities with one whom they never knew, will draw them to this work with a fond interest. Its lively and varied narrative will secure all readers of every class against any thing like weariness in its perusal. All that a book can receive of attractiveness from being a biography of a real and a peculiar character as drawn by itself in personal memoirs and letters, and as illustrated and made distinct by the help of true, admiring friendship, this book certainly has in perfection. To have been an object of such attachment to those who have so affectionately united their tribute in these pages is no inconsiderable token of the merits of their common subject. The Rev. W. H. Channing and R. W. Emerson are the more prominent tributaries, but many other friends have been enlisted in the work. There is a freedom of self-disclosure in the letters of the lady, as well as a frankness of communication on the part of the editors, which give raciness to more than half of these pages. The book is indeed filled with revelations of the heart, and calls out the sympathies on which the enjoyment of its perusal depends.

The book certainly invites and tempts criticism,—a criticism, too, which would not stop with the printed page but would enter largely into the character, the training, the genius, the peculiarities, the opinions, and the influence of her who is the subject of it. Yet who could find it in his heart to apply any severe processes to such an ungenial task. One would need first to exalt some personal traits of a striking and eminently sincere character above their place as idiosyncrasies, into offensive eccentricities, and then to warn those who are in no danger of adopting them against the risk of imitation. It is not to be denied that some few years ago, when Miss Fuller was an object of interest as a prominent member of that dreaded circle of *illuminati* who were called Transcendentalists, some grave and cautious parents hereabouts were afraid that their daughters would suffer from her influence. She was called an impracticable person, an odd person, a dreamy, visionary person. And so perhaps she was. The question

---

*[Charles Mayo Ellis], [Review of *Memoirs of Margaret Fuller Ossoli*], *Christian Examiner*, (March, 1852), 297-98.

was occasionally asked concerning her,—as it is concerning others with similar or different peculiarities,—"What should we do if all were like her?" The obvious answer, calculated to remove all fear on that score, is, that we are not all in any risk of being like her. Such characters are rare, and such gifts as hers are even more rare, in men or in women.

Our readers will find these volumes eminently suggestive. They may see reason to dissent from many of the opinions and views intimated in them, and their minds will be exercised by a running commentary of wonder, pleasure, and curiosity. But all will agree that their subject was no commonplace character. From her childhood to her death, the materials on which she lived were such as but few can gather into the nutriment of their being. Her tragical end, with her husband and infant, in the bosom of the stormy wave, was a termination not wholly discordant with some of the moods and incidents of her life.

# "Memoirs of Margaret Fuller"

**Anonymous**\*

Until we arrived at the third volume, we did not quite comprehend the expectations that could have induced an English publisher to reprint this American book.

Margaret Fuller was one of those he-women who, thank Heaven! for the most part figure and flourish, and have their fame on the other side of the Atlantic. She was an intellectual Bloomer of the very largest calibre. She was an encyclopaedia in cerulean stockings. She understood Socrates better than Plato did, Faust better than Göethe did, Kant's Philosophy better than Kant did—an acquirement by the way not, perhaps, so very, very, difficult—astronomy much better than Adams or Leverrier, ethics better than Aristotle, rhetoric, logic, poetry, better than any professor in any Yankee college. But, alack! the difference between an enclycopaedia bound in calfskin, and an encyclopaedia moving in blue stockings! Every fact, word, thought, idea, theory, notion, line, verse, that crowded in the cranium of Margaret Fuller was a weapon. They shot from her in season and out of season, like pellets from a steam gun. She bristled all over with transcendentalism, assailed you with metaphysics, suffocated you with mythology, peppered you with ethics, and struck you down with heavy history. For our part if one-tenth of what these three volumes say is true, we would just as soon sit in a library, where all the books should be endowed with voice, and all should sing forth their contents continuously, as to find ourselves in the company of any Mrs. Ossoli, or of any Margaret Fuller.

However, Mrs. Ossoli is dead, and a committee of Yankee memoir writers have combined to work her apotheosis. Here she sits upon a cloud, blown by these panting, puffing fame-givers. The bombastic eulogy, well-flavoured as it is by American slang, would be amusing from its exaggeration; but, alas! it disgusts by its vulgarity.

Of course this mighty mass of mind never did anything worth recording. She translated some German and Italian, and helped to edit an American transcendental periodical, but nothing more did Margaret Fuller *do*. The strong-minded lady, however, forced all she knew upon everybody, and obtained an awful respect in society. We question after all whether Margaret Fuller, whom even one of her biographers admits knew very little indeed of one

---

\*Anonymous, "Memoirs of Margaret Fuller," *New Quarterly Review*, 1 (2nd Quarter 1852), 168–170.

of the authors she vapours most about—Shakespeare, had more solid useful learning than many a well-informed English lady, who is quite content to remain a woman and not to be a prodigy.

As to the book, it opens within an autobiographical fragment wherein Miss Fuller describes her father, a Massachusetts attorney, her mother, who "was of a flower-like nature, but was bound by the same law as the blue sky, the dew, and the frolic birds," and herself, whom her father crammed with learning until he destroyed her health, and made her nervous and a sleep-walker for life . . . .

When will American women find out that the men know very well that it is only crass ignorance that induces a certain class of transatlantic females to talk the twaddle of a shop-boys' debating club? It requires no reading to speak the stuff we have just quoted, but in the quiet conversation of half-a-dozen English ladies, as they skim the subjects of the day, and talk of books and music, and passing topics of the hour, there is taste, refinement, and gently-placed illustration that show a quiet power, and evidence a concealed garner-house of study laid up with more care and patience than could be found in a wilderness of "strong-minded women." Contrast such a scene with that wherein Miss Fuller or Mrs. Ossoli, with a loud voice, and a nasal twang loud as the crack of a planter's whip, silences all general conversation, lectures and asserts, utterly contradicts, and contemptuously denies, until she has cleared the room of all except a few weak-minded wonderers, whose instinct it is to lick the dust before some roaring lion.

The third volume contains Mrs. Ossoli's adventures in Europe; and here it is we find what an English public is expected to buy. When she describes contemporaries of note, her sketches have an interest which she herself is, in our eyes, quite incapable of exciting. It is the old story of "Pencillings by the Way," "Notables in Undress," "Private Life in England," "Portraits of People who asked me to Dinner," "What I heard in the Servants' Hall," and such like charming catching titles, wherewith our American guests contrive to improve their experiences, and make money out of a host without stealing his silver forks. Perhaps the lady who has least ground of complaint on the present occasion is Madame Dudevant, for Margaret Fuller has all the rights of a captor and an invader over her. Now, this lady is the reality of that whereof Mrs. Ossoli was only a wretched imitation—a woman of great power and intellect, exercising influence upon her age and generation. How she uses her power, whether her influence be good or bad, may be disputed, and is disputed. But no one denies that the power exists. The strong-minded American evidently bored poor George Sand nearly to death. The Frenchwoman's politeness was a dreadful incumbrance when matched against such an antagonist. In vain did she leave her letter of self-introduction unanswered. Our Americaine was not to be thus put off. She walks into Madame Dudevant's rooms as cooly as Fighting Fitzgerald did into Brookes's after his blackballing, and no hints about printers waiting for copy, could get rid of her "for a good part of the day." We don't wonder that she never saw George Sand uninterruptedly afterwards. . . .

It is scarcely disguised that Mrs. Ossoli thought Thomas Carlyle an intolerant and most intolerable bore. What Mr. Carlyle thinks of Mrs. Ossoli he is probably too polite to say.

We do not quarrel with the lady for thinking Joseph Mazzini "by far the most beauteous person she ever saw," or for revealing how he writes in "Saunder's People's Journal;" nor do we vehemently disapprove the twaddle about Wordsworth and his love for hollyhocks, and her surprise that an old man of seventy-six should live at Rydal Mount, "the retirement of a gentleman, rather than the haunt of a poet." Doubtless, Margaret Fuller had a right to expect to find the poet declaiming in a damp cave, or catching rhymes and rheumatisms in the spray of a waterfall: but we confess we cannot forgive her a monstrous eulogy of Rousseau, the meanest and the basest reptile that ever crawled in the garden of literature. We do not think well of any woman who professes to have read the "Confessions of Rousseau," and who can speak of him without horror. Let the French, who, by the way seldom read any others than his one worst book, admire the shining phrases of the man who tells them in pathetic French how he seduced a servant-girl, and stole some ribbons to offer her as a love gift—and how, when the owner of the ribbons identified them, and prosecuted the poor girl for the theft, the lover, the man of genius, the great apostle of French, and, as it would seem, American ethics, looked on in apathy and saw his victim punished for his crime. When we find a woman eulogising a man in whose history this is but one consistent fact, we are much inclined to be thankful she was not an Englishwoman.

We need hardly say that we do not recommend this book to English family reading. It is false in style and sentiment, and, although free from glaring improprieties, and, perhaps, not amusing enough to be very likely to be read, still we think it is not a nice book for English ladies, and not an entertaining book for English gentlemen.

# "Memoirs of Margaret Fuller Ossoli"

Anonymous*

This book is a perplexity to a reviewer, and if he were malicious he might extract both from its authors and its subject much ill-natured amusement. It is the history of a mystic, mystically written. It is an account of one who lived in an atmosphere of exaggeration, puffed out by three such powerful blowers as Messrs. Clarke, Emerson, and Channing. It is the biography of one whose whole being was disordered and fragmentary, written by biographers who dispense with all observance of order, connection, consecutiveness, or chronology. Each of these gentlemen, in his turn, turns Miss Fuller round and round until he gets her in certain lights familiar or propitious to himself, and then blows a succession of brilliant bubbles. But all this is biographical varnish; you hear much of her spirit, and from her own words and letters you learn something of it—but the life she led, the things she did, the duties she performed, the sacrifices she made and how she made them, her daily environment of circumstances, the nature of her home, her intercourses with her family, or whether she lived with her family, the dramatic embodiments of her character, are not to be discovered in these pages. Through the great bulk of them she is a Muse, or a Sybil, or a Bacchante, or a self-concentrated Mystic, whilst all the time you are provoked by the feeling that it is owing to an act of will, or of discretion, on the part of the biographers that you are not getting the actual and substantial life of the woman. You perceive that they could have told you a much plainer and more solid story, and that whilst hiding the form and structure of her acted being, they are giving you but the colouring and varnish of her portrait. The result is much the same as if the mind had to body forth a landscape from a knowledge of the tints of the sky and the shades of the greens, with the specification of some predominant feature, such as a prevalence of mountains. We are thankful however for what they have chosen to disclose, and in our ignorance cannot judge them for what they have chosen to conceal; for with all her faults they have given us glimpses of a noble woman. We cannot so readily forgive them the confusion of their plan. Each gentleman gives his own impressions and recollections, and begins where he pleases, so that the Life would require a harmony, and it would be no light task to construct one. The materials are

*Anonymous, "Memoirs of Margaret Fuller Ossoli," *Prospective Review*, 8 (April 1852), 199-218.

arranged apparently in studied disorder. Later letters are given before earlier ones, though they are used for no purpose of illustration; and a disregard of accuracy in dates prevails throughout. In a letter bearing the date of April 30, 1848, *Rome*, Miss Fuller and the Roman people are "staring at the broken windows and burnt door of the Pope's Palace;" anticipating an event that did not take place until November of that year. Twenty pages further on the story is told under its proper date. Nor can we compliment these gentlemen upon the tone they adopt towards the object of their admiration. It leaves too much the impression that they assume a right to treat with some familiarity an idol of their own making. A woman whose weakness or misfortune it was to set conventional proprieties too much at defiance, should have had no ridicule attach to her from her own biographers, if they wished to produce a conviction of her real superiority, and of their competency to be its witnesses. We protest against the indecent vulgarity of "Margaret," and "our Margaret," and "our noble Margaret," the style in which she is continually mentioned in these volumes.

The many striking phases of her character that are given, with the scanty information as to her actual life, present strong temptations to the formation of a theory to account for a being so full of eccentricities and inconsistencies, so clever yet so self-centred and short-sighted, so noble and so arrogant, so refined and so audacious, so full of sensibility to beauty and so exaggerated, angular, and inelegant, so full of womanly affections and instincts and so wilfully masculine. One thing is clear, that upon her father's head rests the distortion of the physical, mental, and moral nature of a rarely-endowed child. He was a hard man of the world, who knew nothing of the organization of man or woman, and treated a tender girl, a mere infant, like a machine that had no vital structure of its own, and might be worked without cruelty according to his will. He was her only teacher, and unfortunately for her he was something of a scholar. He was too poor to devote to her instruction the healthy and natural hours of the day, yet so severe and exacting that the lessons were a terror and oppression until they were got over. The long hours of the day were spent in preparation, and fearful anticipation—and the late hours of the evening and often of the night in the formidable examination. The child was dismissed to bed, hours too late, with overwrought brain, with excited nerves, often with wounded feelings, with a craving, restless, unsatisfied heart, to be haunted by spectral illusions and horrid faces, or to fall into hideous dreams and rise in her sleep and go moaning through the house. So ignorant was her father of the meaning of all this, that on awakening her out of one of these wretched wanderings he only told her sharply, "to leave off thinking of such nonsense, or she would be crazy." Her mother is described throughout as a woman of singular tenderness and maternal anxiety, but how she was blind to the cruelty of this management of her child, or ignorant of the terrible sufferings that resulted from it, does not appear. And the book is full of such moral perplexities as this, leading to the conclusion that, after the exaggerated manner of American speaking and writing, in the portraiture of character very liberal presents are made of high qualities. People who, from the description of them, ought to have been everything to her, seem to have been nothing to her. With such a mother as she describes, how comes it that in later years she could speak with such touching melancholy of a childhood without joy, without sympathy, without genial love and care? "Poor child! Far remote in time, in thought, from that period, I look back on these glooms and terrors, wherein I was enveloped, and perceive that I had no natural childhood." Her father, unconsciously and innocently, may have been the skeleton in the house, the spectre and nightmare of her life, but there is not a trace that she had even an alleviation and refuge in her mother, and that the sufferings that could not be averted were even soothed and softened by her presence and her love. The child, with her whole being distorted, turned away from the heart, the fancy, the imagination, from the free life of nature, the rightful realm and heritage of childhood, to severe intellectual studies in languages and authors beyond the range of her unforced sympathies, is seen mournfully by a pitying reader standing in the frame of the garden-gate that looked out into the liberty and mystic joy of the universe, breathing away the wretchedness of her spirit in cravings and longings for some loving communion, the blessed touch of nature opening her heart only to make her feel, without understanding, her perverted condition, her wants, and her hopelessness. We know not a sadder nor a more exquisite picture: and we find in all her after eccentricities, her independence, her wilfulness, her determination to walk in her own way and be satisfied out of herself, her jealous self-assertion, bitterness, and haughtiness, only the natural reaction of her rich, proud, wounded, shut up spirit, against the violence and heart-hunger inflicted upon her childhood . . . .

Many years after we find this great want of her childhood coming in bursting sobs out of her heart, at a time when the very words in which she expresses her lamentation show such a growth in gentle holiness and moral wisdom as might seem to prove her independent of human aid, and to have outlived the sense of its loss. But the want in childhood of a wise love to lean upon, of some one for heart and soul to trust and almost worship, and spend the young powers of our reverence upon, of some one who by meeting and chastening the cravings of our nature prevents their returning in poisonous self-consciousness upon themselves, is a want never to be forgotten by natures of much capability, and, alas, never to be overcome. To all such some sense of bitterness from the chalice of their earliest years, some sore memories of a lonely sorrow that none knew they were tasting, of a repugnance and violence on nature that none knew that the obedient child was resenting and disdaining, some isolation, and hardness, and inability to open freely the depths and fulness of their hearts and live in unreserved sympathy, remains, and, though resisted and mourned over, cannot be dismissed . . . .

Her overtasked childhood, the education of a boy, the severe, intellectual, character of her studies, and the desolate wastes of her young heart, made her at an early age a female prodigy, clever, learned, pedantic, odd, bold, awkward, and bitter;—in most of her outward manifestations, as we collect, a thoroughly dangerous, unsafe, disagreeable, insufferable person. Combined with all this there was unquestionable genius, remarkable power and brilliancy in conversation, great variety and extent of culture, a noble and generous if not a chastened ideal, an entire trust in truth and truthfulness, with a scornful hatred of all insincerity . . . .

The unhappy biasses of her education were strengthened and perpetuated by the early lead that she was compelled to take in the management of her family's affairs. Her father died suddenly, leaving small provision for his widow and children, and she as the oldest in years, and by far the strongest in character, felt that the responsibility of the family maintenance, regulation, and support devolved upon her. This was singularly unfortunate for her. A place of clear subordination and wise heart-guidance might have corrected her faulty tendencies and ripened the rich things that were in her nature: a place of authority, such as in this life must always really fall to the strongest, to the helper and worker on whom others rest, rely, and throw their cares, took her from control, and gave that license to her impulses, which left her fertile and unchastened nature to develop itself in its own wild way. From this time, the household belonged to her—we have again and again the heavy consciousness of her responsibility sighing out—"there is no one to take up my burden if I drop it,"—and though all this called out much noble effort and self-sacrifice, it cannot be doubted that it strengthened her will, and self-reliance, and arbitrariness, and independence. Women who are thrown alone in the world, or, worse than alone, in situations where they must take the lead that naturally ought to fall to others, are often cruelly judged and censured for faults that in them are virtues, or at least inevitable consequences of their severe and unsupported virtues. What exactly she did for her family, and why she was called upon to do so much, does not distinctly appear. We can only collect that in a great variety of efforts and directions she distinguished herself as an instructor of her sex, both in its childhood and its womanhood, and that she often painfully bewails the necessity of these exertions as a bondage on her free movements, a heavy arrest upon the developments of her own nature. She seems always to have had a strong sense that she was unhappily placed, that there was an unfitness and discord between the wants of her nature and not merely the society in which she moved, but any society that America afforded. She was always haunted by the feeling that in Europe she would have unfolded more harmoniously—that she would have been carried more out of herself—that she would have lost her self-consciousness, her awkward antagonism, her easy superiority, her disdain of the ungraced forms which the life around her was assuming. And in this, owing to the peculiarity of her temperament and circumstances, and the early distortion of her nature, she may have been right. . . .

Upon the unnatural pressure and distortion of her early education, three powerful influences, conditions of her consciousness, seem to have been permanently acting. She had an inward passion for refinement, grace and high culture, and everything around her wore an air of meanness and deformity. American Society appeared to her vulgar in all its aspects.—She had the quickest sensibility to beauty, and somehow had come to feel that her extreme plainness had made her a blotch on nature.—She thirsted for sympathy and love and intercommunion of nature, and she believed that personal accidents had cut her off from the most perfect form of this life, that none would ever love her as she could love.—Hence her arrogance and want of humility, her intellectual and aesthetic contempt for the world she moved in.—Hence her exactions, bitterness, and scorn. Hence her lonely pride, her independent ways, her disregard of conventional rules. If she could have breathed in a more congenial atmosphere, if she could have had any filled, unmortified, affections, if the reaction of all her natural desires and wants against the necessities of her state and circumstances had not been so terrible and personally humiliating, the flagrant defects of her character might never have appeared, or might insensibly have melted away in the sweet light of a heart at peace. Her sense of repugnance to her own ugliness, and of the ugliness of everything around her, seems to have amounted to absolute loathing, and this, no doubt, is in itself the sign of a mind constitutionally morbid and unbalanced. She was by her temperament and its abuses, trembling on the verge of insanity, and she found but little outwards to keep her from falling over. And that she was not altogether insane in having an aesthetic repugnance to the most characteristic forms of New England social life, we might cite Mr. Emerson's testimony in evidence. He says that she was ill-timed and mis-mated, that she saw in the life of others no expression of her own, that the only right thing the city of the Puritans had for her was Beethoven's symphony, and that her love of art was mainly a sympathy with the artist "in the protest which his work pronounced on the deformity of our daily manners." If her moral nature had been satisfied and rightly exercised this unhealthy disgust could not have existed, but the striking improvement that came upon her humility—when she had experience of European life and culture, shows that circumstances had, in her condition of disease, much to do in fostering the natural seeds of her scornful egotism. Her self-esteem is almost incredible, and along with her many high qualities, her large attainments and her occasional modesty and deference before such men as Channing and Emerson, presents a moral problem of no easy solution. Emerson describes her as in the coolest way saying to her friends, "I now know all the people worth knowing in America, and I find no intellect comparable to my own." And long after she makes the same remark of Italy, with this difference, that she confines it to her own sex, and admits, in all the most captivating forms of mind, their large superiority over herself. "Among the famous women, I find none with so comprehensive a ken, or such fine instincts, as I; but they are so superior to me in energy and productive talent, that I suppose the world is right to prize them much more, and afford them an easier path." Yet she can be humble before Emerson, of whom she speaks in this mystic, exaggerated, way. "I present to him the many forms of nature, and solicit with music; he melts them all into one spirit, and reproves performance with prayer. When I am with God alone, I adore in silence. With nature I am filled and grow only. With most men I bring words of now past life, and do actions suggested by the wants of their natures rather than my own. But he stops me from doing anything, and makes me think." And to Dr. Channing she confesses her mental relations with modesty enough: "He takes in subjects more deliberately than is conceivable to us feminine people, with our habits of ducking, diving, or flying for truth. Doubtless, however, he makes better use of what he gets, and if his sympathies were livelier, he would not view certain truths in so steady a light. I do not feel that constraint which some persons complain of, but am perfectly free, though less called out than by other intellects of inferior power. I get too much food for thought from him, and am not bound to any tiresome formality of respect on account of his age and rank in the world of intellect. He seems desirous to meet even one young and obscure as myself on equal terms, and trusts to the elevation of his thoughts to keep him in his place. . . ."

We have mentioned her consciousness of her own homeliness as one of the sources of her bitter war with nature, one of the constant protests of her feelings against palpable and disagreeable fact. Mr. Emerson's description of her would seem to imply that this knowledge was forced upon her, for so sensitive a person would not be slow to interpret the unwillingness even to be in her company. "Her extreme plainness,—a trick of incessantly opening and shutting her eyelids,—the nasal tone of her voice—all repelled; and I said to myself, we shall never get far. It is to be said, that Margaret made a disagreeable first impression on most persons, including those who became afterwards her best friends, to such an extreme that they did not wish to be in the same room with her. This was partly the effect of her manners, which expressed an overweening sense of power, and slight esteem of others, and partly the prejudice of her fame. She had a dangerous reputation for satire, in addition to her great scholarship. The men thought she carried too many guns, and the women did not like one who despised them." . . .

The worst reaction of this consciousness was in making her distrust the pure quality of the affections that were given to her, and despair of ever being of essential importance to the life of any one. With all her pride, she knew that she was but a dark moon, until she found her sun. She was apt to think that the friendship that was shown her was of a commercial character, that she was prized only for the wealth she brought, for the thoughts, pictures, amusement that she furnished, and that no one loved her for herself. To this secret of her heart-loneliness all her intimate friends bear record. Mr. Emerson gives the following expression of her sense of doomed isolation:—"I remain fixed to be, without churlishness or coldness, as much alone as possible. It is best for me. I am not fitted to be loved, and it pains me to have close dealings with those who do not love, to whom my feelings are 'strange.' Kindness and esteem are very well. I am willing to receive and bestow them; but these alone are not worth feelings such as mine."—Mr. Channing gives this clue to a portion of her character: "Through the mask of slight personal defects and ungraceful manners, of superficial hauteur and egotism, and occasional extravagance of sentiment, no equal had recognised the rare beauty of her spirit. She was yet alone. Among her papers remains this pathetic petition:—'Oh God, take me! take me wholly!—Take me only awhile. No fellow being will receive me. I cannot pause; they will not detain me by their love. Take me awhile, and again I will go forth on a renewed service. It is not that I repine, my Father, but I sink from want of rest, and none will shelter me.' " And many years before she became a wife and mother, we find this wildly desolate cry:—"Surely a being born wholly of my being, would not let me lie so still and cold in lonely sadness. This is a new sorrow; for always, before, I have wanted a superior or equal, but now it seems that only the feeling of a parent for a child could exhaust the richness of one's soul. All powerful Nature, how dost thou lead me into thy heart and rebuke every factitious feeling, every thought of pride which has severed me from the Universe! How did I aspire to be a pure flame, ever pointing upward on the altar! But these thoughts of consecrations, though true to the time, are false to the whole. I thought ages would pass before I had this parent feeling, and then that the desire would rise from my fulness of being. But now it springs up in my poverty and sadness. I am well aware that I ought not to be so happy. I do not deserve to be well beloved in any way, far less as the mother by her child. I am too rough and blurred an image of the Creator, to become a bestower of life. Yet, if I refuse to be anything else than my highest self, the true beauty will finally glow out in fulness." There are strange revelations of the womanly nature, of the secret bitternesses of many lonely hearts, and are sacredly and reverently to be interpreted.

In 1846 the long desire of her life was gratified, and she came to Europe. The most eventful portion of her history was passed in Rome. There her whole nature softened, mellowed, and ripened. Wandering one evening in the twilight shades of St. Peter's she lost her party, where one might have twenty parties and lose them all, and lingering in perplexity, until left nearly alone with the servitors of the church, she was approached by an Italian gentleman who courteously proffered his services. No carriage was to be found in the Piazza, and the Roman noble escorted the American lady to her lodgings. Such was the first meeting with her future husband, the Marchese Ossoli. His father had lately died, he had two elder brothers, and the property was undivided. The brothers belonged to the conservative party, Ossoli to the republican. He wooed Margaret Fuller, and after a time won her. Her brilliancy and enthusiasm were the complement of his calm, slow, receptive nature. She married him in private, and her marriage was concealed for more than a year after her son was born. To her own mother she gives no earlier information. The only explanation that appears of this is that the Italian post-office could not be trusted, and that if it had been known to the Ecclesiastical authorities, with whom such matters lie, that Ossoli had married a Protestant and a person who had made herself so notorious at Rome for revolutionary sympathies, he must have lost his portion of the paternal property. He waited for a republican triumph, and lost all. He seems to have been a man of a noble nature, simple, high-minded, and affectionate, who had nothing of the culture and intellectual activity which Miss Fuller could so well supply, but in whose large and honest love her overstrained and somewhat artificial being might at last find rest. The change is instant and beautiful. She becomes a new creature, a thorough woman, living now in and from her heart. She blooms, and softens, and flowers, like a rhododendron, or an azalea, taken from a clay soil and a windy site and set down in rich bog and warm exposures....

Her married life was terribly tried. It was during the time of the French siege. Her child was at Rieti; her husband at Rome, exposed to great dangers. She passed from the one place to the other, distracted at either. Her child nearly perished in her absence, through the sordid neglect of its Italian nurse. At Rome she was appointed to the charge of one of the Hospitals, and here the beauty and magnanimity of her character come forth, accompanied with a new humility. She discovers and confesses that there was in her more of the woman than of the heroine. . . .

We must here say that we think her utterly misjudging in her views of Roman politics; and that her lost Memoirs, though doubtless they would have been most valuable for their sketches and incidents, must in our apprehension have been conceived in a mistaken spirit. We think her most unjust to the Pope; and quite misled, as to all probabilities, by her own hot republicanism and idolatrous admiration for Mazzini. We do not mean that she was not right in finding much that is noble in his personal character and daring, but that to Rome and Roman liberty he was an unfortunate friend. We have no more faith in national redemption coming through imported foreign patriots, than through foreign troops; and Mazzini was but an adventurer at Rome. To us it is unspeakably shocking (even in a cause so open to disturbing enthusiasm) to find the heart of a woman so perverted by her judgment, that she could speak of "the satisfaction with which she heard of the violent death" of Rossi, and declare herself to be affected by it as by an act of terrible justice. It is a terrible proof of her presumption—of the danger to man or woman of stepping out of their sphere—and leaves a stain upon the record of her Roman life, which her devotedness in the hospitals cannot quite wipe away.

We do not mean to write the melancholy close of her life. After the fall of Rome, and some happy, pensive, days, with husband and child in Florence, they all embarked together for America, and perished together in the sea. She would have it so. They might possibly have been saved, if she would have borne the necessary separation, with the risk that they might not all meet the same fate, that some might be rescued, and some saved. She would not have it so. In life or death they must be united. What a change had been wrought in the high, bold, daring, philosophic girl! It was wrong; it was weakness; it was unjustifiable disposal of lives not her own, but after what she had suffered, what she had pined for, what she had begun to cling to, and what heroic sacrifices these new affections had already carried her through—ours is not the hand that can sternly write her condemnation.

There is one passage in these Memoirs that ought not to have been left as it now stands. Her biographers ought to have felt that either it shows great ignorance of life, or that it affects the purity of her own mind. It ought not to remain as it is, without a word of comment or explanation. It is the passage in which she speaks of George Sand. It is in the worst tone of false, heartless, morals; a very odious bit of sentimental sepulchre painting. We do not believe that she could have written it after her marriage. It has our unqualified disapprobation.

# "Memoirs of Sarah Margaret Fuller"

Anonymous*

Any one who runs his eye over the monthly catalogue of a London bookseller will find ample proof of an intellectual activity among our Transatlantic brethren, which bids fair to rival, what seems among ourselves to give a pretty full illustration of the proverb, that of making books there is no end. English literature—or, if the term is not sufficiently distinctive, the literature of the English language—has received not a few note-worthy contributions from America within the last few years, and, engrossed as we are with the constant and constantly increasing product of the home book-market, we may, perhaps, be charged by those who have begun to avail themselves of it more regularly, with something like a culpable neglect of their claims. Never were the most prominent contributors to American literature so well known in this country as they now are; never, perhaps, were they so well entitled to notice, except when Cooper and Washington Irving were producing their best works, and then it was scarcely possible for fictions on a novel series of subjects, and published, too, in this country, to escape attention. While these two names have now come to be regarded as familiarly as those of the most popular of our own novelists and essayists, and have been classed, indeed, with the best of them, five years have scarcely elapsed since others who are now in the front rank of their many successors—the most successful and best known among their countrymen—began to be known even to the critical portion of readers among ourselves. The only novelists besides Cooper, whose names were previously familiar to us were Brockden Brown, Dr. Bird, Kennedy, and Ward, and at least three of these may almost be said to belong to the last generation. A much more vigorous and original class of writers has arisen within the last ten years, and with these, although they have all reached the zenith of their fame at home, we are only beginning to form an acquaintance. Every facility is afforded us for doing so. An American book worth knowing cannot now be many weeks published ere we have it reproduced for us, and placed upon our tables in one or other of the forms which the cheap publication movement is taking. Those who are acquainted to any considerable degree with American literature as it is now introduced to us by Messrs. Wiley and Putnam, Mr. John Chapman, or Mr.

---

*Anonymous, "Memoirs of Sarah Margaret Fuller," *Eclectic Review*, 5th series 3 (June 1852), 678–689.

Bohn, can scarcely fail to have been struck with the intellectual activity of the female sex as evinced in the varied character of its contributions to the long lists of American works which these publishers so frequently bring under our notice. To our mind, it constitutes rather a remarkable feature in the civilization of the New World that the number of literary women of note is considerably greater in America than it is among ourselves. True we do not find a Mrs. Somerville, a Joanna Bailie, nor even a Harriet Martineau among them, but in poetry, fiction, and criticism, as well as in the weightier forms of literature, there are many names which deserve to be ranked among the highest of our female writers—names as distinguished, perhaps, as any of those of the living writers of the other sex in America. Some of them have done good service to womanhood throughout the world by eloquent and judicious counsels, which amply compensate for the aberrations of Mrs. Amelia Bloomer, while others, of whom we need only mention Mrs. Sigourney, Alice Carey, Miss Sedgwick, Mrs. Kirkland (the discreet and amusing 'Mary Clavers'), and Mrs. Osgood, have given works which will bear comparison with any in English literature of the classes to which they belong.

Few American writers of either sex are better known in this country than Margaret Fuller, Marchesa d'Ossoli, and certainly few have done so little to be known out of a mere local circle. It may be presumed, however, from the fact of a writer so well known as Ralph Waldo Emerson coming before the world as her biographer, that her character and her life had some features of interest to more than the friends among whom the most active part of her brief career was spent. Our Transatlantic brethren have a *penchant* for magnifying the merits of mere local celebrities; but from what we already know of Mr. Emerson, it may be inferred, we think, that he would scarcely consent to rank among the trumpeters of a Jefferson Brick. The three volumes in which he and Mr. Channing (the nephew and biographer of the celebrated Unitarian preacher and writer,) have given us a record of the remarkable life of their countrywoman Margaret Fuller, will be read, we believe, with great interest, even by those who have hitherto known little or nothing of the subject. The work may, indeed, be considered as, in some sense, a tribute due by Mr. Emerson to one of his most devoted disciples, and we have only to regret that a departure from his ordinary subjects of discourse has been so little of a departure from the hazy style in which he has been accustomed to present such subjects to his readers. There is so little of what we desiderate in a biography to be found in his share of the work, that we are disposed to consider his efforts to make some compensation for the admiring criticisms of Margaret Fuller as in the main abortive, so far, at least, as the reader's interest in the book is concerned. The narrative of a life so full of incident, and the gossip with which it is spiced, must, nevertheless, be interesting, despite of Mr. Emerson's heavy and obscure commentaries; and, regarding the letters and the journal as the best parts of the book, we propose in the outline which we are about to give, to let the accomplished, and in many respects remarkable woman who forms the subject of it, speak for herself. That her lips were closed in death when one of the most interesting periods of her brief existence had just closed, must be deeply deplored by all who knew anything of her energetic temperament, her lively sympathies, and her strong, though but partially developed mind. Much that would now have been valuable, perished with her in the remorseless sea, and in considering her life and labours we feel that we must speak of both as merely indicating what might have been, that we are not tracing the career of a successful writer, but the existence of a remarkable woman, spoiled in a great measure by early training, and taken from the world just when she was beginning to see her true position, and to be emancipated by her experiences from the cold philosophy of those among whom not a little of her life was spent.

Margaret Fuller was born at Cambridge in Massachusetts, in the year 1810. Her father, a lawyer, and for some time a member of Congress, ultimately retired to a farm in the neighbourhood of Cambridge, and divided his attention between the prosecution of agricultural improvements, and the education of his family. His ideas in regard to the latter were, unfortunately, peculiar; and Margaret, the most promising of his children, was unhappily destined to become the victim of an ill-judged attempt to make a prodigy of her, and to fill up the time which ought to have been spent in the sports of youth with Latin verses, philosophy, history, and science. At an age when ordinary children are usually employed in mimicking the serious drama of their future years with the Dutch doll and its tiny wardrobe, poor Margaret was forced to sit with aching head and weary eyes, poring over some musty tome, the leaves of which too soon began to impart their yellow shade to her tender cheek. The details she gives us of this period are painfully suggestive of the misery arising from an unnatural tampering with the growth of the human plant. She looked back upon these days of premature mental excitement and nights of horrible dreams and spectral illusions, the consequences of that excitement, with a kind of shrinking terror, deploring in a tone of affecting pathos that she had no natural childhood. We read this passage of the book before us with pain, and with a feeling of apprehension lest in our educational zeal we forget that something must be left to nature, and that, in our eagerness to diffuse the blessings of intellectual culture, we render these worse than useless by neglecting the development of the real germ of all sound manhood and womanhood. The history of Margaret Fuller's youthful years is that of all who have been the victims of such mistaken views of education. A spirit naturally lively and buoyant was crushed beneath the weight thus laid upon it, and the effect of a departure from the path of nature in her childhood was but too obvious in the oddities and sentimentalities of her opening womanhood. By far too large a portion of the book is taken up with the record of this poetical and eccentric period of her life. Here and there we have glimpses of what she was afterwards to become—indications of a strong and subtle mind, struggling out from among the sickly rhapsodies and outpourings of a not very characteristic enthusiasm, which fill page after page; but we have too much of this. The only object which such a picture can serve is that of instruction and warning, and the lessons could have been given in a third of the space. Mr. Emerson and his associate in the work have obviously thought, however, that they were called upon to give to the world all that they respectively knew of Margaret Fuller; and with very little order or systematic arrangement they each take up the narrative when the subject of it was nearest themselves, and most frequently in their society. Thus Mr. Emerson describes, in his own style, her first visit to Concord, and the share he had in directing her to the proper objects of study, referring with something like a sneer to her 'raptures about scenery, and her attempts to describe its varying aspects,' while Mr. Channing contributes his share of the biography just as he has had opportunities of gathering materials for it.

We do not consider it necessary to follow Margaret Fuller through the changes in her early life. Except occasional criticisms to be found in her journals, letters to her friends, and sketches of certain small celebrities to be met with in the society into which her talents introduced her, there is little that can be interesting to the general reader in the first part of the book. Suffice it to say, that at the time the young authoress (for she had already become known by her contributions to sundry periodicals) was contemplating a journey to Europe, her father died, leaving his family in circumstances somewhat different from those in which they had previously lived. Margaret met this reverse of fortune with a composure which sufficiently indicated her strength of mind, and at once set herself to provide for the wants of her family by literary labours and by teaching. In 1843 she made a journey to Lake Superior and Michigan, and afterwards published her impressions of the scenery, and a narrative of the incidents in her travels in a work entitled, 'Summer on the Lakes.' Besides this she translated 'Eckermann's Conversations with Goethe,' and the 'Letters of Gunderode and Bettine,' the latter unquestionably the best of the three translations now known to the public. For two years she conducted an Emersonian periodical, entitled 'The Dial,' contributing to it some of her best essays, afterwards published under the titles of 'Papers on Literature and Art,' and 'Woman in the Nineteenth Century,' both favourably known in this country. Of her other literary undertakings the most noteworthy were the articles that appeared in 'The Tribune,' which she assisted for some time in conducting.

The highest estimate which can be taken of Margaret Fuller's writings will not place them above the staple of periodical contributions. Her style, though often forcible, is rough and irregular; and although her essays abound with evidences of a well-stored mind, many of them are marked by the obscurity and the turgidity which characterize the works of those with whom she was so closely associated in her literary undertakings, and with whom she so thoroughly sympathized. As a conversationalist she has had few equals. It was well said by one of her own countrymen, that Margaret Fuller combined with the natural loquaciousness of her sex, the affluence of a highly cultivated mind, and the vigour of an imagination which the reader of her works knows nothing of, and can scarcely imagine. In the literary circles of America she was chiefly known as a wonderful talker; and Mr. Emerson gives a long account of her conversational gifts describing the style of her monologues with a good deal of candour. To a stranger she appeared overbearing, and might almost be said to be disagreeable. Our own recollection of her manner, as it at first impressed us, is by no means pleasing. There was a show of knowledge in all she said, and a vaunting of experience which seemed almost to contradict itself. The abruptness and cynicism soon gave way, however, before the warmth and fulness of her sympathies, as, in the felicitous language of her biographer, she 'made green again the wastes of commonplace.' The originality and the richness of her eloquence are brought back to us by many passages from her diaries given in these volumes, and we recal with a feeling of melancholy pleasure the occasion of our last meeting with her. It was at the house of one who, differing widely from her and all her sympathizers on many important subjects, yet prized her society, and that of those whose earnestness and intellectual vigour are sufficiently known to the world. Let the reader imagine a select circle in which a lady of by no means prepossessing exterior, but who at once strikes you as being no ordinary person; a sad-visaged man, with melancholy yet often fiery eyes, and another, of a rougher but still remarkable aspect, are the principal objects of interest. The state of Italy—the emancipation of Italy—is the theme of conversation. With a sweep of speech worthy of such a theme does that large-brained and large-hearted woman discourse on the traditional glories and the republican instincts of the Italian people. Herself a republican, she gathers up from all the epochs of their history great memories with which to magnify the principle, and to strengthen her argument for its modern application. The dark eye of her silent Italian listener glows as he hears his own ideas expressed thus eloquently by such lips; and ere many weeks are over, he gives to the world a grand and striking illustration of their truth which, but for the perfidy of a sister republic, would have gone far to secure for Italy her proper place among the nations and to have changed the face of Europe. But to return to the narrative.

In the summer of 1846, Margaret Fuller came to Europe, and in her letters to her friends at home, we have lively accounts of her travels, and of the remarkable personages to whom she was introduced, and in whose society she frequently mingled while in this country and in France. There are notices of visits to Wordsworth, Joanna Bailie, DeQuincy, Carlyle, and others, interspersed with graphic descriptions of the scenery through which she passed, and her impressions of English and French society. Her studies, and her literary friendships at home, had made her an admirer of Carlyle; but that her admiration was not altogether indiscriminating, we gather from some observations upon one of his books which occur in a letter to Mr. Emerson, and the justice of which must appear obvious to all who have read the more recent works of the Chelsea Cynic. 'Carlyle's book,' she says, 'I have read, it has no valuable doctrine in it except the Goethean,—*Do to-day the nearest duty*. He ends as he began. Everything is bad. You are fools and hypocrites, or you would make it better.' We are not sure that the spirit of Carlyle's writings could have been better expressed. Though a sympathizer with him in many of his ideas, some of the very worst of them, perhaps, Margaret Fuller's heart was still too much of a woman's heart, and her charity too broad and lively to admit of her giving her assent to such doctrines as those of the 'Latter Day Pamphlets,' which were then appearing. She regarded him, not without reason, as the chief exponent of a new dynasty of thought; and yet the accounts she gives of her interviews with him, indicate that she felt such thought to be but a sad and sorry thing for the world after all. . . .

Having visited most of the interesting scenes in the South of Europe, Margaret Fuller arrived at Rome in the Spring of 1848. She continued to reside there, making occasional journies to Florence, Milan, &c., during the whole of the recent revolutionary epoch of European history, and was intimately connected with the gallant defenders of Italian liberty. She saw the beginning of the movement which terminated in the flight of the pope and the proclamation of the Italian Republic; and her warm friendship with the soul of the Italian struggle, Joseph Mazzini, while in London, led her into the very centre of the movement of which it was the result. Ties of a tender personal kind conspired with political sympathies to bind her to the Roman cause. In circumstances of a somewhat commonplace character, while waiting for a carriage, in fact, to convey her from St. Peter's to her lodging in the Corso, she met a stranger, the young Marquis Ossoli, destined to be her future husband. The chance meeting led to many interviews, and an offer of marriage followed. The offer was declined for the time, and Margaret set out with some American friends for Venice and Milan. She soon afterwards returned to Rome, however, and was married to Ossoli. For family reasons, the chief of which was the risk which her husband had incurred through his union with a Protestant, of losing his property in Italy, the marriage was for a time concealed. Inspired by the enthusiasm of his wife, Ossoli enrolled himself on the side of Roman liberty, and was actively engaged in the brief but glorious struggle, taking his station with his men on the walls of the Vatican during the protracted siege of the Eternal City, while Margaret laboured day and night as assistant to the Princess Belgioso in the hospitals for the wounded. Writing to Mr. Emerson amid the terrible days of the bombardment, she again and again refers to the heroism and the wisdom of Mazzini. 'There is one,' she apostrophises, 'who understands thee, Mazzini—who knew thee no less when an object of fear than of idolatry; and who, if the pen be not held too feebly, will help posterity to know thee better.' Those who do not know enough of the brave Italian exile have cause to deplore that the record of his career in Rome, which that pen had prepared, perished with the large-hearted woman who used it so vigorously, and that the only account of her experiences during the brief days of the republic, as well as her opinions on the subject of Italian liberty—a subject as momentous now as ever it was—is to be found in the hurried but eloquent and glowing epistles published in the volumes before us.

All Margaret's hopes fell with the hopes of Italy; and fully did she share in the sorrows and privations of those whom the re-fastening of the chain upon their stricken country had driven once more into exile. When the French were entering Rome, 'the good lady,' as the bleeding soldiers whom she had tended so gently were accustomed to call her, sat with Mazzini in the upper chamber of a private house to watch the scene beneath. 'The triumvir had passed many nights without sleep,' she writes; 'in two short months he had grown old; all the vital juices seemed exhausted; his eyes were all bloodshot; his hair was mixed with grey: but he had never quailed; had protested in the last hour against surrender; great and calm, but full of a more fiery purpose than ever.' And now, while she is thus writing about others, came the crowd of poor Margaret's own sorrows. Ossoli, whose brothers were officers of rank in the Papal service, had renounced all his worldly prospects for the liberal cause, and had been so far compromised as to be forced to seek his personal safety by flight. Alone, deprived of her child, too, her little boy Angelo, and racked by a thousand fears for his safety and that of her husband, Margaret writes to her mother and her friends at home the whole history of her secret marriage and her sufferings. . . .

There is something peculiarly touching in the lines with which she closes this letter to her only parent. 'Write the name of my child,' she says, 'in your Bible—Angelo Ossoli, *born* 5th September, 1848. God grant he may live to see you, and may prove worthy of your love.' An allwise Providence had otherwise decreed. After a sojourn at Rieti and at Florence, quiet, tranquil, and happy, even amid poverty and the remembrance of shattered hopes, rendered memorable, too, by acts of kindness and benevolence, Margaret, with her husband and the little Nino, set out for the home of her youth, now her only home. The chapter in which Mr. Emerson opens for us the 'last scene of all, that ends this sad, eventful history,' is one of touching interest. It was the spring in Italy. 'Spring, bright prophet of God's eternal youth, herald ever eloquent of heaven's undying joy, had once more wrought its miracle of resurrection on the vineyards and olive-groves of Tuscany, and touched with gently-wakening fingers the myrtle and the orange in the gardens of Florence.' 'I am homesick,' Margaret had written years before, but where is that home? The sad family took ship with many misgivings. An Italian fortune-teller had warned Margaret to 'beware of the sea,' and the voyage was undertaken with many presentiments of danger. It was disastrous from the very outset. The captain died on the voyage, and the mate either mistook his reckonings, or was bewildered by the currents that disturbed the ship's course. The little Angelo was seized with severe illness, and all grew dark around them. Again it brightened; the child recovered, but only to share the melancholy fate of his father and mother. The vessel struck upon the beach near Long Island, while the passengers were in bed. They were brought on deck with much difficulty. The captain's widow and some of the crew were saved by planks and by swimming. Still no effort was made to save the others by those who had collected on the beach, eagerly looking out for, and carrying off, the valuables which were washed ashore. . . .

Thus perished one whose gifts and acquirements might have shed a lustre around her name, and contributed worthily to the honour of her country by raising the character of its literature. America has much to regret in the early death of Margaret Fuller. Undeveloped as her intellect in its natural tone may be said to have been, it was sufficiently obvious that there was that in it which is no every-day product. What she has left us in her literary labours was but a promise; her life-labour—her enthusiasm—her high-hearted devotion to truth and nobleness—the strength of character which is born of suffering, was more. If ever there was an earnest liver upon this earth it was Margaret Fuller, notwithstanding all that dreary deadening cramming in her childhood, and that speculative vagueness—that Emersonianism into which she was afterwards dragged. Her large true heart was ever reaching above and struggling to get beyond these, and that her rough share in the battle of life would have enabled her to fight up to a position beyond them, we have no doubt whatever. 'Too soon, too soon was she called from the field,' say we in our blindness; but it was not too soon, for God's voice called her. It is not for us to pierce the veil of the mysterious future. Yet, in our honest admiration of such rare abilities and energy, we look with sad regret on the poor preparation which Emersonianism affords for either the struggles of life or the issues of death, while it turns away with irreverent scorn from Him who has 'brought life and immortality to light.'

# "Vanity *versus* Philosophy. Margaret Fuller Ossoli"

Anonymous*

Margaret Fuller Ossoli should have been by nature a woman among men, but by intellect she was a man among women. Whether in her case the latter will pass current as value for the former on the great 'Change of human nature, we will not take on us to decide; but we would say, that, whatever chance it might have had of such a consummation has been materially diminished by the parties who were selected to collect, write, and edit her memoirs. Not that anything can be taken from intellect where it exists, but much may be added to it which will lessen its value, even as a superfluity of clothing will deform the appearance of man, though the man is still the same, or as the attachment of a few weights will drag down and sink the most buoyant piece of cork, the cork being still the same, only that it is obscured.

These volumes detract much from our idea of Margaret Fuller; and we are certain there is no admirer of her high talents and brilliant capacities but will feel wearied and disgusted with the overweening vanity, inordinate ambition, and capricious characteristics which those books treasure up to her account. We deem it anything but worthy or characteristic of the friendship (which the editors of her memoirs profess to have had for the living), and love for the memory of *their* dead "Margaret," to parade throughout the greater portion of two volumes her idiosyncratic weaknesses and egotism; and we more object to the exercise of the same faculties in the persons of, and as regards those editors themselves. We heartily wish those volumes could exchange places with their subject, and that she were here to defend and save herself from her friends. Samuel Johnson used to say that he would take the life of any person who intended to write his; and indeed, we do not remember a case in which such an act could be perpetrated with more justification, if the party under consideration had been aware of the intention of her "friends," than the publishing of the memoirs before us, always and ever excepting Leigh Hunt's Life of Byron and Lamartine's autobiographical "Confidences."

The "Life" should have been written and edited by more *mere* mortal men than Messrs. Emerson, Channing, and their friends, account themselves. A readable and worthy volume might have been furnished by the hands of more

---

*Anonymous, "Vanity *versus* Philosophy. Margaret Fuller Ossoli," *United States Magazine and Democratic Review*, 30 (June 1852), 513–529.

practical and less transcendental philosophers. They should not have intruded on the public three-fourths of the correspondence printed, very much of which is in the style of thought and phraseology of those New England lights, and the only point of which seems to be the adulation of the writer and receiver of each letter. Things of such small interest to the world will be forgotten by it, and the temporary notoriety such may gain by publication, will only the more hastily and inevitably drag whatever else of good there may be mixed up with them to a more immediate oblivion. We say all this because those parties boast of being the friends and intellectual lovers of Madame Fuller Ossoli. But if they were, they should have more regard for her character as a "philosopher" than for any self-glorification, and should not have printed what, while it only praises them or herself, also ruins her in the estimation of all common-sense readers. For ourselves, who do not profess any such adoration, but who respect and admire the ability while we condemn the vain glory, and who feel proud of her as an American writer, while we blush to see how her intellectual womanhood was overcome in early life by vanity, and afterwards by the acquaintanceship and superficial halo of philosophy of sundry Boston writers—we can but say, that as we suppose the letters and journals are authentic, they reveal Margaret Fuller; and however disgusting their perusal may have been, we congratulate the editors on the excuse they have of being impartial to her, by giving a very full view of her life, and thus praising themselves through her correspondence, and at the expense of her reputation.

Margaret Fuller Ossoli, without doubt, has attained and will hold a position in the young literature of America. Her ripe scholarship, various attainments, forcible style, and strong, though often obscure thought, deservedly claim a rank of no mean order. With such ability and resources she might have become, with more literary skill and less self-conceit, which she mistook for self-reliance, an author of great power, breadth and purpose. As it is, she has written well on various subjects, and acted better, as a true American should, when in Rome during the revolution and the annihilation of the Roman republic by the French; attending on the beseiged freemen at their barricades, or comforting the wounded in the hospitals. She had a strong spirit in her, but in this country it was "philosophized" into wordy audacity by the literary clique into which she fell, and who flattered her young vanity, and talked her into a position she did not really, nor could, occupy . . . .

She displayed more art in the pains she took to inform her friends of her ability than she did in her printed books and writings. Mr. Emerson gives us a clue to the secret. He informs us that

> "Margaret was one of the few persons who looked upon life as an art, and every person not merely as an artist, but as a work of art. She looked upon herself as a living statue, which should always stand on a polished pedestal, with right accessories, and under the most fitting lights. She would have been glad to have everybody so live and act. She was annoyed when they did not, and when they did not regard her from the point of view which alone did justice to her."—*Memoirs*, vol. 1, page 238.

Mr. Emerson means, from the point she *desired* to be viewed from. We are sorry that we cannot view her from such a point, if that point be the one in which she has placed herself, and has been kept by others, in these "Memoirs." She viewed life as an art, everybody as a piece of art, and of course she artistically used the latter, that is, influenced them to her ambition or vanity; made them, in fact, the "polished pedestal" on which her "living statue" was to be fixed for the admiring gaze of poor natural people. It must be a humiliating consideration for Mr. Emerson that he had been very successfully used in this way; he, whose theory and objects were the same, knocked off his centre by the more subtle woman-artist. It might flatter his gallantry to thus have acknowledged a female, if his philosophic pride would not rebel against the harboring of such an intention. . . .

# "Margaret Fuller Ossoli"

Émile Montégut*

To those who like to contemplate the mysteries of human nature, the abysses it discloses, and all the enchanted world of its desires, passions, and hopes, this book will prove an interesting acquisition, as it has been to us. It is a journey into the regions of the soul and the thoughts, which interests and discloses certain secrets of human character, as few other such journeys can do. You are enabled to distinguish and enumerate all the volcanoes which the nineteenth century has opened to us,—love of change, restlessness, pride; in fine, all the youthful passions of modern times, running to and fro with disheveled locks, and brandishing their thyrsi like bacchants. The virtues of the past still live, however, though concealed in retirement, aged, almost exhausted, ready to expire, and tormented in their last hours by pitiless hobgoblins, cries of despair, or mocking sarcasms. The perusal of this work produces in the soul a feeling of sadness—almost of compassion. The most brilliant imagination, united to such inability of realizing its conceptions; so much imperious pride with so many failures; so much eloquence with so much delirium; to reduce to nothing the most precious gifts of nature and providence, by all the caprices and the phantasies of will and character; to pass like a flaming meteor through the midst of men, inspiring them with mingled astonishment and terror; loved only in being feared; considered everywhere as a splendid accident, whose law is unknown—such was the sad and lamentable destiny of Margaret Fuller, Marchioness d'Ossoli, prophet, sibyl, a queen without a kingdom, seeking every where to gather subjects under her sceptre, neophytes to convert to her creed, or slaves to liberate. With her uncommon intelligence, and her entirely misdirected mind, she is the most complete representative of the excellences and defects of the most celebrated women of our time; possessed of true candor, notwithstanding all her pride, of irreproachable conduct, her faults and her merits always remained in a metaphysical state; and this is why she deserves, notwithstanding her singularity, that those who do not share the enthusiasm of her friends—to whom she is neither goddess nor prophetess—should speak of her only with reserve, justice, and sympathy.

Of all the celebrated women of the nineteenth century, (we do not include

---

*[Émile Montégut], "Margaret Fuller Ossoli," *National Magazine*, 1 (October, November, December 1852), 314–320, 409–418, 529–536; first published as "Marguerite Fuller," *Revue des Deux Mondes*, 22 (15 April 1852), 37–73.

Madame de Staël, whose correctness and clearness of mind cannot accommodate themselves to such comparisons, and who should not be mentioned with most other writers of her sex,) Margaret Fuller is certainly the most individual, the least *abandonee*; in short, has the most resistance and character. Proud and imperious, she never abdicated her reason nor her will; she had not the passive, obedient, almost humble nature, of Bettina, whose child-like character only asked to be conquered; she had not the irresistible and equivocal attractions of George Sand; nothing of that overpowering strength which the river possesses when enlarged by storms; she had not the prodigious courage of Lady Stanhope, who threw herself into abysses in order to explore their depths, nor the relative modesty of Rachel de Vainhagan, happy in exercising her influence over a circle of chosen friends, content to be on a footing of equality with them, and freely to express her thoughts to them. She, on the contrary, had only one thought,—to govern; only one ambition,—to reign. A desire of power, misdirected, and always enveloped in the vapors of idealism, penetrates all her words. Give to her life a definite object, withdraw her from her German studies, instead of the world of metaphysicians and poets in which she lived, throw her into the political and active world, and you would have, immediately, the chief of a party, a leader, after the manner of Madam Roland, for example. Give her a strictly religious and Catholic education, and you would see her submit to the most terrible experiences to found or reform some monastic order; and always the governor, employing her powerful will in directing the mysterious flock of tormented souls who have sought repose in cloistered retirement. Instead of the exclusively literary training to which the imprudence of her father condemned her, give her a more *gymnastic* education, if we may so express ourselves, the education of an Amazon instead of that of the scholar, and you would soon see her attempt the most perilous adventures, perhaps withdrawing to the desert to found kingdoms, and undertaking political and military enterprises, after the manner of Lady Stanhope. The circumstances and the manners of her country, her education and the mediocrity of her fortune, prevented Margaret Fuller from launching into these dangers. All the abnormal force which she possessed found nothing on which to exercise itself, happily perhaps for her memory; it remained always in the latent state; unable to display itself outwardly, her moral life slowly consumed, and made her existence one long fever. Margaret should have limited herself to the part of a muse and of Egeria. Is this true? No; these words, which awake the idea of persuasiveness in the mind, of modesty and sweetness, do not belong to her. Even in her character of inspirer, she always finds means to make her superiority and her power felt; there is still more of the magician than of the muse or the beneficent fairy in her composition. Eloquent, proud, gifted with a great power of attraction and moral magnetism, she appears to us, in the midst of her cortége of friends, metaphysicians, poets, gray-haired students, young enthusiasts, and intellectual women, as the Circe of the American literary world and of the idealistic school.

To comprehend the character of Margaret Fuller, this essential trait must be recognized—her love of power. All her words, all her actions, emanate from and circle around this single point. To those who have not understood this original vice or this innate virtue, whichever it may be termed, her character is most complicated,—it is entirely inexplicable. We shall confine ourselves as much as possible to the unfolding of her character, now that we know what was the foundation of it; and the moral lesson, if there is any, will be drawn better from a simple analysis than from a discussion of it.

Before entering into the analysis of these memoirs, however, a few words are necessary upon the book itself, and upon the compilers and arrangers of Margaret's papers. The editors are three in number: one is cousin of Margaret, Mr. James Freeman Clark; the second is a celebrated man, Ralph Waldo Emerson; the third, in place of personal celebrity, bears the illustrious name of Channing. We shall not reproach them with their concealments in certain places, we shall not ask of them the secrets and the facts which they have retained; but we have a right to reproach them with the method which they have employed in the arrangement of these memoirs, and the singular style of narration by which they have patched up among them the fragments left by Margaret. In reading these pages, written in so mystical, extravagant, almost occult and cabalistic a style, it seems scarcely like reading of a being of flesh and blood, but of some fantastic personage from one of the planets; it would be taken for the biography of a mysterious stranger, rather than that of a beloved friend. The work has been written in the style of Novalis's *Disciples de Saïs* and Byron's *Lara*. The associates of Lara could not otherwise relate what they knew of the mysterious page; the disciples of Saïs could not in any other manner have explained the teachings or displayed the science of their master. This style of narrative produces endless suppositions in the mind of the reader, and leaves him with an incomplete knowledge, which easily leads to reverie; but it is not suited to biography. In the second place, the editors have broken the unity of these memoirs by dividing the task; each in his admiration of Margaret Fuller, has desired to say what he himself knew of her. This is doubtless an honorable sentiment, but it increases the dithyrams and repetitions of the book without adding new facts or remembrances. Each in turn recommences the portrait of Margaret, and resumes the strain of eulogy and panegyric which the first had finished. Emerson, doubtless, instructs us the most; and it is to be regretted that he had not the entire arrangement of these memoirs. Emerson saw the most clearly into her character, and he has told us her faults with the least reserve and prudery. He is the most skeptical, the most defying, and the most analytic of the three. We repeat, it is to be regretted that the work is not entirely his own; he would have gained by it, and the character of Margaret Fuller would have lost nothing. The praise and admiration of Messrs. Clark and Channing, on the contrary, are much more prejudicial to it; for they give rise to the suspicion that their friendship has closed their eyes, or at least prevented them from seeing clearly . . . .

Thus terminated, by a horrible catastrophe, the life of this ardent and feverish woman. Margaret Fuller has marked her place in the annals of her country. It is the first time such a character has appeared in the United States.

Among all the symptoms indicative of a desire for change in the manners, moral life, and religion of the Americans, there is nothing more curious than this. We are interested in this question, we Europeans; such an existence may serve us for a moral thermometer, by which to measure the amount of influence which European ideas have had, and are still exciting in the development of transatlantic civilization. The whole history of America is the result of the ideas of Europe:—after Luther and Calvin, who may be regarded as the founders of New-England, came Locke and Voltaire, who may be considered in their turn as the founders of the Union and the fathers of the Revolution. Now it is Kant and Hegel who are the apostles of a moral and intellectual renovation. America is thus a vast workshop of experiments. In moral things, as in physical geography, America is not a distinct and separate world; it is but the second hemisphere of our planet. All that Europe thinks, America applies, whether it be an industrial invention or a system of morals. The Americans have not at present, and probably will not have for a long time to come, any ideas which are properly their own; but they know how to live a cosmopolitan life, and they receive all the influences of Europe. Ideas which would disturb our reason, events which would inflict destruction upon us, have no effect upon their robust temperament and vigorous health; all are useful to them, and nothing is capable of injuring them. So, whatever may have been her mistakes or her faults, Margaret Fuller ought not to be judged too severely. Her influence, which might have been hurtful in Europe, has been, on the contrary, salutary in America. After the revolutions it has gone through, and the shocks it has suffered, the European mind requires to be treated with infinite caution. It must be soothed with prudence when governed; and he cannot too carefully weigh his words, who would address it as a writer or philosopher. But the American mind can be addressed without fear of heating it too violently. There, in that young and vigorous world, words fly more lightly than in our Europe; they are less easily rendered into action, and there is no such need to moderate one's enthusiasm. The influence of Margaret has not died with her; she still lives, she returns to us and will long return to us, under the form of books or essays. She, more than any other individual, has sown the harvest which is beginning to show itself in America and is slowly ripening there. Hence we have spoken of her with minuteness and sympathy, in order that hereafter, when all the facts and ideas which she has scattered in America shall bear their fruit, she also may sustain her share of the responsibility and receive her portion of the praise, for the evil and the good which these ideas and facts may ultimately produce.

# [Margaret Fuller]

Matthew Arnold*

23. Grosvenor St. West [London]
Grosvenor Place
March 21 [18]53.

My dear Clough

..................................................

Margaret Fuller[1] —what do you think of her? I have given, after some hesitation, half a guinea for the three volumes concerning her—partly moved by the low price partly by interest about that partly brazen female. I incline to think that the meeting with her would have made me return all the contents of my spiritual stomach but through the screen of a book I willingly look at her and allow her her exquisite intelligence and fineness of aperçus. But my G—d what rot did she and the other female dogs of Boston talk about the Greek mythology! The absence of men of any culture in America, where everybody knows that the Earth is an oblate speroid and nobody knows anything worth knowing, must have made her run riot so wildly, and for many years made her insufferable.

Notes

1. The estimate of Margaret Fuller (1810–1850) is not wholly distinguished by "urbanity" and "proportion"; but Arnold also properly sets forth her merits. About this same time he wrote his mother, "I have been reading Margaret Fuller, and again have been struck with her sincere striving to be good and helpful. Her address to the poor women in the Penitentiary is really beautiful. 'Cultivate the spirit of prayer. I do not mean agitation and excitement, but a deep desire for truth, purity, and goodness, and you will daily learn how near He is to every one of us.' Nothing can be better than that" (*Letters of Matthew Arnold 1848–1888*, ed. George W. E. Russell [London: Macmillan, 1895], I, 36).

*From *The Letters of Matthew Arnold to Arthur Hugh Clough*, ed. Howard Foster Lowry (London: Oxford University Press, 1932), pp. 131–134.

# [Memoirs of Margaret Fuller Ossoli]

Anonymous*

These two volumes have been sometime before the public, and have served as foundations for good, bad, and indifferent criticism. They can never be popular in any 'UNCLE-TOM' sense of the word. The school and its teachings forbid it. Into this sanctuary of thought but few will care to enter; and on its threshold they must divest themselves of all the common weeds of an every-day experience, and walk in privacy and calmness of judgment.

In style and idea these volumes are completely original. The rhetoric is pithy and masculine; the thought impulsive and suggestive. They are sweet kernels from the nut of Transcendental Literature. No super-refinement is here. Cultivated intellect is married to common-sense, and there is a superlative freshness, which savors of New-England forests wet with morning-dew. The analysis of character is so perfect, so beautifully complete, so regardful of light and shadow, that it is as if we beheld a natural landscape, where every exquisite detail but perfects the unity of the whole.

MARGARET FULLER OSSOLI was born in Cambridgeport, Massachusetts, on the twenty-third of May, 1810. 'My father,' she says, 'was a lawyer and a politician. He was a man largely endowed with that sagacious energy which the state of New-England society for the last half-century has been so well fitted to develop.' Speaking of her mother in the same connection, she beautifully observes, 'She was one of those fair and flower-like natures which sometimes spring up even beside the most dusty highways of life—a creature not to be shaped into a merely useful instrument, but bound by one law with the blue sky, the dew, and the frolic birds. Of all persons whom I have known, she had in her most of the angelic: of that spontaneous love for every living thing—for man, and beast, and tree, which restores the golden age.'

Margaret's education was early cared for by her father, who fell into the common and fatal error of stimulating her intellect to a precocious degree. She ascribes to this, visitations of spectral illusions which defiled nightly before her over-tasked brain, in shapes more hideous than those which for years besieged the Opium-Eater.

She early imbibed a taste for literature—more particularly for the litera-

---

*Anonymous, [Review of *Memoirs of Margaret Fuller Ossoli*], *Knickerbocker Magazine*, 41 (June 1853), 544–548.

ture of southern Europe—believing her intellectual affinities all pointed that way; and DE STAEL, RACINE, PETRARCH, and ROUSSEAU, engrossed a homage which a more liberal and corrected taste afterward bestowed upon the masters of English and German literature.

From the school of Misses PRESCOTT, in Groton, Massachusetts, whither her father had sent her for a time, MARGARET returned to live in Cambridge. Here she applied herself to the culture of her mind, and formed many friendships which endured for life. Her reading and study were extended and severe. She was already acquainted with French, Italian, and Spanish literature, and qualifying herself for the reading of German. In three months from the time she commenced German, she read with ease the flower of its literature. All this reading did not affect her judgment, nor bias, in any considerable degree, her intellect. She thoroughly understood the nature and relations of each author whom she read, and never placed him above or below his true standard. SCHILLER, JEAN PAUL, and NOVALIS, exercised a powerful and invigorating influence over her; but GOETHE—the wonderful, universal, and many-sided—drew her by the force of his superior attraction. 'It seems to me as if the mind of Goethe had embraced the universe. I have felt this lately, in reading his lyric poems. I am enchanted while I read. He comprehends every feeling I have ever had so perfectly, expresses it so beautifully; but when I shut the book, it seems as if I had lost my personal identity; all my feelings linked with such an immense variety that belong to beings I had thought so different.' The effect of Goethe on MARGARET was complete. She was perfectly timed to it. She found her moods met, her topics treated, the liberty of thought she loved, the same climate of mind. Of course, this book superseded all others for the time, and tinged deeply all her thoughts. The religion, the science, the Catholicism, the worship of art, the mysticism and demonology, and withal the clear recognition of moral distinctions as final and eternal—all charmed her; and FAUST, and TASSO, and MIGNON, and MAKARIA, and IPHIGENIA, became irresistible names. It was one of those agreeable historical coincidences, perhaps invariable, though not yet registered—the simultaneous appearance of a teacher and of pupils, between whom exists a strict affinity. Nowhere did GOETHE find a braver, more intelligent, or more sympathetic reader.

The shock and impulse of delight which MARGARET, as well as many others, experienced from the battery of German transcendentalism, was communicated by a master-spirit of the age—THOMAS CARLYLE. In a series of essays of deep and original splendor, this great thinker had challenged the attention of the youthful world of literature to the essential truth which German philosophy symbolized.

Transcendentalism, in its original sense, was a philosophic protest against the teachings of Hume and the materialistic spirit of the age. In its later and more significant sense, it was an appeal from all traditional and sectarian dogmas, to the direct inspiration of the soul by GOD. It eschewed all binding formulas, and proclaimed, as its end, the attainment of absolute freedom. On the stepping-stones of patience, culture, agony of soul, solitude, and long watching for inspiration from the 'wind which bloweth where it listeth,' its disciples sought to ascend to the mystical heights of rapture and ecstasy, to stand upon the prophetic mount, and catch glimpses of the promised CANAAN.

Toward the realization of this result, all nature contributed. Each stone became a sermon; each flower a hint of mystery. Man's body was the temple of the living GOD; man's heart was the Paradise of promise and perfect bloom; and love and poetic rapture constituted at once the sweetest incense and the purest praise. Intuition usurped the seat of logic; and precept and morality were to be realized in active life.

The standard orthodoxy had become divided into a multitude of sects, each of whom claimed to be the receptacle and participant of the entire truth. The division-lines were marked and impassable, and the sentiment of religion, which is spontaneous, overflowing, and pervading, was inextricably interwoven within the meshes of dogmatic controversy, and personal praise and worship were neglected for party wrangling and bigotry. Then came the reäction. The appeal was lost amid the clash and din of contending sects, and its intent and purpose was misunderstood, because its essence could not be bounded by a creed. Day by day it grew stronger, gathering many pure and good into its open and unforbidden communion, and constituting a living church gathered from all sects, and involving the 'spirit of all creeds, and the substance of all formulas.' In short, it was the inception of a new theology, whose hopes embraced all humanity, whose law was love, whose end was absolute freedom and perfection.

Theoretically, transcendentalism is sublime in the extreme. It involves, as a condition of its growth and symmetrical development, the employment of every passion and faculty that is beautiful and noble in humanity. It appeals, with equal reason, to the heart and the intellect. The graces and embellishments of life are not to be sacrified to its sterner and coarser demands; nor, on the other hand, are they to be retained as indispensable to a high culture. Affection and reason divide the empire of being, and GOD and humanity acknowledge no tie but that parental and reverential love which on the one side is pure and perfect, and on the other devoid of fear. The practical philosophy and holy aim of transcendentalism attracted and quickened the finest intellects of the age; and side by side with the names of Emerson, Carlyle, Parker, Martineau, Clarke, and Ripley, who illustrated and still adorn the school, must be placed that of MARGARET FULLER OSSOLI, who, equally by her trustful energies and by her poetic and penetrating genius, exercised a sweet and welcome influence over many kindred hearts.

MARGARET realized in herself the perfect combination of teacher and disciple. Her intellect and soul were open to all the daily aspirations which exhale from the gardens of nature and humanity; and in turn, the flower of her genius and the altar of her heart distilled a fragrance and precious incense which revealed the beauty of the blossom and the purity of the worship. 'The world is the book of woman,' says Rousseau; and it is certain that, much as MARGARET was indebted to literature, her obligations to persons were weightier and of more benefit.

Her conversational powers were of an original and suggestive order. She intuitively perceived the thought and character of her audience, and surprised individuals by this genius of insight, which opened the casket of the inner heart, and revealed treasures which came to one as a memory and a dream. Those who were repelled in the original contact, and those who were prejudiced by hearsay, came at last to be delighted auditors of this Delphian maid and priestess of the soul. Her conversational efforts were the offspring of present excitement, and included a more varied range, a greater depth, and greater life and vigor, than are to be found in her printed works. 'With the firmest tact, she led the discourse into the midst of their daily living and working, recognizing the goodwill and sincerity which each man has in his aims, and treating so playfully and intellectually all the points, that one seemed to see his life *en beau*, and was flattered by beholding what he found so tedious in its worldly weeds, shining in glorious costume. Each of his friends passed before him in the new light; hope seemed to spring under his feet, and life was worth living. The auditor jumped for joy, and thirsted for unlimited draughts. What! is this the dame who, I heard, was sneering and critical? This the blue-stocking of whom I stood in terror and dislike? This wondrous woman, full of counsel, full of tenderness, before whom every mean thing is ashamed and hides itself; this new Corinne, more variously gifted, wise, sportive, eloquent, who seems to have learned all languages—HEAVEN knows when or how—I should think she was born to them—magnificent, prophetic, reading my life at her will, and puzzling me with riddles like this: 'Yours is an example of a destiny springing from character;' and again, 'I see your destiny hovering before you, but it always escapes from you.''

The charity of MARGARET's opinions may be read in her remark on Shelly: 'Had he lived twenty years longer,' says she, 'he would have become a fervent Christian, and thus have attained that mental harmony which was necessary to him.'

It is refreshing to find amid the shallow cant and fashionable persecution of the day, such true perceptions of the inharmonious relations of one whose temperament was as spiritual as that of FENELON, whose heart was as brave as FICHTE's or JEAN PAUL's, and whose defects, and long-seeking for bright views and settled convictions regarding the sublime problems of life and death, are attributable to the sinister influences of a misdirected early education.

We read constantly of MARGARET's enthusiastic admiration of great intellect and great men, and yet she was no hero-worshipper in Carlyle's sense of the term. She did not subscribe to the exaggerated statement that 'society is founded on hero-worship.' She felt, as all feel, the magnetic attraction which adheres to marked personality; and owned—as who does not!—such influence as grows out of the really beautiful and true in human character. But she constantly disowned the imperfection of man. For every word of flattery, she had another of plain, honest, out-spoken truth; and to her clear discernment, the naked soul of the king was revealed through all the disguises and trappings of royalty.

Her nearest and dearest friends were not exempt from this severity. Affection was met by affection, kindness by kindness, caresses by caresses. But then this intimacy was to be strengthened and purified by counsel, advice, and, if need be, stern rebuke. She did this 'boldly and sincerely.' In her estimate, truth was more than friendship, and true friendship she would weigh against the world. And yet she called for equal sincerity on the part of her friends. Truth gives wings to strength; and so, on the stepping-stones of self-knowledge, love, and friendly advice, she advanced into higher kingdoms of perfection, and into atmospheres of perpetual and unclouded beauty.

Margaret's acquaintance with RALPH WALDO EMERSON commenced in 1835, and was productive of benefit on both sides. The philosopher was stimulated by her genius, and puzzled by her character. He observed in her a continual strife between passion and common-sense. Now she was driven into strange assertions, and isolated positions, and an hour following her good sense prevailed, and established harmony of thought and action. This unequal poise of passion and intellect, giving to the one or the other temporal ascendency, constituted her in character and sphinx, whose riddle it was hard to resolve.

She had the popular and unpopular sides. In criticism her writings were characterized by 'directness, terseness, and practicality.' What she wrote for the New-York *Tribune,* the *Dial,* and in published books, was loaded with common-sense, and charged with popularity; but her strong ties of friendship were twisted of the fibres of passion; and in her private correspondence, where she is liberated from the irksome decorum and established formality which beset popular writings, where affection prompted instead of intellect, she unburdens her soul of all its griefs and raptures, and, carried away by her abundant temperament, floats out into the sea of mysticism, and of poetic ecstacy.

But we pause for the present. Farther and concluding remarks upon these volumes must be reserved for our next number.

# "Margaret Fuller Ossoli"

Caroline Healey Dall[*]

The horticulturist glows with delight when Nature offers him a new flower. The statelier its aspect, the more intense its tints, the more difficult its culture, the more cordial is his welcome. While its inspiriting fragrance floats through his conservatory, and lifts the very heads of all other plants, hope kindles in his bosom, and every energy is bent to the perfecting of that germ, which is the vehicle of its immortal type, and which shall transmit its grace, its color, and its God-given charm. He does not stay to ask why the stem is coarse and angular, the leaves heavy and viscous, the root moist with a poisonous juice, the calyx set round with thorns; or if he deals with these matters at all, it is to seek their relation to the continuous life of the plant, and not to find fault with the Creator. What precious fluids flow through that angular channel, what honeyed sweets are exhaled through those viscous organs of respiration, what precious medicament lies hidden in the poison, what possible injury to the young germ the thorny crown repels,—these things, indeed, concern him. Would to Heaven that ordinary human creatures stood thus reverent before a new soul, fresh from that Hand which makes and permits no mistakes; that their eyes opened gladly to the unfading beauty of the immortal; and that the angularity, the bitterness, the individual peculiarity or weakness, with which God defends the youth of His best beloved, were heeded only as they reveal the secret of development, or explain the facts of position! Then had we long since ceased to hear of Margaret Fuller's arrogance, conceit, and irreligion, and recognized her as a noble gift to our time. Now that we have for the first time before us a complete memorial of her, it will be well to review briefly the works which she has left to us,—especially that best of all her works, her life,—and to endeavor, through the pages of this Review, to correct some misapprehensions concerning her which still float on the popular breeze. To those who "wander to and fro on the earth," fulfilling the varied engagements of the Lyceum, these misapprehensions are familiar as household words. Rumor finished her clumsy work long ago, and it is still too early for the historic sponge to clear the board. "Show us anything that Margaret has left, as fine as many of the things that have been said of her, and we will put faith in your vindication," said once an

---

[*][Caroline Healey Dall], "Margaret Fuller Ossoli," *North American Review*, 91 (July 1860), 119–129; reprinted as "Margaret Fuller" in Dall's *Historical Pictures Retouched* (Boston: Walker, Wise, 1860), pp. 226–248.

intelligent clergyman who should have known better. Is it nothing, then, to prompt to the saying of fine things? "This is the method of genius," Margaret writes, "to ripen fruit for the crowd, by those rays of whose heat they complain."

The two volumes of Memoirs, now republished, contain, beside the original matter, a touching life of Margaret's mother, from the pen of her son Richard, and a genealogical record of the Fuller family, which doubtless indicates the force and quality of that blood. It seems to us that the editor is unnecessarily anxious to efface the impression that his father's discipline was so severe as to overtax even Margaret's precocity. In her Autobiography, a species of writing for which she was admirably qualified by nature, she left on record, in regard to this matter, precisely the statement which she desired should survive. Does the editor call the Autobiography a romance? Very well. In its pages the writer sought to convert her own personal experience to universal use. "A more than ordinarily high standard was presented me," she wrote. "My father's influence upon me was great, but opposed to the natural unfolding of my character, which was fervent, of strong grasp, and disposed to infatuation and self-forgetfulness." To foster these peculiarities would have been a worse service than the overstraining, whose results, it seems to us, Margaret naturally enough misjudged, while, by the thorough discipline he maintained, Mr. Fuller brought an influence to bear on her "infatuation," the benefits of which she never ceased to feel, and came ultimately to understand. With her nightmares and somnambulisms, also, this severe *régime* and excessive study had little to do. They belong to such natures as hers. They are a part of the dreamy "self-forgetfulness"; and if an occasional indiscretion added to their horrors, they could not have been wholly escaped, under the most tender indulgence, by one of her class. If not overworked by requirements from without, a mind like hers must have overwrought itself. Madame de Staël wrote standing, that she might not seem to be disturbed when her autocratic father entered her apartment. A gifted woman of the present century spent three years of her youth in copying mercantile letters, the only curb her merchant-father could find for an ideality which he did not comprehend. For all such natures, God provides such discipline. It may look harsh. We can trust Him, that it shall prove wise.

None but poets remember their youth, and we prize this autobiographical fragment more than most else of what Margaret has left us. Very beautiful is the conception of the Memoir, a threefold, yet concurrent testimony, which serves to show her many-sided nature. Very grateful ought our public to be to Mr. Clarke, for the crystalline clearness with which he sets before them the story of his intercourse with his friend. He feels his obligations, and with graceful, manly self-reliance acknowledges them. To her other biographers she ministered delight, to him growth. They stood admiring; he felt the woman in the genius. "This record," he says, "may encourage some youthful souls, as earnest and eager as ours, to trust themselves to their heart's impulse, and enjoy some such blessing as came to us." He will never know how many. Nowhere does the remarkable simplicity of her relations with men and women appear to such advantage as in his pages. Not a shadow of coquetry nor mist of passion hovers over the record. Impetuosity, ardor, and high resolve gleam through the rifts of the correspondence, and grant us clear guesses at what we do not see.

The most common charge brought against Margaret is that of arrogance,—a charge which had some show of truth in it, both as concerns her own peculiarities, and in regard to the temperament which she inherited; but who are we that bring this charge, and what true significance has it? May we not be talebearers, censorious, meddlers in other men's matters? and if so, what is the significance of that fact? For us and her abides the old eternal law. She was human, unlikely therefore to show us perfection, either inherited or attained in the life that now is. The only profitable question is, Did she accept, foster, hug to her bosom her own frailties, or did she in the main, at all events ultimately, see their true nature, and put them under subjection? To this question there can be but one answer. From a manuscript for some time in our possession, we copy the following statement—a very fair one it seems to us—of the impression she sometimes made upon truly noble souls.

> "My nature would always have resented the assumption of superiority; but gladly would I have knelt before the humblest human creature in whom I perceived it. Many a pure-hearted child has bent the knee which only stiffened before Margaret, and this, not because I was not willing to acknowledge her fine ability, her great superiority, but because I knew the highest crown we could either of us inherit, it depended upon our own wills to wear,—because I felt myself as much the child of my Heavenly Father as she. To become truly regal, in my eyes, she must have relinquished the love of power for its own sake, must stretch out generous, sustaining tendrils towards feebler souls. In fine, must break up 'her court,' and enter 'society.' If there was anything in my own temper which bore a likeness to her faults, I only felt, on that account, how necessary it was that she should hold them, as I was trying to hold mine, 'under her heel.' Margaret was, even then, at times, beautifully tender and considerate, but it was from the height of her queenliness that she was so. Her possibilities enthralled me, but never her actual self."

This statement, nowhere so distinctly made in the Memoirs, but involved in facts to which they bear witness, may for the sake of truth be made once, but for the sake of all honor and nobleness it should be for ever after set aside. We balance it, first, by her own words concerning Carlyle, showing how much more just she could be to others than we are to her, and then by the prayer which Mr. Channing quotes from her Diary, under date of the very hour which rang with complaints of her conceit and coldness.

> "His arrogance," she says of Carlyle, "does not in the least proceed from an unwillingness to allow freedom to others. No man would more enjoy a manly resistance. It is the habit of a mind accustomed to follow its own impulse, as a hawk does its prey. He is indeed arrogant and overbearing, but in his arrogance there is no trace of littleness or self-love. It is in his nature, in the untamable energy that has given him power to crush the dragons."

All this was true of her who wrote it, and who, at the moment of misapprehension, wrote also this truly Christianlike prayer: "Father, let me not injure my fellows during this period of repression. I feel that, when we meet, my tones are not so sweet as I would have them. O let me not wound! I who know so well how wounds can burn and ache should not inflict them. Let my touch be light and gentle. Let me not fail to be kind and tender when need is." Here her keen intellectuality detected a pharisaic satisfaction in the very humility of her petition, and her truth breaks through to close in these words: "Yet I would not assume an overstrained poetic magnanimity. Help me to do *just right*, and no more." Do the records of womanhood show us a finer instance of self-knowledge and humble seeking?

Next to be considered is the common charge of an irreligious character. This the volumes before us by no means rebut in so forcible a manner as could be wished. Mr. Clarke's expression of "*almost* Christian" when he speaks of her aim in self-culture, Mr. Emerson's evident want of faith in her religious experiences, of a nature which it was impossible he should understand, and his dwelling so long upon her belief in demonology and fate, in omens and presentiments, have done much to strengthen the popular mistake. She had a Goethe-like faculty of seeming and being all things to all men. The being hardly lived to whom she would have breathed her vital religious experiences in all their force. To the cold and flippant,—before the merely intellectual or philosophic,—she was dumb as death. When she presented to an observer a single glittering surface, she was necessarily misunderstood. She forgot her own past, and did not pause to explain changes. In his usual spirit of fairness, Mr. Emerson offers us the key to the riddle, so far as it concerns himself. "The religious nature remained unknown to you," Margaret writes, "because it would not proclaim itself, but claimed to be divined. The deepest soul that approached you was, in your eyes, nothing but a magic lantern."

It seems to us that Mr. Clarke came nearer to her personally than any of her biographers; and if so, it was on account of the deep religious glow in his own soul, which hers answered with a faint, but decided reflection. He undoubtedly strove to make the truth manifest in this regard, and failed not for lack of material,—for there is an abundance in his pages,—but from some accidental inability to marshal it in effective array. The book followed, as most memoirs do now-a-days, too soon after the death of its subject, and could not meet a public prejudice, not as yet fully recognized.

Margaret's profound truthfulness was religious in its very nature, and she herself perceived the relation. Truth is God-like to our human view; and she expressed an underlying and shaping fact of her own inward life when she wrote, "The man of truth, that is, of God." "She had so profound a faith in truth, that thoughts to her were things," writes Mr. Clarke; and because they were of the essence of God himself, she dealt with them so subtilely, so earnestly, and so unsparingly. It was religious aspiration which spoke in her when she wrote, "No fortunate purple isle exists for me now, and all these hopes and fancies are lifted from the sea into the sky." "Never was my mind so active," she writes a little afterward, "and the subjects are God, the universe, and immortality." Are we to believe that she thought of such things in vain? If her religious instincts failed anywhere, at first it, was in practical recognition of the brotherhood of man; but the walls of Sing-Sing and the pavements of the Roman hospitals cry out with later answers to that charge. One friend she gladly sought for his "compact, thoroughly-considered views of God and the world." "Tangible promises, well-defined hopes, are things of which I do not now feel the need," she wrote once; and on the next page, "Blessed Father! lead me any way to truth and goodness, but if it might be, I would not pass from idol to idol. Lead me, my Father, enable me to root out pride and selfishness."

"Margaret, has God's light dawned on your soul?" some friend questions; and she answers, with a truly Christian humility, "I think it has." Indeed, so far from being irreligious, it might almost be said of her, from the testimony of these pages, that she received a sudden illumination, and was converted in the stricter evangelical sense of the word. It was in experiences like this that Emerson put no faith. Their ecstasy did not suit his cool head, and, in her periods of bitterest anxiety for her husband and child, she wrote from Italy that his fears were justified. Her faith had not lasted. But her own words, written at such a moment, must not be allowed to condemn her. If such feelings sometimes flicker, as we all know, they are none the less real on that account,—they are the seed of a yet profounder experience. It is our human weakness which cries out in Gethsemane, and children of God we still are, whether we can read our family name or not. "I thought I should die," she wrote after her sickness at Groton; "but I was calm, and looked to God, without fear. Nothing sustains me now but the thought of God, who saw fit to restore me to life, when I was very willing to leave it. I shall be obliged to give up selfishness in the end. May God enable me to see the way clear." When she wrote this, she was not accusing herself of any low form of selfishness, only of that intense desire of self-culture which possessed her like a demon, and which it was the will of God, working through circumstances, perpetually to thwart. "I have faith," she says again, "in a glorious explanation, which shall make manifest perfect justice and wisdom." "I reverence the serenity of a truly religious mind so much, that I think I may attain to it." "Like Timon, I have liked to give, not so much from beneficence as from restless love. I return to Thee, my Father, from the husks that have been offered me. But I return as one who *meant not* to leave Thee." In July, 1838, she says: "I partook to-day, for the first time, of the Lord's supper. I had often wished to do so." Were these the utterances of an irreligious spirit? Nay, they came from a profoundly religious spirit, yet one far too individual, to accept commonplace conclusions, or to be content with a second-hand faith. Very slowly did this side of her nature develop, but with soundness and entire freedom. Could she have seen as little children see, when she so bitterly regretted her defeated hope of visiting Europe, she would have known that in all earthly experience, whether of travel, or of artistic or literary culture, there is but one end to be gained,—an end which God inevitably secures for every human soul, though he may sometimes postpone it; and in this faith, every thwarted purpose glows in the light of hope.

Too much is said in these volumes of her own dissatisfaction at her lack of personal charms. She herself said, and said truly, that this was "mere superficial, temporary tragedy!"

It surprises us, also, that one of her biographers should expect impossibilities of her. Strange he thinks it, that she had not studied the natural sciences, and could write only vapid descriptions of "skyscape." But it was never in her to observe or to criticise Nature or Art for itself alone. The subtile change of air, earth, and sea, she heeded only as the aesthetic influence stole over her, and then she described, not Nature's change, but the soothing, recreating power of Nature over the human soul.

> "It remains to say," says Emerson, and we say with him, "that all these powers and accomplishments found their best and only adequate channel in her conversation,—a conversation which those who have heard it unanimously, so far as I know, pronounced to be in elegance, in range and flexibility and adroit transition, in depth, in cordiality, and in moral aim, altogether admirable, surprising, and cheerful as a poem, and communicating its own civility and elevation like a charm to all hearers."

In the third volume of the present series is published "Woman in the Nineteenth Century;" several papers concerning woman and her interests; and some letters from and concerning Margaret, which would more properly have been included in the Memoirs. Some of these last show her religious feeling and her sweet womanliness in so bright an aspect, that we would gladly quote them. "Woman in the Nineteenth Century" is, perhaps, more widely known than any of her works. We shall avoid any lengthened criticism of it, because it must open a discussion of the still unfolding "Woman Question," for which we have neither space nor time. It is doubtless the most complete, brilliant, and scholarly statement ever made upon this subject. Its terse epigrammatic sentences have furnished more than one watchword to the reformers with whom the author herself was never associated. The book is interesting as the strongest expression of the aggressive and reformatory element in her. She was interested in the social pioneers of whom she often spoke lightly, and it was reserved for Italy to teach her the practical value of an abstract idea. In the Preface to this volume, the editor bears touching testimony to her domestic virtues.

The fourth volume contains "Summer on the Lakes,"—her "Letters from Europe to the Tribune," giving the details of Italian politics,—some letters to friends, portions of which had been already incorporated into her Memoirs,— and details of the fatal shipwreck. "Summer on the Lakes" has long been one of our favorite summer classics. It first won us, not more by the vital individuality and grace of the style, in which it stands alone among her lighter works, than by the beauty of the little brown etchings with which her friend Miss Clarke adorned the first edition. In the matter of style, it was Margaret's peculiarity to have none when she spoke from her memory. The narrative portions of her "Letters from Abroad," for example, might just as well have been written by any one else. But once arouse her heart and mind, and out flowed the personality! Let her speak of Mazzini, or describe a fringed flower in the moonbeams, and no one could mistake the author. This volume is especially interesting, as containing all that remains of her Italian experience, her complete work on "Italy" having shared, to our bitter regret, her own fate.

"Art, Literature, and the Drama," is a reprint of the volume which she published on the eve of her departure for Europe. A friendly gift to those she was leaving, it proved, in many respects, the most popular thing she had printed,—and deservedly, for her mind was eminently critical. She was often misled in her first judgment, as in one well-known instance, by the strength of her affection and her sympathy; but let the merit be real, and of a kind which she was glad to recognize, and no one ever did more exquisite justice to thought and to its form. Every word which she ever wrote of Goethe was admirable, and yet what we possess was only *her preparation* for better work. Nothing was ever more tender and true than her sketch of "The Two Herberts" in this volume. Let the reader dwell also on what she has to say of "American Literature," and the "Lives of the Great Composers."

The closing volume of this series, entitled, "Life without and Life within," strikes us as the most interesting portion of her miscellaneous writings, and its contents are almost entirely new to the public. Here we have the best of what remained about Goethe,—pleasant criticisms, and ideal sketches of various kinds,—appeals for the unhappy also, and words which, if the fault-finders will but read them, will show, not merely her spiritual capacity, but, in some respects, the measure of her attainment.

It is impossible, in closing, to criticise these works as they deserve. We repeat what is well known, and has been often said, that their *suggestiveness* is their chief and perpetual charm. No one can read attentively what she wrote, without learning to think for himself. The difference between her written works and her marvellous conversation was well indicated by a compliment paid by the Comte de Ségur to Madame de Staël. "Tell me, Count," she asked in a vivacious moment, "which do you like best, my conversation or my printed works?" "Your conversation, Madame," was the immediate reply, "for it does not give you leisure to become obscure."

Some poems are added to the last volume, and these have been severely criticised. It is quite probable that Margaret never would have published them,—that she would have said of them at last, what she wrote at the first, that her verses were merely "vents for her personal experience." Nevertheless, let them be as faulty in artistic form as the critics would represent them, we are glad to have them, as revelations of her inward life. She wrote never a word to be spared. We feel an unbounded confidence in her, and we thank her brother for sharing in it. One of these poems, at least, seems to us to have exquisite truth and beauty, both in thought and form. We refer to the "Lines" addressed to the lady who illustrated her "Summer on the Lakes."

These volumes are stereotyped clearly, on good paper, in tasteful array. Yet one criticism upon their form we cannot withhold. We deeply regret that all the biographical matter was not thrown together, according to its period, even if Appendix after Appendix had been thus made needful. It is further a matter of regret, that the essays themselves are not dated. We are quite aware that this is not usual; but in this particular case their psychological value would have been much increased by such a means of tracing development. We should have been glad to extract largely from these volumes; but to do it, we must have resigned all hope of speaking at length in regard to Madame Ossoli's personal character, which we were unwilling to pass without our tribute of sincere, yet we trust not undiscriminating, respect and gratitude.

We could hardly believe, till we had turned the six volumes over repeatedly, that the only portrait offered in this complete edition is one from the picture painted by Hicks, during the last few months of her life in Rome. It was well to have this preserved, for there is great ideality and sweetness in the expression,—a certain look we always hoped would dawn and nestle there. Those who saw her after a mother's hope had risen in her heart say that this was a good likeness; but we cannot but miss the old portrait, published, we think, in a former edition of "Woman in the Nineteenth Century." If the later portrait gives an idea of more personal beauty than Margaret possessed, it wholly fails of that majestic, Juno-like curve of the throat, which was more than beauty. If it was, as in the engraved countenance now given us, that her eyes dilated and her lips grew tender when she gazed upon the wounded men in those Italian hospitals, let us know it; but we cannot be satisfied to possess only a likeness which not one of her early friends would recognize.

# "Margaret Fuller"

### A. Bronson Alcott*

THURSDAY, 20.

HORACE GREELEY has just issued from the "Tribune" office a uniform edition of Margaret Fuller's works, together with her Memoirs first published twenty years ago. And now, while woman is the theme of public discussion, her character and writings may be studied to advantage. The sex has had no abler advocate. Her book entitled "Woman in the Nineteenth Century" anticipated most of the questions now in the air, and the leaders in the movement for woman's welfare might take its counsels as the text for their action. Her methods, too, suggest the better modes of influence. That she wrote books is the least of her merits. She was greatest when she dropped her pen. She spoke best what others essayed to say, and what women speak best. Hers was a glancing logic that leaped straight to the sure conclusion; a sibylline intelligence that divined oracularly; knew by anticipation; in the presence always, the open vision. Alas, that so much should have been lost to us, and this at the moment when it seemed we most needed and could profit by it! Was it some omen of that catastrophe which gave her voice at times the tones of a sadness almost preternatural? What figure were she now here in times and triumphs like ours! She seemed to have divined the significance of woman, dared where her sex had hesitated hitherto, was gifted to untie social knots which the genius of a Plato even failed to disentangle. "Either sex alone," he said, "was but half itself." Yet he did not complement the two in honorable marriage in his social polity. "If a house be rooted in wrong," says Euripides, "it will blossom in vice." As the oak is cradled in the acorn's cup, so the state in the family. Domestic licentiousness saps every institution, the morals of the community at large,—a statement trite enough, but till it is no longer needful to be made is the commonwealth established on immovable foundations.

> "Revere no God whom men adore by night."

Let the sexes be held to like purity of morals, and equal justice meted to them for any infraction of the laws of social order. Women are the natural leaders of society in whatever concerns private morals, lead where it were safe for men to

*From A. Bronson Alcott, *Concord Days* (Boston: Roberts, 1872), pp. 77–78.

follow. About the like number as of men, doubtless, possess gifts to serve the community at large; while most women, as most men, will remain private citizens, fulfilling private duties. Her vote as such will tell for personal purity, for honor, temperance, justice, mercy, peace,—the domestic virtues upon which communities are founded, and in which they must be firmly rooted to prosper and endure. The unfallen souls are feminine. . . .

# [Margaret Fuller]

### Harriet Martineau*

In Margaret Fuller's Memoirs there is a letter which she declared she sent to me, after copying it into her common-place book. It is a condemnatory criticism of my "Society in America;" and her condemnation is grounded on its being what she called "an abolition book." I remember having a letter from her; and one which I considered unworthy of her and of the occasion, from her regarding the anti-slavery subject as simply a low and disagreeable one, which should be left to unrefined persons to manage, while others were occupied with higher things: but I do not think that the letter I received was the one which stands in her common-place book. I wish that she had mentioned it to me when my guest some years afterwards, or that my reply had appeared with her criticism. However, her letter, taken as it stands, shows exactly the difference between us. She who witnessed and aided the struggles of the oppressed in Italy must have become before her death better aware than when she wrote that letter that the struggle for the personal liberty of millions in her native republic ought to have had more of her sympathy, and none of the discouragement which she haughtily and complacently cast upon the cause. The difference between us was that while she was living and moving in an ideal world, talking in private and discoursing in public about the most fanciful and shallow conceits which the transcendentalists of Boston took for philosophy, she looked down upon persons who acted instead of talking finely, and devoted their fortunes, their peace, their repose, and their very lives to the preservation of the principles of the republic. While Margaret Fuller and her adult pupils sat "gorgeously dressed," talking about Mars and Venus, Plato and Göthe, and fancying themselves the elect of the earth in intellect and refinement, the liberties of the republic were running out as fast as they could go, at a breach which another sort of elect persons were devoting themselves to repair: and my complaint against the "gorgeous" pedants was that they regarded their preservers as hewers of wood and drawers of water, and their work as a less vital one than the pedantic orations which were spoiling a set of well-meaning women in a pitiable way. All that is settled now. It was over years before Margaret died. I mention it now to show, by an example already made public by Margaret herself, what the difference was between me and her, and those who followed

---

*From *Harriet Martineau's Autobiography*, ed. Maria Weston Chapman (Boston: James R. Osgood, 1877), I, 380–384.

her lead. This difference grew up mainly after my return from America. We were there intimate friends; and I am disposed to consider that period the best of her life, except the short one which intervened between her finding her real self and her death. She told me what danger she had been in from the training her father had given her, and the encouragement to pedantry and rudeness which she derived from the circumstances of her youth. She told me that she was at nineteen the most intolerable girl that ever took a seat in a drawing-room. Her admirable candour, the philosophical way in which she took herself in hand, her genuine heart, her practical insight, and, no doubt, the natural influence of her attachment to myself, endeared her to me, while her powers, and her confidence in the use of them, led me to expect great things from her. We both hoped that she might go to Europe when I returned, with some friends of hers who would have been happy to take her: but her father's death, and the family circumstances rendered her going out of the question. I introduced her to the special care of R. Waldo Emerson and his wife: and I remember what Emerson said in wise and gentle rebuke of my lamentations for Margaret that she could not go to Europe, as she was chafing to do, for purposes of self-improvement. "Does Margaret Fuller,—supposing her to be what you say,— believe her progress to be dependent on whether she is here or there?" I accepted the lesson, and hoped the best. How it might have been with her if she had come to Europe in 1836, I have often speculated. As it was, her life in Boston was little short of destructive. I need but refer to the memoir of her. In the most pedantic age of society in her own country, and in its most pedantic city, she who was just beginning to rise out of pedantic habits of thought and speech relapsed most grievously. She was not only completely spoiled in conversation and manners: she made false estimates of the objects and interests of human life. She was not content with pursuing, and inducing others to pursue, a metaphysical idealism destructive of all genuine feeling and sound activity: she mocked at objects and efforts of a higher order than her own, and despised those who, like myself, could not adopt her scale of valuation. All this might have been spared, a world of mischief saved, and a world of good effected, if she had found her heart a dozen years sooner, and in America instead of Italy. It is the most grievous loss I have almost ever known in private history,—the deferring of Margaret Fuller's married life so long. The noble last period of her life is, happily, on record as well as the earlier. My friendship with her was in the interval between her first and second stages of pedantry and forwardness: and I saw her again under all the disadvantages of the confirmed bad manners and self-delusions which she brought from home. The ensuing period redeemed all; and I regard her American life as a reflexion, more useful than agreeable, of the prevalent social spirit of her time and place; and the Italian life as the true revelation of the tender and high-souled woman, who had till then been as curiously concealed from herself as from others.

# [Margaret Fuller and Hawthorne]

Julian Hawthorne*

... Miss Fuller was at this time in her apogee, and had to be doing something; and accordingly, during the ensuing year, she produced a book in which the never-to-be-exhausted theme of Woman's Rights was touched upon. The book made the rounds of the transcendental circle, and was sufficiently discussed; and doubtless there are disciples of this renowned woman now living who could quote pages of it. But married women, who had in their husbands their ideal of marital virtue, and whose domestic affairs sufficiently occupied them, were not likely to be cordial supporters of such doctrines as the book enunciated. Mrs. Hawthorne and her mother, in letters which happen to be written on the same day, expressed themselves on the subject as follows. I give passages from the former's epistle first:

> "... Mr. Emerson's review of Carlyle in the 'Dial' is noble, is it not? What a cordial joy it must be to Carlyle to find in another such worthy appreciation of his best purposes! In all his writings I have been mainly impressed with his pure humanity, which has made me love the man and listen reverently to all he utters,—though in chaotic phrase, like rattling thunder echoed among ragged hills. If ever a mortal had a high aim, it is certainly he. What do you think of the speech which Queen Margaret Fuller has made from the throne? It seems to me that if she were married truly, she would no longer be puzzled about the rights of woman. This is the revelation of woman's true destiny and place, which never can be *imagined* by those who do not experience the relation. In perfect, high union there is no question of supremacy. Souls are equal in love and intelligent communion, and all things take their proper places as inevitably as the stars their orbits. Had there never been false and profane marriages, there would not only be no commotion about woman's rights, but it would be Heaven here at once. Even before I was married, however, I could never feel the slightest interest in this movement. It then seemed to me that each woman could make her own sphere quietly, and also it was always a shock to me to have women mount the rostrum. Home, I think, is the great arena for women, and there, I am sure, she can wield a power which no king or conqueror can cope with. I do not believe any man who ever knew one noble woman would ever speak as if she were an inferior in any sense: it is the fault of ignoble women that there is any such opinion in the world."

---

*From Julian Hawthorne, *Nathaniel Hawthorne and His Wife* (Boston: Houghton, Mifflin, 1884), I, 252–262.

Mrs. Peabody writes from very much the same standpoint:—

"Margaret Fuller's book has made a breeze, I assure you. Seems to me I could have written on the very same subjects, and set forth as strongly what rights yet belonged to woman which were not granted her, and yet have used language less offensive to delicacy, and put in clearer view the only source (vital religion) from which her true position in society can be estimated. A consistent Christian woman will be exactly what Margaret would have woman to be; and a consistently religious man would readily award to her every rightful advantage. I believe that woman must wait till the lion shall lie down with the lamb, before she can hope to be the friend and companion of man. He has the physical power, as well as conventional, to treat her like a plaything or a slave, and will exercise that power till his own soul is elevated to the standard set up by Him who spake as never man spoke. I think Margaret is too personal. It is always painful to me to hear persons dwell on what they have done and thought,—it is taxing human sympathy too heavily. It is still worse in a book designed for the public. The style, too, is very bad. How is it that one who talks so admirably should write so obscurely? The book has great faults, I think,—even the *look* of absolute irreligion,—yet it is full of noble thoughts and high aspirations. I wish it may do good; but I believe little that is high and ennobling can have other foundation than genuine Christianity."

—I find no further allusion to Margaret in any of the American letters or journals; but fifteen years afterwards, when she was dead, and Hawthorne was in Rome, he came across some facts regarding her marriage which led him into the following interesting and not too eulogistic analysis of her character and career.

## *EXTRACT FROM ROMAN JOURNAL.*

Mr. Mozier knew Margaret well, she having been an inmate of his during a part of his residence in Italy. . . . He says that the Ossoli family, though technically noble, is really of no rank whatever; the elder brother, with the title of Marquis, being at this very time a working bricklayer, and the sisters walking the streets without bonnets,—that is, being in the station of peasant-girls. Ossoli himself, to the best of his belief, was ——'s servant, or had something to do with the care of ——'s apartments. He was the handsomest man that Mr. Mozier ever saw, but entirely ignorant, even of his own language; scarcely able to read at all; destitute of manners,—in short, half an idiot, and without any pretension to be a gentleman. At Margaret's request, Mr. Mozier had taken him into his studio, with a view to ascertain whether he were capable of instruction in sculpture; but after four months' labor, Ossoli produced a thing intended to be a copy of a human foot, but the great toe was on the wrong side. He could not possibly have had the least appreciation of Margaret; and the wonder is, what attraction she found in this boor, this man without the intellectual spark,—she that had always shown such a cruel and bitter scorn of intellectual deficiency. As from her towards him, I do not understand what feeling there could have been; . . . as from him towards her I can understand as little, for she had not the charm of womanhood. But she was a person anxious to try all things, and fill up her experience in all directions; she had a strong and coarse nature, which she had done her utmost to refine, with infinite pains; but of course it could only be superficially changed. The solution of the riddle lies in this direction; nor does one's conscience revolt at the idea of thus solving it; for (at least, this is my own experience) Margaret has not left in the hearts and minds of those who knew her any deep witness of her integrity and purity. She was a great humbug,—of course, with much talent and much moral reality, or else she could never have been so great a humbug. But she had stuck herself full of borrowed qualities, which she chose to provide herself with, but which had no root in her. Mr. Mozier added that Margaret had quite lost all power of literary production before she left Rome, though occasionally the charm and power of her conversation would reappear. To his certain knowledge, she had no important manuscripts with her when she sailed (she having shown him all she had, with a view to his procuring their publication in America), and the "History of the Roman Revolution," about which there was so much lamentation, in the belief that it had been lost with her, never had existence. Thus there appears to have been a total collapse in poor Margaret, morally and intellectually; and, tragic as her catastrophe was, Providence was, after all, kind in putting her and her clownish husband and their child on board that fated ship. There never was such a tragedy as her whole story,—the sadder and sterner, because so much of the ridiculous was mixed up with it, and because she could bear anything better than to be ridiculous. It was such an awful joke, that she should have resolved—in all sincerity, no doubt—to make herself the greatest, wisest, best woman of the age. And to that end she set to work on her strong, heavy, unpliable, and, in many respects, defective and evil nature, and adorned it with a mosaic of admirable qualities, such as she chose to possess; putting in here a splendid talent and there a moral excellence, and polishing each separate piece, and the whole together, till it seemed to shine afar and dazzle all who saw it. She took credit to herself for having been her own Redeemer, if not her own Creator; and, indeed, she was far more a work of art than any of Mozier's statues. But she was not working on an inanimate substance, like marble or clay; there was something within her that she could not possible come at, to re-create or refine it; and, by and by, this rude old potency bestirred itself, and undid all her labor in the twinkling of an eye. On the whole, I do not know but I like her the better for it; because she proved herself a very woman after all, and fell as the weakest of her sisters might.

# "Hawthorne and Margaret Fuller Ossoli"

Frederick T. Fuller*

Biographers have not often the will, even if the power, to inflict such wounds as the friends and relatives of Margaret Fuller Ossoli have received at the hands of the compiler of the recently-issued memoir of *Nathaniel Hawthorne and his Wife*. None of the references to her which he has been able to discover are complimentary; but the climax is capped with the following extract from Hawthorne's Roman journal, written during his visit to that city eight or nine years after her tragic death. He writes:. . . .

This is indeed a "severe portrait," as the index puts it; but if it were true and just, I for one would not lift a finger to change it—though I cannot think that Hawthorne's memory will be the gainer by the disclosure that he was capable, even in thought, of pronouncing such a judgment upon a former friend, long since dead, and a woman. That the judgment must be just, because it is Hawthorne's, I find to be a somewhat common sentiment in some quarters where a suspension of judgment until both sides were heard might perhaps have been looked for. In a recent issue of a publication which if not an undisputed authority in literary matters has at least a large circulation and wide influence, the editorial opinion is expressed that "of Margaret Fuller's contemporaries none has shown so much insight into character in general as Hawthorne, and his judgment of her, severe as it is, wonderfully reconciles all the others." And I have not noticed that this verdict has called forth a protest from any of its readers. Another periodical, usually careful and conservative in its statements, points a moral as to ill-assorted marriages by declaring that even Margaret married "a man whom her friends found to be half an imbecile"—though I am not aware that any other "friend" than Hawthorne ever made so startling a discovery. But perhaps it is possible to attach to such popular endorsements as these too much importance. The words of men of Hawthorne's literary standing are not likely, true or false, to lack echoes—and there are still those who are tired of hearing Aristides called the Just.

Certainly it must be admitted that if Hawthorne has erred in his estimate of Margaret it was not altogether from lack of opportunity to study her character. Their acquaintance—though they had met before—appears to have begun in 1841, when Hawthorne was an ardent worker, and Margaret an occasional

---

*Frederick T. Fuller, "Hawthorne and Margaret Fuller" *Literary World*, 16 (10 January 1885), 11–15.

visitor, at Brook Farm, and to have become somewhat intimate at the time of his marriage in the following year. Her friendship with Sophia Peabody [Mrs. Hawthorne] was, I believe, of somewhat earlier date; and I have seen a letter in which the latter, in May, 1842, confides to Margaret the secret of her engagement with Hawthorne. "Dear, most noble Margaret," she calls her; and writes that the decision was not made till the previous evening, and that she is entitled through "our love and profound regard for you," to be told directly; and she signs herself "Your very true and loving friend, Sophia."

In a letter to Margaret, dated August 28, 1842, and printed in the memoirs now under consideration, Hawthorne himself says:

> There is nobody to whom I would more willingly speak my mind, because I can be certain of being thoroughly understood;

a sentiment which, perhaps, reads rather queerly considering the circumstances (according to the *Memoirs*) of its utterance; but at all events it evidences the existence of something more than a casual acquaintance between the two. There is also a letter from Hawthorne dated February 1, 1843 (which, he says, should have been written a great while before), in which, after declaring his inability just then to do something she had suggested, he says:

> How strange [that I must refuse] when I should be so glad to do anything that you had the slightest wish for me to do, and when you are so incapable of wishing anything that ought not to be!

This would seem to indicate—for surely our new Ithuriel cannot be himself a hypocrite—that Hawthorne could not then have formed the estimate of her which he recorded fourteen years later. And indeed there can be no question, as I learn from a study of Margaret's diary, that the period of real intimacy between the two was limited to a few months of the year 1844, during which she was much in Concord, residing chiefly at her sister Ellen's, but an almost daily visitor at the Hawthornes. Of Hawthorne himself she at first writes little—such casual references as

> H. told me something odious about —— which, if true, stamps him as contemptible as any man can be—

but much about Sophia, and more about the little Una, upon whose beauty, brightness, and pretty baby tricks she descants unweariedly with her characteristic love of children—singular trait that, by the way, in a "coarse" nature, destitute of "the charm of womanhood." "Played with Una," she writes of one of the frequent afternoon calls upon the Hawthornes:

> The child was more sweet and radiant than ever. Sophia told me a truth for which I thank her; she seemed nobly. I walked home with H. through the woods. The skies were sighing and veiling their lids, and began to weep as soon as I was housed.... I have been writing a little note to Sophia about the truth. I will think prayerfully of it.
> Took care of Una while H. and Sophia went out for a walk.... Never was a lovelier or nobler little creature. Next to little Waldo, I love her better than any child I ever saw.

Later, she writes oftener of walks and talks with Hawthorne; and after one of these comes the entry:

> I feel more like a sister to H., or rather more that he might be a brother to me, than ever with any man before. Yet with him it is, though sweet, not deep kindred; at least, not deep as yet.

This is at the end of her stay in Concord; in the autumn of 1844 she removed to New York, where she continued to reside until she went abroad in 1846, and met Hawthorne but seldom, if at all, after the former date. There are other interesting entries in her diary during this period, when although so often Hawthorne's guest, loving and petting his child, rendering little sisterly domestic services to Sophia, bringing little delicacies such as without offence may pass as gifts between intimate friends, and learning to cherish Hawthorne himself as a brother, she did not succeed in leaving in his "heart and mind" "any deep witness of her integrity and purity"—entries which read strangely beside the passage in his Roman journal. Of her former pupils she writes:

> My wish has been more and more to purify my own conscience when near them, give clear views of the aims of this life, show them where the magazines of knowledge lie, and leave the rest to themselves and the Spirit who must teach and help them to self-impulse.

Receiving an unkind reply to a letter she had written, remonstrating with a friend upon some act which seemed to her unworthy, she is moved to copy the correspondence, including her rejoinder, in which she says:

> You are a little sarcastic toward me. This is not quite right. You could not seriously think that in saying any act of yours did not entirely commend itself to me I meant to intimate that I myself am in possession of a higher wisdom.

And later she rejoices that her remonstrance has regained her friend. Of an afternoon with Emerson, she writes:

> But Waldo's oration, oh, that was great, heroic.... It was a true happiness to hear him; tears came to my eyes. The old story of how the blacks received their emancipation; it seemed as if I had never heard it before, he gave it such expression. How ashamed one felt ever to be sad while possessing that degree of freedom which gave them such joy. I felt excited to new life and a nobler emulation by Waldo this day.

And on the leaf of the journal that contains the last entry made before she left home for New York, her mother has written, in an old-fashioned and delicate but trembling hand:

> This day is the last of domestic communion for 1844 with dear ones who have constituted a great portion of the happiness of the golden days of my life. I feel deep gratitude for domestic joys, and commend my first-born child to the guidance of her Father and mine, who is alone able to attend and bless in every stage of her journey from the home of her early life, [from] friends she has merited by disinterested endeavors to improve and increase the happiness of all with whom she has had intercourse. May this goodness be returned a hundred fold into her bosom; and, as all separations are solemn things for the infirm, I give my blessing on this last page of the

journal, as if it were my last, with many acknowledgments for the love and tender care I have experienced at the hands of my dear daughter, praying God to do more and better for her than I can ask or think, and to return her again to me in His own good time.

I must confess that these and the many similar passages in her diary of this year—together with the total absence of thoughts ignoble or unkind—would have led me to a very different estimate of her character from that which Hawthorne gives thirteen years later; but how dispute the dictum of one of whom we are assured that "of all her contemporaries none has shown such insight into character?"

But this unlovely vision of the "Roman Journal" is strangely unlike the sister Margaret of whom my father—the "my good little Richard" of the diaries which record the time when, by her father's early death, Margaret was obliged to bear the burdens of the head of the family—used to tell me. My father was neither a great man nor a novelist, but I think no one who knew him will deny that he was true and just. Remembering him to have been what he was, I can hardly help believing that his estimate of his sister's character was at least sincere. I never heard him say much of Margaret's literary achievements, but very much of her aims and character. He regarded me, and not I fear, without reason, as a somewhat indolent and selfish boy; and he would often try to rouse me to a noble emulation by telling me how my Aunt Margaret had striven against almost insurmountable obstacles of ill health and domestic cares to train and use to the best advantage her mental powers, and how she had labored, watchfully and with prayer, to correct the faults of which she was so conscious, and to become what she was always inciting those about her to be. Often, too, near the anniversaries of the wreck of the ill-fated "Elizabeth," he would call me into his study, and talk to me of how Margaret had cheerfully laid aside her own cherished plans and ambitions, in order to earn and save money for the education of himself and his brother Arthur; and of the wise and tender sisterly counsel, comfort, and reproof with which she used to try, and not altogether unavailingly, to hold them true to high ideals of duty. I must say, too, that the entries which I find in her diary for the period of which he spoke most fit in better with his recollections than Hawthorne's impressions do with her diary of 1844.

> Walked through Mr. Norton's grounds with H. Hedge [she writes]. He said many beautiful things—his appeal to me affected me greatly. Yes, my friend, I will strive to remain independent and true. "And Thou, if I should totter, teach me to stand fast."
>
> I have had a letter from E. [a brother] which was not exactly what I expected, but it was perfectly sincere, which is the most desirable of all attributes. [This from Hawthorne's "great humbug."]
>
> I observe with pleasure a sensible improvement in E. [another of the family, whose lovely character as a woman is the dearest legacy of her children]. She often does, of her own accord, little things for other people, and her fits of passion and asperity are at longer intervals.
>
> This week has been blackened by a fit of anger, about a very trifle, too! I must watch over myself.

> I taught the children four days [of another week]. I began with prayer, and they have done pretty well, yet have I not kept my temper as well as could be desired. Hope to do better this coming week.

This, again, is interesting from one who, says Hawthorne, "had always shown such a cruel and bitter scorn of intellectual inferiority."

> I think a good deal of cousin E., who is here now. A humble, cheerful Christian, doing so much good so quietly, and without praising herself even in her very inmost heart. The influence of the gospel alone, without any other advantages, has sufficed to give her a perfection in her way, which I with so many other lights am far from having attained in mine.

And this, from one who "took credit to herself for having been her own Redeemer, if not her own Creator."

> I here close this volume of my journal, which embraces four months of my existence. I have done little, but felt much. Grant, oh my God, that neither the joy nor the sorrow of this period shall have visited my heart in vain! Make me wise and strong to the performance of immediate duties, and ripen me by what means Thou seest best for the performance of those that lie beyond.

Earlier in the same year she writes:

> Peace—a vitalized peace—well-directed goodness, and ever-widening culture and growing intellect—oh, grant them, Heaven. I speak not of circumstances.

This volume of her diary contains the opening chapters—she was then twenty-six—of a little heart-history which has not, I believe, been referred to by any of Margaret's biographers—perhaps because the mutual attraction which it chronicles never "came to anything;" as the homely phrase goes. By the kindness of some elderly friends, Margaret was treated to a pleasure tour in which her passionate love of nature found a keen delight which permeates every page of her journal. One of her companions was a young man whose appreciation of beauty in natural objects seems to have been equal to her own. The discovery of this mutual affinity led to the disclosure of others also, and for some pages moonlight and daylight walks and talks with this new friend, and possible lover, are a prominent theme of the diary. Under such circumstances, young people are usually forgiven if they fall, for a time, a little below their usual standard of thoughtfulness for the wishes and comforts of third parties. With this in mind, such passages in the diary as the following may be of interest as an indication of character:

> Went up to Mrs ——'s room, and found her quite ill [the illness was not alarming—a headache, probably—as a later passage shows that it passed away in a few hours]. Got her tea and waited upon her. Mr. W. sent up to know if I would go down and see the falls by moonlight, according to promise. I longed to go, but thought it would be selfish, as Mrs. —— had just said it was delightful to have me there; so answered no.

Those who have kept diaries, and read them afterwards, are aware how serious a shock to self-complacency is apt to be involved in the latter operation; how cheaply sentimental appear passages which memory assures us were written in moments of sincere and deep emotion, and how mean, unworthy, and vindictive seem the criticisms which, at the time, we thought the outbreathings of a most righteous indignation. Margaret's diaries bear abundant internal evidence of having been written with the fullest unreserve, and with no thought that any eye but her own would ever read them; but, so far as I have examined them, there is nothing in them for which her friends need blush. The faults—partly inherited, and partly the result of a mistaken early training—which caused many who knew her but slightly to "think of her as a person on intellectual stilts, with a large share of arrogance, and little sweetness of temper," are frankly confessed and deplored, and prayerful efforts at amendment are chronicled, the effects of which were so marked that one [Mrs. Story] who had so judged her was led, upon intimate acquaintance with her soon after her marriage, during this very period of—according to Hawthorne—"total collapse morally and intellectually," to express astonishment at finding her "so delicate, so simple, confiding, and affectionate; with a true womanly heart and soul, sensitive and generous, and, what was to me a still greater surprise, possessed of so broad a charity that she could cover with its mantle the faults and defects of all about her." This was in 1848; but the germs at least of such a character must have existed in her when she wrote in her diary, years before Hawthorne ever saw her:

> Since we have moved into the winter parlor, where I used to see father so much, I realize more that he is gone forever. Oh my father, could I but have known that you would leave me, that I might have made your happiness my first object! My heart is wrung when I think of the many little attentions I might have paid you and did not.

But enough of the diaries, of whose general tone a correct idea is given by the extracts already printed in the memoirs of Margaret which have appeared from time to time. The more I read them, and her letters, the better I can understand the extraordinary tenderness with which her memory is still cherished, thirty-four years after her death, by the few intimate friends who survive her, every one of whom, so far as I am informed, resents Hawthorne's characterization as a base slander—though most of them knew Hawthorne well also.

## THE ITALIAN EPISODE.

Some of the well-known facts of Margaret's stay in Italy, the evidence of which has already been published, should be kept in view in connection with the assertions of Hawthorne's journal. She first visited Rome in the early spring of 1847, and during her short stay there met Ossoli, who was an officer in the Civic Guard, with a prospect of following in the steps of his three elder brothers in obtaining preferment in the service of Pius IX. They were mutually interested in each other, but with no thought of love on her part until he offered himself to her, just as she was leaving Rome for the summer. Then she rejected him, telling him that she would always be his friend, but would not marry. In the early autumn of that year she passed a few weeks at Florence, most of the time severely ill, at the house of Mr. and Mrs. Mozier, of the latter of whom she writes in terms of esteem and affection; and this was her only residence with the Moziers. She returned to Rome in October, 1847, and Ossoli renewed his addresses, the result of which was that they were married, but privately, for family reasons of his, which are fully explained in Margaret's memoirs. That winter was spent in Rome, amid the beginnings of the "Roman Revolution" to which Hawthorne refers. The following summer was spent among the mountains, but she returned to Rome soon after the birth of her child in the autumn, doing all a woman could do for the cause of Italian freedom, by espousing which her husband had forfeited all hopes of the favor of the pope and his own relatives. In April of the following year, during the siege of Rome by the French, she was placed by the "Roman Commission for the Succor of the Wounded," in charge of the hospital of the *Fate-Bene Fratelli*, in which devoted service she continued until the end of the conflict; while Ossoli was proving himself no less brave and active in his own post upon the ramparts. Then they escaped to Rieti, and later to Florence, where they passed the winter of 1849–'50, setting sail from Leghorn, May 17, 1850. This winter, accordingly, Mr. Mozier must have first met Ossoli, and then, if ever, must have occurred the remarkable experiences in his studio. How much truth there is in Mr. Mozier's alleged narrative it is not altogether impossible, even at this distance, to determine. A few of Ossoli's letters to Margaret are fortunately preserved, and some have been printed. Their tone is one of deep but dignified tenderness—contrasting rather favorably, I think, with the "thine ownest," "thy own belovedest" of Hawthorne's own post-hymeneal epistles. The handwriting is evidently that of an accomplished and practiced penman, and no one who examines it could possibly believe for a moment that its possessor could be destitute of the power of imitating a copy set before him to the extent implied in molding a human foot "with the great toe on the wrong side"—this phrase not meaning, I suppose, merely a right foot when the model was a left one. As to the rest, I cannot see why Margaret, who was just about setting sail for America, should consult Mr. Mozier, who was to remain in Italy, about the publication of her manuscripts in America; especially considering her own literary standing and acquaintance. That Margaret was actually at work upon her "History" is attested both by her own letters and the evidence of friends who called upon her while she was so employed. That Mr. Mozier was at all upon any such terms of intimacy with her as he seems to claim, I very much doubt. In a letter to her mother, during this winter, she writes, describing her pursuits and companions:

> The Americans meet twice a week, at the house of Messrs. Mozier and Chapman, and I am often present because of the kindly interest of those resident there;

and I can find no allusion which would intimate any closer relation. When Mr. Mozier invited her to his house, nearly three years before, the fact is gratefully noted in her letters to her home friends, as is every kindness shown her by high or low; and I think the tone of the reference above quoted is fairly good negative evidence, especially as she says, in the next sentence:

> With our friends the Greenoughs I have gone twice to the opera; then I see the Brownings often, and love and admire them both, more and more, as I know them better. Mr. Browning enriches every hour I pass with him, and is a most cordial, true, and noble man.

There is no word anywhere of Ossoli's giving attention to sculpture.

> He is separated from his old employments and natural companions [she writes], while no career is open for him at present.

Her friends write of finding him always with Margaret when they called on her; and that the project of making him an artist was entertained at a time when Margaret was looking forward to an early return to the United States and her anxiety was how their daily bread was to be provided—and when, too, "motives of economy" determined them, in spite of many misgivings, to take passage in a merchantman from Leghorn instead of going by way of France and by steamship—seems hardly more credible than the alleged result of the project. Margaret herself has written of him as the most congenial comrade, in her short trips among the Apennines, she ever had, which would seem to speak well for his appreciation of natural scenery. In a letter in which, with a tender deference to his sense of duty and his judgment, she expresses her doubts whether the attempt to liberate Italy is not premature and rash, she mentions the certain loss of "your uncle's employment" as one item to be taken into account before he decides to join the revolutionists. If any think it likely that the employment was merely menial, I have not now at hand better means of refuting the idea than the fact that, in his hasty notes to Margaret, he uses abbreviations that suggest at once familiarity with the forms of polite correspondence and with the duties of a secretary. As to his education, Margaret has written that he was not familiar with other languages than his own and the French, and others have testified that his mental training was merely such as qualified him for good society of his own rank. The friends who saw him with Margaret, both before and after their marriage, speak particularly of his refined manners and pleasing address, and his tenderness to Margaret and watchful care to render her, two years after marriage, such little services as are the delight of lovers, has also been remarked, as well as his great fondness for their child. But I learn that another and abler pen has undertaken the task of showing Ossoli's character in its true colors, and I will not further anticipate the result.

It is curious to observe the superficial likeness as well as the essential unlikeness existing between the two portraits of Margaret and her husband—the one presented by her parents, brothers, and such friends as James Freeman Clarke (who has lately defended her ably in the *Independent*), Miss Sarah F. Clarke, Ralph Waldo Emerson, Dr. Hedge, Horace Greeley, George William Curtis, Mrs. Dall, Mrs. Story, and others who knew her intimately at different periods of her life—some from early childhood—and whose testimony is corroborated by every word she has left on record in published works, correspondence, and her journals; and the other sketched by Hawthorne alone of those who could claim to know her well, but agreeing not inaptly with the criticisms long ago advanced by some whose acquaintance with her never got beyond the stage at which she impressed them as manifesting "the concentrated disagreeableness of forty Fullers." The resemblance is not unlike that between a photograph and a political cartoon of the better class, in which the familiar features of public men appear with a wonderful likeness, at once their most amusing and provoking characteristic, and yet every lineament so affected by an infinitesimal transformation, under the inspiration of party hate, that everything noble or manly has given place to low cunning or overweening arrogance. So under Hawthorne's graphic pencil what we have thought to be her character in youth, marked by uncommon nobility of purpose and intense outbreathings of affection toward all about her, but disfigured by too great self-esteem—to be delivered from "this egoism" is a suggestive prayer of her journals—and an undue pride of intellect fostered by an unnatural system of early education, becomes a "coarse, heavy, unpliable, and in some respects defective and evil nature;" her efforts with "strong crying and prayer" to reform these faults, under the outspoken criticisms of faithful friends, become a hypocritical purpose to seem noble for the world's applause; the conquest which those who thought they knew her in her later years, after she had passed from Hawthorne's vision, testify that she had effected, becomes a thin veneer, artificially covering all but changing nothing; her husband's family, which she and these friends describe as "noble but now impoverished" becomes "technically noble, but really of no rank whatever" (whatever that may mean); her husband himself, who, according to the same authority, was without other education than was attainable under the tuition of a priest, even without Margaret's literary aspirations, but fully able to sympathize in her noble aims and love of natural and spiritual beauty, brave and devoted without ostentation, tender and true to her and their child, and withal upborne in misfortune and peril by a "simple and child-like faith" on which her own could lean and be strengthened—becomes "a boor," "half imbecile," "a man without the intellectual spark;" her own pitying contempt for groveling aims, and for eyes blinded by petty interests to all true beauty—yet accompanied by a tender and helpful spirit toward all, however lowly, who were sincerely trying to rise—becomes "a cruel and bitter scorn of intellectual deficiency;" her passionate craving for affection, which in childhood made her seem "an odd and sometimes inconvenient adorer" to the Cambridge ladies who befriended her, at whose feet she used to sit and whose hands she covered with kisses, becomes "a rude old potency" which at last overturned everything in the twinkling of an eye; her lack of physical prettiness becomes absolute absence of the charm of womanhood; and her love for Ossoli, which her friends hailed with joy as a proof that at last she had fully succeeded in estimating at their true relative worth nobility of heart and soul and mere intellectual endowments and attainments, becomes a mere passion for a handsome face, and she is judged to have "fallen as the weakest of her sisters might."

Can it be, after all, that the lens through which Hawthorne so saw her was distorted by anything awry in his own nature, or that the pencil which so pictured her was not really that of a friend? One who knew both well has publicly suggested that she must have done or said something to "wound the self-love both of Hawthorne and his son." As for the latter, the date of his birth makes this impossible, except indirectly. He has indeed since written: "The majority of readers will, I think, not be inconsolable that poor Margaret Fuller has at last taken her place with the numberless other dismal frauds who fill the limbo of human pretension and failure;" but that was while smarting under the public reminder of Miss Sarah F. Clarke that his mother had showed better feeling and judgment in her former publication of extracts from Hawthorne's journal; and I think I do Mr. Julian Hawthorne only simple justice in saying that his publication of this extract is to be ascribed to no other cause than that he is not one to spoil a sensation to save a friend. I observe that in the same volume he has, without apparent necessity, cast more than one grievous imputation upon the memory of his father's sister Elizabeth (one would much like, by the way, to hear the poor lady's own side of the story); and since he does not spare his own family, I can hardly in reason complain that he does not regard less binding ties. As to the father, I can as yet find—my search has not been anything like exhaustive—nothing in Margaret's writings, published or unpublished, that would seem to indicate any breach of friendliness of which she was conscious. In fact, the last reference to him which I can discover in her journal is that already quoted where she speaks of him as a brother, but of kindred not deep though sweet. On the same page she writes:

> Oh, it is sad that I shall see Una no more in this stage of her beauty. When I do see her again she will be quite another child;

which confirms my belief that this was really written at the time of the parting which circumstances afterwards made final. There are many passages in Hawthorne's own works, however, which seem to indicate that she may have inflicted such a wound unconsciously, in the habit, which was one of her most marked characteristics, of pointing out to her friends, and urging them to remove, whatever she saw (or thought she saw) in them in conflict with their best possible development.

Since the publication of the *Blithedale Romance* his real though hardly avowed dislike of Margaret has been no secret to those that loved her—for no evasion of his biographer, and no skillful engrafting of alien characteristics and incidents, can conceal the truth that Hawthorne did "mean Margaret" by his Zenobia, and himself by Miles Coverdale—and hardly needed the confirmation which it receives from such passages from his *American Note Books* as this:

> I was invited to dine at Mr. Bancroft's yesterday with Miss Margaret Fuller; but Providence had given me some business to do, for which I was very thankful—

to assure us that his biographer is right in speaking of his father's escape from "the rarefied atmosphere of Emerson and Margaret Fuller" as a welcome relief. Readers of the *Blithedale Romance* will remember Zenobia's "amiable remark"—why not amiable, unless self-love was wounded?—that she "could not conceive of being so continually as Mr. Coverdale is within the sphere of a strong and noble nature without being strengthened and ennobled by its influence," and may readily believe that such a remark, referring to Emerson instead of Hollingsworth and substituting Hawthorne for Coverdale, may have been made by Margaret in Concord. Again, when Zenobia reproaches Coverdale with "a cold-blooded criticism, founded on a shallow interpretation of half-perceptions; a monstrous skepticism in regard to any conscience or any wisdom except his own," those who know the bent of Hawthorne's mind, as shown in his writings, may well imagine that some such warning, bereft of its asperity by the kindly purpose of a friend, may have really been spoken by Margaret. "Faithful are the wounds of a friend," but when the reproof is felt to be just, and yet rejected, few rankle more sorely. May not some such hidden hurt explain the base suggestions in the third chapter of the *Blithedale Romance*? At first, he says, he imputed Zenobia's "free, careless, generous mode of expression . . . to a noble courage, conscious of no harm." Later it seems he saw something which undeceived him.

> Now, just when they had passed the impending bough of a birch tree, I plainly saw Zenobia take the hand of Hollingsworth in both her own, press it to her bosom, and let it fall again! The gesture was sudden, and full of passion; the impulse had evidently taken her by surprise; it expressed all! Had Zenobia knelt before him, or flung herself upon his breast, and gasped out, "I love you, Hollingsworth!" I could not have been more certain of what it meant.

Are such things certain? Let us turn again to Margaret's journal, where she records her leave-taking of Emerson, with his family about him ("My Saadi" she calls him):

> At parting I rose. He still sate with his eyes cast down. His hand I pressed to my heart; it was a gentle vow He looked like the youngest child.

To what lengths Hawthorne could go when moved by a pique which would seem small to most men his works show too clearly; and what links were missing here his son has now supplied. The case that has moved me most is that of old Captain Lee—the "Old Lee" and "notorious liar" of his journal, and the custom-house barnacle, the gourmand, the soulless animal, the belly-worshiper, of the *Scarlet Letter*. One of Hawthorne's old Salem comrades, who is yet alive, was chatting with me the other day of his fishing trips with the great author when he was in the custom-house, and warmly assuring me that the tales of Hawthorne's drinking to excess were wholly unfounded, when suddenly he began to speak of this attack on the old inspector, and his tone changed: "Captain Lee was one of those old men whom everybody loves—genial, obliging, fond of spinning sailor's yarns, and of chatting about the roast chickens and Savoy cabbage that were waiting for him at home; but tender-hearted as a child, and without an enemy in the world except Hawthorne's bosom friend, the mainspring of the custom-house, who wanted his place for another man but could not find a pretext for his discharge because he was so general a favorite and performed his duties so well. He was dead then, and everybody felt for his daughters—beautiful girls, as respected as anybody in Salem—but left poor by their father's death and with no one to defend his memory. It was damnable, and Hawthorne's memory ought to rot for it!" And the kindly old man, himself the counterpart of Captain Lee as he described him, trembled and his eyes filled as he recalled the long-forgotten outrage. And what shall we say of Mr. Upham, whom Hawthorne pilloried as Judge Pyncheon in the *House of the Seven Gables*? Is there not something Quilp-like in the way Hawthorne's polished but poisoned scimetar carves in that ghastly chamber the dumb effigy of the enemy who had a hand in ousting him from his snug berth in the custom-house? Was such provocation always needed, either?—or what then shall we say of the wholesale characterization of "beefy," applied to the English ladies who had lionized the American author—a term which has made him perhaps the best hated Yankee that ever crossed the water! Are such delineations as these the work of the best judge of character among all Margaret's contemporaries?

He who unveils the shams of others should himself at least be true and noble. How then are we to account for Hawthorne's boyish request to his sister to deceive their aunt—rare joke that, his biographer would have us believe; his still more urgent plea to his sister to forward a false excuse that will enable him to get away from college; his idleness there—poor return to the uncle who helped him to an education; or his shameless advice, late in life, to a friend in pursuit of office? Far be it from me to attempt to belittle Hawthorne's genius—our American heroes and saints are not so many that we can afford to turn iconoclasts. One can but wish, though, that his illumined pen had been guided by a higher purpose—perhaps then, to cite one instance, the half-formed intent (of which his son has told us) to write something which should avenge and cure the wrongs of tortured seamen would not have been so languid and so easily turned aside.

But I have no wish to follow this analysis of Hawthorne's character further. Not long ago, when my thoughts were already full of this subject, I entered the Metropolitan Museum in Central Park and paused before the statue of Medea meditating the murder of her children. Almost perfect, of its kind, I thought it, and I felt as I gazed at it a shuddering insight into the inmost recesses of a lost and desperate soul; but there was to me nothing uplifting or ennobling in it. Further on, I stopped before a painting of the Betrayal—a blurred and faded canvas from which gleamed out one wondrous face, portraying to the world, as words cannot, a divine love and pity triumphant over the rankle of that last of injuries, the treason of a friend. The realm of art to which the time-worn painting belongs seemed to me above the other by almost the measure of the impassable gulf; and such, I thought, is the contrast between Hawthorne's work as it is and as he might have made it under the impulse of motives such as Margaret would have wished to waken in him. As I looked, the smart of wounded feeling gave place to a pity and forgiveness such as I believe Margaret herself would feel toward the "brother" who has so cruelly judged and rejected her. His words, I am confident, cannot really harm her; and I am not unhopeful that some may even be led by them, as I have been, to study and know her better, learning to hate and shun her faults as she did, and catching, as so many of her own generation have already done, the inspiration of her noble purpose.

# "Mr. Hawthorne and His Critics"

## Julian Hawthorne*

*To the Editor of the Transcript:* Sir—A few final remarks occur to me in regard to the criticisms made upon sundry features of the Hawthorne Biography. These criticisms are resolved, broadly speaking, into two—that the book contains some objectionable things, and that it objectionably fails to contain some others. The passage referring to Margaret Fuller is most prominent in the former category. Hawthorne held certain opinions about Margaret, which he formulated. I included this statement of his in the Biography. Hawthorne has been blamed in some quarters for thinking as he did about her, and I have been blamed still more for revealing his thought. I transcribed the passage in question deliberately and after due reflection. I hoped that it would be noticed, and I should have been disappointed had no notice been taken of it; for what Margaret Fuller was in herself is of very slight importance, but she represents a large and still surviving class, the existence of which is deleterious to civilization and discreditable to human nature. With the advance of progress this class must disappear, and an exposure of the true grounds of its being (such as is made in Hawthorne's analysis) will serve to hasten that disappearance. It is the class which is inspired with the old Pharisaic spirit, which says, "I am holier than thou;" which covets personal merit in the sight of God; which claims exclusiveness; which antagonizes true society or the profound truth of human brotherhood. It is largely composed of what are technically known as "respectable" people. It is well to expose these absurd and degrading pretensions, and Hawthorne deserves thanks for having so powerfully aided in the exposure. How powerful his aid was may be partly estimated by the outcries of those who find themselves wounded by his arrows.

Now, as to my own part in the matter. I am told that, if there be an evil or imperfect side to an otherwise admirable character, it should be mercifully veiled from public knowledge. I do not admit this claim. What the poet says in irony is true in earnest—"the many-headed Beast *should* know." The many-headed beast is mankind—is each one of us universalized. It has been the curse of our race that we have striven to hide our frailties, first from one another, and finally from ourselves. The act is falsehood and the motive is cowardice. Until

---

*Julian Hawthorne, "Mr. Hawthorne and His Critics," *Boston Daily Evening Transcript*, 5 February 1885, p. 4.

the highest of us has confessed himself morally indistinguishable from the lowest, the first step in man's spiritual emancipation is yet to take. Until we recognize the nature given us by creation, we shall never honestly accept God's aid to rise above it. Let us not try to make heroes of ourselves or of one another. What is heroic in us does not belong to us, and does not come from us; the contrast between it and us is the measue of the difference between infinite and finite. Let us, rather, insist upon that contrast and difference, and never for one moment allow the shows of things, and our own vanity, to blind us to it; to say that we are good, is to say that we are God, and that God is a self-seeking and self-complacent slave . . . .

# [Margaret Fuller]

#### Henry James*

  The unquestionably haunting Margaret-ghost, looking out from her quiet little upper chamber at her lamentable doom, would perhaps be never so much to be caught by us as on some such occasion as this. What comes up is the wonderment of *why* she may, to any such degree, be felt as haunting; together with other wonderments that brush us unless we give them the go-by. It is not for this latter end that we are thus engaged at all; so that, making the most of it, we ask ourselves how, possibly, in our own luminous age, she would have affected us on the stage of the "world," or as a candidate, if so we may put it, for the cosmopolite crown. It matters only for the amusement of evocation—since she left nothing behind her, her written utterance being naught; but to what would she have corresponded, have "rhymed," under categories actually known to us? Would she, in other words, with her appetite for ideas and her genius for conversation, have struck us but as a somewhat formidable bore, one of the worst kind, a culture-seeker without a sense of proportion, or, on the contrary, have affected us as a really attaching, a possibly picturesque New England Corinne?

  Such speculations are, however, perhaps too idle; the *facts* of the appearance of this singular woman, who would, though conceit was imputed to her, doubtless have been surprised to know that talk may be still, after more than half a century, made about her—the facts have in themselves quite sufficient colour, and the fact in particular of her having achieved, so unaided and so ungraced, a sharp identity. This identity was that of the talker, the moral *improvisatrice*, or at least had been in her Boston days, when young herself, she had been as a sparkling fountain to other thirsty young. In the Rome of many waters there were doubtless fountains that quenched, collectively, any individual gush; so that it would have been, naturally, for her plentiful life, her active courage and company, that the little set of friends with whom we are concerned valued her. She had bitten deeply into Rome, or, rather, *been*, like so many others, by the wolf of the Capitol, incurably bitten; she met the whole case with New England arts that show even yet, at our distance, as honest and touching; there might be ways for her of being vivid that were not as the ways of Boston. Otherwise what she would mainly prompt us to interest in might be

---

*From Henry James, *William Wetmore Story and His Friends* (Boston: Houghton, Mifflin, 1903), I, 127–131.

precisely the beautiful moral complexion of the little circle of her interlocutors. That is ever half the interest of any celebrated thing—taking Margaret's mind for celebrated: the story it has to tell us of those for whom it flourished and whose measure and reflection it necessarily more or less gives. Let us hasten to add, without too many words, that Mme. Ossoli's circle represented, after all, a small stage, and that there were those on its edges to whom she was not pleasing. This was the case with Lowell and, discoverably, with Hawthorne; the legend of whose having had her in his eye for the figure of Zenobia, while writing "The Blithedale Romance," surely never held water. She inspired Mrs Browning, on the other hand, with sympathy and admiration, and the latter, writing of her in 1852, after the so lamentable end of her return-voyage, with her husband and child, to America—the wreck of the vessel, the loss of father, mother and small son in sight of shore—says that "her death shook me to the very roots of my heart. The comfort is," Mrs Browning then adds, "that she lost little in the world—the change could not be loss to her. She had suffered, and was likely to suffer still more." She had previously to this, in December 1849, spoken of her, in a letter to Miss Mitford, as having "taken us by surprise at Florence, retiring from the Roman world with a husband and child above a year old. Nobody had even suspected a word of this underplot, and her American friends stood in mute astonishment before this apparition of them here. The husband is a Roman marquis appearing amiable and gentlemanly, and having fought well, they say, at the siege, but with no pretension to cope with his wife on any ground appertaining to the intellect." The "underplot" was precisely another of the personal facts by which the lady could interest—the fact, that is, that her marriage should *be* an underplot, and that her husband, much *decaduto*, should make explanation difficult. These things, let alone the final catastrophe, in short, were not talk, but life, and life dealing with the somewhat angular Boston sibyl on its own free lines. All of which, the free lines overscoring the unlikely material, is doubtless partly why the Margaret-ghost, as I have ventured to call it, still unmistakably walks the old passages.

# "The Real Margaret Fuller"

Anonymous*

We publish in another part of this number a paper by Mrs. Annie Nathan Meyer which was suggested by the recent appearance of Margaret Fuller's love-letters to James Nathan. This paper of Mrs. Meyer's represents the view of those who still cherish an enthusiasm for the personality of Margaret Fuller. In this enthusiasm we must confess that we do not share. In her own day her rather scrappy erudition was easily accepted as profound. Her aggressiveness was admired as indicating force of character. Her incoherent talk was thought to contain a subtle philosophy. Her eccentric ways impressed shallow minds as indicative of originality. Emerson was amused by her; but he saw clearly enough that she was in reality a freak, and he said so in his reminiscences. To-day the woman would be regarded with derision, and her performances would be restricted to women's clubs and the Stetsonian Sisterhood. Her plain and almost unpleasant face, her strange, nervous peculiarities, her nasal twang and her arrogant assumption that she was one of the forces of the age would relegate her instantly to the long category of offensive cranks. Her cheap erudition, based upon some reading of German literature and a very shaky knowledge of the classics, would now appear positively ridiculous in the face of her pretensions. All that we can see in these so-called love-letters is an exhibition of egotism, pleased at finding a new field for its exhibition in long monologues addressed to a young Jewish commission merchant who was cad enough to leave the letters behind him so that they might be published, and afford further evidence of the very flimsy foundation on which their writer's reputation rests.

*Anonymous, "The Real Margaret Fuller," *Bookman*, 17 (August 1903), 564.

# "Margaret Fuller as Known by her Scholars."

### Harriet Hall Johnson[*]

To Margaret Fuller and her biographers the eighteen months of her employment as "Lady Superior" in the Green Street School,[1] Providence, R.I., were little more than an incident in her remarkable and varied career, but to a small group of the old scholars in that school it was a most important epoch in their lives.

The high principles and lofty ideals of the talented woman, whom they began by fearing and ended by loving with intense devotion, inspired them with a conscientious regard for duty and courage to meet the trials and discipline of life, which had a large share in the development of their characters; and through their mutual affection for each other and reverence for their teacher was formed and cemented a friendship which lasted through life, for most of the number a period of nearly sixty years.

This remarkable "school-girl friendship" appears to have crystallized around one of their number with whom a close and intimate correspondence was maintained for all that long period, varied by occasional visits to Providence, and receiving her friends in her own home.

Among a trunkful of old letters has recently been discovered some of the early letters in this correspondence and also letters written by herself to her parents while a member of the school, which give such vivid pictures of the daily work in Miss Fuller's classes, and of her influence upon and personal relations to her pupils, that it has seemed well to reproduce them, in this centennial year of her birth, as a tribute to the woman as well as the genius and scholar.

It should be remembered that these are genuine letters, written in the freshness of youth and the exuberance of new and novel experiences, and as such give the pupil's unbiased opinion of the school and the teacher.

Mary, by and to whom these letters were written, was the eldest daughter of a country minister,[2] himself an educator of some note and influence, with a large family and small salary, who, together with his talented and self-sacrificing wife, was always ready to make every exertion in order to give their children all educational advantages in their power.

A much beloved aunt[3] living in Providence was most happy to give Mary a

[*]Harriet Hall Johnson, "Margaret Fuller as Known by her Scholars," *Christian Register*, 21 April 1910, pp. 427–429.

home while there, and thus make it possible for her to become for a few months a member of the school with the special object of availing herself of Miss Fuller's instructions to the utmost of her ability.

In her letters to her parents is told the story of its accomplishment. The first is dated Dec. 20, 1837:—

> I am delighted with the school so far. . . . Do you know, I am more deficient in history than almost anything? If you could only hear one of Miss F.'s recitations in that branch, you would say, "by all means, study history." I heard the recitation in that and in Smellie,[4] on Tuesday, and cannot find words to express my delight and wonder. It is worth a journey to P. to hear Miss Fuller talk. I was very much pleased with the latter recitation, and, if I have time, I think I shall study it, for I want to be with Miss F. as much as possible. . . . I love Miss Fuller already, but I fear her. I would not for a great deal offend her in any way. She is very satirical, and I should think might be *very severe*.
>
> She formed a class in rhetoric to-day, which I have joined, and which, *with her*, I think will be made very useful and interesting. We are to recite once a week in Whateley's Rhetoric. One of the girls asked her if she should get the lesson by heart. "No," said she, "I never wish a lesson learned by heart, as that phrase is commonly understood. A lesson is as far as possible from being learned by *heart* when it is said to be, it is only learned by *body*. I wish *you* to get your lessons by *mind*." She said she wished no one to remain in the class unless she was willing to give her mind and soul to the study, unless she was willing to communicate what was in her mind, to make the recitations social and pleasant, that we might make them very pleasant by exerting ourselves, that we should let no false modesty restrain us. She said it must not be our object to come and hear her talk. We might think it a delightful thing to her to talk to so many interesting auditors, but that was not the thing: she could not teach us so, *we* must talk and let her understand our minds. She talked as fast as she could about half an hour. I never heard any one who seemed to have such command of language

Mary's next letter is dated Jan. 1, 1838, and contains a very full account of the school in general and of the other teachers. Of Miss Fuller she says: "Miss Fuller is as different as you can imagine. I love her, but in a different way. I consider it a very great privilege to be under her instruction. She is very critical and sometimes cuts us up into bits. When she cuts us all in a lump, it is quite pleasant, for she is quite witty; but woe to the one whom she cuts by herself! I do not know what she would say to this letter. I would not have her see it for five dollars!"

By the time the next letter was written Mary had entered upon the full enjoyment and appreciation of her school life, and was ready for a full account of the school exercises, and especially of Miss Fuller's share in them. It appears wonderfully appreciative and well expressed for a country girl of nineteen, who would be considered to have had few advantages of education or culture.

Jan. 18, 1838, she writes:—

> I can never thank you and mother enough for letting me go to school here this winter. It is *exactly* what I needed,—something to impel me forward, something to give me a start.
>
> Such a constant intercourse with Miss Fuller makes me feel my deficiencies. She is very precise, and we must understand as far as we go, thoroughly. When she first

went to the school, there was a class who thought themselves ready for Virgil, or at least thought they knew a good deal about Latin; but she found they did not, and put them into the grammar, and they have been thirty weeks going through it, and have just begun *Liber Primus*. I am in that class, and, though for a short time I was sorry I began Latin, I am now very glad; for you know I used to like it, though I did not half understand the grammar.

Now I shall want to go on with it, for she makes us understand and apply the rules. I am studying Whateley's Rhetoric, which I like very much because we have such pleasant conversation. The lessons are long and hard, and require a good deal of study. In connection with that study, we write definitions of words, which, though difficult, is very useful. The first we wrote were definitions of Logic, Rhetoric, and Philosophy, as these words were suggested by the conversation. In another lesson something was said about Poetry. She asked us the meaning, and, as no one could tell, she told us to write a definition. Almost all called it a "harmony of words," which she said was very incorrect.

Yesterday she gave us *her* definition, requesting us to write it in our journals; but it was so long I cannot remember more than enough to fill *half a page*. As the words "imagination" and "ideality" were used, she has given us them to define for the next time. I shall not know what to say, but I shall try, as she takes *no excuse for neglect of duty* except ill health. What is not done at one time must be at another. The study I enjoy the most is Wayland's "Moral Science." I do enjoy it exceedingly. There are not more than a dozen in the class and we have such nice times hearing Miss Fuller talk. It is all talk, for our lessons are *very* short. She says we must *think* as well as *study*, and *talk* as well as *recite*. Then we have our poetry class, the exercises of which are diversified. We meet Mondays and Fridays, and I will try to give you a little idea of what we do. Perhaps Monday Miss F. reads us a story to paraphrase, which she has done twice since I have been here, once a long story of Ferdinand, and the other day "Romeo and Juliet," from "Stories from Shakespeare." The day she reads nothing else is done, and a week is given us to write it. If it is not done at the time, she does not like it, and finds much fault, as was the case last Monday, when not more than half brought theirs in. Then sometimes eight are chosen to read for the next time, any piece of poetry they choose, and, when nothing else takes up the time, they read.

Another exercise we have is this,—a very useful one it is. Miss F. gave us each a modern poet to find out what we could about: where born, where died, where they lived, what they wrote,—anything interesting about them.

The most modern poets were exhausted before she came to me, therefore I had Chaucer, and I have become quite interested in the old gentleman and mean to read his writings.

It was probably after one of the "cutting into bits" of which she speaks that Mary and five of her schoolmates sent Miss Fuller a "round robin,"[5] as I have been told, to which they received the following reply. The original little triangular note, yellowed with age, lies before me. It was carefully wrapped in paper, and, with a private letter from Miss Fuller, was one of Mary's most valued treasures.

To M. W. A., S. F. H., E. M., M. M., M. D. M., M. D. A.
WEDNESDAY.

*My dear Girls*,—I suppose you are more than half in jest, but I will answer you in earnest.

I often regret that you have not a teacher who has more heart, more health, more energy to spend upon you than I have; for truly I esteem you worthy of much more. If I were as fit to meet and use life as I was only three or four years since, I should cultivate the acquaintance of many of my scholars. I should wish to know you in your domestic relations and to help you much more and in more ways than I can now. But my duties in life are at present so many, and my health so precarious, that I dare not be *generous* lest I should thus be unable to be *just*, dare not indulge my feelings lest I should fail to discharge my duties. Since I thus act by you in so miserly a spirit, giving to each and all only what the letter of my obligation requires, let me take this opportunity to say that it is not because I do not value you and even (I use not the word lightly) love you. If I did not wish to *give* my love, some of my scholars would *gain* it by their uniformly honorable conduct and engaging manners. And you will do me justice in believing that I generally feel much more regard than I express. And, though I cannot do for you all that another might in my place, let me assure you that, if, while under my care, or after you leave me, you should feel that I can, by any counsel or words of instruction or act of kindness, benefit you where others could not, my ear and heart will always be ready to attend to your wishes.

Give my love to J. I hope I was not too rough with her this morning. Could I but teach her more confidence and self-possession, I should be satisfied with her as much as I am now interested in her.

Affectionately yours,<br>S. M. FULLER.

This tender and affectionate note deeply affected these warm-hearted, intelligent girls, and enlisted their affections for life, besides making them devoted to her at the time, as her most appreciative scholars, and in the later experiences of the school, her unwavering supporters.

In April, Mary writes again:—

We go on about the same at school, though we hear that it is to be broken up, on account of the heretical doctrines taught there; that is to say, because Mr. and Miss Fuller go to no particular church, and so, of course, come sometimes to ours or Mr. F.'s. One teacher is a member of Dr. —'s church, not orthodox, and he threatens to break up the school immediately.

Perhaps it was partly owing to this condition of affairs that the next letter says:—

Miss Fuller, who is always doing something for the good of her scholars, has just commenced a Bible class, entirely independent of the school, though chiefly composed of the scholars, and devotes more than an hour a week of her precious time to us.

She has it on Thursday afternoon after school at night. We have met at her room twice, and in those two lessons have glanced over the whole of the Old Testament, which is the only part of the Bible she intends to teach.

Next time we are going to begin with the creation, and read and talk about it. She has devoted a great deal of time to the study of the Bible, though not so much, she says, as she would have liked. She intended to make it her chief study for four years, with the best authors, but circumstances prevented after the first year, and she has a closet full of books which she will never use. I shall be sorry not to be able to study it longer with her, for she makes everything so clear and plain. You cannot tell how much I love her.

Miss Fuller was not always the severe critic and uncompromising preceptress, for in the same letter Mary says:—

> We talked of having a May party on Tuesday, both scholars and teachers; but we have concluded to postpone it till we have brighter skies and softer air. Miss Fuller is going to write us a song to sing round the maypole. The worst of it is that we shall have to give up school for it, and I had rather go to school than go maying.

Soon after this a great sorrow came to Mary, and at the end of the term she left school, and came in touch with it only now and then through correspondence with former schoolmates.

One of them writes, Oct. 28, 1838:—

> I cannot find words to express to you my love for dear Miss Fuller, you who know her so well can better conceive it than I describe. She is everything to me,—my teacher, my counsellor, my guide, my friend, my pillar on which I lean for support when disheartened and discouraged, and she allows me to look upon her as such. . . . I had no idea she had so much heart, but it is overflowing with affection and love.

Another, the J. to whom Miss Fuller alluded in her note, in a long letter devoted almost entirely to Miss Fuller's influence upon herself, says:—

> I have thought much of late of Miss Fuller's situation. It seems to me that she will not remain long where she is, for, the better I become acquainted with the infinite capacity of her mind, the more I see of her glorious endowments. I feel that her situation is not that for which she is fitted: it seems to me that she finds not here the sympathy which her spirit craves, the minds around her do not, cannot, sympathize with hers. She cannot exercise her brightest, highest powers, for they cannot be understood; and, when she is obliged to bury, as it were, that which is most congenial to her mind, and bring it to a level with the minds round her, it must be a most irksome task, so sadly uncultivated as many of them are. . . . I do not know the motives by which she actuated [to take the place she occupied]. I cannot conceive, perhaps, the principles by which she is guided; but . . . something within tells me that it is a noble philanthropy which actuates her; that she looks not to the present, but to the future; that she regards it, in the words of Dr. Channing, as "the noblest work on earth to act with an elevating power on a human spirit.". . . . I shall ever feel it one of my greatest privileges to have been under her instruction.

That the writer just quoted was right in believing Miss Fuller would not long remain in her present situation was soon proved, for only a few weeks later came letters from each of the two girls, telling to one whom they knew would feel it as they did, of the final parting with their beloved teacher. With these touching descriptions of the last, under date of Nov. 15, 1838, the same writer gives the following interesting record of the last day, in which she had gathered all her older pupils together, a short time before she gave up her situation and left the school.

> I passed the day at school yesterday. O how I wish you and Sarah could have been there. I thought before I went that it would seem very different to me from what it did when I was a scholar there; . . . but I was mistaken, for it seemed so much the same that I could hardly feel I was not a scholar still. I went again into that recitation room where we have passed together so many happy hours, and heard again from Miss Fuller's lips that never-wearying flood of goodness and eloquence. O the goodness, the tenderness of that heart! Could her pupils have been sensible of the privilege they enjoyed, what a little heaven upon earth would that place be!

In the moral science class Miss Fuller read some letters that she had requested them to write to her upon the manner in which they thought the Sabbath should be spent. She made some remarks upon them and gave her own views. She spoke of her feelings in regard to religion, and expressed in her never-to-be-forgotten tone and manner her deep interest in its truths and her desire that it might be the guide of her pupils. She then made them a most affecting request: that they would keep these letters for her sake, and that in one year from the coming Christmas they would read them and think of her, think whether they had been guided by the rules there laid down, whether they had progressed in the path of goodness, in the preparation for another and a better world. Miss Fuller spoke of our "sweet Mary" in the class, and more highly she could not have spoken of her rigid conscientiousness and her devotion to truth.

Another friend writes movingly of Miss Fuller's farewell to her scholars, thus complementing Miss Fuller's own descriptions of the same scene, and giving it from the pupil's standpoint a deeper and tenderer significance.

Under the date of Dec. 22, 1838, after speaking of a gift the members of the poetry class presented to Miss Fuller,—an elegant copy of Shakespeare and a ring,—she says:—

> Wednesday, which was her last day, S. and J. went with me to see her. She talked to us beautifully in the rhetoric class, but said she should say more to us at twelve, when she wished all the oldest girls to be present. When the time came, the room was filled to overflowing. she began to speak by alluding to the circumstances under which she came here, the many difficulties she had to contend with in finding the scholars so ignorant. She spoke of her manner of teaching, so different from every other; then of her manner to us generally, that she feared it had sometimes been harsh, sometimes too ironical, but that she had never felt either towards us; that the former she had found absolutely necessary to insure obedience to her commands, and the latter she had made use of, not to wound our feelings, but to awaken in us a sense of our deficiencies, to make us feel how little we knew, comparatively, and to stimulate us to exertion. But she said she feared she had wounded many tender natures. "But for this," said she, "I humbly ask your pardon, and I can sincerely say that it was never intentional." She then spoke of what she had done for us, and how much more she had wished to do, yet she thought the time was not wasted, that it had not passed without great improvement. She then spoke of her own trials, of the disappointment of her own brilliant prospects, of her most cherished hopes, and then, oh, how beautifully, did she speak of the *faith* that had supported her through them all! Her eyes were filled with tears, her voice choked with emotion, and often was she obliged to stop; but she talked to us long of the blessedness of that religion which can alone support us in this sorrowing world. She said she had not introduced the subject very often, but it was on account of her own peculiar views that she had refrained from it, and, although they were everything to her, she did not wish to influence any of us. Yet, she said, her whole aim had been to inspire us with a love and respect for religion, to look upon it as the only thing on which we could lean for consolation and peace here and for happiness hereafter! You know, dear M., how the words flow from her lips, how full they are of eloquence and beauty, and you can imagine how she talked much better than I can describe it. After once more begging *our pardon* for whatever in her had seemed harsh or unjust, after having expressed to us how much affection she really felt for us all, and how much she should ever feel for us, and having given us her blessing, she said, "*For the last time, my girls*, I say to you, you

may go." No one moved, every heart was almost bursting with grief, all eyes were swollen with weeping. After a few moments had elapsed, Miss Fuller rose, went to each one, and, kissing her, said some kind word to cheer her, and then left the room. The girls soon followed, all except a few of our own little circle, the M's., J., and I. We sat there talking and weeping alternately for a long time; and is it wicked, dear M., if I compare ourselves to that little band of disciples after the crucifixion of their Master? Their sorrow was no doubt deeper, but it could not have been *more sincere*. Such moments are worth everything when the purest and best feelings of our nature are called forth. No words can tell how much I wished you there.

Thus the little group of girls to whom allusion was made in the beginning parted from their beloved teacher; but her words of instruction and admonition went with them and no doubt helped them to lead lives of usefulness and self-sacrifice, and gave them strength to bear the discipline of life and to be faithful unto the end.

Notes

1. The school in which Margaret Fuller taught at Providence was the Green Street Academy, founded by Col. Hiram Fuller, a gentleman in no way her relative—*T.W. Higginson*.

In the spring of 1837 M. F. was invited to fill an important post in the Green Street School at Providence, R.I. Her connection with the school lasted two years. Her success in this work was considered very great, and her brief residence in Rhode Island was crowned with public esteem and with many valued friendships.—*Julia Ward Howe*.

M. F. was born 23 May 1810 and so was about twenty-eight years old at this time.

2. Rev. Joseph Allen of Northborough, Mass.

3. Mrs. Edward B. Hall (Harriet Ware).

4. "The Philosophy of Natural History," by William Smellie (1740–1795).

5. It is believed that the "Round Robin" was written to vindicate a schoolmate of rare excellence and character, but so reserved and diffident that she could not always do herself justice, and so far removed in temperament from Miss Fuller that *she* failed to comprehend her true character, and was impatient with her apparent lack of acquirements. Her schoolmates, feeling that if Miss Fuller realized her mistake she would be too just to persist in it, took this method of calling her attention to it. The "round robin" probably does not exist, and I know of no copy.

# [Margaret Fuller and Emerson]

O. W. Firkins*

Between 1836 and 1846, Margaret Fuller was "an established friend and frequent inmate of our house, and was accustomed, during this period, to come, once in three or four months, to spend a week or fortnight with us." The remarkable person who impressed strongly the New England of her time and who had the knack of eliciting homage from people far abler and worthier than herself remains, at our present distance, one of the most inscrutable of personalities. There is no lack of clear-cut, even of poignant and mordant, traits, but in the wilderness of attributes one searches fruitlessly for the evasive character: one chases Margaret through Margaret in vain. It is not merely that her published writings give slight indications either of intellectual eminence or of that temperamental vigor which would account for her mastership in conversation,—that they suggest, indeed, either an astonishing good luck with her contemporaries or a grave misadventure with posterity,—but that even the "Memorabilia" which the piety of her friends has compiled do not convey the impression which they obviously wish to convey. Poor Emerson conducts his share of the "Memoirs" in a ceremonious, laborious fashion, praising assiduously, compunctiously, almost apprehensively, bringing up each new excellence for the inspection of the sceptical reader with an anxious "There, will that convince you?" When he tells us that she wore her friends "like a necklace of diamonds about her neck," that she resembled "the queen of some parliament of love," and that "persons were her game," his intentions are quite void of malevolence. He does not withold the evidence of her childish superstitions (she was given to omens and amulets), of her colossal egotism which found in America, after painstaking search, no intellect comparable to her own, of her social veracity which skirted the magnificent and the brutal in the same breath.

The facts half persuade us to believe that Miss Fuller, in spite of a coating of masculinity, was at heart profoundly feminine, that she was indeterminate, that she shared in that receptiveness and plasticity, that dependence on suggestion, which has been attributed, more or less plausibly, to women so eminent as George Eliot and George Sand. The possession of considerable ability and of a masterful temper enabled her to screen this formlessness and instability from the eyes of her admiring contemporaries. Her abilities, her pursuits, her ardors, were loose, versatile, and tentative. Hence that splendor in conversation—that

*From O. W. Firkins, *Ralph Waldo Emerson* (Boston: Houghton Mifflin, 1915), pp. 82–85.

response to the mood, the hour—which had too little reality or stability to be capable of transference to the printed page or of reproduction in spoken words on the ensuing day. She was not a strong soul with speech as its appropriate and exclusive vehicle; she was a formless being to whom speech imparted the semblance of organization.

These criticisms apply chiefly to the New England Margaret, the prodigy and prophetess, the precocious child pampered on Latin and Greek, the student of art, the literary critic, the editor of the "Dial," the leader of exalted conversations, and the cultivator of friendships on the high level and the grand scale. In Italy, 1847–50, she was lucky both in fortune and misfortune. She won the love and accepted the hand of Angelo Ossoli, a plain, affectionate, and faithful young man, in whom these merits lost none of their worth by association with an Italian countship; she bore a child; she aided Italian freedom by faithful and admirable service in hospitals during the siege of Rome; and, under the humanizing influence of contact with the plainer and sterner order of realities, becomes for the first time really interesting. She perished with her husband and her child off Fire Island Beach, Long Island, in the wreck of the Elizabeth, on which the party had taken passage for America.

That Emerson admired and valued Miss Fuller is certain, though, as often happens in commerce, the stock curiously shrank when tested by an inventory; whether he "liked" her is another question. Mr. Cabot is probably right in supposing that "a slight shudder qualified the pleasure with which he welcomed her visits to his house." She taught him nothing and the stimulus she brought was rather galvanic than intellectual. But Emerson's gratitude for stimuli included even influences that were momentarily perturbing or distracting, and he was always magnetized by the gift of spontaneous and eloquent conversation. In animated speech the air seemed tremulous with possibilites; a dialogue held for him the palpitant interest of a *séance*. Margaret Fuller and other such dominating personalities affected him with a vague but kindling sense of power, like the rush of unseen wings in the air, or the reverberation of the tread of hurrying multitudes in a remote street.

# "Margaret Fuller, Rebel"

#### Vernon Louis Parrington*

    The fame of Margaret Fuller has waned greatly since her vivid personality was blotted out in the prime of her intellectual development. Misunderstood in her own time, caricatured by unfriendly critics, and with significant facts of her life suppressed by her friends out of a chivalrous sense of loyalty, the real woman has been lost in a Margaret Fuller myth and later generations have come to underestimate her powers and undervalue her work. Yet no other woman of her generation in America is so well worth recalling. She was the completest embodiment of the inchoate rebellions and grandiose aspirations of the age of transcendental ferment; for to the many grievances charged against the times by other New England liberals, she added the special grievance of the stupid inhibitions laid upon women. Transcendental radical and critic, like Emerson and Thoreau and Parker, she was feminist also; and to the difficult business of freeing her mind from the Cambridge orthodoxies, she added the greater difficulty of freeing her sex.

    The written record that Margaret Fuller left is quite inadequate to explain her contemporary reputation. In no sense an artist, scarcely a competent craftsman, she wrote nothing that bears the mark of high distinction either in thought or style. Impatient of organization and inadequately disciplined, she threw off her work impulsively, not pausing to shape it to enduring form. Yet she was vastly talked about, and common report makes her out to have been an extraordinary woman who creatively influenced those with whom she came in contact. Like Alcott, her power lay in brilliant talk. Her quick mind seems to have been an electric current that stimulated other minds to activity, and created a vortex of speculation wherever she passed. Hungry for ideas, intellectually and emotionally vibrant, she caught her inspirations from obscure impulses of a nature thwarted and inhibited from normal unfolding; and in her sensitive oscillations she was often drawn away from polar principles to which she would later swing back. There was quite evidently a fundamental unrest within her, a conflict of impulses, that issued in dissatisfaction; and this contradiction was aggravated by intense emotions, which both quickened her mind and distorted it.

---

*Vernon Louis Parrington, "Margaret Fuller, Rebel," *The Romantic Revolution in America 1800–1860* (New York: Harcourt, Brace, 1927), pp. 426–434; from *Main Currents in American Thought*, Vol. II, by Vernon Louis Parrington, copyright, 1927, by Harcourt Brace Jovanovich, Inc.; renewed, 1955, by Vernon L. Parrington, Jr., Louise P. Tucker, and Elizabeth P. Thomas. Reprinted by permission of the publisher.

A product of Cambridge bookishness, Margaret Fuller was both a wonder and a riddle to a generation that made little account of the psychology of sex. She was commonly looked upon as an intellectual monstrosity, the most fearful of Yankee bluestockings, and a later Bostonian has gone so far as to suggest that she was "an unsexed version of Plato's Socrates" (Wendell, *Literary History of America*, p. 300). But to present-day psychology her character is an extraordinarily suggestive document, and a recent critic has read her seeming contradictions like an open book.[1] Before Miss Anthony's penetrating analysis the Margaret Fuller myth vanishes, and a very real, natural, and unfortunate woman takes its place. She came of vigorous stock, independent, out-spoken, opinionated. Her grandfather was a clergyman who was unfrocked by his church for being lukewarm in the Revolutionary War. Her father, Timothy Fuller, and her four uncles, worked their way through Harvard. In Timothy Fuller there was a large measure of Puritan grimness and severity that locked the door on the passions of his heart, that none might know of them; yet there seems to have been a volcano in the man who held off the world so brusquely. The rebel was strong in him. The Fullers were not of Brahmin stock and had no wish to please their social superiors. While a Harvard undergraduate, Timothy Fuller turned Jeffersonian republican and lost his place as first honor man by joining in an undergraduate protest against certain hated regulations. As a lawyer and politician he repudiated respectable Federalism, and although he was representative in Congress for four terms and enjoyed certain other offices, his non-conformity in the end cost him dear. No doubt he had counted on that, for he was stubborn oak that might break but would not bend. The tragedy of Margaret Fuller's life seems to have been sketched before in the life of Timothy Fuller.

To an extraordinary degree the daughter was the child of the father, in ideas and sympathies as well as blood. Like him she was a rebel, but for the daughter to turn rebel involved greater hazards than for the father. Her sex was a heavy handicap, for the experience of Fanny Wright and Lucretia Mott had revealed that American chivalry had definite bounds; it did not shield the woman who ventured beyond the pale. Yet considering her blood and training, how could she help thus venturing into freer fields without? From her earliest years her father treated her as a comrade and gave her the training of a boy. In her studies he dealt with her as James Mill dealt with his brilliant son. Perhaps it was a mistake to force her into the rigid groove of classical learning when she should have been playing with her dolls. From it she got very unusual acquisitions, but overstimulation broke her health, and isolation turned her mind in upon itself and made her the victim of somnambulism and freaks of imagination. The result was the development, on one side of her nature, of a female counterpart of Cotton Mather—precocious, domineering, moody, visionary, given to long hours of greedy reading, gorging herself on books and well-nigh ruining her intellectual digestion as well as her health. Against this unfortunate overstimulation her vigorous nature struggled for years, and never quite successfully. Her emotions were forever embroiling her intellect. To conceive of her as sexless is curiously to miss the point of her emotionalism. She was rather the victim of sex. Her ardent friendships with other women, her flashes of mystical experience, her fondness for children, her love of luxury and creature comforts, her eager love affair with James Nathan who unchivalrously found safety in flight, her friendship with Mazzini and her more intimate friendship with Count Ossoli, that ended in an unconventional marriage after her situation rendered it necessary—such reactions can be explained on no other hypothesis. Her ardent nature was the victim of disastrous frustrations, rendered the more acute by premature development. If she had married early, as Harriet Beecher did, and her excessive energy had been turned into domestic channels, her life must have been less tragic, whatever the effect might have been on her intellectual development.

The acutest contemporary analysis of her contradictory character is that given by her friend William Henry Channing, who found his clue in the clash between endowment and environment:

> Here was one fond as a child of joy, eager as a native of the tropics for swift transition from luxurious rest to passionate excitement, prodigal to pour her mingled force of will, thought, sentiment, into the life of the moment, all radiant with imagination, longing for communion with artists of every age in their inspired hours, fitted by genius and culture to mingle as an equal in the most refined circles of Europe, and yet her youth and early womanhood had passed away amid the very decent, yet drudging, descendants of prim Puritans. Trained among those who could have discerned her peculiar power, and early fed with the fruits of beauty for which her spirits pined, she would have developed into one of the finest lyrics, romancers and critics, that the modern literary world has seen. This she knew; and this tantalization of her fate she keenly felt. (*Memoirs of Margaret Fuller Ossoli*, by R. W. Emerson, W. H. Channing, and J. F. Clarke, Vol. II, pp. 36–37.)

This disastrous clash between endowment and environment is strikingly exemplified in her delight in Europe when at thirty-four she found herself there—in her admiration for Georges Sand, and in particular the extravagance of her love for Rome, where her starved heart found satisfactions she had long dreamed of. "Italy receives me as a long-lost child, and I feel myself at home here," she wrote in 1847; and a few weeks later, "I find how true was the lure that always drew me towards Europe. It was no false instinct that said I might here find an atmosphere to develop me in ways I need. Had I only come ten years earlier! Now my life must be a failure, so much strength has been wasted on abstractions, which only came because I grew not in the right soil" (*ibid.*, Vol. II, p. 225). She was too eagerly pagan to be satisfied with either Puritan or Yankee Cambridge. The pale ethicism of New England was thin gruel for such an appetite for life. Even Emerson she found cold, and her stomach rebelled at the food he throve on. But this was only half the story; the other half was this:

> But the tragedy of Margaret's history was deeper yet. Behind the poet was the woman,—fond and relying, the heroic and disinterested woman. The very glow of her poetic enthusiasm was but an outflush of trustful affection; the very restlessness of her intellect was the confession that her heart had found no home. A "book-worm," a "dilettante," a "pedant," I had heard her sneeringly called; but now it was evident that her seeming insensibility was virgin pride, and her absorption in studying the natural vent of emotions, which met no object of life-long attachment. At once, many

of her peculiarities became intelligible. Fitfulness, unlooked-for changes of mood, misconceptions of words and actions, substitutions of fancy for fact . . . were now referred to the morbid influence of affections pent up to prey upon themselves. And, what was still more interesting, the clue was given to a singular credulousness, by which, in spite of her unusual penetration, Margaret might be led away blindfold. As this revelation of her ardent nature burst upon me, and . . . I saw how faithful she had kept to her life purposes,—how patient, gentle, and thoughtful of others, how active in self-improvement and usefulness, how wisely dignified she had been,—I could not but bow to her in reverence. (*Ibid.*, Vol. II, p. 37.)

The inchoate rebellions in her heart were stimulated and given form by her reading. From the English, French, and German romantics she drew much of her intellectual food. The long hours spent with her father over Jefferson's letters were the best of preparation for Rousseau and Mary Wollstonecraft, and French romanticism provided an excellent introduction to the German. Her emotions were in high ferment when she came upon the German school, and she yielded her heart to it without reserve. Novalis, Richter, above all Goethe, became a passion and swept her along the path that Hedge and James Freeman Clarke were following. For years she gathered materials for a life of Goethe, but a feeling of self-distrust held back the project. Her love for him was the great literary enthusiasm of her life. "It seems to me," she wrote in 1832, "as if the mind of Goethe had embraced the universe. . . . I am enchanted while I read. He comprehends every feeling I have ever had so perfectly, expresses it so beautifully; but when I shut the book, it seems as if I had lost my personal identity; all my feelings linked with such an immense variety that belongs to things I had thought so different" (*ibid.*, Vol. I, p. 119). Later, with more critical analysis of Goethe, she found her enthusiasm modifying; she was repelled by his calm, aloof intellectuality;[2] but she never wavered in loyal recognition of his commanding powers.

Her romantic idealism was in full career when the transcendental movement caught her up and put its stamp upon her. It came as an emotional appeal to the vague aspirations of a life inadequately motivated, and she threw herself eagerly into the new philosophy and became the most hectic of its expounders. The intellectual foundations of her transcendentalism were so slight in comparison with the equipment of Hedge and Parker as scarcely to justify her pretentions to their fellowship. But what she lacked in knowledge of Kant and Fichte she made up in enthusiasm, and none questioned her right to speak for the group. The editorship of the *Dial* provided a convenient safety valve for her energy, but it neither absorbed her nor sufficed to satisfy her limitless desires. She needed to espouse a cause more concrete and dramatic, personal in its demands, calling for high sacrifice. Abolitionism was at hand, but it repelled her by its narrow dogmatisms. Garrison was never a hero of hers. She regarded him with "high respect" for his "noble and generous" course; but "he has indulged in violent invective and denunciation till he has spoiled the temper of his mind" ("Frederick Douglass," in *Life Without and Life Within*, p. 122). Later, when she was in Europe, she looked back half regretfully at her indifference to the movement.

> How it pleases me here to think of the Abolitionists! I could never endure to be with them at home; they were so tedious, often so narrow, always so rabid and exaggerated in their tone. But, after all, they had a high motive, something eternal in their desire and life. (*Memoirs*, Vol. II, p. 229.)

Even Brook Farm repelled her as much as it attracted her. Though she loved many of the members, bore her share in the discussions preliminary to its establishment, and often visited there, she would not join the venture. She had had enough of farm life at Groton. To open a road to Utopia with a common plow was, perhaps, too prosaic a business for her romantic nature, and when the Fourier Phalanx was introduced she grew skeptical. Fourierism seemed to her too mechanical a conception, in spite of her sympathy for the humanitarian spirit that lay behind it. As she looked back upon it from the vantage point of her French experience, she modified her judgment somewhat, although the old transcendental bias that Emerson had voiced still colored her views.

> The more I see of the terrible ills which infest the body politic of Europe, the more indignation I feel at the selfishness or stupidity of those in my own country who oppose an examination of these subjects,—such as is animated by the hope of prevention. Educated in an age of gross materialism, Fourier is tainted by its faults; in attempts to reorganise society, he commits the error of making soul the result of health of body, instead of body the clothing of the soul; but his heart was that of a genuine lover of his kind, of a philanthropist in the sense of Jesus; his views are large and noble; his life was one of devout study on these subjects, and I should pity the person who, after the briefest sojourn in Manchester and Lyons, the most superficial acquaintance with the population of London or Paris, could seek to hinder a study of his thoughts, or be wanting in reverence for his purposes. (*Ibid.*, Vol. II, p. 206.)

It was in part from Fourier, certainly from the collectivistic theories discussed so generally by the transcendental group, that she received her equipment for the cause which, more than any other except the dramatic Roman revolution, appealed to the deeper rebellions of her soul. She had dealt much with the woman question in her "Conversations," and in 1844 she published *Woman in the Nineteenth Century*, a work that made a great stir in America. The "little book was the first considered statement of feminism in this country" (Katharine Anthony, *Margaret Fuller*, p. 80), and its novelty was emphasized by its boldness. The question of woman's place had emerged sharply from the Abolition movement, when the appearance of women on the platform had aroused opposition even from radical reformers, and Angelina Grimké had encountered insults when she spoke at Abolition meetings. But Margaret Fuller was the first since Mary Wollstonecraft, fifty years before, to undertake a reasoned defense of the claims of woman to emancipation from man-made custom. It was a somewhat shocking book to fling at respectable Boston bluestockings—male as well as female—for not only did she discuss equality of economic opportunity and equality of political rights for women, but she went further and spoke frankly about sex equality, marriage, prostitution, physical passions—pretty much everything that was taboo in Boston society. It was a bold thing to do, needing more courage even than to engage in a Fourieristic onslaught upon the conventions of private property. Only a first-class rebel would have had the temerity to offer such morsels to wagging tongues.

This was her parting shot at the world that had done its best to stifle her. Thenceforth her field was to broaden out immensely. In 1844 she went to New York to live in the family of Horace Greeley and write critical reviews for *The Tribune*—a shift that marked the beginning of her intellectual maturity, the end of her mystical sentimentalism. She was thirty-four years of age, and she plunged vigorously into the work of criticism, never perhaps very successfully, certainly never with high distinction. Her judgments were penetrating and individual, she awakened some Cambridge animosities by her comment on certain Cambridge poets, but she was not a notable critic. A fine craftsmanship she never attained. A light touch she could never command. Nevertheless the experience was sobering. Honest, practical Horace Greeley, with his pugnacious fondness for social reform, was an excellent antidote to Concord transcendentalism; and an awakening sociological interest discovered ample opportunities in New York for the expression of her mother-instinct. She took to her stormy bosom the inmates of Sing Sing prison, the poor and outcast of the city. At last she went to Europe, fell in with Mazzini, and found a cause dramatic enough and real enough to satisfy her rebellious instincts. She was profoundly stirred by the Roman revolution, took charge of one of the hospitals, and spent her strength freely. On the tragic failure of the revolt she started home with her husband and child, only to perish on the sandy shores of Fire Island—a fate she did not turn her finger to escape. Perhaps it was well. She had only too good reason to be fearful of her reception and of the future. Tongues that had wagged before would certainly have risen to a virtuous gabble over her misadventure in Italy. On the whole one must be glad that her friends refused to permit her good name to be thrown to the gossips. Why shouldn't gentlemen lie stoutly if by so doing they can cheat the salacious?

A sensitive emotional nature offers the best of social barometers, and Margaret Fuller's tragic life, despite its lack of solid accomplishment, was an epitome of the great revolt of the New England mind against Puritan asceticism and Yankee materialism. She was the emotional expression of a rebellious generation that had done with the past and was questioning the future. Not a scholar like Theodore Parker, not a thinker like Thoreau, not an artist like Emerson, she was a ferment of troubled aspiration, an enthusiasm for a more generous culture than New England had known—the logical outcome of the romantic revolution which, beginning with Channing's discovery of humanitarian France, and leading thence to idealistic Germany, was to break the indurated shell of life in New England, and release its conscience and its mind. She was the spiritual child of Jean Jacques even more than of Goethe—a fact that she eventually came to realize. Writing from Paris in 1847, she said:

> To the . . . Chamber of Deputies, I was indebted for a sight of the manuscripts of Rousseau, treasured in their library. I saw them and touched them,—those manuscripts just as he has celebrated them, written on fine white paper, tied with ribbon. Yellow and faded age has made them, yet at their touch I seemed to feel the fire of youth, immortally glowing, more and more expansive, with which his soul has pervaded this century. He was the precursor of all we most prize. True, his blood was mixed with madness, and the course of his actual life made some *detours* through

villainous places; but his spirit was intimate with the fundamental truths of human nature, and fraught with prophecy. There is none who has given birth to more life for this age; his gifts are yet untold; they are too present with us; but he who thinks really must often think with Rousseau, and learn him ever more and more. Such is the method of genius,—to ripen fruit for the crowd by those rays of whose heat they complain. (*Memoirs,* Vol. II, pp. 206–207.)

The rebel pays a heavy price for his rebellions, as Margaret learned to her cost. She suffered much in her daily life, but it was her art that suffered most. She was evidently a far richer nature than her printed works reveal. Intense in her extravagant demand upon life, a radical humanitarian in all her sympathies and instincts, generous in response to whatever was fine and high, living unduly an inner life as became a daughter of Puritanism—Margaret Fuller was too vivid a personality, too complete an embodiment of the rich ferment of the forties, to be carelessly forgotten. The deeper failure of her career—its vague aspirations and inadequate accomplishment—was a failure that may be justly charged against the narrow word that bred her. Perhaps no sharper criticism could be leveled at New England than that it could do no better with such material, lent it by the gods.

Notes

1. See Katherine Anthony, *Margaret Fuller. A Psychological Biography* (New York: Harcourt, Brace and Howe, 1920).

2. See *Life Without and Life Within* (Boston: Brown, Taggard and Chase, 1860), pp. 23–60.

# "A Conversation in Boston"

## Granville Hicks[*]

Dr. Nathaniel Peabody, until lately dentist of Salem, dusted the books and arranged the chairs. One of the chairs, he noted, needed mending. Well and good, he could fix anything, as Nathaniel Hawthorne was one day gratefully to acknowledge. There were a dozen things waiting to be done now, but first he must make the bookshop clean and neat. It was unlikely that many customers would be in to buy or borrow books that morning, though ordinarily one could count on a breathless and head-splitting visit from Orestes Brownson, a shy call from Dr. Channing, a leisurely chat with Waldo Emerson, or a lofty debate carried on by three or four young intellectuals. But everyone knew that Wednesday was the day of Margaret Fuller's conversations.

Dr. Peabody could hear his wife and daughters moving about upstairs. Elizabeth and Mary would be down soon, but Sophia, the invalid of the family, was unlikely to appear until it was time for the class to begin. How well these girls had done—with their knowledge of languages, their familiarity with the newest ideas, their easy association with the more or less great of Boston! But the boys: two of them dead and the third by no means a scholar!

Elizabeth entered the store just as her father was leaving, and looked with pleasure at the books on the shelves. This was her idea. Herself eager for the latest publications of France and Germany, she had conceived the plan of selling foreign books. The circulating library, too, was her creation. This business, now the mainstay of the family, might, Dr. Peabody thought, be reasonably profitable; but Elizabeth had little business sense, and he was no hand to drive a bargain. It was difficult to charge every possible cent when one was profiting so richly from the conversation of those who bought and borrowed books.

Elizabeth was large, and she would grow larger, but her square, massive face carried the marks of intelligence. Dr. Peabody loved her intransigent zeal for learning, her enthusiasm for new ideas, especially in education, even her dreamy impracticality. He had rejoiced when she persuaded Emerson to teach her Latin and Greek, when she became a sort of literary assistant to Dr. Channing, when she attached herself to Bronson Alcott's ill-fated school. He was ready to support her if she undertook the publication of the *Dial*, already

---

[*]Granville Hicks, "A Conversation in Boston," *Sewanee Review*, 39 (April–June 1931), 129–143; reprinted by permission of the publisher.

tottering on the edge of failure, and he would willingly prepare the copies for mailing with his own hands.

Dr. Peabody had scarcely gone when Sophia Ripley entered and greeted Elizabeth. The wife of the Rev. George Ripley had undertaken a kind of guardianship over these classes of Margaret Fuller's. It was to her that Margaret had gone for advice when, a year before, she had first conceived the project. Women were studying, Margaret had said, but they seldom had an opportunity to state what they thought. Thus their education was incomplete. Did Mrs. Ripley think that she, Margaret, could bring together a score of women to discuss what they were born to do? Mrs. Ripley did think so, and she had watched with pleasure those conversations on mythology which Margaret had conducted the preceeding winter. Now, in November of 1840, the second series was beginning, and Mrs. Ripley was there to observe and to participate in their progress.

Sophia Ripley was tall, graceful, fair. Her father was a Dana, her mother a Willard; and these aristocratic families whence she sprang viewed with misgiving her passionate progress in the world of social reform. Her marriage to a pleasant young Unitarian minister, of inferior social standing, had been bad enough, but when she threw herself, with an enthusiasm that even George Ripley could not equal, into a violent struggle for world improvement, they were puzzled and depressed. They would have been even more chagrined if they had known what Sophia and George, at that very time, were planning. And what pain it would have given them if they could have foreseen their Sophia standing at a Brook Farm washtub, nursing a Brook Farm leper, teaching in the Brook Farm school. For some time George Ripley had dreamt of a community where men and women could live in that spirit of simple Christian fellowship which it was so exceedingly difficult to maintain in Boston. Now the dream was assuming substance: a location had been tentatively selected, a plan sketchily drawn up. Sophia was as excited as her husband, and already she viewed the project with that loyal enthusiasm which was in no small degree responsible for such success as Brook Farm had.

She brought the same enthusiasm and the same cheerful energy to Margaret Fuller's classes, and when Margaret arrived that November morning, there were her two principal supporters to receive her. Margaret, very, very near-sighted, had to look twice before she could recognize Elizabeth and Sophia. They, of course, would have known her if they had seen her across Boston Common, for she walked like a queen. But she was homely, there was no question of that. To them there was nothing strange in the black alpaca dress, or in the tight, smooth coiffure, but even their love could not ignore the rangy build, the sharp features, the peering eyes. Yes, she was even awkward, despite the grandeur of her manner. And yet there was the radiance in her face, expressive of the self-assurance and happiness that had come, after her exile in Groton and in Providence, with her return to the society that she loved.

People were beginning to come: the wife of the Collector of the Port of Boston, the wife of the next president of the Massachusetts Senate, the daughter of Dr. Channing, the daughter of Dr. Tuckerman, the daughter of Judge Jackson. It was a gathering almost as eminent socially as it was distinguished intellectually. Unpopular as Margaret was in Boston, her following among the women was not confined to the little circle of Transcendentalist radicals. While Margaret asked Mary Channing about her father's health and Sarah Tuckerman about her father's work with the poor, Mrs. Bancroft and Mrs. Quincy politely overlooked the fact that the husband of one was a Democrat and the husband of the other a Whig. Political differences counted for little here. Judge Charles T. Jackson might look on abolitionists as incendiaries, but his daughter Marianne, beautiful, gifted, and sadly destined to die young, fraternized gladly with Louisa Loring and Lydia Child.

At the hour of noon Margaret began, expressing her gratitude at seeing so many present. She referred to herself. She had, she said, changed in some ways since they had last met. They, doubtless, were also changed. She found herself looking at all things less objectively and more as if she were identified with the laws that controlled the universe. That was true progress, from the circumference of being, where we found ourselves at birth, to the center of being. Such an advance was enacted poetry. That was the true path: prose there must be, but poetry was the way of life.

There would be, everyone perceived, little discussion that morning, for Margaret was too full of her subject to encourage interruption. This would be a monologue, but they were not loath to listen, since she was at her best, brilliant, gracious, profound. The topic this winter would be the fine arts. They would divide the subject so and so; they would discuss this and that. Margaret mentioned the conversations of the preceeding winter, summarizing their results and remarking that they had necessarily been superficial. This year they would go deeper. Most of the women—especially, perhaps, the younger ones—listened as if under enchantment, and Margaret went on and on.

Occupied as she was with her theme, Margaret could not but observe with satisfaction that many of the women present had come from some little distance and at considerable inconvenience. There, for example, was Susan Burley, who had come in from Salem. One of Elizabeth Peabody's special friends, she commended herself to Margaret by her learning and her zeal for securing the highest culture for women. She had founded in Salem a club for the discussion of philosophy, modeled after the Boston Transcendental Club. Hawthorne had been taken to one of its meetings, to sit nervous and distraught through the conversation. He had gone again, however, braving the intellectuals in the company of the Peabody sisters. Susan had not failed to profit by her Salem experiences; she was one of those who needed little urging to talk.

The Concord delegation consisted of two staunch admirers of Ralph Waldo Emerson, his wife and Elizabeth Hoar. Equally self-effacing, they had served more than once as audience for the soaring colloquies of Margaret and Waldo. Lydian could not sufficiently praise Margaret's eloquence and the affluence of her knowledge. Elizabeth admired Margaret's wit, the rapidity with which she amassed her quantities of information, the severe mental discipline which ruled her life, the love of beauty which guided her studies. But perhaps both Elizabeth and Lydian had their reservations when they spoke of Margaret.

One wonders if Lydian, recalling the savage orthodoxy of her childhood training, sometimes asked herself how she had chanced to escape into this liberal, lively, and fundamentally cheerful world of Concord and Boston. She had married the thoughtful young widower who had come courting her in Plymouth, and she had made his gods her gods, even to the extent of naming her daughter for that first wife that lay in the Sleepy Hollow burying ground. Her rôle in this new world was largely that of observer, sometimes a little puzzled, no doubt, by the sphinx-like husband who called her "mine Asia" and wrote Thomas Carlyle that she was the incarnation of Christianity. But she accepted, she appreciated, she understood. Only she could withdraw enough to look with calm humor on the extravagances of Waldo's friends.

Elizabeth seemed, as Hawthorne was to remark, more at home among spirits than among fleshly bodies. She thought of her brothers, Ebenezer, just admitted to the bar, and George still in his teens, and of Waldo's brother, Charles, who was to have been her husband. But he had died, and she was committed to a career of sisterhood, a sister to those solid, stolid Concord conservatives, a sister in the spirit to the Waldo who humbly called her "Elizabeth the Wise." She had moved between two worlds and lived in her own. Her code was the code of gentleness, and she condemned radicalism only insofar as it sinned against refinement. If she saw Margaret's faults, she forgave them. As for Margaret, she wearied a little of "that expression of unbroken purity."

Margaret began to explain why one must never regard poetry as a mere relaxation, as an ornamental fringe on the garment of life. It was amazing how enthusiasm grew, how eloquence came to her, in this atmosphere of friendship and admiration. Here was neither scorn for her ideas nor condemnation for her manners. On such a person as Sarah Clarke, for example, one could depend. Sarah had, as Emerson observed, her full proportion of the native frost, but there was stability and candor in her nature. She could nurse Margaret through a sick headache, or she could listen with patience and intelligence to a rhapsody on art. Margaret had called on her to contribute to the *Dial*, and she enjoyed the distinction of studying under Washington Allston. Less stimulating perhaps, than her brother James, she was quite as satisfactory as a friend. "Her neighborhood," said Margaret, "casts the mildness and purity too of the moonbeam on the else parti-colored scene."

If Sarah Clarke was soothing and restful, Amelia Barlow was lively and amusing. In Margaret's Cambridge days, she and Amelia had vied for the leadership of their company of young intellectuals, Margaret claiming it by right of intelligence, Amelia by the right of beauty. After Amelia had married handsome David Barlow, and he had been settled in the Unitarian church at Lynn, she and Margaret had maintained an enthusiastic and intimate corresondence. Barlow, who had won notoriety by composing a Harvard Phi Beta Kappa poem which he required forty-seven minutes to deliver, left the ministry, and left his wife, and Amelia came back to Cambridge with three children to care for. Of course tongues wagged, all the more limberly because she had lost none of her attraction for men and none of her fondness for their society. She could pay rapt attentions to the conversations, but she shone in a more animate gathering. Brook Farm was in her mind, for she saw in its proposed school an opportunity to secure an education for her children, while its promised fellowship appealed to her gregariousness.

With Amelia was Mrs. Farrar, wife of the Harvard professor of mathematics. Margaret looked upon her with the warmest gratitude, for Mrs. Farrar had meant much to her when she was growing up in Cambridge. What wonders Mrs. Farrar had seen, what great men and women she had looked upon in France and England! She had been born in France, though her father was a native of Nantucket, and she had mingled in famous literary circles before she was established in her salon in Cambridge. It was at her house that Margaret had met many of these women; at her house too, that she had seen Harriet Martineau and many another celebrity. Mrs. Farrar was not only the associate of authors but an author herself: "The Young Lady's Friend" and "The Youth's Letter-Writer" had shaped morals and manners for more than one aspiring young woman.

Mrs. Farrar had had her fling at shaping Margaret, too. How gauche the brilliant young daughter of Timothy Fuller had seemed in her teens! Full of the erudition which her father had crammed into her at the sacrifice of health for them both, she was utterly without knowledge of how to conduct herself in polite society, and she had tried to make up in arrogance what she lacked in polish. Mrs. Farrar had tactfully hinted and admonished, and she had even supplied a model to guide the proposed reformation. Her cousin, Anna Barker, trained in the society of New York and New Orleans, had been visiting Mrs. Farrar, and she conspicuously possessed the qualities Margaret lacked. The two girls had been thrown together, with, Mrs. Farrar hoped, some profit to both the stubborn intellectual and the talented beauty.

Elizabeth Peabody, Margaret noticed, was sitting with an expression on her face that might signify either sleepiness or rapture. Elizabeth had that mannerism; at the Concord School of Philosophy, forty years later, visitors would swear she was napping during the addresses, but when the speeches were over, she invariably asked profound and pertinent questions. It was much the same at these conversations: if there was an opportunity for discussion, Elizabeth would take the leading part. But one could not tell what occupied her dreamy mind as Margaret's words went on and on.

Perhaps Elizabeth, who took personal pride in these meetings, was making a mental list of the women present. She, too, would rejoice that so many had come. She would note the size of the West Roxbury contingent. Mrs. Francis George Shaw and her sister-in-law, Anna Shaw, sat with Mrs. George R. Russell and her sister-in-law, Ida Russell, and with them was the large, comfortable wife of their pastor. Mrs. Theodore Parker, whose mildness led her husband to call her Bearsie, and whose ample person seemed to Hawthorne stuffed full of tenderness, was scarcely an intellectual, in Margaret's sense of the word. She regretted a little Theodore's insatiable devotion to books, but she shared his humanitarian zeal. And her understanding of people amazed the husband who had accepted her limitations. Her naivete was reflected in the gentle expression of her almost immature features.

Bearsie Parker, though it would not have occurred to her to take part in the conversation, enjoyed Margaret's flights. She felt secure with Mrs. Shaw and Mrs. Russell, for she knew they were as unpretentious as she. She loved these women, whose husbands so firmly supported her husband. Frank Shaw and George Russell had settled near each other in West Roxbury in order to enjoy each other's company and to escape the crowded streets of Boston. They were both business men by training, but Russell had retired—at the age of thirty-five—and Shaw paid more attention to literature than he did to business.

George Russell, son of the late minister to Sweden, had gone, after graduating from Brown in 1821, to South America to help the revolutionists, but he had soon returned, determined to make his fortune. Ten years in Canton and Manilla served his purpose, and in 1835 he married Frank Shaw's sister, Sarah, and devoted himself to literature and the rural life. His wife was tranquil, self-possessed, free from artificiality. Together they quietly encouraged this philanthropy and that reform. His widowed mother, who lived in Milton, visited the conversations on occasion, and his sister, Ida, a handsome and agreeable young lady, was often present.

Associated with Russell by marriage, nearness of residence, and community of interest, Frank Shaw in many ways resembled his older friend. His father was a prosperous merchant, and Frank was trained for the business. He possessed the kind of executive ability which had built up the firm, but neither the long voyages to the East, nor the days of bookkeeping and bartering had attracted him. It was, he found, better to devote himself to translating George Sand and Fourier. Fourier was just beginning to attract him, and he stood ready to lend his support to Fourier's disciples, just as later he would give his aid to Henry George. His wife was born a Sturgis, a cousin of the three Sturgis girls who were present that morning. His sister Anna was to perpetuate the family tradition for radicalism by marrying that eccentric clergyman William Batchelder Green.

Margaret was talking about the prose of life, of the impossibility of escaping sordid concerns with money. She might have thought of those merchant Shaws and Russells and of her young friend Sam G. Ward, who, only a month before, had married her erstwhile model, Anna Barker. Ward was fond of saying to Margaret that his father had spoiled him by sending him to Harvard and then giving him an opportunity to travel in Europe. He might once, he said, have made just as good a business man as his father, but he lacked the undivided zeal. Of course, now that he had a wife to support, he would go to work for the Barings, and he would do well, but he enjoyed the society of Emerson more than the society of the merchants who drank Madeira at his father's club. He could write bills of lading, but he preferred to write poems for the *Dial*. Though he had been frightened of Margaret when he first met her, he was fond of her now, and he was glad that both his wife and his sister went to her conversations. Anna was there this morning, as beautiful and gracious as ever.

There was, Amelia Barlow thought, permitting her attention to wander from Margaret's remarks, much material in this group for gossip. Leaving to one side her own uncertain affairs, and this recent marriage of Sam Ward, there were various courtships to be studied with interest. Mary Channing, it was said, was about to marry Frederick Eustis, a clergyman whose views were too radical for his church. Maria White, rumor had it, was receiving sonnets from the Cambridge Sir Galahad, James Russell Lowell. Maria was herself a poet and an idealist. She had converted Lowell to the anti-slavery cause, but she could not make a Transcendentalist of him. She was a pretty, unworldly young girl, Mrs. Barlow thought, and it was no wonder that the Cambridge youths referred to Lowell and Miss White as the King and Queen.

And, of course, there were the Peabody girls. Everyone who frequented the bookstore knew that the author of *Twice-Told Tales*, now, thanks to George Bancroft, a measurer at the Boston Customs House, was moving slowly toward marriage with Sophia. Sophia may well have blushed when she thought of the love letters which she was preserving upstairs, but she knew she had company, for a serious young widower was calling upon her sister Mary. The secretary of the Massachusetts Board of Education, tall, spare, and square-jawed, came not infrequently, in his long black coat, to the house on West Street. Sophia may have thought them a strange pair of lovers—her own romantic, shy, hesitant Mr. Hawthorne, and Mary's dyspeptic, dogmatic, terrifying Mr. Mann.

Amelia Barlow would have been amused if she could have foreseen the sequel to two of the these courtships. Loyal as Maria White and Sophia Peabody were to Margaret Fuller, they could not control their husbands' opinions of her. James Russell Lowell was rather too much the gentleman to care to have his wife associating with radicals, and he was careful to insist that she was never really a Transcendentalist. But a natural distaste for Margaret was intensified when she, refusing to be imposed upon by the mellifluousness of his verse, expressed her disdain in the columns of the New York *Tribune*. The result was the searing portrait of her in "The Fable for Critics."

Of Hawthorne perhaps all we can say is that he did not like her. We have Sophia's letter to Margaret, telling her that Mr. Hawthorne rejoiced because, when they were in Concord, Margaret could visit them, but we also have the direct statements in the Journal and the little disguised portrait in *The Blithedale Romance*. It seems as if Hawthorne, "in the midst of his emotions," as Sophia puts it, quite forgot himself, or as if Sophia, in the midst of her emotions, with marriage at last in sight, ignored the need for accurate statement.

But neither Mrs. Barlow nor Margaret could read the future, and Margaret, absorbed in this nice distinction between prose and poetry, would have cared but little if she had known. Margaret was particularly pleased to see that Mrs. Samuel Ripley was present. It was not often that she could leave the half dozen children in the Waltham parsonage, declare a vacation for the boys she and her husband were preparing for Harvard, and come into the city for a few hours of talk. A stranger seeing this tall woman in a black dress, with a lace cap on her graying hair, would have found it easy to believe in her domestic accomplishments, but would have thought it strange that she should be here among the youthful intelligentsia. Margaret knew better. How puerile much of this talk must have seemed to the daughter of Captain Gamaliel Bradford, who had taught herself Greek and Latin, French, Italian, and German! She longed to know Hebrew, and at the age of seventy she would be reading *Don Quixote* in Spanish. Just at present she was reading Spinoza's *Tractatus Theologicus*. She had read Euripides while she nursed her babies, and when she sat down to mend stockings she propped Virgil before her and translated it for the children. One of her pupils remembered that she examined him while she shelled peas, and with one foot rocked the cradle of her little grandson.

Though perhaps the most erudite woman in the room, Sarah Ripley never wrote a book, whereas fully half the others had written or were to write for publication. It was a distinguished literary gathering. Lydia Maria Child had written two or three novels, a treatise on household economics, and an attack on slavery. Mrs. Farrar had half a dozen books to her credit. Mrs. Samuel Putnam, Lowell's sister, was soon to write *The Tragedy of Errors* and *The Records of an Obscure Man*. Mrs. Thomas Lee, daughter of the illustrious Joseph Buckminster, whose biography she was to write, had already published a life of Richter and a historical novel, and *Naomi, Parthenia,* and *Florence* were still to come.

Margaret could not help but be brilliant in such a company, but she laid bare her mind rather for her personal followers and admirers than for these established literatae. Ellen Hooper was one of the few to whose heart Margaret felt she spoke directly. Margaret had been proud to publish her "Poet" in the *Dial*, and she could only regret that so little came from her pen. The daughter of a merchant and the wife of a physician, Ellen Hooper would seem to have found her poetic aspirations mercilessly in contrast with the social and intellectual tone of her family circle. But she could attribute something of her unconventionality and her sympathy with unpopular causes to the example of her father. Old Captain Sturgis, whose firm dominated more than half the trade between the Atlantic seaboard and the West Coast and China, had come sailing into port nearly forty years ago as the master of his own ship at the age of nineteen. It had taken only five years for him to rise to his captaincy, and it took but a few years more to amass the fortune which made possible the establishment of Bryant and Sturgis. He abandoned the sea in 1810, abandoned the long voyages and the fights with pirates, married the daughter of Judge Davis, and settled down to a half century as merchant prince. Popular rumor made him out a stern, intolerant man, but friends knew of the causes to which he had silently given. No one could call him a radical, but when, three years before, Wendell Phillips had stood in Fanuiel Hall, striving for a chance to damn forever the bloody slavery sentiments of Attorney-General Austin, it had been William Sturgis who restrained the cat-calling mob, and gave the young orator his opportunity.

Three daughters of Captain Sturgis were in Miss Peabody's bookstore that noon. Ellen was probably the most brilliant of the trio, but her unmarried sister, Caroline, had also written for the *Dial*. Caroline was the friend whom Margaret sought when she had in view a vacation in the open air. Not long before they had spent a fortnight together camping on the Merrimac, and they would spend another in Fishkill, N.Y., while Margaret completed her *Women in the Nineteenth Century*. It would have saddened Margaret to know that Caroline, who married William Tappan in 1847, brought out of her literary skill only a little verse and a few books for children.

The third of the Sturgis girls had also married a Hooper—Samuel Hooper, Robert's brother—a bright young man who had had the good sense to go into business with his father-in-law. Anne did not display the literary talent of her sisters; her gifts fitted her to aid her husband as he rose in the tensely competitive worlds of commerce and politics.

Margaret had finished her remarks on poetry and prose in life. One could not, she said, always be poetic in life, but one might and should be poetic in thought and intention. The man who could not perfectly weave his thought of beauty into his life—and who could?—wrote it in stone, drew it on canvas, breathed it in music, or built it in lofty rhyme. One must not in life be always consciously seeking beauty, for to seek it was often to miss it, but one should strive to live as harmoniously with the great laws of the universe as one's social and other duties permitted. Then the vision which was only incompletely rendered in the terms of daily existence could be expressed in art, or, if one were denied the privilege of creating, one could solace oneself with the creations of others.

Lydian Emerson, though listening carefully, looked about her. There was George Bancroft's wife, a suitable partner, Lydian thought, in the far-reaching career which everyone was predicting for this schoolmaster in politics. Lydian had known her in Plymouth, when they were Lydia Jackson and Elizabeth Davis. Elizabeth had married Alexander Bliss, a promising lawyer who had been a junior partner in Daniel Webster's firm. He had died, leaving her with two sons, and then Bancroft, a widower of only a few months, had come to Boston and won her.

Lydian observed another personal friend, Belinda Randall. Her father was a doctor, her brother a poet. She was a special friend of Elizabeth Hoar's, and when she came to Concord everything else was dropped while she played or sang. She was rather like Elizabeth, not exactly an intellectual but with something in her character which the more discerning of the intellectuals found worthy of respect.

Margaret moved towards her peroration, outlining the topics which she hoped to discuss in subsequent meetings. Ednah Littlehale, the youngest of the group and one of Margaret's most unreserved admirers, listened as if to divine revelation. With her was her squint-eyed friend Mary Ann Haliburton. For three years Ednah came regularly to these meetings, and with similar fidelity attended the lectures of Emerson and the other Transcendentalists. She would marry Seth Cheney, the artist, and a long life of writing books, lecturing to women's clubs, working for feminism, stretched before her; but at the end of her life—after the beginning of the new century—she would still remember Margaret's manners and Margaret's wisdom.

Lydia Child began to formulate the question she would ask when Margaret had finished. She had formerly been popular and prosperous, with her novels, her *Juvenile Miscellany* for children, and her "Frugal Housewife" for their mothers. But in 1833 she had published "An Appeal for That Class of Americans Known as Africans." Her friends had ostracized her, and indignant fathers had cancelled subscriptions to the *Miscellany*. She had need for frugality then. But she continued her writing, while her husband, a lawyer by training, undertook the cultivation of sugar beets. In these years she only occasionally visited Boston, but when she was there she eagerly sought out Margaret Fuller. They had known each other for more than a decade, and years before had planned to read together the philosophy of Locke. Mrs. Child had taken peculiar pleasure in the conversations on mythology which had been carried on the year before, for she was already considering the treatise on comparative religions which it required seven years to write.

For many Bostonians the meeting would have been sufficiently damned by Mrs. Child's presence, but it acquired further odium from the fact that she was accompanied by two of her abolitionist friends, Ann Terry Phillips and Louisa Loring. The young woman who converted Wendell Phillips to the anti-slavery cause was not well enough to mingle often in society. Mrs. Loring, however, was likely to be found wherever liberal causes were advocated. Like her husband, who lent to the abolitionists all his legal knowledge and skill, she counted no sacrifice too great if it was directed toward the destruction of slavery. Ideas as such interested her less than causes, but she enjoyed the fervor of Miss Fuller's talk and the transient brilliance of the occasional sparks she drew from her followers.

Margaret had finished, and a few minutes remained. She did not have to wait long for a response to her remarks. Most of the members of the group, it was plain to see, were moved by what she had to say, and two or three of them were ready with comments that sounded rather like testimonials. Warmth and sympathy pulsed in the gathering. A few questions came. Elizabeth Peabody asked if the search for beauty was not likely to result in a dilettantish attitude toward life. Yes, said Margaret, we must distinguish carefully; she was tired, she said, of young ladies who were always sighing after being beautiful. What was the greatest of the arts? Music, she cried, for that conveyed from soul to soul the most secret motions of feeling and thought.

But the time for questions was brief, and soon Margaret stood up and prepared to go. There was again a rustling of trailing skirts, as the women swirled about their leader; but she felt exhausted; she had given too much already. Accompanied by Mrs. Farrar, she left, tall and proud and walking like a queen. The others began to go, with many words about Margaret's talk. Yes, she was at her best today; such fire! such depth! How much the winter seemed to promise! What had she meant when she said—? Where was Elizabeth Peabody, and could she recommend such and such an article in the *Revue des Deux Mondes?* But at last they had all departed, and Elizabeth went upstairs, whither Mary had already escorted Sophia. Dr. Peabody appeared and began to clear the room.

Margaret sat back limply while Mrs. Farrar told her what a noble meeting it had been. Their glistening eyes, their responsiveness, their love—it was a splendid, purposeful, integrated group. They were, Mrs. Farrar said, remarkable women. They had won their erudition by their own efforts, learned their languages, planned their courses of reading. And their loyalty to Margaret and her purposes was so fine. When Professor Farrar's residence was reached, Margaret went to bed with a nervous headache. Mrs. Farrar attended anxiously upon her. Would it be so all winter, she asked. If it is, Margaret answered, I do not care.

# "Margaret Fuller and Ralph Waldo Emerson"

## Harry R. Warfel[*]

"Yesterday Margaret Fuller returned home after making us a visit of three weeks," Emerson noted in his Journal on August 12, 1836. To this brief statement of fact he added these few words of characterization: "A very accomplished and very intelligent person."[1] She had sought for two years to make Emerson's acquaintance. On October 6, 1834, she had written that the Rev. Frederick Henry Hedge

> spoke with due admiration of the Rev. W. Emerson, that only clergyman of all possible clergymen, who eludes my acquaintance. *Mais n'importe.* I keep his image bright before my mind.[2]

Sometime later she had sent a translation of Goethe's *Tasso* to Hedge with the suggestion that he transmit it to Emerson for his perusal and criticism.[3] At another time she complained that Emerson had preached in her home church when she was out of town.[4] Late in 1835, probably through the good offices of Harriet Martineau, they were introduced.[5] But it was not until she had maneuvered tactfully by an exchange of letters with Mrs. Emerson[6] and had gained the help of mutual friends that she attained the honor of intimacy with the mind she most respected in America.

Miss Fuller was twenty-six years of age when she entered the Emerson home. In all essentials, as Emerson stated, she was at this time completely formed intellectually.

> Each of the main problems of human life had been closely scanned and interrogated by her, and some of them had been much earlier solved.[7]

Her experience and her self-training fitted her to meet Emerson as an intellectual equal.

She came not, therefore, to sit as a student at the feet of Emerson. Wide knowledge she had already attained, and her eager reading never ceased; always she attempted the new, the abstruse, and the difficult. Frequently she meditated on the shortcomings which prevented her attainment of absolute

---

[*] Harry R. Warfel, "Margaret Fuller and Ralph Waldo Emerson," *PMLA*, 50 (June 1935), 576–594; reprinted by permission of the Modern Language Association of America.

genius. "Who," she once asked archly of Emerson, "would be a goody that could be a genius?"[8]

She came to Emerson for a solution of her personal problems, particularly how she, a woman fettered by the conventionalities, might make her life rich, full, and meaningful. From Harriet Martineau she had sought assistance, but their plans for an educational tour through Europe had been frustrated by her father's death. Her queries remained unanswered. Unwilling to remain in a prison either of her own or society's making, she sought another who might direct her future footsteps into proper paths. A romantic notion, perhaps, it arose from a fundamental psychological need. As early as 1833 she had written to James Freeman Clarke:

> How often have I thought, if I could see Goethe, and tell him my state of mind, he would support and guide me! He would be able to understand.[9]

Two years later she wrote again:

> I sigh for an intellectual guide. Nothing but the sense of what God has done for me, in bringing me nearer to Himself, saves me from despair. . . . I had hoped some friend would do—what none has ever yet done—comprehend me wholly, mentally and morally, and enable me better to comprehend myself. I have had some hope that Miss Martineau might be this friend, but cannot yet tell. She has what I want—vigorous reasoning powers, invention, clear views of her objects—and she has been trained to the best means of execution. Add to this, that there are no strong intellectual sympathies between us, such as would blind her to my defects.[10]

Having failed to acquire self-comprehension from Miss Martineau, Margaret turned the more eagerly toward Emerson in the hope that she might attain the orientation this fearless theological rebel demonstrated. His calm enunciation of principles, his steady view of life, his insistence upon individual self-sufficiency, his personal integrity, and, above all, his luminous seminal thought—these qualities which she had found in his sermons led her to believe that he alone was her fit counsellor. It was for this reason that she had sharpened every weapon in her armory to assail the doors of his house and mind for admittance.

In one of her frank letters she explained why she had sought him out: "It is partly because yours is an image in my oratory . . . and I must pray."[11] Emerson was a saint, or a priest in a confessional, to whom she might go to gain release for emotional pressure. She had learned from Bacon that "no receipt openeth the heart but a true friend, to whom you may impart griefs, joys, fears, hopes, suspicions, counsels, and whatsoever lieth upon the heart to oppress it, in a kind of civil shrift or confession." But the person to whom she could unburden herself could be no mere friend. She had a dozen preachers and lawyers among her close acquaintances, men whose daily task demanded the giving of such counsel as she wanted. She required a spiritual adviser with the authority of an archbishop of Canterbury, of a Pope. Emerson alone in New England fulfilled her high requirements.

It was with a sense of triumph that Margaret Fuller entered the Emerson home in July, 1836, as the guest of Mrs. Emerson. She had connived successfully to come near her saint; now, she felt, the mental illumination that she so greatly craved would be hers. But she reckoned not the nature of her host.

> She and Mr. Emerson met like Pyramus and Thisbe, a blank wall between.[12]

At thirty-three Emerson was almost completely formed: he too had scanned all life and had settled its main problems. He had sent his first book, *Nature*, to the printer a few days before her arrival. The main structure of his philosophy had been built; the years might add new parts, but the original design would not be altered. With firmness and kindness he enunciated his principles and avowed his purposes. He recognized his shortcomings, too. One of these was his coldness, his "porcupine impossibility to contact," his unwillingness to open the doors to the inner recesses of his heart and mind.

Of this first visit Emerson has left a record:

> I still remember [he wrote in 1851] the first half-hour of Margaret's conversation. She was then twenty-six years old. She had a face and frame that would indicate fulness and tenacity of life. She was rather under the middle height; her complexion was fair, with strong fair hair. She was then, as always, carefully and becomingly dressed, and of lady-like self-possession. For the rest, her appearance had nothing prepossessing. Her extreme plainness—a trick of incessantly opening and shutting her eyelids—the nasal tone of her voice—all repelled; and I said to myself, we shall never get far.[13]

Margaret usually evoked unpleasant feelings in her new acquaintances, but this repugnance was soon lost.

Margaret's conversation scintillated like the heavens on a summer evening. Stars of thought twinkled, and an occasional, unexpected streak of lightning zigzagged through the air. All knowledge had been her province, and she hesitated not to discuss matters either very abstruse or very personal. She had a trick of electrifying a discussion. By plays of wit and fancy she could accelerate the rhythm of talk or turn to humorous use a serious proposal. She mimicked the idiosyncrasies of their mutual friends. Emerson objected to the way she made the twigs crackle under the pot: she made him laugh more than he liked. For, says Emerson,

> Margaret, who had stuffed me out as a philosopher, in her own fancy, was too intent on establishing a good footing between us to omit any art of winning. She studied my tastes, piqued and amused me, challenged frankness by frankness, and did not conceal the good opinion she brought with her, nor her wish to please.[14]

Apollonious the scholar looked into the eyes of Lamia and at once called her a serpent-woman. Emerson thought he had done the same; he had found her out; her little game would not succeed. She was, he must have thought, no better than the other visitors who sought acquaintance with him. Every person of moment then, as now, was fair game for the souvenir hunter or the campaigner seeking support for a new reform. But Margaret fitted none of these categories fully, although she was—according to her biographers—snake-like, was anxious to know the great, and was a reformer. She had, as has been said, a personal problem to which only Emerson could give a solution. He might graciously dismiss her, but, until he gave the "open sesame" by which she might know herself, she would cling to him.

The topics of conversation during these days of the first visit can be imagined. Emerson's gardening, the chores of the house, the neighboring woods and their inhabitants offered easy topics to these lovers of nature. A discussion of the many reforms and reformers gave Margaret an opportunity to speak of her desire for the improvement of the status of women in society. To this generalization he doubtless objected in equally general terms:

> It is folly to imagine that there can be anything very bad in the position of woman compared with that of man.[15]

Goethe was spoken of early, for here were two of the limited number of Goethe readers in America. Emerson recalled that Margaret had sent him a translation of *Tasso* and thanked her. They discussed and argued, for Emerson refused to grant Goethe the highest literary honors. Goethe lacked dependence upon soul; he was devoted "to truth for the sake of culture" and not "to pure truth."[16] She retorted vainly that Goethe was the great liberating personality of the nineteenth century, the only writer who freed his readers from the tyranny of the narrow ideas of the time. They spoke also of that great host of oversea writers who were now first attracting attention in America. There was Carlyle, who had beckoned both to a study of German literature. Emerson told of his visit to the lonely Scotch cottage and filled avid ears with personalia about Thomas and Jane Carlyle. He smilingly recounted his unsatisfactory meeting with Wordsworth, now first fully appreciated in America. Last, but not least in importance, might have been the topic of religion, an ever recurrent theme of discourse in the educated homes of New England. "The unhappy plight in which the Unitarian church then found itself"[17] became in this year the initial problem of the Transcendental Club.

These were hours and days filled with vivacious talk, but probably, to Margaret, not soul-satisfying talk. Emerson was, on his side, too anxious to be gracious; he doubtless talked more than he liked and little to Margaret's purpose. On her side, Margaret tried to please too much by ingratiating and witty remarks. The first visit was not an entire failure, but it was not the great success Margaret had expected.

The one tangible result of the visit was Emerson's introduction of Margaret to Amos Bronson Alcott, who was then conducting a school on new principles in Boston. On Emerson's recommendation she was engaged to teach Latin and French and to report stenographically the conversations between Alcott and the pupils. The winter, therefore, found Margaret in Boston where she might be near her new friends.

Upon her return home Margaret wrote a letter of appreciation to the Emersons and solicited a regular correspondence. What could not be won vis-à-vis might be attainable by letter. She adopted immediately a friendly and familiar tone. In September, shortly after she had entered upon her work in Alcott's school, she proposed that Emerson drive her to Groton for a Sunday visit. That she was uncertain of Emerson's kindly disposition towards her can be gleaned from the half-mocking postscript to her letter:

> You must not make a joke of my anxiety about next Sunday, but must take it seriously as I am feeling. It is a great gain to be able to address yourself directly, instead of intriguing as I did last year.[18]

During the winter of 1836–1837 Emerson lectured in Boston, and Margaret took every opportunity to see and hear him. A note in her December Journal indicates with what eagerness she compared all other men with Emerson. She had passed the evening with Dr. Channing.

> He was more eloquent on the subject of faith and hope, than I have ever heard him in the pulpit. I could not but contrast his tone with that of Mr. E. on the same subjects of conversation I had with him a few weeks ago. Oh man of expediency: how poor and faded are thy once fair words, beside those of a man of principle![19]

Miss Fuller's frail health was severely taxed by her work with Alcott. When an opportunity came in the spring to transfer to the Greene Street School at Providence, she withdrew, April, 1837, from Boston to Groton for a period of rest. To Emerson she wrote, in a letter accompanying one of many packages of books that passed between them,

> I look to Concord as my Lethe and Eunoë. After this purgatory of distracting petty tasks, I am sure you will purify and strengthen me to enter the Paradise of thought once more.[20]

This letter doubtless evoked or confirmed a second invitation to visit at Concord late that month, for on May 4 Emerson recorded in his Journal that Margaret had left for home.[21] To a friend she wrote during the visit: "The excitement of conversation prevents my sleeping."[22] Their rich and full talk again centered about German, for Emerson noted somewhat cynically:

> Among the many things that make her visit valuable and memorable, this is not the least, that she gave me five or six lessons in German pronunciation, never by my offer and rather against my will each time, so that now, spite of myself, I shall always have to thank her for a great convenience—which she foresaw.[23]

Having failed to win the hoped-for illumination through ordinary friendly interchange of ideas, she applied herself to secure her ends by teaching a bit of needed knowledge. It was with a shrewd calculation of human nature that she thus sought to penetrate the reserves of her "priest." On Sunday she drove with Emerson to Watertown,[24] where he doubtless went to preach. She omitted no art of pleasing, and lost no opportunity. But at the end of her visit she was as far from her goal as she had been before she had met Emerson. For, a few days after her return home, she again addressed to him a breezy letter; on this he made the notation, "What shocking familiarity."[25]

The persistency with which Margaret continued her efforts to enlist the sympathy and understanding of Emerson can best be understood in the light of a letter sent about this time to James Freeman Clarke.

> You question me [she began] as to the nature of the benefits conferred upon me by Mr. E's preaching. I answer, that his influence has been more beneficial to me than that of any American, and that from him I first learned what is meant by an inward life. . . . That the "mind is its own place," was a dead phrase to me, till he cast light upon my mind. Several of his sermons stand apart in memory, like landmarks in my spiritual history. It would take a volume to tell what this one influence did for me.[26]

Margaret's fertile mind nourished the seeds of Emersonian thought; the prejudices of home and environment, the thoughts gleaned from books, and her own ideas were rudely jostled by Emerson's sermons and lectures. Her worries about practical affairs, her desire to be of concrete service to her fellow citizens, were brought into sharp conflict with Emerson's optimistic and seemingly successful philosophy of individualism: "Trust thyself: every heart vibrates to that iron string"; trust God, nor be afraid. The conflict was that which results from the meeting of ideal and real, theoretical and practical thinkers. Margaret looked upon society as the source of evil; Emerson looked upon the individual as the creator or destroyer of his own happiness. Which attitude was the correct one, she wondered. All about her were the many practical reformers, the socialists, the watercureists, the graham-bread-eaters, the abolitionists; they seemed to be doing a good work. And here was the wisest American of the era taking the position that such reforms were foolish. His challenge to religion, too, sent her back to her own mind. Not books, not received opinion, not custom, but the truth to one's highest self he demanded. In that very demand he announced by implication the impossibility of one person's controlling another. But Margaret did not understand that this statement applied to her; as a self-appointed disciple she wanted the master to lay down for her concrete principles of thought and action.

During the year 1837—the exact date cannot be learned—Miss Fuller was admitted to the Transcendental Club, a group of New Englanders that met at the convenience of Dr. F. H. Hedge to discuss matters of religion, reform, and philosophy. Called together first on September 8, 1836, this group had neither a constitution nor a definite name. Likeminded folk were invited to attend, and no restrictions were placed upon the free flow of conversation. "Revelation, Inspiration, Providence, Law, Truth, and other generalities were treated openly and candidly."[27] Its membership included Emerson, Alcott, the Ripleys, Parker, Hedge, and others. Later members included Thoreau, Miss Sophia Peabody who married Hawthorne, Hawthorne, and Miss Fuller. This group sought through talk a solution for the world's ills. Unconscious of the part they were playing in furthering New England culture, they wasted no time in recording their transactions. From their discussions, however, arose in 1840 the twin children of transcendentalism: *The Dial*, a magazine for the recording and propagation of their ideas; and Brook Farm, an experiment in Utopian and communistic living. In these meetings Miss Fuller took her place on an equality with the other members, and she demonstrated that the mind of at least one woman in nineteenth-century America did not yield in firmness of opinion or in richness of knowledge to the Harvard graduates about her.

In June, 1837, Margaret took up her teaching duties at Providence. Not yet fully recovered in health, she thought longingly of her stay at Concord.

> Concord, dear Concord, haven of repose, where headache, vertigo, other sins that flesh is heir to, cannot long continue.[28]

Who but Emerson, she thought, should give the address upon the occasion of the dedication of the new school? It was her suggestion, doubtless, that led to his engagement. On June 10 Emerson spoke to the students and patrons on "Culture." Margaret, eager disciple that she was, looked about and discovered that the "good word" had fallen on barren ground; she wrote, therefore, to Alcott that, since she had been "much cheered and instructed," she hoped to be the means of fertilizing the thought there sown.[29] She would be the Emersonian vicar at Providence, teaching to the devotees of Animal Magnetism the master's message.

Transplanted, Margaret was not transformed. She still asked: Who and what am I? She appealed again to Emerson to explain how she might best go about the tantalizing job of orienting herself. Like a rubber ball cast to earth, she rebounded after rebuffs or denials. In a letter so carefully phrased that he copied it into his Journal and used part of it later in "Self-Reliance," he wrote:

> Power and aim seldom meet in one soul. The wit of our time is sick for an object. Genius is homesick. I cannot but think that our age is somewhat distinguished hereby, for you cannot talk with any intelligent company without finding expressions of regret and impatience that attack the whole structure of our worship, education, and social manners. We all undoubtedly expect that time will bring amelioration, but whilst the grass grows the noble seed starves, we die of numb palsy.
>
> But ethics stand when wit falls. Fall back on simplest sentiment, be heroic, deal justly, walk humbly, and you do something and do invest the capital of your being in a bank that cannot break, and that will surely yield ample rents.[30]

To Margaret, who could characterize herself as the possessor of "a great share of Typhon to the Osiris, wild rush and leap, blind force for the sake of force,"[31] this letter with its generalities must have seemed poor advice indeed. How could she who arose in the morning in jubilant spirits and went to bed with a nervous prostration, the spasms of which totally incapacitated her—how could this passionate intellect be calmed with oracular words like "walk humbly" and "fall back on simplest sentiment"? It could not be done that way.

For nearly a month she sulked or smiled at the advice given her, and then frankly wrote to Emerson that she had not written with customary promptness because she had not desired to write. She thrust directly at him with her explanation:

> I have been in an irreligious state of mind, a little misanthropic, and skeptical about the existence of any real communication between friends. I bear constantly in heart that text of yours—"Oh *my friends*, there are no friends," but to me it is a paralyzing

conviction. Surely we are very unlike Gods in "their seats of eternal transquillity" that we need illusions so much to keep us in action.[32]

Then, as if to dull her weapon, and with the intention of trying again after a year's failure, she added that she desired to see her "dear *no friends*, Mr. and Mrs. Emerson," and would be glad, since they had invited her, to make another visit to their home.[33]

With the exception of occasional visits to Boston, Margaret spent the entire time between September, 1837, and December, 1838, in her Providence school. New friends she made, of course; she wrote to Jane Tuckerman of a "gentleman not young, but noble in form and mind, and more rich in intellect than any person I have known since Mr. Emerson."[34] Her thoughts, it is evident, turned frequently to Emerson; all men were to be judged by comparison with him. Letters passed frequently between them. Their reading, their friends, their duties, their new gleanings in nature were discussed. Emerson during this period had sent two new challenges to American thinkers, "The American Scholar" and "The Divinity School Address." He was busy lecturing, and these two new declarations of independence were part of a full year's work. The furore the latter aroused was less important to Margaret than the problem which still worried her. She wrote with urgency: "I must see you, and still more hear you." She demanded that he lecture in Boston when she could be present, or that he send her his lectures on "Holiness" and "Heroism." It was in this letter that she wrote: "Yours is an image in my oratory . . . and I must pray."[35]

During the last days of December, 1838, Margaret left her school for ever and went to Groton to rest. She again plunged into her studies. A collection of copies and prints of great works of art having been given to the Boston Athenaeum, she immersed herself in the study of the history and interpretation of the fine arts, a subject she had become interested in much earlier through her reading of Goethe. To be nearer her friends, she took a place in Jamaica Plains, near Boston. From this suburban point of vantage she could sally out daily to meet her friends or to read in the library. The immense activity of her earlier years continued. She planned great literary works. She read widely, wrote much, and visited frequently. No form of expression—book, art, sermon, or lecture—escaped her attention. Nor did she let her friends escape the impact of her enthusiasm.

> I pleased myself [Emerson noted] in seeing the pictures brought in her portfolio by Margaret Fuller.[36]

It was a season of great interest in art, and Margaret and Emerson spent many occasional hours in the study of the works of the great Italian artists. Naturally Margaret led in the discussions.

> I remember [Emerson wrote] that in the first times I chanced to see pictures with her, I listened reverently to her opinions.[37]

Later he realized that she offered interpretations which the pictures did not justify.

> Her taste in works of art, though honest, was not on universal, but on idiosyncratic grounds.... Her fancy and imagination were easily stimulated to genial activity, and she erroneously thanked the artist for the pleasing emotions and thoughts that rose in her mind.[38]

Her opinions, Emerson confessed, were worth hearing for their original and interesting quality, if not for their accuracy.[39]

The year 1839 seems to have been a happy one in Margaret's life. Her Goethe studies bore fruit in a volume of translation, *Eckermann's Conversations with Goethe*. She wrote many essays and sketches which did service later in *The Dial* and the *Tribune*. She had made definite progress toward that high goal in authorship she had set for herself. She began in November her Conversations with such success that they were repeated annually for five years. Not unimportant was the solid foundation of her friendship with Emerson. He could note in his Journal late at night the visit of Alcott and Margaret.

> Very friendly influences these, each and both. Cold as I am, they are almost dear. [But he distrusted his jubilation and added] What is good to make me happy is not however good to make me write. Life too near paralyzes art.[40]

Three weeks later he lamented his "porcupine impossibility of contact with men."[41] He was as close to Margaret as he could be to any person. Although the *rapport* was not so complete as Margaret could wish, Emerson's earlier feeling of distance and restraint had largely passed. Margaret was less bumptious, for she withheld a letter and a poem she had written because she was afraid they "might destroy relations."[42] There were communal tasks to be performed, and on Margaret alone could Emerson depend for assistance. It was to her that he turned in these last days of 1839 when the long-projected magazine was to be launched.

*The Dial* was not the offspring of a moment's thought. Such a periodical had been conceived—as many earlier American magazines like the *Monthly Anthology* and the *Port Folio* had been planned—as a coöperative organ for the dissemination of the ideas of a like-minded group. As early as 1833 the Reverend Frederick Henry Hedge had sought by correspondence to organize a magazine. Margaret had then offered to contribute, provided that Hedge would give her a subject. Two years later she again offered to aid. In 1836 at the bi-centennial celebration of Harvard College, Hedge drew Emerson, George Ripley, and George Putnam into a conference to discuss the narrowing tendencies of the Unitarian church. Out of this discussion grew the Transcendental Club. Early in 1839 Brownson's *Boston Quarterly Review* so aroused the members that they felt they too might put to use much vacant talent and publish to the world the ideas which circulated in their association. John A. Heraud's British *New Monthly Magazine* became the immediate model. At a club meeting, September 18, Margaret "gave her views of the proposed *Dial*."[43] On October 20 Alcott and Margaret drove to Concord to confer all day with Emerson on the feasibility of the project. On January 1, 1840, she wrote to her friends to announce the new quarterly journal. Emerson, she was careful to say, would contribute to each issue. She begged for materials of so excellent a character that the first number might justify its publication. It is a commentary on man's ambitions that Hedge, who for seven years had nursed the idea of a magazine, was one of the tardiest contributors. The date for publication was to be April, 1840, but the poor response delayed the first number until July.[44]

During these six months Margaret corresponded with every possible contributor, accepted or rejected copy, revised or offered suggestions, even to Emerson, and in general carried out with fortitude the almost thankless task of organizing the editorial department of the paper. To Emerson, who acted as consulting editor, Margaret went frequently with her troubles and plans.

They examined every detail with some care until the first issue was ready to go to press. Then Margaret went away and trusted—as amateurs do to their sorrow—to the accuracy of the printer. Numerous small errors in type font, arrangement, and word drew a quick apology from Margaret to Emerson.[45] Her meekness in this respect was compensated by her frankness in editing the master's copy. "I think," she wrote Emerson in regard to proofs for the second issue, "when you look again you will think you have not said what you meant to say."[46] She supported her statement with a list of specific corrections. In some ways Margaret, although she attempted to interpret and popularize his ideas, was Emerson's harshest critic. She knew his personal weaknesses and his lack of continuity in writing. No worshipper ever sought more earnestly to give life to the clay feet of his God than did Margaret. She attempted

> to teach this sage [that] all he wants to make him the full-fledged angel [is] to make him forego these tedious, tedious attempts to learn the universe by thought alone.[47]

As literary editor of Horace Greeley's *Tribune* she took delight in praising "the sage of Concord"[48] while yet appraising his work disinterestedly.[49] No American critic has distributed more justly both praise and blame to Emerson's writings.

To *The Dial* Margaret and Emerson contributed, during her editorship, a large portion of the material. The sixth number contained, of a total of one hundred thirty-six pages, eighty-five from Margaret's pen. Much of this material was old or hastily written. Emerson, for his part, complained of the extreme fatigue he suffered from filling gaps at the last moment.[50]

It is not our purpose here to appraise *The Dial* or Margaret's part in it except so far as it shows how she and Emerson were drawn together into more simple and direct relations. The frequent letters between them and their hurried visits indicate that they attained an informality that stopped short of confidences. Emerson carried family messages for her, and he was trusted to look in upon Richard Fuller at Harvard on every visit to Cambridge. She petulantly chided her family for failing to make use of Emerson in the office of postman.[51]

When the burden of conducting the magazine was handed over to Emerson in March, 1842, he realized to the full Margaret's devotion to the paper. He came to realize, too, the utter justness and impartiality with which she had conducted it; and by letter she let him know his own shortcomings as an editor by referring to her experiences.[52] As guide, counsellor, and friend she sought to serve the best interests of Emerson, as well as of *The Dial* and herself. Emerson's loyalty to *The Dial*, if we judge by his letters to Carlyle, "seemed inseparably connected with his loyalty to her."[53]

These busy days did not bring to an end her questions about herself. Early in 1840 she sent him a little parable and added:

> Why do I write thus to one who must ever regard the deepest tones of my nature as those of childish fancy or worldly discontent?[54]

She continued to press her questions and in October drew from him a long letter in which he attempted to explain their relation:

> Concord, October 24th, 1840
>
> I have your frank and noble and affecting letter—and yet I think I could wish it unwritten. I ought never to have suffered you to lead me into any conversation or writing on our relation—a topic from which with all persons my Genius ever sternly warns me away. I was content and happy to meet on a human footing a woman of sense and sentiment, with whom one could exchange reasonable words, and go away assured that wherever she went was light and force and honor. That is to me a solid good: it gives value to thought and the day; it redeems society from that foggy and misty aspect it wears so often, seen from our retirement; it is the foundation of everlasting friendship.
>
> ... But tell me that I am cold or unkind, and, in my most flowing state I become a cake of ice; I can feel the crystals shoot and the drops solidify. It may do for others, but it is not for me to bring the relation to speech. Instantly I find myself a solitary, unrelated person, destitute not only of all social faculty but of all private substance. I see precisely the double of my state in my little Waldo, when, in the midst of his dialogue with his hobby-horse, in the full tide of his eloquence, I should ask him if he loves me—he is mute and stupid.... I take it for granted that everybody will show me kindness and wit, and am happy in the observation of all the abundant particulars of the show to feel the slightest obligation resting on me to do anything or say anything for the company. I talk to my hobby, and will join you in harnessing and driving him; but ask me what I think of you and me, and I am put to confusion.... There is a difference in our constitution. We use a different rhetoric. It seems as if we had been born and bred in different nations. You say you understand me wholly. You cannot communicate yourself to me. I hear the words sometimes, but remain a stranger to your state of mind. Yet we are all the time a little nearer. I honor you for a brave and beneficent woman, and mark with gladness your steadfast good-will to me. I see not how we can bear each other anything else than good-will, though we had sworn to the contrary. And now, what will you? The stars in Orion do not quarrel this night, but shine in peace in the old society. Are we not much better than they? Let us live as we always have done, only ever better, I hope, and richer. Speak to me of everything but myself, and I will endeavor to make an intelligible reply....
>
> Yours affectionately
> R. W. Emerson[55]

A year later Emerson was again disturbed. On one of her frequent visits Margaret went into the library to secure a book. Instead of reading she wrote the following letter:

October 1841

Dear Waldo,

 I know you do not regard our foolish critiques, except in the true way to see whether you have yet got the best form of expression. What do we know of when you should stop writing or how you should live? In these pages I seem to hear the music rising I so long have wished to hear and am made sensible to the truth of the passage in one of your letters, "Life, like the nimble Tartar &c."

 I like to be in your library when you are out of it. It seems a sacred place. I came here to find a book, that I might feel more life and be worthy to sleep, but there is so much here I do not need a book. When I come to yourself, I cannot receive you, and you cannot give yourself: it does not profit. But when I cannot find you the beauty and permanence of your life come to me.

 "The (Poesie) has ascended from the depths of a nature, and only by a similar depth, shall she be apprehended!"—I want to say while I am feeling it, what I have often (not always) great pleasure in feeling—how long it must be before I am able to meet you.—I see you.—and fancied it nearer than it was, you were right in knowing the contrary.

 How much, much more I would fain say and cannot. I am too powerfully drawn while with you, and cannot advance a step, but when away I have learned something. Not yet to be patient and faithful and holy, however, but only have taken off the shoes, to tread the holy ground. I shall often depart through the ranges of manifold being, but as often return to where I am tonight.

Margaret F.
 Oct. 1841
Letter written at
Concord from
room to room.[56]

**Emerson noted in his Journal on October 12 with a tinge of despair:**

I would that I could, I know afar off I cannot, give the lights and shades, the hopes and outlooks that come to me in these strange, cold-warm, attractive-repelling conversations with Margaret, whom I always admire, most revere when I nearest see, and sometimes love—yet whom I freeze, and who freezes me to silence, when we seem to come nearest.[57]

Ten days later he recorded the opinion that she was "a being of unsettled rank in the universe."[58] She seemed to have become a kind of sphinx, a living riddle. When he was surest of a solution, he was furthest away from the truth. She disturbed his equanimity as no one else had done, except possibly Aunt Mary Moody Emerson. Was he thinking of Margaret when he wrote: "Better be a nettle in the side of your friend than his echo"?[59]

Meantime there had been, as there would be hereafter, many good letters between them. Emerson, indeed, wrote that he "wishes letters every day from Margaret Fuller."[60] He tells her of his experiences as a gardener, his hoeing of corn and potatoes,[61] of his impending trip to Waterville, Maine, to deliver a lecture ("For which of my sins?" he asked jocosely),[62] of his pleasure in again being at the ocean,[63] and of his joy in her praise.[64] More interesting to her must have been his suggestion that they coöperate in founding a school (really a college on the plan recently adopted by Rollins College) in which instruction would be given by lecturers only. Ripley, Hedge, Parker, and Alcott could assist them.[65] When one recalls that Emerson wished for a professorship of rhetoric, it can be understood with what eagerness he awaited Margaret's reply. He too could confide in her, for, as she wrote him, she knew how to keep confidences.[66]

Late in 1840 the Reverend George Ripley withdrew from his pastorate and organized the Brook Farm Community in an attempt "to bring cultivated, thoughtful people together, and make a society that deserved the name."[67] Margaret and Emerson, as well as the other members of the Transcendental Club, were invited to join. Neither joined although each wished the colony well, and each visited it and spoke to the assembled members. Some of the meetings of Margaret and Emerson took place there, as Hawthorne recorded in his notebooks.[68]

Margaret's mental growth, as Emerson perceived, was visible.[69] The Conversations required a popular treatment of scholarly information and a ready command of her material. Her reserves needed to be stronger than her marshalled, prepared papers. She was at her best when a learned opponent called her forth. The vinous quality of her talk led her friends to urge her to publish in carefully organized form these brilliant *ex tempore* expressions. Her first task, after having been relieved from the onerous duties of *The Dial*, was to prepare these books. First came the translation of the correspondence of Fräulein Günderode and Bettine von Arnim, another branch of the Goethe tree she was growing. This book was published in 1842. She set to work on her *Woman in the Nineteenth Century*, the basis of which had appeared in *The Dial* as "The Great Lawsuit." In 1843 she made her pilgrimage to the West, the record of which is to be found in her third book, *Summer on the Lakes*. In 1844 *Woman* came from the presses. With four books to her credit, she was at thirty-four one of America's leading writers.

Margaret's new ardency in propagating feminist notions did not please Emerson. After a meeting with her, he wrote in his Journal:

> The conversation turned upon the state and duties of Woman. As always, it was historically considered, and had a certain falseness so. For me, to-day, Woman is not a degraded person with duties forgotten, but a docile daughter of God with her face heavenward endeavoring to hear the divine word and to convey it to me.[70]

Earlier he had written:

> Woman should not be expected to write, or fight, or build, or compose scores: she does all by inspiring man to do all.[71]

As generalizations, Margaret doubtless remarked, these statements were very attractive, but the individual woman could not be content to suffer, as she herself had suffered, to see her own property managed by a man simply because she was a woman; to suffer regret because she could not attend college; and to suffer the odium of gossip because she had acquired an education equal to a man's. There were practicable solutions possible, and these solutions she would demand. Against her ideas Emerson naturally opposed all his belief in the uselessness of method. They differed, but they did not quarrel. Her thinking had carried her beyond Emerson. Hers was a crescive mind; she could no longer tarry within Emersonian limits.

After the room-to-room correspondence Margaret seems not to have harassed Emerson for further explanations. Her visit to Concord in August, 1842, several months after the death of little Waldo, is happily to be reconstructed from one of the few extant portions of her diaries. It is evident that they met as friendly contemporaries and not as master and follower. She had come to write, and Emerson promptly put her to work. On the day following her arrival she walked with Emerson to Walden Pond. Their new "relations" can be understood from her notation:

> I feel more at home with him constantly, but we do not act powerfully on one another. He is much a better companion than formerly, for once he would talk obstinately through the walk, but now we can be silent and see things together.[72]

On an evening they walked to the river.

> We had an excellent talk: we agreed that my God was love, his truth.[73]

On another day she wrote:

> Waldo and I have good meetings, though we stop at all our old places. But my expectations are moderate now; it is his beautiful presence that I prize, far more than our intercourse.[74]

"My expectations are moderate now!" In that phrase Margaret explained to herself the new basis of their association. It was no longer to be a pursuit after a phantom. The old demand was no longer to be made; she was content with the realization that friendship with Emerson had to exist on his principles and not on hers. In the chatty letters that passed between them while she was at home, in New York City, and in Europe there was a continuous flow of friendly personal items. They had demonstrated to each other—Emerson reluctantly and with embarrassment—that they cared for, indeed loved, each other in their own way. With that knowledge Margaret had to be satisfied, and she thus versified her thought:

> TO R. W. EMERSON, JULY 1844
> Slight is the token, yet it should bring
> Thoughts of trust unbroken, hopes of Eternal Spring
> Of Love no word be spoken, it is too cold to sing.
>     May the coming day,
>     To my now clearer way,
>     Bring a ministry
>     More worthy thee;
>     Bring to thee
>     Truer thoughts of me.
> Gifts to the Giver
> Rain-drops to the parent river:
>     From absence they borrow
>     The tearful, pearly joy of sorrow.[75]

Of Margaret's year and a half as a critic on the *Tribune* we need remark no more than that only Poe in these years equalled her as a critic. Her just appraisal of Emerson as a poet and prose writer has already been alluded to. Of her years in Europe, her marriage, and her service to the Italian revolutionary cause as a nurse we need only say that these incidents fulfilled the expectations one might have of the high-spirited and noble young woman. Her tragic death by shipwreck within a few rods of the American coast closed at the age of forty the career of America's most brilliant woman of the era. It is not to Emerson's memoir of Margaret that we need to turn for his characterization of their relations, fine as that account is. This one sad sentence, written when he first learned of her death, contains in its first clause the simplest statement of his loss: "I have lost in her my audience, and I hurry now to my work admonished that I have a few days left."[76]

Notes

1. *Journals of Ralph Waldo Emerson*, ed. Edward Waldo Emerson and Waldo Emerson Forbes (Boston: Houghton Mifflin, 1909–1914), IV, 79–80.

2. MS. Works of S. M. F. Ossoli, 5 vols., I, 17, preserved in the Harvard College Library.— Permission to quote from these MS. volumes has been graciously given by Mrs. Gertrude Fuller Nichols.

3. Thomas Wentworth Higginson, *Margaret Fuller Ossoli* (Boston: Houghton, Mifflin, 1884), p. 64.

4. Higginson, *Margaret Fuller Ossoli*, p. 53.

5. [Ralph Waldo Emerson, William Henry Channing, and James Freeman Clarke], *Memoirs of Margaret Fuller Ossoli* (Boston: Phillips, Sampson, 1852), I, 201.

6. *Memoirs*, I, 201.

7. *Memoirs*, I, 291.

8. 20 October 1837, *Journals*, IV, 333.

9. *Memoirs*, I, 112.

10. *Memoirs*, I, 153.

11. Higginson, *Margaret Fuller Ossoli*, p. 90.

12. Caroline H. Dall, *Margaret and Her Friends* (Boston: Roberts, 1895), p. 13.

13. *Memoirs*, I, 202.

14. *Memoirs*, I, 202–203.

15. *Journals*, IV, 405.

16. *The Works of Ralph Waldo Emerson* (Boston: Houghton, Mifflin, 1903–1904), IV, 260–270.

17. Lindsay Swift, *Brook Farm* (New York: Macmillan, 1900), pp. 7–8.

18. MS. letter, dated Boston, 21 September 1836, preserved in the Boston Public Library. [Actually a copy; the original is at Harvard: see Robert N. Hudspeth, "A Calendar of the Letters of Margaret Fuller," *Studies in the American Renaissance 1977*, ed. Joel Myerson (Boston: Twayne, 1978), p. 62 (Ed. Note).]

19. 5 December 1836, MS. Works of S. M. F. Ossoli, I, 403–405.

20. 11 April 1837, Higginson, *Margaret Fuller Ossoli*, pp. 68–69.

21. *Journals*, IV, 225.

22. *Woman in the Nineteenth Century*, ed. Arthur B. Fuller (Boston: Roberts, 1874), p. 351.

23. 4 May 1837, *Journals*, IV, 225.

24. *Woman*, p. 351.

25. MS. letter, dated Groton, 30 May 1837, preserved in the Boston Public Library. Emerson regularly endorsed every letter he received. [Actually a copy; the original is at Harvard: see Hudspeth, "Calendar of Fuller Letters," p. 63 (Ed. Note).]

26. *Memoirs*, I, 194–195.

27. Swift, *Brook Farm*, p. 9.

28. Higginson, *Margaret Fuller Ossoli*, p. 80.

29. MS. letter, dated 27 June 1837, preserved in the Boston Public Library. [Actually a copy; the original is at Harvard: see Hudspeth, "Calendar of Fuller Letters," p. 63 (Ed. Note).]

30. *Journals*, IV, 256–257.

31. *Memoirs*, I, 237.

32. MS. letter, dated Providence, 14 August 1837, preserved in the Boston Public Library. [Actually a copy; the original is at Harvard: see Hudspeth, "Calendar of Fuller Letters," p. 64 (Ed. Note).]

33. 14 August 1837, Boston Public Library.

34. 21 September 1838, MS. Works of S. M. F. Ossoli, I, 89.

35. Higginson, *Margaret Fuller Ossoli*, pp. 89–91.

36. 8 June 1838, *Journals*, IV, 465. Emerson at this time was attempting to determine his own critical standards in the judgment of works of art. Margaret's excessively romantic interpretations taught him the need for "perfect equilibrium of mind."

37. *Memoirs*, I, 267–268.

38. *Memoirs*, I, 268.

39. *Memoirs*, I, 268.

40. 21 October 1839, *Journals*, V, 292.

41. *Journals*, V, 325.

42. Memoirs, I, 230. Cf. MS. letter to Caroline Sturgis, dated 25 November 1839, preserved in the Boston Public Library [not listed in Hudspeth, "Calendar of Fuller Letters," p. 69 (Ed. Note)], in which Margaret sent a poem and some leaves from her Journal: "I hesitated about sending you any papers now because you are busy writing, but then I reflected that you would not wish your mind strained up to your subject all day, but might like some grove of private life into which you might step aside to refresh yourself from the broad highway of philosophy."

43. Higginson, *Margaret Fuller Ossoli*, p. 147.

44. Higginson, *Margaret Fuller Ossoli*, pp. 130 ff.

45. Higginson, *Margaret Fuller Ossoli*, pp. 155–156.

46. Higginson, *Margaret Fuller Ossoli*, p. 157.

47. James Elliot Cabot, *A Memoir of Ralph Waldo Emerson* (Boston: Houghton, Mifflin, 1887), I, 276, Cf. MS. letter dated Groton, 7 January 1838, preserved in the Boston Public Library, in which she rebuked Emerson in humorous terms for adjourning a lecture because he had lost a night's rest as a result of a slight indisposition: "Imagine my indignation: lost a night's rest! as if an intellectual person ever had a night's rest." See, also, in the same place an undated letter in which she comments upon a criticism offered upon his *Essays:* "There is something obviously wrong in this attempt to measure one another, or one another's act."—Cf. also *Memoirs*, I, 240–241, in a letter to Emerson, dated December 1842, anent her unwillingness to send Dante's *Vita Nuova* in the original Italian to him: "It has never seemed to me you entered enough into the genius of the Italian to apprehend the mind, which has seemed so great to me, and a star unlike, if not higher than all others in our sky."

48. Ossoli, *Art, Literature, and the Drama* (Boston: Roberts, 1874), p. 304.

49. *Art, Literature, and the Drama*, pp. 195–196.

50. Higginson, *Margaret Fuller Ossoli*, p. 165.

51. MS. Works of S. M. F. Ossoli, II, 257, 551, 643, 657, and 663–665. For example, "During the two months that Mr. E. will lecture here I can always send by him" (pp. 663–665).

52. Higginson, *Margaret Fuller Ossoli*, pp. 166–167.

53. Higginson, *Margaret Fuller Ossoli*, p. 171.

54. 23 February 1840, *Memoirs*, I, 291.

55. Cabot, *Emerson*, I, 367–369.

56. The letter is preserved in the Boston Public Library. The endorsement, as usual, is in Emerson's hand. [Actually a copy; the original is at Harvard: see Hudspeth, "Calendar of Fuller Letters," p. 76 (Ed. Note).]

57. *Journals*, VI, 87.

58. *Journals*, VI, 97.

59. "Friendship," *Works*, II, 208.

60. Cabot, *Emerson*, II, 267.

61. Cabot, *Emerson*, II, 65.

62. Cabot, *Emerson*, II, 67.

63. Cabot, *Emerson*, II, 82–83.

64. Cabot, *Emerson*, II, 95–97.

65. Cabot, *Emerson*, II, 27–28.

66. MS. letter, dated 5 February? July? 1840, preserved in the Boston Public Library. [Actually a copy; the original, dated 5 July 1840, is at Harvard: see Hudspeth, "Calendar of Fuller Letters," p. 72 (Ed. Note).] This letter is of interest because it reveals the fact that another young lady sought out Emerson for counsel in a private matter somewhat similar in nature to Margaret's problem.—Cf. *Memoirs*, I, 214: "She never confounded relations, but kept a hundred fine threads in her hand, without crossing or entangling any."

67. Swift, *Brook Farm*, p. 9.

68. *The Works of Nathaniel Hawthorne* (Boston: Houghton, Mifflin, 1883–1891), IX, 252, 308.

69. Cf. Hawthorne, *Works*, IX, 334: Mr. Emerson "spoke of Margaret Fuller, who, he says, has risen perceptibly into a higher state since their last meeting." Cf. also *Memoirs*, I, 215, where Emerson wrote: "The day was never long enough to exhaust her opulent memory; and I, who knew her intimately for ten years . . . never saw her without surprise at her new powers."

70. March 1843, *Journals*, VI, 369.

71. November 1841, Journals, VI, 134.

72. MS. Works of S. M. F. Ossoli, III, 165.

73. MS. Works of S. M. F. Ossoli, III, 169.

74. MS. Works of S. M. F. Ossoli, III, 175–177.

75. MS. Works of S. M. F. Ossoli, I, 459.

76. Denton J. Snider, *A Biography of Ralph Waldo Emerson* (St. Louis: William Harvey Miner, 1921), p. 333.

# "Nemesis and Nathaniel Hawthorne"

Oscar Cargill*

No literary quarrel in European annals surpasses for rancor the American one which involved the Peabodys, the Channings, the Hawthornes, and Margaret Fuller in the second quarter of the nineteenth century. That Nathaniel Hawthorne finally came to hate Margaret Fuller and that the Hawthorne family were willing to pillory her is clear enough from the well-known passage in the Roman *Note-books*[1] in which he calls her young Italian husband, the Marquis Ossoli, a "boor" and a "clown" and in which, among other things, he says that Margaret herself was without

> the charm of womanhood.... She had a strong and coarse nature, which she had done her utmost to refine, with infinite pains; but of course it could be only superficially changed.... She was a great humbug.... She had stuck herself full of borrowed qualities.... She set herself to work on her strong, heavy, unpliable, and, in many respects, defective and evil nature ... but ... she could not recreate or refine it.

Yet it is not equally clear, as a modern psycho-analyst has told us, that Hawthorne's "immoderate dislike of Margaret is only comprehensible as a symptom of his hidden misery, a cover for his fascinated interest in the Bacchante type."[2] To trace Hawthorne's malice towards Miss Fuller wholly to perverted attraction for her is, as we shall see, too facile an explanation.

To begin with, the evidence that Hawthorne was fascinated by a Bacchante type is most sketchy. It is based entirely upon a misinterpretation of the character of Donatello in *The Marble Faun*. In presenting Donatello, Hawthorne was absorbed by an idea which he had previously set forth in the character of little Pearl in *The Scarlet Letter*. This tiny wood-sprite, this elf, after cavorting in a most charming fashion about her harassed mother and the distraught minister, suddenly becomes a normal human being after receiving a kiss from her dying father.[3] One suspects that here Hawthorne has merely taken liberties with certain broad conceptions of Calvin and Rousseau:[4] that the kiss symbolizes Original Sin without which we would all be primitives and mænads. Similarly, the Faun is transformed from a Romantic Savage, from a

---

*Oscar Cargill, "Nemesis and Nathaniel Hawthorne," *PMLA*, 52 (September 1937), 848–862; reprinted by permission of the Modern Language Association of America.

wild innocent, into a *human being* by his sin of casting Miriam's persecutor from the parapet of the Capitoline Hill. No one but Hawthorne would have occupied himself with a synthesis of Natural Goodness and Original Sin, yet it does not follow that the New England novelist was warped or neurotic. He merely took as seriously the sages of Geneva and Montpellier as Emerson took Goethe. To assume, as the Freudians do, that Hawthorne was fascinated by the "Bacchante type" as represented by the male faun and the little child Pearl (said to be drawn from his daughter Una)[5] is to hint at horrid perversions such as only disciples of the Id can imagine. It would seem to be a duty of criticism to forestall such constructions by setting forth without bias, if possible, the facts.

Hawthorne first clashed with Margaret Fuller in 1834 before the two were acquainted. In October of that year George Bancroft published in the *North American Review* an article on "Slavery in Rome" in which he charged Brutus with sycophancy, time-serving, cruelty, and avarice. Margaret, as well read in Roman history as Bancroft himself, attacked the article in the Boston *Daily Advertiser*, defending Brutus with spirit.[6] Three days later "some big-wig from Salem" who signed himself "H" (her words)[7] replied to her in the same paper. It was thus, in all probability, that Hawthorne first attracted the attention of Bancroft, which led to his appointment under the latter in the Boston Customs House as weigher and gauger in 1839.[8] In her first relationship with the novelist, Margaret Fuller served him rather well, but at the same time she acquired a knowledge of his willingness to truckle which she could put to use later if she chose.

Hawthorne's Boston appointment brought the two into close relationships. Before leaving old Salem, Hawthorne had fallen in love with pretty, talented Sophia Peabody,[9] his future wife. This girl's sister Elizabeth, after teaching school for the eccentric Alcott,[10] had set up a bookshop at No. 13 West Street, Boston, which then served as a meeting place for literary folk. Elizabeth had become infatuated with the brilliant Margaret Fuller some time before Hawthorne's advent, it would appear, possibly in 1836, when Margaret succeeded her as a teacher in Alcott's school.[11] All who knew Miss Fuller speak of her personal magnetism, particularly for members of her own sex. Thus Emerson writes, "The loveliest and the highest endowed women were eager to lay their beauty, their grace, the hospitalities of sumptuous homes, and their costly gifts at her feet"; and he quotes a friend of her teaching days as remarking, "Had she been a man, any one of those fine girls of sixteen, who surrounded her here, would have married her: they were all in love with her, she understood them so well."[12] In her journal, Margaret comments significantly upon the powerful attachment one woman may feel for another:

> It is so true that a woman may be in love with a woman, and a man with a man. I like to feel sure of it, for it is the same love which the angels feel, where—
> "Sie fragen nicht nach Mann und Weib."
> It is regulated by the same law as that of love between persons of different sexes; only it is purely intellectual and spiritual . . . I loved ———, for a time, with as much

> passion as I was then strong enough to feel . . . I do not love her now with passion, but I still feel towards her as I can to no other woman.[13]

Waiving altogether the question of whether such a love as Margaret Fuller was capable of stimulating towards herself was healthful for Elizabeth Peabody, we know positively that it gave her own career a set-back. Elizabeth Peabody was ambitious to make a literary reputation; Theodore Parker who knew both women well, thought her more talented than Miss Fuller.[14] Yet to invite Margaret Fuller to give "conversations" in her bookshop meant that Elizabeth Peabody yielded a right to which she had prior claim, having herself conducted "conversations" in 1833 and 1836.[15] It must have been a severe test of her devotion to Margaret Fuller to see the latter's talks enormously successful, so that they were repeated for five successive winters.[16] Not only did Elizabeth's affection survive this test, however, but it withstood the more severe one of Margaret Fuller's scorn—since Margaret might have been expected to be at least grateful to her worshipper. Miss Fuller's attitude was so contemptuous and so obviously unfair that it called forth a rebuke from Doctor W. E. Channing:

> Miss Fuller, when I consider that you are all Miss P. wished to be, and that you despise her, and that she loves and honours you, I think her place in Heaven must be very high.[17]

Yet far from changing her attitude, Channing's rebuke seems to have aroused her ill-will, for during the *Dial* days she tried to dissuade Emerson from publishing anything of Elizabeth Peabody's, as a postscript to one of her letters of April, 1842, reveals:

> Let me before I forget it guard you, if need be, against trusting E.P.P. to write the slightest notice or advertisement. I never saw anything like her for impossibility of being clear and accurate in a brief space.[18]

Boston was not big enough, apparently, in Miss Fuller's estimation, to support two women of genius.

Now, when Hawthorne's fiancée, Sophia Peabody, came up to Boston, she too fell under the influence of the glamorous Margaret. And her admiration for this exotic was as great as her sister's. Indeed, when Sophia, on May 11, 1842, confided to Margaret Fuller by letter her wedding plans, she enclosed a sonnet addressed "To a Priestess of the Temple not Made with Hands" which closes with this couplet:

> Behold! I reverent stand before thy shrine
> In recognition of thy words divine.[19]

Hawthorne, whose visits to Sophia at the West Street home were doubtless impeded by the "conversationalists," early resented the hold that Margaret Fuller had upon the affections of the sisters, as one of his love letters to Sophia indicates: "And what wilt thou do to-day, persecuted little Dove, when thy abiding place will be a Babel of talkers? Would that Miss Margaret Fuller might lose her tongue! or my Dove her ears, and so be left wholly to her husband's golden silence!"[20] Thereafter the novelist made persistent efforts to break Sophia's infatuation, not by direct assault, but by making Margaret Fuller appear arrogant or ridiculous. Perhaps the most memorable of these efforts was the letter whch he addressed Sophia from Brook Farm on April 16, 1841:

> Belovedest, the herd has rebelled against the usurpation of Miss Fuller's heifer... She is not an amiable cow; but she has a very intelligent face, and seems to be of a reflective cast of character. I doubt not that she will soon perceive the expediency of being on good terms with the rest of the sisterhood....[21]

Hawthorne's hand is revealed to us when we learn from Higginson that this heifer did not exist.[22]

Yet in time Hawthorne seems to have become reconciled to Sophia's admiration for Margaret Fuller; after he and Sophia were married, they frequently entertained Margaret at the Old Manse in Concord,[23] and Hawthorne even seems to have enjoyed her company.[24] Mrs. Hawthorne was to tell a "truth" to Margaret about her husband which was to make Margaret "feel more like a sister to H... than with any man before."[25] Moreover, Margaret Fuller was on such good terms with the Hawthornes that, in view of their poverty, she dared to suggest, in August, 1842, that they take her brother-in-law and his wife, Ellery Channing and Ellen Fuller Channing, as boarders at the Old Manse. Mrs. Hawthorne rather favored the plan, but Hawthorne vetoed it very diplomatically: "Dear Margaret:... Had it been proposed to Adam and Eve to receive two angels into their paradise, as *boarders*, I doubt whether they would have been pleased to consent...."[26]

Despite Miss Fuller's treatment of Elizabeth Peabody and despite Hawthorne's wariness, there might never have been an explosion had it not been for Ellery Channing. Even in the most judicious view this man was something of an ass. Apparently supported throughout his life by wealthy relatives,[27] he devoted himself entirely to poetry and peripatetics. Failing to secure lodgings with the Hawthornes, he settled in a house belonging to Thoreau and soon was talking and walking the elite of Concord—Thoreau, Emerson, and Hawthorne—out of breath.[28] Emerson called him a "Hamlet in the Fields." Hawthorne, though he was forced to tag along, frankly did not greatly admire Ellery Channing. The most unflattering analysis of the poet appears in the *Note-books:*

> He is one of those queer and clever young men whom Mr. Emerson... is continually picking up by way of a genius. There is nothing very peculiar about him—some originality and self-inspiration in his character, but none, or very little, in his intellect. Nevertheless, the lad himself seems to feel as if he were a genius.... I like him well enough, however; but after all, these originals in a small way, after one has seen a few of them, become more dull and commonplace than even those who keep the ordinary pathway of life....[29]

Sophia Hawthorne, however, had known Ellery Channing for a long time, having once been under the medical care of his father, Dr. Walter Channing,[30] and was much more favorably disposed towards him than was her husband.

When Hawthorne recorded in his *Note-book* that, as a companion, Ellery Channing was "but a poor substitute for Mr. Thoreau,"[31] Sophia wrote in the journal of April 23, 1843:

> I think perhaps he will prove more worthy and interesting a companion than thou supposed, dearest husband. He has to me a pleasanter way of saying things than Mr. Thoreau, because so wholly without the air of saying anything of consequence.

She and Ellery had a common interest in painting, both having studied under Washington Allston;[32] but perhaps the fact that Ellery had married Margaret Fuller's sister was as powerful an influence with Mrs. Hawthorne as any. It is significant that when Sophia Hawthorne edited the novelist's *Note-books* after his death she deleted the hostile passage on Ellery Channing. Elizabeth Peabody declared that Mrs. Hawthorne "was for some years the single influence that tamed Ellery Channing."[33] But we shall see how appreciative he was of that influence.

Ellery, whose real nature was fond, obsequious, sycophantical, and weak, made every effort to court Hawthorne's favor, as he did that of other prominent literary men.[34] Mrs. Hawthorne records in the journal, May 23, 1843, "Ellery shines, and seems perfectly to idolize my darling husband." In "Poems of the Heart" Ellery draws a portrait of "Hawthorne in the Old Manse" that is meant to be wholly flattering. The lines—

> New England's Chaucer, Hawthorne fitly lives,
> The gentlest man that kindly Nature drew.[35]

possibly gave rise to the legend that Hawthorne was a "gentle Fanny," so often repeated by other poets of the day.[36] A total misconception of his character, these lines must have irked the novelist, for the poet hastened to write another tribute to him, this time addressing him as "Count Julian"—a reference to that stalwart hero of Spain during the Moorish invasions, whom Landor had made the central figure in a verse drama. Now Hawthorne's "pure, slight form" that had "a true Grecian charm"[37] is conceded to be "Yet sinewy, and capable of action."[38] This and the assertion that—

> ... neither time nor place nor poet's pen
> Nor sculptor's chisel e'er can mould again

a figure like Hawthorne's so won the savage ironist's heart that he somewhat unbent towards Ellery, and modesty not permitting him to name his son after himself (as Mrs. Hawthorne doubtless would have wanted) he named him Julian Hawthorne!

In passing, it is worth noting that Ellery Channing's effusive praise of Hawthorne's genius was not sincere, and that privately he was jealous of Hawthorne's success. He remarked to Emerson, and the latter faithfully recorded it in his *Journal* that "he is a lucky man who can write in bulk forty pages on a hiccough, ten pages on a man's sitting down in a chair, like Hawthorne, etc., that will go."[39] Meanwhile Hawthorne, probably intending to do Ellery a kindness, had put the latter in the introductory sketch of *Mosses from an Old Manse*. He recalled fishing excursions with him on the Assabeth river, in which their talk gushed "like the babble of a fountain." Then he thoughtlessly, but truthfully added:

> The evanescent spray was Ellery's; and his, too, the lumps of golden thought that lay glimmering in the fountain's bed and brightened both our faces by the reflection. Could he have drawn out that virgin gold, and stamped it with the mint-mark that alone gives currency, the world might have had the profit, and he the fame. My mind was richer merely by the knowledge that it was there. . . .[40]

In "P's Correspondence," later in the book, Hawthorne applies what he has here said about Ellery Channing's talk to the latter's poetry as well:

> . . . some of the poems have a richness that is not merely of the surface, but glows still the brighter the deeper and more faithfully you look into them. They seem carelessly wrought, however, like those rings and ornaments of the very purest gold, but of rude, native manufacture which are found among the gold dust from Africa. I doubt whether the American public will accept them; it looks less to the assay of metal than to the neat and cunning manufacture.[41]

And finally, in "Earth's Holocaust" the novelist places Ellery in the flattering company of Shelley, Lord Byron, and Tom Moore, when they consign their writings to the everlasting flames. In the case of the American versifier, however, Hawthorne's comment is shaped by the awareness that two poems in the latter's volume are addressed to himself. Fire surely would not affect these verses as it did the others:

> I especially remember that a great deal of inflammability was exhibited in a thin volume of poems by Ellery Channing; although to speak the truth, there were certain portions that hissed and spluttered in a very disagreeable fashion.[42]

It is clear that these gratuitous allusions to Ellery and his poetry in *Mosses from an Old Manse* are the efforts of an older and better established writer to call attention to his junior and to administer at the same time a friendly reprimand for slovenly workmanship so that the junior might realize some of the promise that his friends saw in him; nevertheless Ellery missed the intention and felt only the criticism. He may have been able to conceal his fancied injury, but it rankled with him and later provided the poison which unhinged his reason.

After Hawthorne became famous in the world and notorious in Salem through the publication of *The Scarlet Letter* and withdrew to Lenox in the Berkshires to work, Ellery Channing visited him there and Hawthorne took at least one more walk with him.[43] The novelist, however, had felt the success of his book was more or less a fluke and was anxious to realize from his popularity with the reading public before he lost favor. *The House of Seven Gables* and *A Wonder Book* were written prior to Ellery's visit; Hawthorne had other projects in view, including the removal of his family to West Newton, and it seems likely that, without intentional brusqueness, he may have intimated to Ellery that he was too busy for further peripatetics. This is conjecture, but what followed is not.

Thoroughly hurt, and suddenly aware of his old wound, Ellery Channing penned a protest to Hawthorne entitled an "Unfaithful Friendship" in which he makes the novelist say to the poet:

> Thy silly jests for idlers' ears are fit
> And only silence complements thy wit.
> I love thee at arm's-length; my quarantine
> Declares pacific measures, and divine.
> I would it were not so—poor helpless thing,
> That like a blue jay can but shriek or sing
> Those lamentable ditties that refuse
> To call themselves productions of the Muse!
> Nay! walk not with me in the curling wood!
> I stride abroad in quest of solitude.
> I love my friends far off; when they come near,
> Too warm! too warm the crowded atmosphere.[44]

For this product of injured sensibility Channing might have been forgiven had he not stupidly and with deplorably bad manners accused Mrs. Hawthorne of being responsible (as he fancied) for the novelist's change of attitude towards him. He makes the "unfaithful friend" say:

> . . . sad Poet! what art thou to me?
> More—I have married an angelic wife,
> Who wreathes with roses my enchanted life;
> Thou art superfluous—come not thou too near!

This was not only execrably bad taste but sheer madness, for had he known Hawthorne, he would have realized the latter could never overlook this. Hawthorne would strike back and strike through the one where the blow would hurt most. The novelist never forgave an injury. Mr. Lee, one of the Inspectors in the Salem's Custom House, "a notorious liar,"[45] Hawthorne savagely lampooned in *The Scarlet Letter* as a creature possessing but a "very trifling admixture of moral and spiritual ingredients . . . in barely enough measure to keep the old gentleman from walking on all fours"[46]—all because he suspected the old gentleman of complicity in his own dismissal. Further, he retained this picture after Mr. Lee's death,[47] blandly asserting in the Preface to the Second Edition,

> It appears to him, that the only remarkable features of the sketch are its frank and genuine good humor, and the general accuracy with which he has conveyed his sincere impressions of the characters therein described. As to enmity or ill feeling of any kind, personal or political, he utterly disclaims such motives.

This ill assorts with his letter to his publisher, Fields, on March 7, 1850, before the book was issued, "I shall catch it pretty smartly from my ill-wishers here in Salem on the score of this old Inspector . . ."[48] The Reverend Mr. Charles Upham, who was connected with the same affair in Hawthorne's mind, was made hideous as Judge Pyncheon in *The House of Seven Gables*.[49] With the passage of time the fierceness of Hawthorne's temper has been forgotten. He was irresistible when aroused, and a frightened skipper with whom he had a run-in at Salem is said to have demanded of the authorities, "What in God's name have you sent on board my ship as an inspector?"[50] In "Monsieur du Miroir," a self-analytical study, he speaks of a temper that sometimes rose "to blood heat, fever heat, or boiling water heat, according to the measure of wrong which might seem to have fallen entirely on myself."[51] Not without cause his publisher used to call him a "boned pirate."[52] Ellery Channing knew not what he had baited.

Hawthorne's opportunity to strike indirectly and to hurt came with the death of Margaret Fuller from drowning off Fire Island on July 19, 1850. Miss Fuller, after editing the *Dial,* had gone to New York to work for Greeley on the *Tribune*. There she had fallen in love with a young Jew, James Nathan, and when he had gone abroad, had followed him with the intention of joining him in Europe, only to discover that he had (somewhat dishonorably) transferred his affections to another.[53] To forget this affair she had gone to Italy, plunged into the struggle for Italian freedom, and in the course of events met a young Italian marquis, whom she married and to whom she bore a child. The Marquis Ossoli, the wife, and son were lost when the *Elizabeth,* conveying them to America, was wrecked upon a sand bar in sight of land. Margaret died because she would not be parted from her husband and child.[54]

While the grief of relatives and friends "was yet green," Hawthorne published the devastating satire of Margaret Fuller found in *The Blithedale Romance*. As in the case of *The Scarlet Letter*, he again avowed his innocence so far as any personal satire was concerned.[55] Yet no one of any intelligence was deceived by this. "Zenobia," says Thomas Wentworth Higginson, "in Hawthorne's *Blithedale Romance*. . . . will be identified with Margaret Fuller while the literature of the English language is read."[56] And that is precisely what Hawthorne intended. For the materials of his story Hawthorne reverted to his Brook Farm experiences—that communistic colony which only he joined after Emerson, Margaret Fuller, and Elizabeth Peabody discussed it enthusiastically.[57] Margaret Fuller was never an active Associationist, not being willing to do the work required there,[58] yet she spent a surprising amount of time at Brook Farm where she held "conversations" and led discussions.[59] For Hawthorne's purposes this was enough to connect her with the Farm.

In *The Blithedale Romance*, Zenobia, represented as an ardent champion of woman's rights, exerts a powerful fascination upon the younger members of her own sex. "A brilliant woman," comments Hawthorne, "is often the object of the devoted admiration—it might almost be termed worship or idolatry—of some young girl,"[60] and he makes this the magnetism in his story which has drawn a little seamstress from Boston to the bleak farm community to worship at the feet of the militant feminist, Zenobia. Who can doubt that he had in mind Margaret Fuller's influence over his own wife, over Elizabeth Peabody, and over other women, any more than that he had in mind Miss Fuller's championship of woman's rights in *Woman in the Nineteenth Century* when he drew the character of Zenobia? As the story unfolds itself, Priscilla, the seamstress, substitutes for this unnatural love for Zenobia a strong passion for Hollingsworth, the blind philanthropist at the head of the community. The result is that Zenobia, who also loves Hollingsworth with a wild and unrestrained ardor, commits suicide by drowning herself in the brook behind the farm—a death which must forcibly have reminded his readers of Margaret Fuller's end.

To be doubly sure that every reader made the identification he desired, Hawthorne reinforced the similarity of Zenobia and Margaret Fuller at every possible point—that is, at every point he could without flatly declaring the portraiture. For example, Zenobia not only resembles Margaret Fuller physically but is represented as always wearing exotic flowers in her hair—a habit of Miss Fuller's.[61] When Priscilla first engages the attention of Hollingsworth, Hawthorne says that he caught on the face of Zenobia "a look that would have made the fortune of a tragic actress could she have borrowed it for the moment when she fumbles in her bosom for the concealed dagger...." Then he dismisses this fancy, for this is New England *not Italy*[62] —the country indissoluably connected with Margaret Fuller's name. As it develops in the story that Priscilla is half-sister to Zenobia, the narrator is suddenly struck with the resemblance of Priscilla to Margaret Fuller—here named specifically.[63]

Those who have made a study of the story have neglected altogether the central episode where a man by the name of Westervelt, a flashy, disagreeable stranger, comes to Blithedale, talks with Zenobia, then later as a spiritualist uses Priscilla for a medium in a seance—until Hollingsworth breaks up the show and rescues the maiden. This is not a satire of an actual event, but it is an elaborate takeoff of an extended passage in one of Margaret Fuller's popular books. In her *Summer on the Lakes*, published in 1844, Miss Fuller tells of reading a narrative by Justinus Kerner, called *The Seeress of Prevost*, and then writes a dialogue between herself, as Free Hope, and Good Sense, Old Church, and Self Poise, on the merits of Spiritualism, in which she defends it, remarking, "You sometimes need such a field in which to wander vagrant."[64] She then adds that in the New West where she is, "the Germans, the Norwegians, the Swedes" bring the mysticism of the Old World to the New and make a belief in it more plausible.[65] Now Hawthorne got the name *Westervelt* from the list of those lost on the ship *Elizabeth* where the record is: "Henry Westervelt, seaman (Swede)."[66] Thus the whole episode makes it clear that Hawthorne's malice was aimed chiefly at Margaret Fuller.

The most reprehensible part of the satire in *The Blithedale Romance* hints broadly at Margaret Fuller's early and unfortunate love affairs, first with Sam Ward, who betrayed her,[67] and then with Nathan, who deserted her. Of Zenobia, Hawthorne writes:

> One subject, about which—very impertinently, moreover—I perplexed myself with a great many conjectures, was, whether Zenobia had ever been married.... If the great event of woman's existence had been consummated, the world knew nothing of it, although the world seemed to know Zenobia well.[68]

And he concludes, "Zenobia is a wife—Zenobia has lived and loved!"[69] —a conclusion he lets the events of the book reinforce. Malice, in lieu of any evidence, could go no further than the insinuations of *The Blithedale Romance*. However much Hawthorne resented the verses of Ellery Channing, he had no justification for this.

Thus in *The Blithedale Romance,* which both Henry Adams and Henry James have praised for its literary merits beyond the novelist's other books, Hawthorne took the fullest possible vengeance for his wounded feelings. From the deep he drew the body of Margaret Fuller and abused it to torment her relatives who had attacked him through his wife. But he did this with a temerity of which only he was conscious, for the man at heart was a devout Puritan, a firm believer, as story after story of his proves, that vengeance belongs to the Lord. Hence there remains a chapter to be added to the tale.

Hawthorne had enjoyed his revenge for but a few weeks[70] when a most awful punishment was visited upon him, best described by Sophia Hawthorne in a letter to Mrs. Peabody, on Friday, July 30, 1852:

> My dearest Mother,—This morning we received the shocking intelligence that Louisa Hawthorne [the novelist's favorite sister] was lost in the destruction of the steamer *Henry Clay* on the Hudson on Wednesday, July 27. She has been at Saratoga Springs and with Mr. Deke for a fortnight, and was returning by way of New York, and we expected her here for a long visit . . .
> . . . All at once he [Julian] got up and went to the study—he had the intention of consoling his father . . . but his father had gone on the hill. . . .

Hawthorne was seen no more that day according to his son, and according to Conway (who married his wife's cousin) was "greatly affected" by Louisa's tragic death[71] —she had died from *drowning* after leaping from the burning boat, it was later learned. More indicative of the effect upon Hawthorne, however, is the fact that he wrote no more fiction for six years, and then was uncertain and ineffective in his work. Yet in the end his hatred still burned, increased perhaps by resentment, and in the *Italian Note-books* he pronounced a judgment upon Margaret Fuller's character which remains a permanent clue to his own. Pettiness, vindictiveness, and superstition, rather than sexual perversion, are the explanation. No wonder Emerson, who knew all the facts, hoped some day the man would display "a purer power"[72] than he ever did. Force and subtlety are in the novelist, but charity and justice are lacking. He is not here indicted; he indicted himself.[73]

Notes

1. First published by Julian Hawthorne in *Hawthorne and His Wife* (Boston: Houghton, Mifflin, 1885), I, 259–262. F. T. Fuller, nephew of Margaret Fuller, in a communication addressed to the *Literary World* (XVI, 11–15), of 10 January 1885, writes, "Biographers have not often the will, even if the power, to inflict such wounds as the friends and relatives of Margaret Fuller Ossoli have received at the hand of the compiler of the recently issued memoir of *Nathaniel Hawthorne and His Wife* . . . I think I do Mr. Julian Hawthorne only simple justice in saying that his publication

of this extract is to be ascribed to no other cause than that he is not one to spoil a sensation to save a friend."

2. Katherine Anthony, *Margaret Fuller, A Psychological Biography* (New York: Harcourt, Brace, and Howe, 1920), p. 92.

3. "Pearl kissed his lips. A spell was broken. The great scene of grief, in which the wild infant bore a part, *had developed all her sympathies....*" *The Scarlet Letter,* ed. M. S. L. (New York, 1919), p. 263. See pp. 267–268 for Pearl's later *normal* life.

4. For Hawthorne's reading see George Parsons Lathrop, *A Study of Hawthorne* (Boston: James R. Osgood, 1876), pp. 164–165 and Appendix. For his Calvinism, see Austin Warren, *Nathaniel Hawthorne: Representative Selections* (New York: American Book Company, 1934), pp. xix–xxxiv.

5. So Julian Hawthorne, *Hawthorne and His Wife,* quoting *American Note-books,* 29 July 1849. Cf. *The American Notebooks,* ed. Randall Stewart (New Haven: Yale University Press, 1932), pp. 206–210.

6. Boston *Daily Advertiser,* 27 November 1834.

7. Letter to Dr. Hedge, 6 March 1835. See Thomas Wentworth Higginson, *Margaret Fuller Ossoli* (Boston: Houghton, Mifflin, 1884), pp. 48–50.

8. *Hawthorne and His Wife,* I, 195.

9. Lathrop, *Hawthorne,* p. 181; *Hawthorne and His Wife,* I, 195–199.

10. Alcott's unpublished diary, 2 August 1836. Quoted, Higginson, *Margaret Fuller Ossoli,* p. 74.

11. Higginson, *Margaret Fuller Ossoli,* pp. 75–80.

12. [Ralph Waldo Emerson, William Henry Channing, and James Freeman Clarke], *Memoirs of Margaret Fuller Ossoli* (Boston: Phillips, Sampson, 1852), I, 281.

13. *Memoirs,* I, 283–284.

14. F. B. Sanborn, *Recollections of Seventy Years* (Boston: Richard G. Badger, 1909), II, 548. Quotation from Parker's journal of 1839 in Clarence L. F. Gohdes, *The Periodicals of American Transcendentalism* (Durham: Duke University Press, 1931), p. 144.

15. Gohdes, *Periodicals,* p. 146; Henry Barnard, *American Journal of Education* (Hartford), XXX, 584 ff.

16. Higginson, *Margaret Fuller Ossoli,* p. 114.

17. *Journals of Ralph Waldo Emerson,* ed. Edward Waldo Emerson and Waldo Emerson Forbes (Boston: Houghton Mifflin, 1909–1914), VIII, 118.

18. Gohdes, *Periodicals,* p. 71, quoting M. F. Ossoli MSS, in Boston Public Library.

19. *American Notebooks,* ed. Stewart, p. 315, quoting a letter in the Harvard Library.

20. *American Notebooks,* ed. Stewart, pp. 293–294, quoting *Love Letters of Nathaniel Hawthorne 1839–1841* (Chicago: Society of the Dofobs, 1907), I, 232.

21. *American Note-books,* ed. Sophia Hawthorne (Boston: Houghton, Mifflin, 1883), p. 229.

22. Higginson, *Margaret Fuller Ossoli,* p. 179.

23. *Memoirs,* I, 218; *American Notebooks,* ed. Stewart, pp. 159, 169, 315. F. T. Fuller, who corroborates this from Margaret's diary, adds that she took care of the baby Una while Hawthorne and Sophia went out for walks. Of Una, Margaret wrote, "Next to little Waldo [Emerson], I love her better than any child I ever saw" (*Literary World,* XVI, 12).

24. *American Notebooks,* ed. Stewart, pp. 160, 315, 317.

25. *American Notebooks,* ed. Stewart, p. 315; also F. T. Fuller, *Literary World,* XVI, 11–15.

26. *Hawthorne and His Wife,* I, 252–256; Moncure D. Conway, *Life of Nathaniel Hawthorne* (London: Walter Scott, 1890), p. 95.

27. Ellery Channing, *Poems of Sixty-five Years,* ed. F. B. Sanborn (Philadelphia and Concord: James H. Bentley, 1902), pp. xiv, xix–xx, xliii.

28. Channing, *Poems*, pp. xxxv–xxxviii.

29. *American Notebooks*, ed. Stewart, p. 168.

30. *American Notebooks*, ed. Stewart, p. 312.

31. *American Notebooks*, ed. Stewart, p. 175.

32. *Hawthorne and His Wife*, I, 248; Channing, *Poems*, pp. xx–xxi; see also *American Notebooks*, ed. Stewart, p. 312.

33. *Hawthorne and His Wife*, I, 64.

34. "I have but one reason for settling in one place in America; it is because you are there." Channing to Emerson, *Poems*, p. xx. See also pp. 87, 104–127, 137, 175, etc.

35. Channing, *Poems*, p. 111. This poem is No. I in "Poems of the Heart" in *Poems: Second Series* (Boston: James Munroe, 1847), pp. 108–110, where its position indicates the poet's affection for the novelist.

36. For example, in Lowell's *A Fable for Critics*, 11. 226–243, and Holmes' "At the Saturday Club," 11. 105–120. These men were not intimate with Hawthorne.

37. See Walter Savage Landor, "Count Julian," *The Works and Life of Walter Savage Landor* (London, 1876), VII, 45–100.

38. Channing, *Poems of Sixty-five Years*, p. 113. This poem is No. VII in *Poems: Second Series*, pp. 114–115.

39. *Journals*, VIII, 257.

40. *The Works of Nathaniel Hawthorne* (Boston: Houghton, Mifflin, 1882), II, 27–31.

41. *Works*, II, 149. Called to my attention by N. F. Adkins, whose knowledge of Hawthorne has been of great service to me.

42. *Works*, II, 170.

43. 29 October 1851, *American Note-books*, ed. Hawthorne, p. 408; the Hawthornes left Lenox on 21 November 1851.

44. Channing, *Poems of Sixty-five Years*, pp. 118–119. The poem is not addressed to Hawthorne by name, yet there is no escaping the fact that it was addressed to him. It is one of the group called "Poems of the Heart," in which the poet pays tribute to Emerson, Hawthorne, Alcott, Elizabeth Hoar, and Thoreau—one of whom is meant as an unfaithful friend. No quarrel can be shown with the others; indeed, in later life Channing wrote tributes to all the others save Hawthorne. On the other hand, it can be shown that Hawthorne changed his attitude towards Ellery Channing between 1850 and 1856. In the "Custom-House" sketch in *The Scarlet Letter* (1850), p. 25, Hawthorne refers to Ellery very much as he had done in *Mosses from an Old Manse*, but in the *English Note-books* (Boston: Fields, Osgood, 1870), entry for 5 April 1856, Hawthorne writes, "As for Mr. Douglas Jerrold, he often reminded me of E—— C——, in the rich veins of the latter, both by his face and expression, and by a tincture of something at once wise and humorously absurd in what he said. But I think he has a kinder, more genial, wholesomer nature than E——."

Further, the portrait fits the novelist. Who loved solitude, retirement, etc., more than Hawthorne? Note that, in line 3 of the poem, Channing calls the unfaithful friend "the Student"— an epithet like "a scholar of rare worth" in line 4 of "Hawthorne in the Old Manse." None other of the group is called student or scholar. Note especially how appropriate to Hawthorne, because of his connection with the Salem Custom House, is the phrase, "my quarantine."

Moreover, the unfaithful friend had some connection with Lenox, where Ellery visited Hawthorne. The sonnet, "An Estranged Friend," which immediately precedes "Unfaithful Friendship," "was written, says the manuscript, 'in the road between L. and S.,' which I take to be Lenox and Stockbridge. The year must have been 1845 or 1846" (Sanborn's headnote). Sanborn was unaware that Channing was in Lenox in 1851. Discretion would not have kept the poem out of the 1847 volume of Channing's verse had it been written at that time.

45. *American Notebooks*, ed. Stewart, p. 123.

46. *The Scarlet Letter*, pp. 15–17.

47. William B. Cairns, *A History of American Literature* (New York: Oxford University Press, 1912), p. 312.

48. Conway, *Hawthorne*, p. 106.

49. *American Notebooks*, ed. Stewart, pp. liv, 228.

50. Conway, *Hawthorne*, p. 106.

51. Hawthorne, *Works*, II, 174.

52. Conway, *Hawthorne*, p. 92. This is also attributed to Tom Appleton.

53. See *Love-Letters of Margaret Fuller 1845–1846*, with an introduction by Julia Ward Howe (New York: Appleton, 1903); Margaret Bell, *Margaret Fuller* (New York: Boni, 1930), pp. 171–208.

54. *Memoirs*, II, 341–352.

55. "These characters . . . are entirely fictitious. It would, indeed (considering how few amiable qualities he distributes among his imaginary progeny), be a most grievous wrong to his former excellent associates, were the author to allow it to be supposed he has been sketching any of their likenesses . . ." Preface, *The Blithedale Romance* in *Works*, II, vii.

56. Higginson, *Margaret Fuller Ossoli*, p. 173. F. T. Fuller accepts the identification.

57. The first discussion of the project was at Emerson's with Alcott, Miss Fuller, and George Ripley in attendance (Higginson, *Margaret Fuller Ossoli*, pp. 180–181). Miss Fuller, after a first enthusiasm (*Memoirs*, I, 57), became skeptical (*Memoirs*, I, 72–75) much like Hawthorne himself later on. For Elizabeth Peabody, see: "A Glimpse of Christ's Idea of Society," *Dial*, II (October 1841), 214 ff.

58. "My position would be too uncertain here as I could not work." *Memoirs*, II, 75.

59. See *Memoirs*, II, 73–80; Higginson, *Margaret Fuller Ossoli*, pp. 179–186; Julia Ward Howe, *Margaret Fuller* (Boston: Roberts, 1883), pp. 97–99; Octavius Brooks Frothingham, *George Ripley* (Boston: Houghton, Mifflin, 1882), pp. 150–151.

60. *The Blithedale Romance*, p. 43.

61. At "receptions to literary friends" she presided as "a gracious hostess with a white japonica in her hair" (Higginson, *Margaret Fuller Ossoli*, p. 211). Note especially Miss Fuller's "flower sketches" written for the *Dial* and other magazines (see Higginson, pp. 96–97): "Inheriting a love of flowers. . . . she gave to them meanings and mysticisms of her own."

62. *The Blithedale Romance*, pp. 94–95.

63. *The Blithedale Romance*, p. 64.

64. *At Home and Abroad*, ed. Arthur B. Fuller (Boston: Crosby, Nichols, 1856), pp. 69–75.

65. *At Home and Abroad*, p. 75.

66. *At Home and Abroad*, p. 451.

67. Bell, *Fuller*, pp. 113–115. Note that Margaret in the company of Sam Ward once called upon the Hawthornes (*American Notebooks*, ed. Stewart, p. 169).

68. *The Blithedale Romance*, pp. 57–58.

69. *The Blithedale Romance*, p. 59.

70. He finished the novel, 1 May 1852, and read proof on it throughout May (*American Notebooks*, ed. Stewart, p. 335). It was apparently published in June 1852.

71. Conway, *Hawthorne*, p. 143.

72. 24 May 1864, *Journals*, X, 40.

73. Ellery Channing had the final word in the controversy, but was so weak that he could not make up his mind whether it was expedient to assail Hawthorne or not. Consequently, under "Personalities" in his *Thoreau: The Poet-Naturalist* (Boston: Roberts, 1873) he writes of the novelist: ". . . He [Thoreau] wasted none of his precious jewels, his moments, upon epistles to the class of Rosa Matilda invalids, some of whom like leeches fastened upon his homely cuticle, but did not draw. Of this gilt vermoulu, the sugar-gingerbread of Sympathy, Hawthorne had as much. There was a blank simper, an insufficient sort of affection, at your petted sorrow, in the story-teller—more

consoling than the boiled macaroni of pathos. Hawthorne—swallowed up in the wretchedness of life, in that sardonic puritan element that drips from the elms of his birthplace—thought it inexpressibly ridiculous that anyone should notice man's miseries, these being his staple product. . . . It is believed that Hawthorne truly admired Thoreau. A vein of humor had they both; and when they laughed, like Shelley, the operation was sufficient to split a pitcher. Hawthorne could have said: 'People live as long in Pepper Alley as on Salisbury Plain; and they live so much happier than an inhabitant of the first would, if he turned cottager, starve his understanding for want of conversation and perish in a state of mental inferiority.' Henry would never have believed it . . . [Thoreau] never went to nor voted at a town meeting . . . nor often did things he could not understand. In these respects Hawthorne mimicked him. The Concord novelist was a handsome, bulky character, with a soft, rolling gait. A wit said he seemed like a *boned pirate*. Shy and awkward, he dreaded the stranger in his gates; while, as inspector, he was employed to swear oaths *versus* English colliers. When surveyor, finding rum sent to the African coast was watered, he vowed he would not ship another gill if it was anything but pure proof spirit. Such was his justice to the oppressed. One of the things he most dreaded was to be looked at after he was dead. Being at a friend's demise, of whose extinction he had the care, he enjoyed—as if it had been a scene in some old Spanish novel—his success in keeping the waiters from stealing the costly wines sent in to the sick. Careless of heat and cold indoors, he lived in an aeolian-harp house, that could not be warmed: that he entered it by a trap door from a ladder is false. Lovely, amiable, and charming, his absent-mindedness passed for unsocial when he was hatching a new tragedy. As a writer he loves the morbid and lame. The "Gentle Boy" and "Scarlet Letter" eloped with the girls' boarding schools. His reputation is master of his literary taste. His characters are not drawn from life; plots and thoughts are often dreary, as he was himself in some lights. . . ." (pp. 257–259).

# "Hawthorne, Margaret Fuller, and 'Nemesis'"

Austin Warren[*]

Professor Cargill's spirited article (*PMLA*, LII, 848–862) emits heat as well as light; much of the "rancor" developed during the literary quarrel which he chronicles has transferred itself to the chronicler. In final intent he designs, apparently, to show Hawthorne's capacities for hatred and revenge, and to represent Margaret Fuller as the novelist's victim; but, if such be the intent, it is blurred by apparent spleen toward "Margaret" and her brother-in-law, Ellery Channing, as well as toward Hawthorne: unintentionally, perhaps, Cargill leaves the final impression that all three were rather unlovely specimens, and all the contestants got about what they deserved. The article, albeit fully documented, sometimes wrests evidence, offers conjectures as authoritative, and advances "views" necessarily unprovable. I should like to add a few disagreements and assents.

The passages cited (in note 14) do not establish that Parker thought Miss Peabody more talented than Miss Fuller. We learn from Higginson, says Cargill, that the famous Fullerian heifer (disclosed in the *American Note-Books*) did not exist outside of Hawthorne's perverse imagination. But the same Higginson reports (*Margaret Fuller Ossoli*, p. 179) that "Mr. Ripley, founder of Brook Farm, was fond of naming his cattle after his friends, and may, very likely, have found among them a Margaret Fuller." The long passage quoted (in note 73) from Ellery Channing seems neither vindictive assailment nor obsequious flattery: it is a not unpenetrating interpretation, and can hardly be cited as evidence for Ellery's pettiness of character.

The causes—or the ingredients—of Hawthorne's dislike for Margaret were various. Cargill's article convinces me that a chief cause was the magnetic influence Margaret exerted over the Peabody sisters, especially the future Mrs. Hawthorne. But it should be added that Hawthorne did not, in general, like "literary" people, that he had a persistent distrust of Transcendentalists and distaste for their "mystical" diction and their "progressive" doctrines, and finally that he heartily disapproved of feminists, including his sister-in-law, Elizabeth Peabody.[1]

Cargill overstates and oversimplifies Hawthorne's relation to Margaret. He

---

[*]Austin Warren, "Hawthorne, Margaret Fuller, and 'Nemesis,'" *PMLA*, 54 (June 1939), 472–476; reprinted by permission of the Modern Language Association of America.

asserts, as fact, that the two first clashed in 1834 over an article by George Bancroft; but the evidence offered is slight and unconvincing. That "H" of Salem, defending Bancroft's article against Margaret's attack, was Hawthorne rests upon no stronger ground than that, five years after, Bancroft gave Hawthorne a post under him in the Boston Custom House. "In her first relationship with the novelist," writes Cargill, "Margaret Fuller served him rather well, but at the same time she acquired a knowledge of his willingness to truckle which she could put to use later if she chose." What does this mean? Miss Fuller did not attribute the letter to Hawthorne; "I flatter myself," she says, that it was "by some big-wig,"—assuredly not a term applicable to Hawthorne before the publication of *Twice-Told Tales;* and Hawthorne's "willingness to truckle" exists, to the best of my knowledge, only in Cargill's mind. In the next place, the *Blithedale Romance* is not a "devastating satire" of Miss Fuller; and I see no reason to think that Hawthorne deliberately waited till her death for his "opportunity to strike indirectly and to hurt" Ellery Channing[2] or that he intended "to pillory" Margaret for all time, or that he drew from the deep the body of Margaret and "abused it to torment her relatives. . ." These are not matters that can be proved or disproved. It is true that Hawthorne was a man of strong hostilities; but he was equally a man of strong friendships: if he took savage revenge upon Upham, he demonstrated his loyalty to Franklin Pierce when such loyalty had its liabilities. Furthermore, he satirized Upham and Lee while they were living; I cannot believe that, cold-bloodedly, he waited till Margaret's death to wreak revenge upon her.

In calling the tragic death of Hawthorne's sister Louisa a "nemesis" upon him for his treatment of Margaret, Cargill is of course falling—for melodramatic purposes—into the kind of "superstition" which he attributes to his victim; and when he attributes to Louisa's death the "fact" that Hawthorne "wrote no more fiction for six years, and then was uncertain and ineffective in his work," he is almost certainly mistaken. Though *The Marble Faun* cannot rank with *The Scarlet Letter*, it requires more than a negation or two for its disposal; and Cargill fails to mention that during most of the "six years" of silence Hawthorne was occupying, conscientiously and patiently, the consular office at Liverpool. Furthermore, Hawthorne's whole life, after his engagement to Sophia Peabody, was a sequence of practical extraversions alternating with creative introversions. He could not write when a farmer in West Roxbury or when a "weigher and gauger" in the Boston Custom House at Brook Farm. His three earlier Romances had been written not during his surveyorship at the Salem Custom House but after his dismissal from it. "Uncertain and ineffective" the posthumous Romances certainly are; but the causes have more to do with the Civil War, it seems, than with Louisa or Margaret.[3]

That Miss Fuller furnished the creative "hint" for Zenobia I do not doubt; and I find several of Cargill's additional corroborations plausible,—notably the fact that "Westervelt," the exotic name of Yankee Zenobia's husband (or lover) was that of a Swedish sailor who perished, with Margaret, at the sinking of the *Elizabeth*.

Though scholarship is sometimes heavy-handed in attempting equations of fictional characters with possible prototypes, the evidence for the equation of Zenobia with Margaret Fuller is varied in kind and convergent. Two testimonies seem to me of especial importance,—that of Margaret's nephew (*Literary World*, XVI, 11–15) and that of Henry James (*Hawthorne*, p. 78), who, himself a novelist, may be trusted to know the way in which the imagination transforms and transmutes hints from life. It is "tolerably manifest," writes James, having read the Fuller *Memoirs*, that Margaret "was, in his imagination, the starting-point of the figure of Zenobia; and Zenobia is, to my sense, Hawthorne's only very definite attempt at the representation of a character. The portrait is full of alteration and embellishment; but it has a greater reality, a greater abundance of detail, than any of his other figures, and the reality was a memory of the lady whom he had encountered in the Roxbury pastoral or among the woodwalks of Concord. . ."

The parellelisms between characterizations in the *Blithedale Romance* and in Hawthorne's final psychograph, published by his son in 1884, are striking. Says Coverdale: "I recognized no severe culture in Zenobia; her mind was full of weeds. I malevolently beheld the true character of the woman, passionate, luxurious, lacking simplicity, not deeply refined, incapable of pure and perfect taste." But of Zenobia, Coverdale also says: "Her poor little stories and tracts never half did justice to her intellect. . .", and "Passionate, self-willed, and imperious, she had a warm and generous nature." The reader is left with the choice of thinking that Hawthorne's view of Miss Fuller grew steadily more harsh (the *Blithedale Romance* representing no final estimate) or that Zenobia is, in character as well as physical appearance, a creative modification of her prototype. Certainly Zenobia is not a "devastating satire" of any one. She is no more villainess than heroine, but a turbulent personality of mixed egotism and benevolence, headstrong in purpose but, as befits the true woman, dominated by her affections. Said George Hillard, the Boston critic (*Hawthorne and His Wife*, I 448), "Zenobia is a splendid creature, and I wish there were more such rich and ripe women about."

Notes

1. I am considering Hawthorne's estimates of his Concord acquaintance in a Wisconsin dissertation, now in progress.

2. "Nemesis and Nathaniel Hawthorne," *PMLA*, 52 (September 1937), 857.

3. Julian Hawthorne, *Nathaniel Hawthorne and His Wife* (Boston: Houghton, Mifflin, 1885), II, 265.

# "Margaret Fuller—
# Transcendentalist Interpreter
# of German Literature"

Arthur R. Schultz[*]

A study of the work of Margaret Fuller as critic and interpreter of German authors is necessary to establish the influence of German literature, as distinct from theology and philosophy, in the complex of forces that went to make up American Transcendentalism. Men like Parker and Ripley were interested primarily in German Biblical scholarship, and none of the early group was so active as Margaret[1] in bringing German literature into the orbit of Transcendentalist interests.

In outward circumstances her life parallels that of Parker and Clarke. Of exactly their age, and reared in the liberal atmosphere of Cambridge, she was subjected to the same intellectual influences as were her clerical friends. The early schooling administered by her father in the classical languages, grammar, and composition, together with her own wide reading, gave her fully as thorough a literary grounding as her contemporaries were receiving in the halls of Harvard College. Even at the age of thirteen she impressed F. H. Hedge as being a remarkably energetic, robust personality, a mind of "mighty force."[2] She was, so to speak, an unofficial member of the famous Harvard Class of 1829, for she knew personally the students and professors who were identified with the new spirit. Besides Hedge—William Henry Channing and James F. Clarke among the students, and Professors Everett, Ticknor, Follen, Beck, and Gräter were her friends and mentors.[3] By 1832, at the age of twenty-two, she was ready to welcome the new European influences at that moment crowding in upon Unitarian Boston. Just as the young theologians in the Divinity School were responding to the pious emotion and high spirituality of Herder and Coleridge in the field of theology, so she became, about 1832, receptive to the warm, enthusiastic accounts of German literature then being trumpeted "by the wild bugle-call of Thomas Carlyle, in his romantic articles on Richter, Schiller, and Goethe."[4]

Apparently no man had so great a direct influence upon her as did the early Carlyle,[5] though Hedge, who had known her since 1823,[6] did much to

---

[*]Arthur R. Schultz, "Margaret Fuller—Transcendentalist Interpreter of German Literature," *Monatshefte für Deütschen Unterricht*, 34 (April 1942), 169–182; copyright 1942 by the Board of Regents of the University of Wisconsin System and reprinted by permission.

encourage her study of German literature. But personal considerations were a strong contributory factor; for as yet she had found no sphere of activity that engaged her active mind and her well-trained talents. Her first period of study of the German language and authors took the form of a release from the confines of her circumscribed existence.

> "For bitter months a heavy weight had been pressing on me,—the weight of deceived friendship. I could not be much alone,—a great burden of family cares pressed upon me; I was in the midst of society, and obliged to act my part there as well as I could. At that time I took up the study of German, and my progress was like the rebound of a string pressed almost to bursting. My mind being then in the highest state of action, heightened, by intellectual appreciation, every pang; and imagination, by prophetic power, gave to the painful present all the weight of as painful a future."[7]

She occupied herself with the masterpieces of French, Italian, Latin, and Spanish literature as well as with the German, but to her passionate and essentially romantic nature, it was soon evident that the recent German literature spoke more directly than any other.[8] Though self-taught,[9] she gained proficiency in reading in a short time, and thereafter immersed herself in a course of uninterrupted study of the greatest figures in German literature. Clarke reports in detail on her study of 1832:

> "I believe that in about three months from the time that Margaret commenced German, she was reading with ease the masterpieces of its literature. Within the year, she had read Goethe's Faust, Tasso, Iphigenia, Hermann and Dorothea, Elective Affinities, and Memoirs; Tieck's William Lovel, Prince Zerbino, and other works; Körner, Novalis,[10] and something of Richter; all of Schiller's principal dramas, and his lyric poetry . . . The thought and the beauty of this rich literature equally filled her mind and fascinated her imagination."[11]

During the years 1833–1836 Margaret tempered the monotony of farm life at Groton by turning, as often as she could, to her favorite studies, which continued throughout these years to be her German authors, Dr. Hedge and James Clarke lending her many volumes from their libraries. In addition to the continued study of the works mentioned above, she became acquainted with the following: Lessing's *Miss Sara Sampson, Emilia Galotti,* and *Minna von Barnhelm;* some of the tales and poems of Jean Paul, including *Titan;* Heine; the poems of Uhland; those works of Goethe which she had not previously read, principally *Wilhelm Meister,* the *Campagne in Frankreich* and *Kunst und Altertum,* and the *Italiänische Reise;* and Klopstock.[12]

By July, 1836, Margaret had made the acquaintance of Emerson. It was his opinion at the time when he wrote the *Memoirs* that she knew German books "more cordially than any other person.[13] Between 1834 and 1838 she demonstrated her thorough command of the language by successfully teaching it both in private and in Alcott's school.[14]

> "To one class I taught the German language, and thought it good success, when, at the end of three months, they could read twenty pages of German at a lesson, and very well. This class, of course, was not interesting, except in the way of observation and analysis of language.

> With more advanced pupils I read, in twenty-four weeks, Schiller's Don Carlos, Artists, and Song of the Bell, besides giving a sort of general lecture on Schiller; Goethe's Hermann and Dorothea, Goetz von Berlichingen, Iphigenia, first part of Faust,—three weeks of thorough study this, as valuable to me as to them,—and Clavigo,—thus comprehending samples of all his efforts in poetry, and bringing forward some of his prominent opinions; Lessing's Nathan, Minna, Emilia Galeotti [sic]; parts of Tieck's Phantasus, and nearly the whole first volume of Richter's Titan.[15]

The number of works is remarkably large for a session of twenty-four weeks; the list is confined on the whole to works which since that day have established themselves as universal favorites. For Margaret merely to have chosen these works at a time when the teaching of German literature was only in its formative stages is a testimony to her critical discrimination. In the face of all the adverse criticism of Goethe in the 'thirties,[16] she chose to give him a larger share of the classroom time than any other writer. Her success as a teacher was a support and encouragement to Margaret in these years. It is clear that her temperament was well fitted to the task of guiding the young, for inspiring them with a desire for knowledge and understanding, and for revealing to them the central meanings of the great works of literature. In 1836 she wrote:

> "It is my earnest wish to interpret the German authors of whom I am most fond to such Americans as are ready to receive. Perhaps some might sneer at the notion of my becoming a teacher; but where I love so much, surely I might inspire others to love a little; and I think this kind of culture would be precisely the counterpoise required by the utilitarian tendencies of our day and place.[17]

Thus during the 'thirties Margaret earned the reputation of being "Germanico" to the point of eccentricity. Higginson tells an anecdote to the effect that Margaret's successor in Alcott's Temple School was once confronted by a lady who claimed with great admiration, "Miss Fuller says she *thinks* in German; do you believe it?" The rejoinder was, "Oh, yes! I do not doubt it; I myself dream in Cherokee."[18] Horace Greeley, writing after Margaret's death, seriously put forth the theory that her knowledge of German hampered her expression in English.[19] Remaining in Boston to 1844, Margaret took it for her mission to spread the gospel of German literature. Even as early as July, 1833, she was hoping to find an organ suitable for the publication of her contemplated essays. Writing to Hedge in March, 1835, she mentioned the "periodical" and promised to "lend a hand" whenever it should be organized, though she felt constrained to apologize for her excessive German enthusiasm: "I fear I am merely 'Germanico' and not 'transcendental.' "[20] When, in 1836, she again discussed the subject, she indicated clearly her idea that one of the primary functions of the publication should be to introduce German literature to the American public.

> "I hope a periodical may arise, by and by, which may think me worthy to furnish a series of articles on German literature, giving room enough and perfect freedom to say what I please. In this case, I should wish to devote at least eight numbers to Tieck.... I should like to begin the proposed series with a review of Heyne's [sic] letters on German literature, which afford excellent opportunity for some preparatory hints ... I could engage ... to furnish at least two articles on Novalis and Körner."[21]

To draw New England into its proper relationship with the totality of Western culture was one of the fundamental aims of the *Dial*, of Ripley's series, *Specimens of Foreign Standard Literature*, and Hedge's *Prose Writers of Germany*.

Throughout the years of her residence in Boston, she referred to herself as the herald of German literature. It is not recorded how many of her public "Conversations" were on the subject of German literature; the only indication is that "Goethe" was named as one of the topics. But undoubtedly German literature came up often in the course of the discussions, even when the topic was some such generality as "Culture" or "Ethics."[22] In a review of *Faust* in the second volume of the *Dial* Margaret wrote: "We cannot but wonder that anyone who aims at all at literary culture can remain ignorant of German, the acquisition of which language is not a year's labor with proper instruction, and would give them access to such wide domains of thought and knowledge."[23] Even as late as 1846, she made a particularly clear statement of her intent:

> "It has been one great object of my life to introduce . . . the works of those great geniuses, the flower and fruit of a higher state of development, which might give the young who are soon to constitute the state, a higher standard in thought and action than would be demanded of them by their own time. I have hoped that, by being thus raised above their native sphere, they would become its instructors and the faithful stewards of its best riches, not its tools or slaves. I feel with satisfaction that I have done a good deal to extend the influence of the great minds of Germany and Italy among my compatriots."[24]

Though German literature had found its champion in writers before Margaret Fuller wrote for the *Dial*, the proportion of material on the subject was nowhere so high as in that magazine. Rare individuals like Hedge and Ripley needed no further instruction on the subject, but others, even some of the most advanced members of the movement, such as Emerson and Parker, had much to learn from Margaret. Theodore Parker represents the opposite pole in the combination of intellectual forces that make up the Transcendentalist movement; for, while he used German theological *Wissenschaft* to an inordinate extent, he had a remarkably dull ear for the message of German *Dichtung*.[25]

In the first months of her stay at Groton, Margaret had been so delighted with Goethe's *Tasso* that, with the encouragement of Hedge, she undertook to translate it into verse. It was completed by March, 1834, but not published during her lifetime. In *Tasso* Goethe spoke directly to Margaret's heart; she identified her isolated existence with that of the frustrated, misunderstood poet.

> "Poor Tasso in the play offered his love and service too officiously to all. They all rejected it, and declared him mad, because he made statements too emphatic of his feelings. If I wanted only ideal figures to think about, there are those in literature I like better than any of your living ones. But I want far more. I want habitual intercourse, cheer, inspiration, tenderness. I want these for myself; I want to impart them."[26]

In her preface Margaret made abundant apologies for the shortcomings of her work. It does not follow the metrical pattern exactly; there are many broken lines, omissions, condensations of thought, and a few misunderstandings of idiomatic expressions. Yet on the whole it does justice to the structure and tone of the original, and it is rendered into clear and simple verse. Her English version strives to be as restrained, luminous, and well-poised as the German, but turns out thinner in substance and less subtle. Obviously the translator was taking Coleridge's treatment of *Wallenstein* as her ideal of translation.

Margaret's first publication was a translation, published in 1839, of Eckermann's conversations with Goethe, which appeared as volume four of Ripley's series. She shortened the work slightly, omitting references to the *Farbenlehre* and certain other topics.[27] This volume, throwing light as it did on the little-known later years of the German poet, revealed an entirely new side of him to the New England public of that day. Many of the younger Transcendentalists must have felt as did T. W. Higginson, when he said, "For one, I can say that it brought him [Goethe] nearer to me than any other book, before or since, has ever done."[28] In 1841 Margaret began to translate the partly fictional correspondence of Fräulein Günderode and Bettina von Arnim, and in the next year appeared a thin pamphlet of 86 pages containing about a quarter of the whole text.[29] Margaret was much attracted by the personality of the gentle, melancholy, and mystical Canoness Günderode, and her career paralleled, or threatened to parallel, that of the German woman, during the critical, indecisive years from 1833–40.[30]

The long struggle to understand Goethe involved the reading of all his works, memoirs, and letters available to her. She recognized that in him there spoke a wise and experienced authority, who, observant and penetrating as he was, taught a doctrine of realism and renunciation very difficult either to refute or accept. This, together with her fear of the impulses within her that seemed dangerously close to his own "paganism," made the study of Goethe a serious occupation which involved a full decade of Margaret's life. Her "favorite Goethe," "our Master, Goethe," with whom she alternately "solaced her soul" and then became impatient,[31] was her greatest literary experience. By 1838 she had collected a large mass of notes and observations on the story of his life, which she tentatively promised to write for Ripley's *Specimens*, but which was never completed. There was no personality, either in books or among her acquaintances, who did more to emancipate her soul from the limitations of New England morality than this man. Obviously she was destined, after such a long period of preparation, to give one of the most authoritative criticisms of Goethe that could in her day have been written in America, or in England either, for that matter. George Ripley wrote a fine article on Goethe,—but that had to wait until twenty years later. In his and Parker's earlier testimonials to the value of German literature, Goethe was not treated with sufficient fullness and understanding. Everybody before Margaret was ready to give at least partial assent to Menzel's charges;[32] it was left to her to justify the ways of this man to the New England conscience.[33] Parker and Ripley started from a conviction that they could show him to be devout, even Christian, at heart; but they had to censure him on the score of morality for his personal conduct toward Friederike and Lili, and in his marriage. Margaret knew Goethe well enough to see that he had a morality and a religion of his own that not only excused him but called forth admiration. She defined morality, not as did the others, as the conformity to absolute rules laid down by the religious authority, but as conformity to the individual's own code of conduct. From this point of view the life of Goethe was, as she said, "active, wise, and honored."[34] Goethe taught her to minimize the importance of what Emerson called "moral Evil" and to grow beyond the bounds of Puritan morality altogether.

It is from this point of view that she wrote the essays on Goethe in the *Dial* and her preface to the *Conversations* with Eckermann. They are not criticisms of separate literary works, but interpretations of the total personality of this man. First in point of time came the preface to the *Conversations*,[35] in which in a brilliant attack on all classes of his critics, she met the charges arranged under four heads:

> "He is not a Christian.
> He is not an Idealist.
> He is not a Democrat.
> He is not Schiller."

Unlike Parker, who cited the "*Bekenntnisse einer schönen Seele*" to show that Goethe was a Christian, Margaret readily admitted that the master was a "Greek" in spirit and as such was not to be judged on Christian standards. She pointed out that this is at the bottom of his aversion "for the worship of sorrow," and that his creed is one of self-reliance and calm acceptance—hence not moralistic at all in the usual sense of the word. As to the second charge, she pointed out that his plan was never to "alter or exalt Nature" and implied that this is a justifiable way of looking at the universe. As to his being aristocratic, she is not alarmed at the appearance of acquiescence to tradition in the old sage; she excuses it on the theory that an artist needs repose to do his work, and that by nature Goethe was reflective not active, and conservative because his study has been the world as it is, not as he would dream it should be. For those who want the other, there is Schiller; but one Schiller was enough.

> "I am not fanatical as to the benefits to be derived from the study of German literature. I suppose, indeed, that there lie the life and learning of the century, and that he who does not go to these sources can have no just notion of the working of the spirit in the European world these last fifty years or more; but my tastes are often displeased by German writers, even by Goethe—of German writers the most English and the most Greek ... I wish that we could learn from the German writers habits of more liberal criticism, and leave this way of judging from comparison or personal prejudice ... Generally, the wise German criticises with the positive degree, and is well aware of the danger in using the comparative."[36]

Applying this critical principle, she attempts a just statement of Goethe's powers and virtues. She sees that he stresses the perfection of the few, a belief in man's continual effort, thought not reformist action, nature not providence. He is the best German stylist, a fine critic of art and literature, an observer of human beings and of external nature. His mind sees well the individuality of character and the universality of thought. On the negative side, she admits she is disturbed, as were many of his readers, by his aversion to pain and by the isolation of his heart. She would not claim that there were any holy or heroic elements in him.

Margaret continued her work of delineating the personality of Goethe in "Menzel's View of Goethe," printed in the third number of the *Dial* (1841). She insists over and over, that we are not fitted to judge him unless we have studied him long and well.

> "He obliges us to live and grow, that we may walk by his side; vainly we strive to leave him behind in some niche of the hall of our ancestors; a few steps onward and we find him again, of yet serener eye and more towering mien than on his other pedestal . . . We doubt whether the revolutions of the century be not required to interpret the quiet depths of his *Saga*."[37]

She explains his career as *the* one necessary to bring German literature to its fruition; though again she is careful to show the limits of his gifts, deploring the fact that he was not a poet-prophet, but "only a sage."[38]

> "Men should be true, wise, beautiful, pure, and aspiring. This man was true and wise, capable of all things. Because he did not in one short life complete his circle, can we affort to lose him out of sight? Can we, in a world where so few men have in any degree redeemed their inheritance, neglect a nature so rich and so manifestly progressive?"[39]

Subsequent discussions of Goethe elaborated and clarified this point of view. The article "Goethe" which followed in the *Dial* six months later is the most impressive of them all.[40] It is particularly noteworthy for its masterly discussion of some of the larger works. Margaret moves through the worlds of *Faust* and *Werther, Meister, Iphigenie,* and *Die Wahlverwandtschaften* with such assured knowledge of the central import of each, that she can explain their profound meaning for the life of their author and his age. By sympathetic analysis and a bold defense of the position that literature must embrace the entire field of reality, she absolves *Meister* and *Die Wahlverwandtschaften* of the charges of immorality and coldness. One point of view that was particularly appealing to her was the idea that the rôle of women in society could be charted and illustrated by taking such Goethean types as Philine, Marianne, Therese, Natalie, Makarie, Ottilie, and Margarete as basic symbols for the whole range of feminine qualities. She made effective use of this method in her feminist treatise, *Woman in the Nineteeth Century* (1844).[41]

The central doctrine that Margaret learned from Goethe was self-reliance, self-culture. It was this that liberated her from New England standards of personal conduct and helped her to resist the social pressure which was stifling her nature. From Goethe too she learned to take the cosmopolitan view of literature—to look upon the advent of a *Weltliteratur* as the distinctive development of the future.[42] No less important for her was that which he taught her about the nature and history of art, of the great tradition of modern and classical painting, sculpture, and architecture.[43]

Yet Goethe's liberalism, his precept of "extraordinary, generous seeking" alone never satisfied the demand for high idealism which was part of Margaret's nature, her inheritance from New England Protestant culture. Furthermore, she belonged to a generation of romanticists, while Goethe stood only on the threshold of that movement; he was too calm, too patient with the reality of life, too aloof. Many times she reproved him for his unconcern with the ideal. "Yes, O Goethe! but the ideal is truer than the actual. This changes and that changes not."[44] When under his influence, Margaret was enabled to make an earnest effort to master her volatile feelings, to learn the lesson of resignation.[45] But her sympathy for the Romantic School in literature shows that this was not constantly in her power.[46] The reading of Novalis and Körner "is a relief, after feeling the immense superiority of Goethe."

> "It seems to me as if the mind of Goethe had embraced the universe. I have felt this lately, in reading his lyric poems. I am enchanted while I read . . . but when I shut the book, it seems as if I had lost my personal identity; all my feelings linked with such an immense variety that belong to beings I had thought so different. What can I bring? There is no answer in my mind, except 'It is so,' or 'It will be so,' or 'No doubt such and such feel so.' Yet, while my judgment becomes daily more tolerant towards others, the same attracting and repelling work is going on in my feelings. . . . But now the one-sidedness, imperfection, and glow, of a mind like that of Novalis, seem refreshingly human to me.[47]

When Goethe described what he termed *"das Dämonische"* she understood him completely; but she divined that she was more under the power of the "magnetic fluid" that he was, that she was better fitted for the rôle of prophet of the kingdom of the spirit than he. "With me, for weeks and months, the demon works his will."[48] On the matter of the appreciation of nature, she was able to learn much from the master. His Spinozistic pantheism had much in common with her feeling for the God immanent in nature, though his *Farbenlehre* appealed to her not because it was a scientific empirical study, but because she could interpret it as a mystical treatise. She looked on the forms of nature symbolically and mystically as did Novalis, and had no sympathy with the 'botanizing, geologizing, and dissecting" of the scientist.[49] Though she appreciated the classical beauty of structure in *Tasso, Iphigenie,* and the *Wahlverwandtschaften,* she was at times more immediately responsive to the chaotic formlessness of Jean Paul and Tieck. She felt fully as much at home in the Thessaly of *Faust II* as in the bright, clear atmosphere of Attica.[50] These facts make the examination of her response to the romantics a necessary counterbalance to the foregoing sketch of her interest in Goethe.

Jean Paul was the most loved and best known of the German romantics in America between 1825 and 1845. Margaret's delight in his tenderness, fancy, and rich brilliance made direct sympathy with his message and point of view inevitable. She prescribed his *Titan*—a most difficult and obscure work—to be read by the children in her advanced class at Alcott's school. From Groton she wrote to Clarke:

> "How thoroughly am I converted to the love of Jean Paul, and wonder at the indolence or shallowness which could resist so long . . . In every page I am forced to

> pencil. I will make me a book, or, as he would say, bind me a bouquet from his pages, and wear it on my heart of hearts, and be ever refreshing my wearied inward sense with its exquisite fragrance. I must have improved to love him as I do."[51]

As early at 1833 she had written the poems on Richter which she published in the *Dial* in 1840. In these criticisms in verse, she celebrated Jean Paul as the "Poet of Nature," fanciful, delicate, a painter of scenes in the gorgeous style of Titian, a man "with Raphael's dignity" and "celestial love." She finds him equal to "devotion's highest flight sublime," the priest of a natural religion, a "magnetic influence!" Is there in him a "want of order," as his detractors say? No, "not of *system* in its highest sense," for he has the order and plan of the universe itself, being coequal to it and its perfect mirror. One need only love nature to love him.

> "Nature's wide temple and the azure dome
> Have plan enough for the free spirit's home!"[52]

Thus she found in Richter the romantic subjectivity, the sublime striving, the enthusiasm and moral earnestness which Goethe could not provide. Her Italianate soul,[53] which had learned from Goethe to appreciate the art of Italy and Greece, responded to Jean Paul's high coloring, his pure and sensitive heroes, his extravagant, rhapsodic passages of description, his fondness for omens, puzzles, premonitions, and apparitions.

To become acquainted with Novalis and Tieck was to indulge some of the same preferences. In 1832 she compared Novalis with Goethe:

> "I feel as though I could pursue my natural mode with him, get acquainted, then make my mind easy in the belief that I know all that is to be known. And he died at twenty-nine . . . And his life was so full and so still . . . I have wished fifty times to write some letters giving an account, first, of his very pretty life, and then of his one volume, as I re-read it, chapter by chapter."[54]

In 1836 she was still anxious to do some articles on Novalis.[55] His religion of nature, his view of the external world as the image of the inward being, the mystical significance he attached to flowers, stones and minerals,[56] his idealism and personal beauty of character—these made the attraction for him irresistible to Margaret.

Lesser figures among the German romantics similarly attracted her interest. Fully forty pages of *Summer on the Lakes* (1844), ostensibly an account of her travels in the West, were devoted to a discussion of Justinus Kerner's *Seherin von Prevorst*. This book, virtually the case-record of an invalid German visionary with unusual psychic powers, held extraordinary interest for Margaret, for she, from childhood a somnambulist herself, was looking for a rationale and analysis of the phenomenon of second-sight and prophecy. Then there were Uhland and Tieck, whom she read, as we have noted, though they do not figure prominently in her critical writings. On her "favorite Körner," the author of patriotic songs, she wrote a warmly enthusiastic sketch, which appeared in the Western Messenger in 1838.[57] A long paper entitled "Romaic and

Rhine Ballads" in the *Dial* for 1842 testifies to her interest in folk poetry as the basis for a national literature.[58] She shared the romanticists' interest in the ballad and folk-song, and in several reviews pointed out how the use of native folk themes and materials might contribute to the strength and genuineness of American letters.

There has been no difficulty in identifying American Transcendentalism with the broader tendencies toward romanticism that characterized the early decades of the nineteenth century. Margaret Fuller belonged to her generation and took her inspiration from the same springs of thought and feeling as had nourished the recent romantic revolt in the several Western nations. Her guiding philosophy was a soaring ethical idealism based on the old dualistic Puritan supernaturalism. Despite her acquaintance with the Goethean relativistic and naturalistic ethics, her political-ethical beliefs were formed by such prophets of the ideal as Coleridge and Carlyle; Schiller, Körner, and Freiligrath among the Germans; Lamennais, Rousseau, and George Sand among the French; and above all by the Italian Mazzini. Her literary favorites, along with the ancient classics and Goethe, were Shakespeare, Milton, Wordsworth, Novalis, and Jean Paul. Like the German Romantic School, she did not find it necessary to reject Goethe even in the act of finding him insufficient. In close accord with Novalis' and Jean Paul's subjectivity and mysticism, she nevertheless learned from Goethe to see the world of nature with clearer, sharper eyes. She gratefully drew on his vast stores of valuable instruction; profited from his revelations of artistry in literary composition, his mellowed judgment in matters of esthetic appreciation, and his dispassionate analysis of human types and the manifestations of the human spirit under new and unrecorded circumstances. Like so many of her generation, she was the earnest student and champion of Goethe, but by no means his perfect disciple. The personality of the mature Goethe, Olympian and sage as she correctly saw, remained enigmatic and unsympathetic to her.

Margaret's preoccupation with German literature forms only a chapter—an early one—in the record of her relation to the thought of her age. Her study of the Germans, however, gains in significance from the fact that it came so early as to count for a definite part of her literary education and as one of the primary formative influences on her mind. In later years, even though the circumstances of her life drew her away from literary criticism, her efforts attained a wide effectiveness through the work of younger Transcendentalist disciples. By her example of faithful translation from the German classics, she encouraged Brooks and Dwight, to name the most prominent, to undertake similar projects, and by her discriminating critical labors she hastened the process of assimilation of the German authors into the receptive but nonetheless provincial Boston community. With the exception of Carlyle, there was no one who before 1845 had revealed to the English-speaking readers in such an authoritative, stimulating, and informative manner the nature of German literary achievements of the recent past.

# Notes

1. Following the practice established by her contemporaries, we may take the liberty of referring to her by first name alone, without thereby implying the least disrespect or unseemly familiarity.

2. [Ralph Waldo Emerson, William Henry Channing, and James Freeman Clarke], *Memoirs of Margaret Fuller Ossoli* (Boston: Roberts, 1874), I, 91.

3. "From some of these men Margaret Fuller had direct instruction;... she was... formed in a society which was itself formed by their presence."—Thomas Wentworth Higginson, *Margaret Fuller Ossoli* (Boston: Houghton, Mifflin, 1884), p. 33.

4. *Memoirs*, I, 114.

5. See Higginson, *Margaret Fuller Ossoli*, pp. 45, 69; also Mason Wade, *Margaret Fuller* (New York: Viking, 1940), pp. 30, 35, 144, 155.

6. *Memoirs*, I, 90.

7. Written in 1838, in reference to the year 1832.—*Woman in the Nineteenth Century* (Boston: Roberts, 1893), pp. 358–359.

8. See *Memoirs*, I, 112–113, and Harold Clarke Goddard, *Studies in New England Transcendentalism* (New York: Columbia University Press, 1908), pp. 93–97, for a full account of Margaret's reading.

9. *Memoirs*, I, 241.

10. The "Lehrlinge zu Sais," and *Heinrich von Ofterdingen.*—*Memoirs*, I, 120.

11. *Memoirs*, I, 114. See also, I, 108.

12. *Memoirs*, I, 121–122, 130, 147–148, 160, 165, 167, 169–170; Higginson, *Margaret Fuller Ossoli*, pp. 44, 45, 309; and *Life Without and Life Within* (Boston: Roberts, 1895), p. 308.

13. *Memoirs*, I, 204.

14. She had four private pupils at Groton in March 1834.—*Memoirs*, I, 150. And while teaching in Alcott's Temple School she likewise gave private instruction in the language, besides teaching it in regular classes.—Wade, *Fuller*, pp. 34–37.

15. *Memoirs*, I, 174.

16. For a concise account of the early reputation of the German writers in America, see S. H. Goodnight's *German Literature in American Magazines Prior to 1846* (Bulletin of the University of Wisconsin, Philology and Literature Series, vol. 4, no. 1) (Madison: University of Wisconsin, 1907), pp. 40–55, 61–104.

17. *Memoirs*, I, 168. See *Life Without and Life Within,* pp. 95–96, 103, for Margaret's opinions on the advisability of early teaching of foreign languages to children.

18. Higginson, *Margaret Fuller Ossoli,* p. 84.

19. "She always wrote freshly, vigorously, but not always clearly; for her full and intimate acquaintance with continental literature, especially German, seemed to have marred her felicity and readiness of expression in her mother tongue."—*Memoirs,* II, 154.

Margaret's style has generally been criticized for a lack of clarity. Readers who do not understand are struggling as much with the thought she is trying to express as with her mode of expressing it. She was an exceedingly subtle psychologist; her mind moved suddenly and brilliantly from the central theme to tangential observations; and she had little gift for shaping her thoughts into any kind of external orderliness. She did not revise and was always too impatient to polish her expression. As Poe remarked, her writing had the style of her conversation, but with this difference, that when one heard her, he could understand because of the emphasis she gave by gesture and intonation, while on the printed page these helps were lacking. Poe, a severe critic of expression, readily admitted that he admired her style, though he too found in it "frequent unjustifiable Carlyleisms."—See *The Works of Edgar Allan Poe,* ed. Edmund Clarence Stedman and George Edward Woodberry (Chicago: Stone and Kimball, 1894–1895), III, 81.

The so-called German influence is rather to be seen as the mark of her essentially romantic attitude toward the problems of writing. She admired Novalis and Jean Paul, despite—or perhaps because of—their fondness for far-fetched metaphors, symbolism, dark allegory, and bad habits of discursiveness and "want of order," which she defends by saying that it results in a higher kind of beauty than is possible in clear, precisely ordered expression. Had her nature been so constituted, she might have emulated the classic, objective style of Goethe which she knew so well—and thus avoided the charge of German subjectivity and mysticism altogether; but this was not possible for her, for her inner being was too restless, non-plastic, "musical" in its essence.

20. Higginson, *Margaret Fuller Ossoli*, p. 141.

21. *Memoirs*, I, 168–169.

22. See *Memoirs*, I, 351.

23. *Dial*, 2 (July 1841), 134.

24. *Art, Literature, and the Drama* (Boston: Roberts, 1889), Preface, p. 7. See also *Life Without and Life Within*, p. 96. Many must have felt sympathetic with Lowell, when in his *Fable for Critics* he set up his satiric portrait of "Miranda" as a presumptuous, self-appointed teacher of literature, making her say,

"I myself introduced, I myself, I alone,
To my Land's better life authors solely my own,
Who the sad heart of earth on their shoulders have taken,
Whose works sound a depth by Life's quiet unshaken . . ."

But attacks such as these also indicate that Margaret was causing enough stir to be noticed. Those who were unsympathetic made her the butt of many unfortunate jests. Hawthorne contributed not a little by his hardly disguised picture of Zenobia in the *Blithedale Romance*. But people were always amazed, too, to find out when they came to know her, she proved worth listening to.—See Higginson, *Margaret Fuller Ossoli*, p. 203.

25. Indeed, he had no use for the abilities of a person like Margaret, and put her low on the list of possible contributors, when he planned his *Massachusetts Quarterly Review*. Bracketed with Thoreau and W. E. Channing, she was labelled, "Certain but not Valuable."—See Clarence L. F. Gohdes, *The Periodicals of American Transcendentalism* (Durham: Duke University Press, 1931), pp. 165, 168.

26. *Memoirs*, I, 287.

27. *Conversations with Goethe in the Last Years of His Life* (Boston: Hilliard, Gray, 1839), Preface, pp. xxiii-xxv.

28. Higginson, *Margaret Fuller Ossoli*, p. 189.

29. Apparently there was not enough patronage to lead her on, though in 1861 the whole work, in a translation completed and revised by Mrs. Minna Wesselhoeft, was published in Boston. See Higginson, *Margaret Fuller Ossoli*, p. 192.

30. Margaret prepared translations of poems, essays, and extracts from long volumes as incidental illustrative material for her reviews and columns. She never pretended to any literary excellence in these works, though on the whole they are done in excellent taste and with fine understanding of the German. Several, especially those from Goethe, were written with no thought of publication, but entirely for her own pleasure; as Professor Frederick Augustus Braun points out, in his book *Margaret Fuller and Goethe* (New York: Henry Holt, 1910), pp. 216–241, they reveal much about her struggles over the fundamental questions of religion at the time when she was looking to Goethe for guidance. Other poems she translated for the purpose of making their authors better known to the American public. The published records of her writings indicate that Margaret translated the following: "Das Göttliche," "Prometheus," "Eins und Alles," "Dauer im Wechsel," "Adler und Taube," and other poems of Goethe; and one poem each of Uhland, Chamisso, Körner, and Schiller.

31. See Higginson, *Margaret Fuller Ossoli*, pp. 135, 111; and *Memoirs*, I, 146, 160–161.

32. As made known in Professor Felton's translation of Menzel's recent work on *German Literature*. See Higginson, *Margaret Fuller Ossoli*, pp. 282–284.

33. It should be noted that Margaret admired the writings of Lessing and Schiller; but she could contribute little to their fame, for they had been made well known by the essays of Carlyle and had been available in translation since 1805. She accepted both as established classics, and, as we have seen, devoted to them a large portion of the time in her classes at Alcott's school. Besides his poetry and dramas, she admired Schiller's historical works (see *Memoirs*, I, 148). His high idealism and moral fervor found a response in her own high idealism, and there was much less conflict between her nature and his than there was between the more complex, worldly, relativistic Goethe and herself. It is this that, on one occasion in 1833, made her exclaim, "I don't like Goethe so well as Schiller now. I mean, I am not so happy in reading him. That perfect wisdom and *merciless* nature seems cold, after those seducing pictures of forms more beautiful than truth." (*Memoirs*, I, 117).

For further references to Schiller as dramatic technician, see *Art, Literature, and the Drama*, pp. 111, 210.

34. *Memoirs*, I, 197.

35. *Conversations with Goethe*, pp. vii–xxvi. Other pieces of Goethe-criticism include the following: a review of *Egmont* as translated anonymously (Boston: James Munroe, 1841), in the *Dial*, 3 (January 1842), 394; a short notice of a translation of *Faust*, *Dial*, 2 (July 1841), 134; a review of almost two columns of George Calvert's translation of the *Correspondence Between Schiller and Goethe*, vol. 1 (New York and London: Wiley & Putnam, 1845), in the *New York Tribune* for 14 March 1845; a review of Samuel Gray Ward's translation of Goethe's *Essays on Art* (Boston: James Munroe, 1845), in the *Tribune* for 29 May 1845.

36. *Conversations with Goethe*, p. xvii.

37. 1 (January 1841), 340–347; reprinted in *Life Without and Life Within*, pp. 13–22; p. 14.

38. See her remark on the "Lili-episode": "right as a genius, but wrong as a character."—*Life Without and Life Within*, p. 350.

39. *Life Without and Life Within*, p. 15.

40. 2 (July 1841), 1–41.

41. Goethe's ideal of woman, "das ewig Weibliche," is to her a key to the interpretation of woman's essential character. In *Woman in the Nineteenth Century* she draws on her knowledge of a whole gallery of feminine figures from the life and writings of Goethe: Frau Aja, Cornelia, Duchess Amalia, Lili Schönemann, Margarete in *Faust*, the Leonoras in *Tasso*, Iphigenia, and the several female figures of *Meister*. Here, as elsewhere, Makarie is placed at the apex in the scale of virtues and spiritual nobility.—See pp. 64, 80, 100, 110, 125–128, 129.

42. The crucial importance of Goethe in the solution of her personal problems and her decision to challenge as she did the New England ethical standards is discussed at length in two special studies: Braun, *Margaret Fuller and Goethe*, chapters 2 and 3, pp. 41–147, and Harry Slochower, "Margaret Fuller and Goethe," *Germanic Review*, 7 (April 1932), 130–144. The tendency of Professor Braun's book is to assert that Margaret was completely and solely the disciple of Goethe and, consequently, to deny that she was a Transcendentalist at all. However, it is clear that the movement which goes by that name was broad enough to include her along with such widely divergent personalities as Parker, Emerson, and Thoreau. Her pioneer work as first editor of the *Dial* and her personal influence over so many men of both her generation and the following is sufficiently well established to secure her place in the movement. Only by overlooking her fundamental differences from the Goethian point of view can it be maintained that she was entirely his pupil.

43. The Goethian attitude towards cosmopolitanism in literature is reflected in *Life Without and Life Within*, pp. 109, 215; with respect to her interest in his writings on art, see *Memoirs*, I, 149, 266.

44. Higginson, *Margaret Fuller Ossoli*, p. 289; also, p. 284; "As to Goethe. . . I do not go to him as a guide or friend, but as a great thinker who makes me think" (1837). For further similar

utterances, see *Memoirs*, I, 167, and *Woman in the Nineteenth Century*, p. 124, where she reflects the Goethian aloofness towards questions of social reform.

45. See *Memoirs*, I, 262.

46. *Memoirs*, I, 160–161.

47. *Memoirs*, I, 119. See also I, 120–121.

48. *Memoirs*, I, 224. See also the passage, I, 224–226; 218.

49. Of the *Farbenlehre* she said: "The facts interest me only in their mystical significance."—Higginson, *Margaret Fuller Ossoli*, pp. 101–102. She continues: "There was a time when one such fact would have made my day brilliant with thought. But now I seek the divine rather in love than law." (Written in 1841).

50. See *Memoirs*, I, 230.

51. *Memoirs*, I, 130. Of *Titan* she wrote in 1836: "It is a noble work, and fit to raise a reader into that high serene of thought where pedants cannot enter."—*Memoirs*, I, 169–170.

52. 1 (July 1840), 135; printed also in *Memoirs*, I, 147–148.

53. See Wade, *Margaret Fuller*, pp. 205–217, on the subject of Margaret's attachment to Italy; see also Katherine Anthony, *Margaret Fuller* (New York: Harcourt, Brace, and Howe, 1920), p. 155.

54. See *Memoirs*, I, 118–121, 123.

55. *Memoirs*, I, 169.

56. Note her flower-fantasies, "Yuca Filamentosa" and "The Magnolia of Lake Pontchartrain," and her poems, the "passionflower," "The Dahlia, Rose, and Heliotrope," "The Flower and the Pearl," and "Lines" (*Life Without and Life Within*, p. 375). These contain symbolism derived from Novalis ("*die blaue Blume*") and Goethe's *Faust* ("the mothers"). See Higginson, *Margaret Fuller Ossoli*, pp. 96–97, 99, 305; *Memoirs*, II, 92–94. Margaret was especially fond of the symbol of the carbuncle as used in *Heinrich von Ofterdigen* (*Woman in the Nineteenth Century*, p. 343; *Memoirs*, II, 95). The pearl was her symbol for herself.

57. 4 (January 1838), 306–311, 369–375. Like so many of her generation, she admired Ferdinand Freiligrath. When in London in 1846, she visited his house—in the spirit of a pilgrim at a shrine of liberty.—*At Home and Abroad* (Boston: Roberts, 1874), p. 180.

58. This was a review of Karl Simrock's *Rheinsagen aus dem Munde des Volkes und Deutscher Dichter* (1842) and of Wilhelm Müller's translation of the *Neu-Griechische Volkslieder*. *Dial*, 3 (October 1842), 137–180.

# "Margaret Fuller's Criticism of the Fine Arts"

Roland Crozier Burton[*]

Although Margaret Fuller remains of interest chiefly because of her literary criticism, as a transcendental exponent of the unified aesthetic sensibility, she frequently touched upon the drama, painting, sculpture, the ballet, and music. Published in the *Western Messenger* (1835–38), the *Dial* (1840–44), the *New York Tribune* (1844–46), and her *Memoirs* (1852) are the discussions, sometimes purely incidental but frequently quite extended, which entitle her to the status of a pioneer American critic of the arts. In this less familiar province she often speaks with less warranted authority than in literature, but her comments are no less significant in revealing her traits of mind.

## I

The tone of her criticism is established by "A Short Essay on Critics," her initial contribution to the *Dial*. Her appeal for a "comprehensive" outlook in literature—a view undistorted by "subjective" and "apprehensive"[1] influences—defines the objective toward which she pointed all her criticism of the arts. In declaring that her comprehensive critic is one who shall be able "to perceive the analogies of the universe, and how they are regulated by an absolute principle,"[2] she immediately reverts to the mysticism which consistently hindered her progress on the course that she had charted. She seemed ever on the threshold of a fertile synthesis of aesthetic principles, yet never attained it; and her criticism remains today a series of unconscious adaptations from European writers. The existence of an absolute principle once affirmed, her mind leaps into the blue empyrean to proclaim that her ideal critic "must be inspired by the philosopher's spirit of inquiry and need of generalization, but he must not be constrained by the hard cemented masonry of method to which philosophers are prone."[3]

Her statements indicate familiarity with the ideas of leading English and Continental authors of the eighteenth and nineteenth centuries. Usually without acknowledgment of indebtedness, she paraphrased their theories in tran-

[*]Roland Crozier Burton, "Margaret Fuller's Criticism of the Fine Arts," *College English*, 6 (October 1944), 18–23; copyright 1944 by the National Council of Teachers of English. Reprinted by permission of the publisher and author.

scendental terms. Thus she made use of Reynolds' distinction between the sublime and the beautiful; of Rousseau's theory of emotional states evoked by natural beauty; of Lessing's pronouncement upon the expression of pain and transitory emotion; of Schiller's discrimination between the naïve and sentimental and between classic harmony and romantic discord; of A. W. Schlegel's delimitation of the boundaries between finite and infinite aspiration; of Novalis' identification of poetry with absolute reality; and, most important of all, of Goethe's injunction, which she freely applied in all the arts, "To appreciate any man, learn first what object he proposed to himself; next, what degree of earnestness he showed with regard to attaining that object."[4] Each of these points of reference served its turn in the attempts by which "we do not seek to degrade but to classify an object by stating what it is not," without, at the same time, being "constrained by the hard cemented masonry of method."[5]

## II

Fundamental to her conception of unity in the arts is the idea, borrowed from the more romantic theorists, relating to the organic succession of forms. In this context Margaret Fuller found the botanical analogy particularly appropriate: "There is, perhaps, a correspondence between the successions of literary vegetation with those of the earth's surface, where, if you burn or cut down an ancient wood, the next offering of the soil will not be in the same kind, but raspberries and purple flowers will succeed the oak, poplars the pine."[6] Comparison of her various papers shows that she consistently adhered to this belief that each particular age would bring forth its own characteristic form of artistic expression. According to the principle, she found the drama most alien to the introspective tendencies of the day. "European life tends to new languages," she asserted, "and for a while neglecting this form of representation, would explore the realms of sound and sight, to make to itself other organs which must for a time supersede the drama."[7] It belonged, rather to the age of Elizabeth, when an appreciation of individual greatness had pervaded society. Contemporary architecture and sculpture, which received little of her attention, evinced to her no more than imitative power, as did painting, in which her low estimate did not, however, prevent a more sustained interest. In poetry she found hopeful portents, especially in that verse which foreshadowed the future greatness of the common man; and she praised the ballet extravagantly, partly because she saw in it "body made pliant to the inspirations of spirit,"[8] and partly because of her abhorrence of the prudery which had objected even to exhibitions of statuary: "everything tends in the civilized world to a reinstatement of the body in the rights of which it has been defrauded."[9]

More illuminating in revealing ideas and attitudes are Margaret Fuller's attempts to order and synthesize her impressions of painting, an art toward which she exhibited one of her most consistent inclinations. Landscape painting, wherein character and incident are subordinated, appeared to give her the most difficulty. Evidently placing it in an inferior category, she was content with representation rather than expression or interpretation. By this criterion she judged Allston's scenes: "Here the painter is merged in this theme, and these pictures affect us as parts of nature, so absorbed are we in contemplating them, so difficult it is to remember them as pictures."[10] Or, in a manner reminiscent of Rousseau's aesthetic preoccupations, she associated pictorial effects upon the beholder with emotions supposedly induced by natural objects, saying that "every part of nature has its peculiar influence. On the hill top one is roused, in the valley soothed, beside the waterfall absorbed."[11]

As a means of classifying paintings, Margaret Fuller used the terms "sublime" and "beautiful"—terms obviously derived from Sir Joshua Reynolds' *Discourses*. Judging by the tone of her comments on ideal portraits, she placed such works—and, inferentially, landscapes—in the inferior category of the Beautiful. She appreciated the delicacy and grace of canvases like Allston's "Beatrice," "Lady Reading a Valentine," and "Rosalie." In the lesser virtues she recognized his merit: "The Beautiful is Mr. Allston's dominion. There he rules as a genius."[12]

In the "grand historical style," which she associated with the Sublime, she considered Allston's best attempts "imposing rather than majestic."[13] Here, only Raphael and Michelangelo, as workers in the pictorial and plastic arts, completely met her expectations. Raphael was the apostle of the Finite, "whose life is all reproduced; nothing was abstract or conscious."[14] Michelangelo was the prophet of the Infinite. "Like thy own Moses," she apostrophized, "even on the mount of celestial converse, thou didst ask thy God to show now his face, and didst write his words, not in the alphabet of flowers, but on stone tables."[15] That art which affirmed most unequivocally the primacy of the "Ideal," the "Infinite"—that which subordinated representation to expression and sense to spirit—was the truly Sublime.

There is traceable, among the disparate and variously oriented statements on the pictorial and plastic arts, a slight tendency toward growth that is unique in her aesthetic criticism. Early in her career, during the flush of her Goethean enthusiasm, she expanded her favorite critical standard into a logical absurdity. Comparing Martin's "Destruction of Nineveh" with one of Raphael's Madonnas, she asserted that if "the one is intended to excite the imagination, and the other to gratify the taste; that which fulfills its object most completely must be the best, whether it give me pleasure or no."[16]

A more rewarding use of her sources is recorded in 1840, when, obviously under the influence of Lessing, she considered the expression of pain and emotion. She found Allston's "Massacre of the Innocents" unpleasant: "not only is the main figure offensive to the sensual eye, thus violating one principal condition of art; it is incapable of any expression at such a time beyond that of physical anguish during the struggle of life suddenly found to re-demand its dominion." Under such conditions, "the mind must reason the eye out of an instinctive aversion, and force it to its work,—always an undesirable circumstance."[17] Five years later, however, she had grown to believe that this same depiction of human agonies might contribute to a deeper experience. Writing on "The Nubian Slave," in 1845, she said: "It is only necessary that pain and dread should be subordinated to some meaning of a permanent dignity, and we think it is so in this instance."[18] That the fluctuations of opinion should at length attain this higher level of comprehension betokens a maturation of viewpoint not discernible in relation to the other arts.

Such lack of fulfilment is most notable in her criticism of music. Her theory of organic succession in the arts proclaimed music as the most authentic and original voice of her own age, the culmination of finite aspiration, and the glorious expression of modern yearning toward the infinite. In her gallery of individual heroes—Goethe, Wordsworth, Shelley, Emerson, and the like—she admired a musician, Beethoven, the most consistently and least critically.[19]

In moments of highest enthusiasm she felt that music could supplant, not only the other arts, but other fields of human knowledge as well: "What other arts indicate and Philosophy infers, this all-enfolding language declares."[20] Her exaltation of music, as reflected in her writing, does not appear to be implemented by soundness of knowledge or acuteness of perception. She attempted to characterize the various instruments in terms of emotional and imaginative suggestion: the oboe was the "sweet pastoral instrument";[21] the violin was "tearful";[22] and in the cello, "the wonderful union of deep and grave passion with soft aerial vanishing notes . . . . made the instrument impressive as a spiritual presence in itself."[23] Her praise of "the *Sehnsucht* of music";[24] her confusion of musical, with conceptual, ideas; and her almost complete indifference to harmonic and formal structure—all corroborate an impression which is further strengthened by her frequent preoccupation with the incidental matters of financial support, the decorum of audiences, and the personal mannerisms of concert artists:[25] music was for her, in spite of pretensions to the contrary, little more than a sensuous pleasure and a stimulant toward free imaginative association with all elevating experiences.

### III

The social implications of a universally diffused aesthetic sensibility, a persistent theme in Margaret Fuller's writing, has led some of her admirers to regard her as the precursor of twentieth-century Marxian criticism.[26] The general drift of her sympathies is, to be sure, undeniable. "This poetic sensibility ought to be common to every one," she said, "and we perceived distinctly that, at some periods of history, it has been far more so than at present."[27] She was consistently eager to verify, among the "popular poets" such as William Thom and John Critchley Prince, this diffusion of artistic taste. She confessed, moreover, her alliance with "the 'extreme left' of the army of progress,"[28] and she looked forward, in her most exuberantly prophetic moments to the eventual abolition of class distinctions, when "there may still be in the future many low and mean men, but no lower classes."[29]

These proletarian sympathies, however, existed contemporaneously with more conservative attitudes. It is noteworthy, not only that she remained aloof from active participation in the restricted collectivism of Brook Farm, but also that she later published extremely orthodox social views. Such, for example, were her commendation of charity for the "Ideal Rich Man"[30] and of patient reconciliation with his lot for the "Ideal Poor Man."[31] Even her stand on social classes fluctuated. Though in July, 1845, she had prophesied the end of inequality, in the following February she proclaimed the necessity of distinctions: "Our nation is not silly in striving for an aristocracy. Humanity longs for its upper classes. But the silliness consists in making them out of clothes, equipage, and a servile imitation of foreign manners, instead of the genuine elegance and distinction that can be produced by a genuine culture."[32]

## IV

In extenuation of Margaret Fuller's relative inadequacy as a critic of the arts, one might cite the paucity of opportunities for enjoyment of the arts other than literature. A listing of the cultural resources of Boston and New York during the 1830's and 1840's, while quantitatively impressive, would not be remarkable for quality. Margaret Fuller did her best with what was available; indeed, her willingness to generalize was out of proportion to her actual experience with works of art. All that she had to say bore some of the naïveté and freshness of novel experience. Although, for example, she had witnessed theatrical performances by the Keans, the Kembles, Maria Tree, Macready, and Vandenhoff, the drama was for her essentially an armchair entertainment: "Till men shall carry Shakespeare and Molière within their own minds, they will wish to see their works represented."[33] Her remarks on painting and sculpture were based chiefly upon her study of the Athenæum casts and the Flaxman and Retzsch engravings. Her musical experience was bounded by the music lessons of her childhood, the oratorios that she heard in Boston, and the occasional concerts and operas that she attended in New York. Her reading "about" the arts was much richer than her experience "with" the arts.

The riches of her literary background as compared with her restricted acquaintance with kindred arts suggests a fundamental weakness of her criticism in these other fields. All of them were judged in terms of literature. However powerful the emotional stimulus awakened by a particular work, she remained somewhat perplexed until she could discover a literary theme. Were not all forms of art simply languages by which "the presence of the highest genius makes all mediums alike transparent"?[34] She drew from this principle a corollary that the "language" must of necessity be a literary language. "What does the picture mean to say?" she queried, upon inspecting Allston's "Witch of Endor"; and, upon finding the artist's reading of the text at variance with her own, she disparaged the painting as conveying "no distinct impression."[35] With facile assurance she translated the meaning from one art to another. Concerning Beethoven's "Fifth Symphony," she said: "What the Sibyls and Prophets of Michel Angelo demand, is in this majestic work made present to us."[36] Again, in encompassing the Creation theme, she found that her own imagination, fired by the scriptural text, was more nearly adequate to the conception than was either a literary, a musical, or a sculptural transcription: "Haydn fell short of Milton, who falls short of what we know how to expect. An Adam and Eve we hardly hope to see, for even Michel Angelo's, while they transcend our demand, only stimulate, not satisfy our thoughts."[37] The pervasive literary standard, blurring the distinctions among the arts and uniting them under a false premise, operated to prevent the formulation of a genuinely "comprehensive" aesthetic theory.

Margaret Fuller's critical essays are the adventures of an active and intelligent but essentially unspeculative mind in a strange field. The conflicts and cross-purposes that in her literary criticism are seemingly transcended—resulting in singularly just estimates of individual writers—are brought to the surface in her criticism of the other arts; and the basic weakness becomes apparent. Though her appraisals of such men as Longfellow, Lowell, Poe, and Emerson were at variance with the majority opinion of her own day and notably prophetic of significant twentieth-century estimates, her opinions in these other fields lapsed into the genteel orthodoxies of her own time and ours.

In its entirety Margaret Fuller's criticism of the arts bears the impress of a mind that seeks to assert the unity of the aesthetic sensibility and to base the criticism of art on broadly comprehensive principles. She perceived many of the basic issues in aesthetics. Inquiries concerning representation versus expression, the Sublime and the Beautiful, content versus form, the distinction between aesthetic and conceptual ideas, the sociological implications of art, moral versus aesthetic judgment—all are adumbrated in her published writings; yet none of these questions can be pursued far enough to suggest thorough assimilation of sources, if, indeed, the pursuit does not at length reveal a contradictory attitude. By brushing aside all sustained and systematic investigation of any one of her hypotheses, and by relying entirely upon what she thought to be her individual intuitions, she involved herself in contradictions, ambiguities, and false assumptions, ending in the very type of conventionality that she professedly disliked. Whether temperamental limitations primarily, or a climate of opinion unfavorable to methodical inquiry, prevented the fulfilment of her program cannot yet be confidently asserted. In either event, the program outlined in "A Short Essay on Critics" remains the vision of an edifice that she could not build.

## Notes

1. *Dial*, 1 (July 1840), 5–6. Bernard Smith (*Forces in American Criticism* [New York: Harcourt, Brace, 1939], pp. 116–117) rightly considers the term "subjective" as analogous to the currently used term "impressionistic," and "apprehensive" as comparable to "expressionistic."

2. "A Short Essay on Critics," pp. 6–7.

3. "A Short Essay on Critics," p. 8.

4. "Menzel's View of Goethe," *Dial*, 1 (January 1841), 344. Resemblances in verbal expression and in meaning indicate that these authors, in the light of Margaret Fuller's reading, are the probable immediate, rather than ultimate, sources of the ideas.

5. "A Short Essay on Critics," p. 8.
6. "The Modern Drama," *Dial*, 4 (January 1844), 310.
7. "The Modern Drama," p. 310.
8. "The Modern Drama," p. 311.
9. "Entertainments of the Past Winter," *Dial*, 3 (July 1842), 64.
10. "A Record of Impressions," *Dial*, 1 (July 1840), 82.
11. "A Record of Impressions," p. 80.
12. "A Record of Impressions," p. 79.
13. "A Record of Impressions," p. 77.
14. [Ralph Waldo Emerson, William Henry Channing, and James Freeman Clarke], *Memoirs of Margaret Fuller Ossoli* (Boston: Phillips, Sampson, 1852), I, 274.
15. *Memoirs*, I, 274.
16. "Philip Van Artevelde," *Western Messenger*, 1 (December 1836), 399.
17. "A Record of Impressions," p. 76.
18. "The Nubian Slave," *New York Weekly Tribune*, 28 June 1845. Previous studies of Margaret Fuller's criticism do not reveal detailed examination of her many contributions to the *Tribune*, for which she wrote from December 1844 to August 1846.
19. See her *Memoirs*, I, 233. In Bettina von Arnim (1785–1845), with whom Margaret Fuller felt a temperamental kinship, she had a European exemplar in this admiration.
20. "Lives of the Great Composers," *Dial*, 2 (October 1841), 151.
21. "Entertainments of the Past Winter," p. 63.
22. "Entertainments of the Past Winter," p. 58.
23. "Entertainments of the Past Winter," p. 59.
24. *Memoirs*, I, 275.
25. See "German Opera at Palmo's Opera House," *New York Daily Tribune*, 11 December 1845.
26. Smith (*American Criticism*, p. 120) pays tribute to her proletarian sympathies thus: "Those who have fought on the side of humanity are never wholly forgotten."
27. "Books of Travel," *New York Daily Tribune*, 18 December 1845.
28. "Der Volks-Tribun," *New York Daily Tribune*, 17 January 1846.
29. "Prince's Hours with the Muses," *New York Weekly Tribune*, 26 July 1845.
30. "The Rich Man—An Ideal Sketch," *New York Daily Tribune*, 6 February 1846.
31. "The Poor Man—An Ideal Sketch," *New York Daily Tribune*, 25 March 1846.
32. "The Rich Man—An Ideal Sketch."
33. "Entertainments of the Past Winter," p. 47.
34. "Lives of the Great Composers," p. 153.
35. "A Record of Impressions," p. 79.
36. "Entertainments of the Past Winter," p. 62.
37. "Entertainments of the Past Winter," pp. 54–55.

# "Margaret Fuller's Ideas on Criticism"

**Wilma R. Ebbitt**[*]

Margaret Fuller's last piece of formal literary criticism, an essay entitled "American Literature; Its Position in the Present Time, and Prospects for the Future," was written just before she left America on August 1, 1846. It was the one essay composed especially for *Papers on Literature and Art*, a collection of reviews that had first appeared in magazines and newspapers.[1] Many of the original manuscripts of these pieces, together with a wealth of letters, poems, and other material, are now in the Margaret Fuller Collection of the Boston Public Library.[2]

In the course of her analysis of the conditions for a national literature, Margaret Fuller evaluates her own contribution to the "ripening of a new and golden harvest":

> We are sad that we cannot be present at the gathering in of this harvest. And yet we are joyous, too, when we think that though our name may not be writ on the pillar of our country's fame, we can really do far more towards rearing it, than those who come at a later period and to a seemingly fairer task. *Now*, the humblest effort, made in a noble spirit, and with religious hope, cannot fail to be even infinitely useful. Whether we introduce some noble model from another time and clime, to encourage aspiration in our own, or cheer into blossom the simplest wood-flower that ever rose from the earth, moved by the genuine impulse to grow, independent of the lures of money or celebrity . . . the spirit of truth, purely worshipped, shall turn our acts and forbearances alike to profit, informing them with oracles which the latest time shall bless.

One hundred years after her death her wistful prophecy appears remarkably accurate. In her translations and reviews she brought the civilizing influence of ancient and contemporary European literature to bear on a culturally immature nation; as editor of the *Dial* and literary critic for the New York *Tribune* she encouraged the growth of a genuine native literature; and in her estimates of American writers she was faithful to her critical standards. Recent studies of her criticism have clarified her contribution as interpreter of German literature and have established the validity of many of her specific judgments.[3] It is the purpose of this paper to outline her theory of criticism and to indicate the consequences of this theory for her critical method.

[*]Wilma R. Ebbitt, "Margaret Fuller's Ideas on Criticism," *Boston Public Library Quarterly*, 3 (July 1951), 171–187; reprinted by permission of the Trustees of the Boston Public Library.

Although only one of the books published before her death represents her as a critic, Margaret Fuller wrote reviews over a period of eleven years. But her conception of the purpose of these reviews was a broad one, and in many articles that ostensibly dealt with specific works she took occasion to discuss the more basic problems of the nature of art, the function of criticism, and the validity of critical standards. Unlike some writers who have treated these problems, however, she was essentially a practicing critic rather than a theorist. The tension created by the interplay of high-level speculation and her recognition of the practical necessities and purposes of book-reviewing is frequently more interesting than the specific literary judgments at which she arrived in these reviews.

In two periods particularly—periods when she held responsible positions—in 1840-41, the first year of her editorship of the *Dial*, and in 1845, when she was in the midst of her work as literary critic for the *Tribune*—she wrote a series of articles in which she reflected on the larger questions of criticism. These two periods, accordingly, will be taken as focal points for the exposition of her ideas.

Margaret Fuller's central statement of her theory of criticism is "A Short Essay on Critics."[4] Published in the first number of the *Dial*, this article comes chronologically midway between her earliest literary criticism in the *Western Messenger* in 1835 and the last literary notices that she wrote for the *Tribune* in 1846. It is clear, however, that in her early work she was moving toward the principles that she formulated in this essay, and it is also clear that in her later work she constantly faced the problem of the practical application of these principles.

"A Short Essay on Critics" has three sections: a classification of critics, a definition of the true critic, and an analysis of the function of criticism in periodicals.

She groups critics in three categories: subjective, apprehensive, and comprehensive. Subjective critics merely record their feelings about a work: "They love, they like, or they hate: the book is detestable, immoral, absurd, or admirable, noble, of a most approved scope. . . . . " They react, and, worse still, they express themselves with dogmatic authoritativeness, "as those who bear the evangel of pure taste and accurate judgment, and need be tried before no human synod." From her point of view, such impressionistic criticism, conditioned as it is by the temperament of the writer and the influence acting upon him, has no value beyond the incidental one of characterizing the critic.

In the next group are the "apprehensive" or reproductive critics. "These can go out of themselves and enter fully into a foreign existence. They breathe its life; they live in its law; they tell what it meant, and why it so expressed its meaning." Their work is valuable as a re-statement or re-creation of the original work; in fact, the re-statement may give more pleasure than the original, "as melodies will sometimes ring sweetlier in the echo."

The third group, the "comprehensive" critics, encompass but go beyond reproductive criticism. After performing the function of the apprehensive critic—after entering into the nature of another and judging his work by its own law, after ascertaining the author's purpose and the degree of his success in fulfilling it—the comprehensive critic detaches himself from the work and assesses the worthiness of its aim. "And this the critic can only do who perceives the analogies of the universe, and how they are regulated by an absolute, invariable principle." In judging by absolute standards, the comprehensive critic goes beyond the appreciative affirmations of the apprehensive critic and points out what the work is not as well as what it is.

In the second section of the essay Margaret Fuller defines the critic as the necessary mediator between the poet and his audience. "The maker is divine; the critic sees this divine, but brings it down to humanity by the analytic process." The true critic, compounded of poet, philosopher, and observer, has a "love of ideal perfection" which forbids him to be content with mere beauty of details. The true critic is thus clearly identified with the comprehensive critic, and the "analogies of the universe" are roughly equivalent to the "ideal perfection" that he hopes to find embodied in works of art.

These first two sections of the essay form the most complete and systematic statement of critical theory that Margaret Fuller achieved. The oracular tone in which she proclaims her extremely idealistic concepts is to be attributed to the special occasion for which the essay was written. As a critical manifesto for a Transcendental literary venture, it says, appropriately enough, that it will settle for nothing short of the ideal. But the problem of critical method was not solved by this apparently definitive statement. The last section of the essay subtly undermines the hierarchic structure established by the classifying of critics. After condemning coterie criticism and editorial bias, after defining the proper aims of criticism in periodicals—to sift, not to stamp a work; to stimulate readers, not to dictate to them—she concludes her account of the activities of such a critic:

> He will teach us to love wisely what we before loved well, for he knows the difference between censoriousness and discernment, infatuation and reverence; and while delighting in the genial melodies of Pan, can perceive, should Apollo bring his lyre into audience, that there may be strains more divine than those of his native groves.

This sentence is the key to all her later speculation on the subject of critical method. It implies the need for a more adaptable approach than is provided for by the clear-cut distinctions she has already established. In the presence of Pan, the critic will be appreciative, affirmative, reproductive; when Apollo appears, he will make an adjustment in his critical method.

In developing the position that she had stated theoretically in "A Short Essay on Critics"—where she does not refer to any critic, poet, or specific work—Margaret Fuller turned to the dialogue, a literary form that she found more flexible than the essay. It gave her the opportunity of expressing opposing points of view, and, it must be granted, permitted her to pose problems that she was not at the moment prepared to solve. The first of these dialogues,[5] published in the year following "A Short Essay on Critics," offers no satisfactory resolution to the issue between poet and critic. In a very brief exchange the poet attacks the critic for his "perpetual analysis, comparison, and classification" and finally for the negative judgments that he makes. The critic defends his place in the order of nature and justifies his negations by appealing to the spiritual quest that motivates his criticism:

> The law of my being is on me, and the ideal standard seeking to be realized in my mind bids me demand perfection from all I see. To say how far each object answers this demand is my criticism. . . . An object that defies my utmost rigor of scrutiny is a new step on the stair I am making to the Olympian tables.

Although the critic has the last word, the point at issue—the validity of comprehensive criticism—is left doubtful, for the poet vanishes and the critic is stifled in the folds of his own banner.

In a much more ambitious dialogue[6] that appeared in the *Dial* six months later, no *deus ex machina* is called in to end the argument. In her review of *Festus*, a poem by Philip James Bailey, Margaret Fuller gives a lesson in practical criticism. As a dramatic sketch, the dialogue has no merit: but the failures in consecutiveness and the re-hashing of issues after they have presumably been closed indicate her scrupulous effort to represent fairly two different critical approaches.

The first question treated here, that of the validity of criticism *per se*, is settled by the now familiar expedient of defining the critic as mediator between poet and audience. After the preliminary skirmish, the real issue is stated: comprehensive criticism *vs.* reproductive criticism. Aglauron, the comprehensive critic, would focus his attention on the work itself and would evaluate it by comparison with his touchstones, Milton and Dante and Shakespeare. Laurie argues that the only "noble way" is the reproductive. Comprehensive criticism, he says, is applicable only to "the *conscious* triumph of genius." *Festus*, according to the author's own modest statement, is simply the record of one period in the writer's development and so should be judged not as a work of art, not as "triumphant artist-growth," but simply as "a leaf from the book of life."

The discussion proceeds haphazardly through various aspects of the poem. After analyzing the poet's intention and comparing the poem with a more successful work on a similar theme, Goethe's *Faust*, the critics agree that the poet has not fulfilled his ambitious purpose. Laurie, defender of reproductive criticism, recognizes the lack of organic completeness and the shallow philosophical insight, but he is not seriously disturbed by these flaws and turns appreciatively to the "fine leadings" inspired by the character of Festus. The expression is likewise found to be defective. By comparison with Milton and Shakespeare, Bailey writes verse that is bombastic, careless, and thin. Again Laurie cheerfully admits its faults, and again he brings the discussion back to an analysis of its merits—sincerity, unpretentiousness, and a "pathetic beauty of tones and cadences."

Laurie finally wins Aglauron to his point of view; Aglauron admits that reproductive criticism has been the more fruitful approach to a poem of this kind. Laurie on his part admits handsomely that he errs on the side of indulgence but justifies his leniency by the spiritual insight gained from re-creating the poet's experience:

> The poet, my friend, the poet, ah! he is indeed the only friend, and gives us for brief intervals an Olympic game instead of the seemingly aimless contests that fill the years between. Yet that they are only *seemingly* aimless his fulfillment shows. We date from such periods, where we saw the crown on worthy brows. We cannot adjudge the palm to the aspirant before us, yet will not many thoughts and those of sacred import take birth from this hour? We have not criticized; we have lived with him.

The dialogue on *Festus* established the appropriate procedure for the critic faced with a work that is clearly not of the highest class. But there remains a conflict between the two critical approaches when the work is, or seems to be, marked by genius. The most interesting example of this conflict in Margaret Fuller's own criticism appears in her essay, "Goethe,"[7] published in the *Dial* in the same year. She had vigorously defended Goethe's right to be judged from the reproductive point of view on two previous occasions. In the preface[8] to her translation, *Eckermann's Conversations with Goethe* (1839), she ranged the charges brought against him—that he was not a Christian, not an idealist, not a democrat, and not Schiller—and set up in opposition positive statements of what he was. She assumed the same defensive position in the peremptory opening of an essay[9] in the *Dial* in 1841. "Menzel's View of Goethe," she says, "is that of a Philistine." In refuting Menzel she takes her cue from Goethe himself and asks whether he lived up to his own standard, not whether he lived up to hers. But, after she has vindicated him from the charges of "Epicurean sage" and "debauchee" by referring to the circumstances of his life and time, and after she has pointed to his works as the record of his essential spirituality, she admits that she cannot "meet the objections of those who measure him, as they have a right to do, by the standard of ideal manhood."

"The standard of ideal manhood" is precisely the point that proves to be the stumbling-block when she turns from her admirable work in defence of Goethe to her own positive appraisal of him. "Goethe" is the longest, most thoughtful critique she ever wrote on one author, and in much of the essay she adopts successfully the attitudes and methods of the apprehensive critic. She considers the influences on the writer of his family, his education, and his friends; she analyzes the political *milieu* of the time; she discerns the symptoms of the mature writer in his early work; and she makes a sympathetic examination of his works in the order of their production. But juxtaposed with this sympathetic re-creation of the poet and his work is a tone of querulous complaint. In her strictures she is not guilty of the gross error of which she had accused Menzel as well as most New Englanders; that is, she does not judge Goethe by her own standards of personal morality. Instead, she finds a turning-point in his own work, a "Parting of the Ways," that is attributable to his decision to attach himself to the Court of Weimar, and she contrasts regretfully the poetic artist of the later period with the prophet-poet foreshadowed in the early work.

The whole essay oscillates between appreciation of Goethe, the man and the poet, and regret that he did not fulfill the Transcendental ideal of Man and Poet. The same ambivalence is evident in her treatment of Goethe's separate works and is illustrated particularly well in the analysis of *Elective Affinities*.

First she defends it valiantly from the charge of "gross immorality"; it is, on the contrary, she says, "a work especially what is called moral in its outward effect, and religious even to piety in its spirit." This she demonstrates by an analysis of the fate of the characters. Then she goes on in her best vein of appreciative, reproductive criticism:

> I cannot express my sense of the beauty of this book as a work of art . . . The perfect picture always before the mind of the chateau, the moss hut, the park, the garden, the lake, with its boats and the landing beneath the platan trees; the gradual manner in which both localities and persons grow upon us, more living than life, inasmuch as we are, unconsciously, kept at our best temperature by the atmosphere of genius, and thereby more delicate in our perceptions than amid our customary fogs; the gentle unfolding of the central thought, as a flower in the morning sun; then the conclusion, rising like a cloud, first soft and white, but darkening as it comes, till with a sudden wind it bursts above our heads . . .

But in the next paragraph, as her ecstatic salute to Art is abruptly modified, she reveals more completely than in any other passage in her writing the essential difference between her apprehensive criticism and her comprehensive criticism:

> For myself, I never felt so completely that very thing that genius should always make us feel, that I was in its circle, and could not get out till its spell was done, and its last spirit permitted to depart. I was not carried away, instructed, delighted more than by other works, but I was there, living there. . . . Others, it would seem, on closing the book, exclaim, "what an immoral book!" I well remember my own thought: "It is a work of Art!". . . . At this moment, remembering what I then felt, I am inclined to class all my negations just written on this paper as stuff. . . . Yet that they were not without foundation I feel again when I turn to the Iphigenia; a work beyond the possibility of negation: a work where a religious meaning not only pierces but enfolds the whole; a work as admirable in art, still higher in significance, more single in expression.

In the final analysis, then, the work that is "higher in significance," the work that represents Goethe's "higher tendency," is superior.

Margaret Fuller recognized Goethe as the greatest of contemporary writers. Because he was so rich a genius, she tried him by her highest standards. It is obvious that these standards, based as they are on a Transcendental faith in the infinitude of man rather than on the highest artistic achievements of the ages, will never be satisfied. The essay on Goethe illustrates the futility of the effort to arrive at any completely affirmative judgment within the Transcendental frame of reference.

The group of essays from the *Dial* that we have been considering points up an ambivalence in method that is less characteristic of either her earlier or her later work. In the reviews that she wrote before 1840 she showed considerably less concern about the soul and its destiny and considerably more respect for the more functional aspects of her critical system. Her criticism of *Philip Van Artevelde* by Henry Taylor,[10] published in 1835, illustrates the method of comparative criticism that underlies most of her work. Early in the review, as a preface to an attack on subjective criticism, she makes a statement which foreshadows her later distinction between apprehensive and comprehensive criticism but which makes provision for fruitful discussion in terms other than those of "ideal perfection."

> The natural process of the mind in forming a judgment is comparison. The office of sound criticism is to teach that this comparison should be made, not between the productions of differently constituted minds, but between any one of these and a fixed standard of perfection. Nevertheless it is not contrary to the canon to take a survey of the labors of many artists with reference to one, if we value them, not according to the degree of pleasure we have experienced from them, which must always depend upon our then age, the state of the passions and relations with life, but according to the success of the artist in attaining the object he himself had in view.

In order to arrive at the works pertinent to the comparison, she makes a survey of the dramatic writings of the past sixty years and sets up the broad classification of "classical" and "romantic." At this point she admits a strong preference for the restraint, the economy, and the powerful concentration of the classical school. These qualities she illustrates from a number of the works of Alfieri, Goethe, and Schiller, and in the course of her appreciative comment she makes comparisons between one work and another. Finally, two-thirds of the way through her review, after accounting for a number of other dramas that do not fit her scheme of classification, she comes to the work that heads her review. She is willing to meet the author on his own ground and finds much to admire in the picture of the age and in the vividness of the character portrayal.

In its lack of proportion and in the relatively perfunctory treatment given to the work ostensibly under consideration, this piece is an extreme example of the discursiveness of Margaret Fuller's critiques. It provides, however, a good illustration of her critical method and of her notion of the function of a review. In order to help her readers acquire the proper perspective, she presents "a cluster of objects," as she says, around the work.

The method of classifying works and ranking them in hierarchies is utilized more legitimately in another essay that she wrote in her early period. In "Modern British Poets,"[11] published in 1836, she groups nine poets in three categories: the singers—Campbell, Moore, and Scott; the indices to "particular sufferings" of their time—Crabbe, Byron, and Shelley; and the pilot-minds of the age—Southey, Coleridge, and Wordsworth. For the later development of her critical theory there are two points of interest in the essay. One is her frank admission of a lack of sympathy with Crabbe's scientific view of life and human nature, a view "softened by no cool shadow, gladdened by no rose-light" and mirrored by the "strange bleak fidelity" and the "cold tints" of his descriptive passages. After making a perceptive analysis of the realistic qualities of his work, she concludes: "It is difficult to do Crabbe justice, both because the subject is so large a one, and because tempted to discuss it rather in admiration than in love." She confesses here her failure to surrender completely to the poet and his intention, the first condition for apprehensive criticism.

The other point of interest is her contrast between the poems that Wordsworth and Shelley wrote on the subject of the skylark. After lengthy quotation from each, she writes, "Should we not say from the samples before us that

Shelley, in melody and exuberance of fancy, was incalculably superior to Wordsworth? But mark their *inferences.*" And after drawing the moral in the words of the poets—Shelley's desire for the gift of "harmonious madness" and the lesson of cheerful submission in "plodding on" through life that Wordsworth learns—she makes one suggestive comment: "If Wordsworth have superiority then, it consists in greater maturity and dignity of sentiment." The *if* seems to indicate some doubt. The hierarchic ordering of the three classes does, however, indicate that the pilot-minds of the age, the philosopher poets, are generally superior to the singers. At the same time, she appreciates the singers for what they are; she does not condemn them for not being philosophers.

The habit of classification remained with Margaret Fuller throughout her career; again and again it prevents her from falling into the excesses of enthusiasm that are natural to the apprehensive critic. In her survey of contemporary drama[12] she first establishes the fact that the English drama is going through a period of "After Muse," an appendix period that results naturally from the ending of the great productive period of the Elizabethan age, and that the attempts in American drama are an even paler reflection of that glory. But though all contemporary drama fails to measure up to the highest standard, its humbler merits are yet worthy of examination. Thus she groups English and American plays into those written for the glorification of individual actors and those written for the closet. The second group she subdivides further into the "dialogued monologues" of Byron, Shelley, and others and historical plays. Her habit of carefully indicating the range of talent available permits her to express full appreciation of work of minor merit but prevents her from giving such works acclaim that could not be substantiated by absolute excellence.

This flexibility served her well when she came to the most challenging work of her career. She recognized the opportunity that was open to her when Horace Greeley in 1844 asked her to join the staff of the New York *Tribune* as literary critic and commentator on the cultural activities and social conditions of New York;[13] and she turned her attention more seriously to the task of educating the taste of her readers and, at the same time, doing justice to native American literature. During the twenty months in which she wrote reviews, she often took the occasion to indicate the standards she considered appropriate to newspaper reviewing. Although fundamentally alike, three of these statements, all written in 1845, are worth considering fully because of their differences in emphasis. Taken together, they add up to another "Short Essay on Critics" which, at some points, contrasts interestingly with the intransigent idealism of the earlier *Dial* essay.

In two lengthy reviews entitled "English Writers Little Known Here,"[14] Margaret Fuller introduced to her *Tribune* readers the writings of Richard Monckton Milnes, Walter Savage Landor, and Julius Hare. The first of these reviews begins with a statement of the dual function of literature: first, to preserve what is of permanent value, "the flowers of life which came to perfect bloom in minds of genius"; and, second, "as affording the means of interpreting contemporary minds to each other on a larger scale than actual conversation in words or deeds furnishes." Between writers at these poles, "between geniuses and men of healthy energy merely," are the gentlemen and scholars who serve as "audience to the genius, interpreter to the multitude, cultivated friends for those who need such." And in this middle group she places Milnes, Landor, and Hare.

The second statement appears in a review of the poems of William Thom, a British weaver.[15] In a passage remarkable for its wealth of metaphor, she establishes two concepts of literature and two corresponding critical methods. The first tolerates only what is excellent, "the Iliads and Odysseys of the mind's endeavor," and demands nothing less than perfection of form and content—"golden apples, served up on silver dishes." The other view sees literature as "the great mutual system of interpretation between all kinds and classes of men" and uses one principle in evaluating all "letters," whether written by the "prisoner" in "soot and water, illustrated by rude sketches in charcoal" or by "nature's nobleman" in "letters of gold, with the fair margin filled with exquisite miniature." This principle expressly gives content priority over form; each work is valued "*first*, in proportion to the degree of its revelation as to the life of the human soul, *second*, in proportion to the perfection of form in which that revelation is expressed." She confesses her allegiance to the "genial and generous" tendency of the second view as opposed to the "hypercriticism and pedantry" of the first. And so, after this expansive welcome to proletarian literature, Margaret Fuller finds something to admire in the sincere, if inartistic, efforts of William Thom.

The third declaration of critical approach, prefaced to a review of Longfellow's poems,[16] begins with a definition of poetry. "Poetry is not a superhuman or supernatural gift. It is, on the contrary, the fullest and therefore most completely natural expression of what is human." Obviously this definition is wide enough to include both "humblest minstrels" and "great bards"—the men of healthy energy and the geniuses of the earlier review. But here Margaret Fuller makes a significant qualification, a criterion that any poetry must meet: ". . . this alone we claim, and can welcome none who cannot present this title to our hearing; that the vision be genuine, the expression spontaneous." The criterion of sincerity gives her the opportunity to launch a violent attack on mock poetry, which can be recognized primarily by the jingling rhymes and dragging, stumbling rhythms of its forms, and incidentally by the bombast, the affected simplicity, the sickly sentiment, or the borrowed dignity of its content. Having eliminated merely imitative productions, she returns to her hierarchy and again establishes a middle group, "men of little original poetic power, but of much poetic taste and sensibility, whom we would not wish to have silenced. They do no harm, but much good, (if only their minds are not confounded with those of a higher class,) by educating in others the faculties dominant in themselves. In this class we place the writer at present before us." The whole point of the attack on Longfellow in this review and in others, an attack that made Margaret Fuller notorious to her generation, finds it *raison d'être* in the parenthesis. Longfellow had, at the time, the reputation of a poet of the first order. Judged as such, according to her, he fails miserably. She demonstrates his failure in the rest of the review by analyzing the derivative and bookish quality if his imagery. Judged as a writer of the second class, he is admirable, she grants, for his fine poetic taste which can be employed most usefully in making translations and compiling anthologies.

In the hundred or more literary reviews that she wrote for the *Tribune*,[17] Margaret Fuller adheres faithfully to the method outlined in these statements. In judging the work of a minor writer, she gives credit to any genuine product of his mind or heart, any accurate reflection of his experience, and she confines her attack on imitativeness. Typical of a great many such comments is the following on Charles Seatsfield's *Tokeah:*[18]

> What merit he has is genuine, for he notes down his impressions just as they are received; this merit we must mention wherever we find it—it is so rare at a time when the fear of public opinion and the spirit of imitation make so large a part of literature hacknied or vapid. A book may be coarse and low, but still if it is *something*, there is a satisfaction and a life even in rejecting it, which cannot be derived from these sad painted shadows of sometime somethings.

For all such books she follows her principle of placing content before expression, and such a comment as the following on William Hosmer's poem *Yonnondio* contrasts interestingly with the careful scrutiny of form in the review of Longfellow's poems:[19]

> The book has, as a literary production, many defects. But we greet it with more pleasure than many that are free from such, as being a sincere transcript of what had interested the author. It is thus that an American literature may grow up; if men will write of what is rooted in their real lives, instead of copies from foreign models or ideals which rest only on the clouds above them.

But in spite of her praise of sincerity, Margaret Fuller never lost sight of her basic distinction between poets and men of poetic inclinations, nor did she forget her definition of art as the "ripest fruit of human experience," a transmutation of experience rather than experience itself. In a review[20] of Charles F. Henningsen's *The White Slave*, she reminds her readers:

> The character of the book is one of living reality. There is none of the productive power of genius—no *re*-presentation.

And even as she gives credit to talent, she reiterates the distinction between talent and genius in a review of William Hazlitt's *Table-Talk*:[21]

> Hazlitt is the oracle of the men of talent. They like his richness of observation better than genius, and his sparkling suggestions better than truth.

The basic dualism is even more evident in a review of the poems of Elizabeth Barrett.[22] After warmly praising the lyrics, she turns to two more ambitious poems:

> In the 'Drama of Exile' and the 'Vision of Poets,' where she aims at a Miltonic flight or Dantesque grasp—not in any spirit of rivalry or imitation, but because she is really possessed of a similar mental scope—her success is far below what we find in the

poems of feeling and experience; for she has the vision of a great poet, but little in proportion of his plastic power.

The weakness in artistic execution is demonstrated by the comparison with Milton and Dante. Here she is exercising the function of the comprehensive critic, but the standards are the works of great poets rather than "ideal perfection."

Although her work on the *Tribune* taught her greater flexibility of critical method and more leniency in evaluation, the ambivalence of the essay on Goethe reveals itself whenever she approaches works that have real merit. In a lengthy essay on French novelists of the time,[23] she concludes her recreation of historical circumstances and her sympathetic treatment of the novels of de Vigny, Eugene Sue, Balzac, and George Sand with the precepts:

> To read these or any foreign works fairly, the reader must understand the national circumstances under which they were written. To use them worthily, he must know how to interpret them for the use of the Universe.

Margaret Fuller never did forget that the purpose of literature was to exert a spiritually expanding influence on life. In her criticism she was never more than casually concerned with technique, for ultimately the effect of great literature on her was spiritual rather than aesthetic. She came close to recognizing that, at least for her, this was a real distinction. One of the most significant sentences in all of her critical comment occurs in the dialogue on *Festus*. Aglauron has expressed dissatisfaction with the poem because, in spite of the ambitiousness of its scope, it has failed to indicate the steps through which man passes to spiritual purification. He protests to Laurie, "You smile; one must always expect to be ridiculed when addressing you Aesthetics from the moral point of view." The distinction is not developed, but here she is at the crux of the difference between her own apprehensive criticism and comprehensive criticism. Laurie wins the argument only because *Festus* is not a great poem.

In her criticism of work just short of genius, she is content to be an apprehensive critic, and apprehensive criticism is aesthetic in the broad sense of that term. It requires a full surrender to the intention of the author; it takes into account as many of the historical circumstances of its production as can be recovered; it can achieve its full purpose only by a complete identification of the critic with the work or by re-creation. But the comprehensive critic, in referring to a standard outside the author's intention in order to evaluate the work, is in a nonaesthetic realm. This realm may be moral philosophy; it may be political ideology; it may be something as mistily defined as her "analogies of the universe." Philosophically, it is as far from aesthetic appreciation as Plato is from Croce.

In theory, Margaret Fuller tried to bridge the gap between the two methods by insisting that the comprehensive critic first perform the function of the apprehensive critic; in practice, she solved the problem in most of her reviews by first classifying the work and then applying the method appropriate to the class. But for the reader the practical solution, though it accounts for much of the restless vitality of her writing, is never wholly convincing. What she really wanted to do, perhaps, was to identify Beauty with Truth, but the fusion of the aesthetic and the spiritual is never quite accomplished.

Notes

1. *Papers on Literature and Art* (New York: Wiley & Putnam, 1846), II, 122–165. Since Margaret Fuller herself revised the papers that appear in this book, its text will be quoted for the essays reprinted in it. Later collections of her criticism included other essays with numerous alterations of her text; therefore, for this material the original newspaper or magazine articles will be quoted.

2. For an account of Margaret Fuller's life based on the Boston Public Library Collection see Margaret Munsterberg, "Margaret Fuller Centenary," *Boston Public Library Quarterly*, 2 (July 1950), 245–268.

3. On the range of Margaret Fuller's literary interests and the validity of her judgments, see particularly Helen Neill McMaster, "Margaret Fuller as a Literary Critic," *University of Buffalo Studies*, 7 (December 1928), 35–100; Mason Wade, *Margaret Fuller* (New York: Viking, 1940), chapters 6 and 9: Arthur Schultz, "Margaret Fuller—Transcendentalist Interpreter of German Literature," *Monatschefte für Deütschen Unterricht*, 34 (April 1942), 169–182.

4. *Dial*, 1 (July 1840), 5–11; *Papers on Literature and Art*, I, 1–8.

5. "A Dialogue," *Dial*, 1 (April 1841), 494–496; *Papers on Literature and Art*, I, 11–14.

6. "Festus," *Dial*, 2 (October 1841), 231–261.

7. *Dial*, 2 (July 1841), 1–41.

8. *Conversations with Goethe in the Last Years of His Life*, translated from Eckermann (Boston: Hilliard, Gray, 1839), pp. vii–xxvi.

9. "Menzel's View of Goethe," *Dial*, 1 (January 1841), 340–347.

10. *Western Messenger*, 1 (December 1835), 398–408.

11. *American Monthly Magazine*, n. s. 2 (September, October 1836), 235–250, 320–333; *Papers on Literature and Art*, I, 58–99.

12. "The Modern Drama," *Dial*, 4 (January 1844), 307–349; *Papers on Literature and Art*, I, 100–150.

13. For the influence of the *Tribune* and its circulation, see McMaster, "Fuller as Literary Critic," Appendix.

14. *New York Tribune*, 4 and 28 March 1845.

15. *New York Tribune*, 22 August 1845: *Papers on Literature and Art*, II, 1–9.

16. *New York Tribune*, 10 December 1845: *Papers on Literature and Art*, II, 150–159.

17. For a partial list of Margaret Fuller's contributions to the *Tribune*, see *The Writings of Margaret Fuller*, ed. Mason Wade (New York: Viking, 1941), pp. 596–600. Wade lists 187 items, some erroneously, and omits 69 of her contributions. Only a little more than one-third of these were literary reviews and notices. [This listing has been superseded by Joel Myerson, *Margaret Fuller: A Descriptive Bibliography* (Pittsburgh: University of Pittsburgh Press, 1978) (Ed. Note).]

18. *New York Tribune*, 28 June 1845.

19. *New York Tribune*, 11 December 1844.

20. *New York Tribune*, 10 September 1845.

21. *New York Tribune*, 30 April 1845.

22. *New York Tribune*, 4 January 1845; *Papers on Literature and Art*, II, 22–30.

23. *New York Tribune*, 1 February 1845.

# [Margaret Fuller and Germany]

Henry A. Pochmann[*]

## EARLY INTELLECTUAL INTERESTS

In evaluating the influence of German literature as distinct from theology and philosophy in the complex of forces that went to make up New England Transcendentalism, the career of Margaret Fuller, the Aspasia of the Transcendental high council, is highly significant. More than any other single influence, her activity as reviewer, translator, and conversationalist was the agency that brought German literature into the orbit of the Transcendentalists' interests. Just as the young theologians in the Divinity School were receptive to the pious emotion and high spirituality of Herder and Coleridge, so she was taken with the warm, enthusiastic accounts of German letters then being trumpted "by the wild bugle-call of Thomas Carlyle."[1]

Early in her prodigious program of German studies she perceived that metaphysics would be of inestimable value to her. She looked into Locke "as introductory to a course of English metaphysics, and then [Mme] de Staël on Locke's system," and progressed soon to Kant and the post-Kantians as necessary to one engaged in studying Lessing, Schiller, and Novalis and "meditating on the life of Goethe," but these first excursions into German transcendental speculation left her optimism a bit dashed. By 1836 she was ready to admit the inadequacy of her metaphysical preparation, and the thought that she had considered "*writing* a life of Goethe" now "shocked her."[2] However, the propagation of the "spiritual philosophy" had gone so far in her day that, while it proved insufficient to plumb the deepest meanings of critical transcendentalism, it provided her with confidence in her own intellectual resources, even to the point that she could declare, with perfect sincerity, that she found in America "no intellect comparable to her own."[3] Much that she believed was not only intuitional in the sense in which Parker used the term, but was communicated to her in flashes of mystical insight, and her communication of that "truth" was in turn couched in metaphorical, dark, and obscure language. Yet at bottom there lies the great tradition of German idealism from Kant and Jacobi to

---

[*]Henry A. Pochmann, [Margaret Fuller and Germany], *German Culture in America* (Madison: University of Wisconsin Press, 1957), pp. 440–447, 760–768; reprinted by permission of the University of Wisconsin Press.

Hegel.⁴ On occasions she wrote of "faith" as contrasted with "understanding,"⁵ thereby recalling the Carlylean re- or misstatement of Kant. Again, she would affirm, "Our lives should be considered as a tendency, an approximation only," and in so doing, call up an image of Kant's *Idee*, dimly apprehended.⁶ She conceived of the unity of existence as "the natural life of the soul,"⁷ as "the law and plan of God";⁸ or (what is highly characteristic) she borrowed a term from the German to call it simply the life of "Poesie" or "Poesy." Though the archaism "poesy" was rarely used among the English romantics and was uncommon in modern English generally, it was a Germanism that Margaret became exceedingly fond of, and which she came to employ as a key element in her thought. In German (as antonym to *Prosa* and synonym for *Dichtung*) *Poesie* had been revived by recent romantic critics and poets, and was a favorite of Bettina, Novalis, Schelling, and Goethe. After 1836 Margaret used it freely to denote all forms of the aspiration toward the ideal, the fulfillment of the highest spiritual potentiality of man. It is, she would say, "the ground . . . of the true art of life; it being not merely truth, not merely good, but the beauty which integrates both."⁹ In the end it became a term by which she could establish the identity of the aesthetic and the religious impulses (in their purest state): she called it directly "the spirit of religion. . . . In their essence and their end these [poetry and religion] are one."¹⁰

Thus the gradual elaboration of her concept of "poesy" as suggested by her German studies foreshadowed a marked growth of her interest in the arts as avenues to the spiritual life. Especially after removing in 1839 to Jamaica Plain her preoccupation with poetry, art, and music was pronounced. In the Boston community she had ready access to museums, galleries, and concert halls; she read Flaxman and Retzsch and made the acquaintance of Allston.¹¹ Though she undertook, at the urging of Dr. Channing, to make translations of the German philosophers, her enthusiasm for the study of the arts drew her attention away from metaphysics,¹² and she never completed any of these translations. The necessity, occasioned by her work on the *Dial*, for orienting herself in the basic principles of literary criticism, accentuated this tendency.¹³ She never engaged in a concentrated study of philosophy as a pursuit in itself, and her cry in 1836, "O for a safe and natural way of intuition," represents a point of view she maintained for the rest of her life.¹⁴

In German literature she became speedily more expert, Emerson observing that she knew the subject "more cordially than any other person."¹⁵ Between 1834 and 1838 she demonstrated her command of German by teaching it both in private and in Alcott's school.¹⁶ She was convinced that her vocation was to be teaching,¹⁷ however difficult that would be in an age when all posts in the higher schools were held by men.¹⁸ By 1836 she wrote on the subject of teaching that it was her earnest desire "to interpret the German authors of whom I am so fond to such Americans as are ready to receive," their "kind of culture" being "precisely the counterpoise required by the utilitarian tendencies of our day and place."¹⁹ She soon earned the name "Germanico."²⁰ As early as 1833 she recognized the need of a suitable organ for her purposes, and by March, 1835, she was actively planning, chiefly with Hedge, the "periodical" that eventually became the *Dial*, the fundamental aim of which was to draw New England into a closer relationship with the totality of western culture. Freely offering to "lend a hand" whenever it should be launched, she made clear that if the projector accepted her help, she would emphasize German literature.[21] "I fear I am merely 'Germanico,' and not 'transcendental.' "[22]

## GOETHE AND SCHILLER

Her first tangible step toward popularizing German authors in America was an effort to bring Goethe out from under the cloud cast over him by Menzel's attack on his morality. To this end, she made a verse translation of *Tasso*. As soon as she completed it (March, 1834), she asked Hedge to submit it to Emerson, who read it but recorded no impression of it. All efforts to secure a publisher failed until the appearance of the second volume of her *Works*, edited posthumously by her brother, in 1859.[23] *Tasso* spoke directly to Margaret's heart, and she responded warmly to the human sympathy displayed by Goethe toward the problems of the artist. She did more. She identified her isolated existence with that of the frustrated, misunderstood poet.

> Poor Tasso [she wrote to Emerson] in the play offered his love and services too officiously to all. . . . If I wanted only ideal figures to think about, there are those in literature I like better than any of your living ones. But I want far more. I want habitual intercourse, cheer, inspiration, tenderness. I want these for myself; I want to impart them.[24]

Emerson, who preserved the New England reticences, while regretfully confessing his "porcupine impossibility of contact" with other personalities, doubtless read this confession warily and counted it an embarrassing instance of her overwarm nature, which throughout the period of their friendship half-irritated him and impelled him to keep her at arm's length.[25]

Margaret's first publication was a translation of Eckermann's *Conversations with Goethe* (1839). She shortened the work slightly, omitting references to the *Farbenlehre* and certain other topics. Throwing light on the little-known later years of Goethe and displaying to full advantage the ripe wisdom, the humanity and profundity of his character, this work revealed an entirely new side of him; and many of the younger Transcendentalists must have felt as did Thomas W. Higginson: "It brought him nearer to me than any book, before or since, has ever done."[26]

Her publication in 1842 of a small portion of Bettina (Brentano) von Arnim's *Günderode* in English translation affords a glimpse into some special enthusiasms in the field of German literature about which she otherwise wrote very little. Margaret was fascinated by this German woman who had achieved success as an interpreter of the inner lives of the romantics.[27] She pored eagerly over Bettina's revelations about Goethe and the extended account of her love affair with the elderly poet, and found herself even more carried away by Bettina's second book, a fictionization of her correspondence with the melancholy young poetess Karoline von Günderode.[28] While somewhat shocked at the sensationalism and candor of the *Correspondence with a Child*,[29] she was delighted with the affecting and beautiful account of the friendship between two gifted girls as recorded in *Günderode*.[30] She saw in it a parallel to the intimacy and tender spiritual response that she herself was attempting to establish in her relations with the young girls who flocked about her in Boston.[31] Without pausing to consider whether the work would have any appeal to an American audience, she set about preparing a translation, the first installment of which she put on sale in Elizabeth P. Peabody's shop, though without identifying herself as translator. Thus the "somewhat angular Boston sibyl," as Henry James once characterized her,[32] not only attained a certain release from emotional tension which had been built up in her but made a covert appeal to have her kind of high-minded sensibility understood and recognized by unsympathetic Boston. She was revealing the strong undercurrents of genuinely romantic emotionality that linked her in spirit with such feminine rebels of her time as George Sand, Rahel, Mme de Staël, and Bettina. Needless to say, *Günderode* failed of its purpose.

The salutary effect of her criticism was that, through her continual attention to European writers and modes of thought, she was able to lead the writer and reader away from parochialism toward subjects and attitudes of universal validity. She defined the critic's function as an activity paralleling that of the creative writer, in which they strive together to realize the objective ideal standard that lies outside and beyond them both.[33] The critic, she says, must be accepted in the community of thinkers as one who keeps up a protestant spirit in the literary church. All literature is required to pass muster in the light of reason. This she considered a universal basis of criticism, and its best justification—a conception where both critic and writer are brought before the same bar and permitted to settle their differences on equal terms.[34] From this lofty critical eminence, she sought to review the literary productions of her time. From this point of view, American literature was for her but a small area of the totality of western culture. Her success on the *Tribune* under such an exacting master as Horace Greeley is a signal achievement in American letters, one that has given her the reputation of being "the best critic produced in America before 1850,"[35] only Poe disputing the position with her.

From the German romantic critics, Schlegel and Tieck, and from Goethe, she learned to apply the laws of historical development in the realm of literature even while, like them, she clung to the ideal principle as the ultimate goal.[36] She used both the ideal and objective criticism with success. The former principle, she held, is consonant with New England absolutism; the second is the naturalistic, organic, and at the same time artistic approach of Goethe and the historical school.[37] The former is in agreement with classical tradition in the drama, the latter with Shakespearean-historical tradition.[38]

Margaret's long struggle to understand Goethe involved the reading of all available works, memoirs, and letters. She recognized that in him there spoke a wise and experienced authority on the problems of life, who, observant and penetrating as he was, taught a doctrine of realism and renunciation very difficult either to refute or to accept. This dilemma, together with her fear of the impulses within her that seemed dangerously close to his own "paganism," made the study of Goethe a serious occupation for a full decade of her life. He alternately "solaced" and "disquieted" her soul, yet provided for her the greatest literary as well as spiritual experience.[39] By 1838 she had collected a large mass of notes on Goethe's life, which she tentatively promised to write for Ripley's *Specimens*, but which she never completed. There was no personality, either in books or among her acquaintances, who did more to emancipate her soul from the limitations of New England morality and the restrictions of femininity.

Critics before her were at a loss how to answer Menzel's charges, how to justify the ways of this man to the Puritan conscience.[40] She knew Goethe well enough to see that he lived by a morality and a religion of his own. She completely shifted the ground of argument: she defined morality, not as did the others, as conformity to absolute rules laid down by religious authority, but as conformity to the individual's own code as prescribed by his personality. From this point of view Goethe's life was, as she said, "active, wise, and honored,"[41] as consistent and beyond reproach as the Gods on Olympus. Her essays on Goethe in the *Dial* and her Preface to the *Conversations with Goethe*[42] are not principally criticisms of separate works but rather interpretations—remarkably modern in tone and depth of understanding—of the total personality of the man.[43] She was no "blind admirer" of the man, but her vision was not obscured by the search for values which he does not profess to have. In her essay on "Menzel's View of Goethe"[44] she continued her work of defining the limits and range of Goethe's mind, affirming again and again that we are not fitted to judge him unless we have studied him long and well. "He obliges us to live and grow, that we may walk by his side.... We doubt whether the revolution of the century be not required to interpret the quiet depths of his Saga." She predicted that the caviling at this or that fault in him will end "in making more men and women read these works and [go] 'on and on,' till they forget whether the author be a patriot or a moralist, in the deep humanity of the thought, the breathing nature of the scene."[45] She explained his career as determined by the environmental influence of his youth—as *the* one necessary to bring German literature to its fruition; though, again, she was careful to show the limits of his gifts, deploring the fact that he was not a poet-prophet, but "only a sage."[46]

Particularly appealing to her was the idea that the role of woman in society could be charted and illustrated by taking such Goethean types as Philine, Marianne, Natalie, Makarie, Ottilie, and Margarete as basic symbols for the range of feminine qualities and types. Goethe's ideal of woman, "das ewig Weibliche," was for her a key for interpreting woman's essential character and potentiality. In her feminist treatise *Woman in the Nineteenth Century* she made effective use of the Goethean gallery of female characters, drawing on her vast knowledge of those women who figured in the actual life of Goethe as well as on the creatures of his imagination. In the area of feminism, where

Emerson failed her dismally, Goethe was able to supply her with the orientation and illumination which she so much desired, and which, more than anything else, became the mainspring of her genius and power. In short, the central doctrine that Margaret learned from Goethe (not Emerson) was self-reliance, self-culture.[47] It was this that liberated her from New England puritanism and taught her to resist the pressure of social convention under which her nature felt stifled. It encouraged her to take a bold stand on the "woman question," for it taught her that for all their well-meant chivalry, the men of her society were putting unfair restrictions on the lives of women. From Goethe, too, she learned to take a cosmopolitan view of literature—to look upon the advent of a *Weltliteratur* as the distinctive development of the future. Her discussion of American writers, her praise and blame of individual authors, are predicated on the conviction that the local and national must be harmonized with the ideal and unversal.[48] Finally, she learned from Goethe much about the nature and history of art; only through him did she come to appreciate the great tradition of modern and classical sculpture, architecture, and painting.[49]

## THE ROMANTIC SCHOOL

Yet Goethe's liberalism, his precept of "extraordinary, generous seeking" alone never satisfied the demands of her idealistic nature. She belonged to a generation of romanticists, while Goethe stood apart from that movement, not at its center; he was too calm, too patient with the reality of life, too aloof.[50] Under his influence she could make heroic efforts to master her volatile feelings, to learn the lesson of resignation; but her glowing enthusiasm for Beethoven and her sympathy for the Romantic School show that this was not constantly in her power.[51] The reading of Novalis and Körner she found "a relief, after feeling the immense superiority of Goethe." She was enchanted while she read him, but found "when I shut the book, it seems as if I had lost my personal identity." At such times "the one-sidedness, imperfection, and glow of a mind like that of Novalis" seemed "refreshingly human" to her.[52] The part of her nature that was repulsed by Goethe's tepid equanimity turned, with true spiritual kinship, to the romantic sentiments of Jean Paul, Novalis, and Bettina and, above all, to the "Titanic utterances" of Beethoven.

Margaret's delight in the tenderness, fancy, and rich brilliance of Jean Paul made for direct sympathy with his message and point of view.[53] She found him the priest of natural religion, a "magnetic influence." Her Italianate soul[54] responded to Jean Paul's high coloring, his pure, sensitive heroes, his extravagant, rhapsodic passages of description, and his fondness for omens, puzzles, premonitions, and apparitions.

To become acquainted with Novalis was to indulge some of the same preferences. In 1832 she was studying Novalis and Goethe, and there were moments when she felt much more sympathy for the "wondrous youth" than for the old "master."[55] His religion of nature, his view of the external world as the image of the inward being, the mystical significance he attached to flowers, stones, and minerals—these found many echoes in her own thought. They gave stimulus and direction to the development of her esoteric mystical studies, which even to her closest friends remained an obscure, imperfectly realized phase of her thought.[56]

Her interest in Justinus Kerner also springs from her addiction to the occult. The lengthy account of his *Seherin von Prevorst,* inserted in *Summer on the Lakes* (pp. 125–164) presents the results of some pseudo-scientific investigations into spiritualistic and so-called "electrical" phenomena. A somnambulist from childhood, she could not let the occasion offered by Kerner's book pass without giving her observations to her readers.[57] All in all, she made no favorable impression on the public by displaying her preoccupation with these mysterious phenomena. It was precisely her penchant for mysticism,[58] nature-worship, and spiritualism that caused her New England neighbors—who possessed more of the witch-hunting spirit than they realized—to look upon her as a foreign creature, a Baccante entirely out of place in the realities of American life.[59]

In her treatment of the ballad literature of Germany, Margaret performed a service to the literary culture of America. Her review of Simrock's *Rheinsagen* (1842)[60] showed an insight into the significance of folk poetry as a basis of a national literature. While most enthusiastic about *Rhein-Romantik,* she also emphasized the importance of the *Volkslied* as a social phenomenon,[61] and urged American writers to follow the German example of paying more attention to their own heritage, including the fast-vanishing Indian lore.[62] She made a strong case for an indigenous American literature, rooted in the native past, and not merely imitative of the European.[63]

## GERMAN MUSIC

The romanticism of her nature is revealed most clearly in her passionate response to music. To hear the symphonies of Beethoven was, as she described it, the supreme spiritual and aesthetic experience of her life in New England.[64] In Beethoven she recognized a genius fired with the high idealism of the age, and in his music she heard the surging romantic affirmation of the universality and prophetic power that she demanded in the highest poetry. Knowing Beethoven, she could say that music was the highest of the arts.[65] She would have the soaring aspirations of her nature expressed not in imperfect words, but in appropriate music. The musical genius was the man completely dominated by "das Dämonische." Music transported her completely; it was a rapture, a fulfillment of her strongest "Sehnsucht."[66] It was for her the embodiment of that religion of nature wherein nothing is negation, and all is seen as the substance of the divine; in a sense, her form of Transcendentalism.[67] Her intense experience in music goes far beyond anything that we find in the other major Transcendentalists. Her dependence on it as a ministrant to the soul reveals her a person closely identified with romanticism in a pure and drastic form. Her utterances on the subject (often private poems not intended for publication[68]) lay bare the irrationalism and desperate romantic loneliness which are strong components of her mind. For a number of years she explored the possibility of finding the meaning and fulfillment of her life in art, above all in music. That this endeavor was difficult and indeed finally unsatisfactory is demonstrated by the fact that after 1844 she altered the direction of her interests and began to take an active part in practical issues, in prison reform, pauperism, education, and European political movements.[69]

Margaret Fuller's influence was exerted in many ways. Not the least was her personal impact on leaders of the Transcendental movement—on Emerson, above all, but also on Clarke, Ripley, W. H. Channing, and their younger associates. Anyone interested in music or art or foreign literature knew what Margaret Fuller had said on these subjects, for as Emerson remarked, "All the art, the thought, and the nobleness of New England, seemed . . . related to her and she to it."[70] It was her distinctive achievement to do for American criticism and literary culture what Parker did for American theology. The wide international viewpoint which she fostered became another strong characteristic of American Transcendentalism. German literature, which was in the ascendancy in that day, received the largest share of her attention because she recognized it as the fountainhead for the newer European movements.[71] In later years, after her removal to Italy and her sudden death in 1850, her efforts attained a wide effectiveness through the work of younger Transcendentalist disciples. By her example of faithful translation of the German classics, she encouraged Brooks and Dwight, to name the most prominent, to undertake similar projects; and by her discriminating critical labors, she hastened the assimilation of German authors into the receptive but nonetheless provincial community. In J. F. Clarke, who decades after her death was to become an authority in the field of primitive religions and mythology, we can see the shaping influence of her mind. Emerson's debt to her was at least as great as hers to him. W. H. Channing, another of her close friends, shared her sensitivity to the beauty of European art and literature. W. E. Channing the younger, C. P. Cranch, C. T. Brooks, Bayard Taylor, and John Weiss can be considered as direct inheritors of her position in New England life, for they continued her pioneering work in translation and criticism from the point where she left it.[72]

American interest in German literature generally was in the ascendancy until well into the 50's though the attention focused on different groups of writers at different times. The high point of interest in theology was reached earliest—in the writings of Parker, Ripley, and Hedge. Then followed, with the stimulus of Margaret Fuller's essays, the study of Goethe and the German romantics. This phase culminated before 1865, by which time most of the larger pieces of translation from the German classics had been completed. After the Civil War came a wave of popularizing and imitation of relatively unimportant contemporary writers of fiction. The members of the Genteel Tradition—reared mainly by the Transcendentalists, to be sure, but developing a different social attitude altogether—now set up a new authoritarianism in taste. The deep, firsthand inspiration which the older generation had drawn from Germany had almost disappeared, leaving in its place a mere curiosity for the entertaining or the sentimental.

This superficial worshipfulness of all things German, of course, had already a long history before the so-called Genteel tradition became operative. The temptation on the part of the meagerly gifted to draw upon German materials in the vain hope thereby to give their effusions a certain afflatus as a substitute for what was inherently lacking goes back to the time when German literature first attracted attention. During the early years of the nineteenth century there was a rash of *Werther* adaptations and of Gothic productions faintly reminiscent of German horror. Later, and running parallel to the flow of books that came from the better Transcendentalist writers, there was a steady stream of second- and third-rate books that claimed descent from the same spiritual source, and that had, indeed, a superficial overlay of Germanic inspiration. Examples that come to mind run from Mrs. L. H. Sigourney's *Zinzendorff* (1836) and Philip James Bailey's *Festus* (1839) to John Lothrop Motley's *The Chevalier de Satiniski* (1844) and Sylvester Judd's *Margaret* (1845). Representatives of a later generation are men like Richard Henry Stoddard and Thomas Bailey Aldrich, who, while they stood basically outside the Germanic tradition, did not entirely escape the contagion. Besides writing a biography of Alexander von Humboldt, Stoddard invested several of his poems in a German locale and apparently wrote his ballad "The Wine Cup" on the model of Uhland's "Glück von Edenhall"; while Aldrich's drama *Judith and Holofernes* appears to be a watered-down version of Hebbel's *Judith*. Meanwhile, on a more popular level, certain distinctive concepts originally derived from German books had become popular possessions, so that the Rev. Henry Ward Beecher, in sermons to his Plymouth Church in Brooklyn during the seventies, explained his emotional entanglements to his parishioners in terms of "elective affinities," and presumably was both understood and forgiven. Already in 1856, when Moncure D. Conway preached his farewell sermon in Washington he took his text "from Mignon's song in *Wilhelm Meister*" and quoted Mephistopheles, and assumed that his audience knew enough of Goethe to grasp his allusions. Years later, when he reported to his free-religionist congregation in Cincinnati his meeting with David Friedrich Strauss and explained the latter's "purely anthropological view of immortality," he again presumed that his auditors comprehended him; but it does not follow that either he or his congregation had any longer the intense interest in the several schools of German Biblical criticism that had inspired the generation of Parker, Ripley, and Norton. These instances, and a hundred like them that could be cited, betoken an ever-widening popularity or speaking-acquaintance with concepts or tendencies stemming from Germany, but often lacking the intensity and absorption of interest of an earlier day. That is to say, there was, except among several groups of specialists, a certain dilution of that once clear stream of Germanic influence as it flowed through the thirties and forties, when it provided for many an exhilarating, sometimes intoxicating stimulant, until during the seventies and eighties it was taken, in many quarters, as a kind of postprandial concoction. In literary circles, a dash of German allusiveness served admirably for garnishment, ornamental embellishment, and a universally recognized sign of literary sophistication.

The Transcendentalists on the whole resisted this relative lowering of appreciation and taste; they stood out conspicuously as the only group (with the exception of professional teachers of German literature) whose interest in Goethe, for example, increased rather than diminished; but some of the youngest among them—men like C. T. Brooks and T. W. Higginson—no longer possessing the inspiration of the original Transcendentalists, followed in the easier ways of the Genteel traditionalists.

Notes

1. Ralph Waldo Emerson, William Henry Channing, and James Freeman Clarke, *Memoirs of Margaret Fuller Ossoli*, 2 vols., Boston: Roberts, 1881), I, 114. Apparently no one impelled her more than the younger Carlyle to a study of the German writers, though F. H. Hedge, who had known her since 1823, encouraged her to study German and lent her books from his library. Even when she was only thirteen, Hedge had been impressed by her energetic, robust personality—her mind of "mighty force" and her "independent spirit full of extravagant enthusiasms for great literature." *Memoirs*, I, 90–93. Except for her periods of residence at Groton, Massachusetts, in 1824–1826 and 1833–1836, she moved in the social and intellectual circles of Cambridge throughout the formative years of her life. She was virtually a member of the famous Class of 1829, for she knew personally the students and professors identified with the new spirit at Harvard at that period. Besides Hedge, W. H. Channing, and J. F. Clarke among the students, Professors Everett, Ticknor, Beck, Follen, and Gräter were her friends and mentors. See Thomas Wentworth Higginson, *Margaret Fuller Ossoli* (Boston: Houghton, Mifflin, 1884), pp. 33, 44–45.

About 1832 there was a crystallization of the slowly developing tendencies toward the study of German. In that year Ripley, Parker, and Clarke were first attracted to it, and Margaret's mind was ready to approach the Germans sympathetically. As yet she had found no sphere of activity fully to engage her active mind and well-trained talents. Her first period of study of the language proved a welcome release from the confines of what she considered her circumscribed existence, compounded of what she called "a heavy weight of deceived friendship" and "a great burden of family cares." She likened her progress in German to "the rebound of a string pressed almost to bursting."—*Woman in the Nineteenth Century*, ed. by Arthur B. Fuller (Boston: Roberts, 1893), pp. 358–359. She occupied herself with the masterpieces of French, Italian, Latin, and Spanish literatures as well as with the German, but to her passionate, essentially romantic nature it soon became evident that the recent German literature spoke more directly than any other.—*Memoirs*, I, 112–113. Though self-taught, she gained proficiency in German in a remarkably short time. Clarke reports in detail on her studies in 1832: within the year she has read Goethe's *Faust, Tasso, Iphigenie, Hermann und Dorothea, Die Wahlverwandtschaften*, and *Dichtung und Wahrheit*, as well as substantial portions of the works of Tieck, Körner, Novalis, Jean Paul, and Schiller. Even during 1833–1836, while living at Groton, cut off from the intellectual atmosphere of Cambridge, she went on with her studies uninterruptedly, Hedge and Clarke sending her books from their own libraries. Thus she added to her knowledge the dramas of Lessing, the poetry of Heine, Klopstock, and Uhland, and other writings of Goethe, Jean Paul, Novalis, and Schiller's chief plays, as well as the historical and critical works of Goethe and Schiller. For details see *Memoirs*, I, 108, 121–122, 130, 147–148, 150, 160, 169–170, 174, 242–244; Higginson, *Margaret Fuller Ossoli*, pp. 89–90; and Harold C. Goddard, *Studies in New England Transcendentalism* (New York: Columbia University Press, 1908), pp. 93–97.

2. *Memoirs*, I, 55, 127, 123–124. She got Fichte and Jacobi, but found she "could not understand [Fichte] at all, though the treatise. . . . was one intended to be popular," while Jacobi she could

understand only "in details, but not in system." Even "consulting Buhle's and Tennemann's histories of philosophy and dipping into Brown, Stewart, and that class of books" proved unsatisfactory.—*Memoirs*, I, 127–128, 165. She took up the study of De Wette and Herder as early as 1833, but she quickly learned that neither provided the "system" that answered her needs. During her residence at Groton, too, she dipped into German theology and read Eichhorn and Jahn in the original. She was attempting to study the "evidences of Christianity" at a time when, as she wrote Dr. Hedge, she "doubted the providence of God, but not the immortality of the soul." Her translating the German theologians, chiefly De Wette and Herder, for Dr. Channing one evening a week during 1836 and her reading of De Wette's *Theodore* (which she put aside without finishing) likewise left no permanent impression on her mind.—*Memoirs*, I, 175, 245–246; Higginson, *Margaret Fuller Ossoli*, p. 45.

3. *Memoirs*, I, 234; also I, 236–238.

4. The instrumentality of Coleridge, as well as of her Transcendentalist friends, notably Emerson, in the formulation of her private creed is apparent. Never systematically formulating her philosophy, she did adumbrate a philosophical position that has points in common with German idealism in general and with Fichte's social ethics and Schelling's pantheistic *Identitätsphilosophie* in particular. Hers was a view which saw the universe as a continuous process, with gradations of being ranging from "nature" at the bottom through "man" to "Spirit," or "higher existence," at the summit. This universe was a kind of idealist absolute under the aspect of eternity, but from the temporal aspect it was in process of becoming. The human will was the agency that carried forward the movement from nature to Spirit, and it is Spirit that ascends through, though "not superseding nature." Margaret placed strong emphasis on the organic unity, the oneness and interdependence of parts, with which she viewed the life process. Phrases to the effect that "life and thought" are man's "means of interpreting nature and aspiring to God" point up her conception of the duty of effort and discipline in the struggle toward perfection. Nature is a system whose laws demand man's active work of "interpreting," and God, together with other "intelligences," is a transcendent principle, to which man aspires, but which is hardly encompassed by human understanding. This basically Emersonian metaphysical structure underlies her thought throughout the period of her work in New England. See her "Credo" in *Memoirs*, I, 88–89; also I, 77, 123, and the summary of her argument in *Woman in the Nineteenth Century*, given in Mason Wade, *Margaret Fuller, Whetstone of Genius* (New York: Viking, 1940), p. 289.

5. *Memoirs*, II, 85.

6. *Memoirs*, II, 74.

7. *Memoirs*, I, 342.

8. *Memoirs*, II, 133.

9. *Memoirs*, I, 340–341, 342. Changes wrought on this theme are to be found in all that Margaret wrote, especially in *Woman in the Nineteenth Century*, where the passages are too numerous to list. Poesy was "the always baffled, always reaspiring hope of the finite to compass the infinite," the "Sehnsucht of music."—*Memoirs*, I, 175. It found expression in "External Nature; the Life of Man; Literature; The Fine Arts."—*Memoirs*, I, 327. Again, in another formulation, she wrote of "Religion, in the two modulations of poetry and music," which "descends through an infinity of waves to the lowest abysses of human nature."—*Art, Literature, and the Drama* (Boston: Roberts, 1889), p. 16.

10. *Memoirs*, II, 134; see also I, 120; II, 39.

11. *Memoirs*, I, 189–191, 265, 278, 319–320.

12. *Memoirs*, I, 186.

13. One of the concrete results was her translation, made about 1841, of Schelling's famous lecture *Über das Verhältnis der bildenden Künste zur Natur*, the effect of which can be traced in the fragmentary accounts and snatches from her Conversations that we have in her memoirs (*Memoirs*, I, 319–351, esp. pp. 324–327, 340–345). Ironically enough, as Dr. Wellek observes, she might have saved herself the labor if she had recalled, from her reading of Coleridge's *Literary Remains* in 1837, that Coleridge's paraphrase in his lecture, "Poesy or Art" already made this

treatise available.—René Wellek, "The Minor Transcendentalists and German Philosophy," *New England Quarterly*, 15 (December 1942), 678–679. Sara Coleridge's edition of Coleridge's *Notes and Lectures* (1849) lists the parallels between Schelling and Coleridge. It is worth observing that Coleridge's "Poesy or Art" offers one of the few instances, if not the only one, where he employs the word "poesy," and insofar as Schelling stood close to the forefront of his mind at the time when he wrote the lecture, the German origin of the term seems as inescapable in his case as in Margaret's. In 1847, when Dr. Hedge published his *Prose Writers of Germany*, he used J. E. Cabot's translation of Schelling's lecture,and Margaret's remains still unpublished.

14. *Memoirs*, I, 171. In her journalistic work in New York, after the autumn of 1844, she wrote very little on philosophy, theology, or science. There is a review by her of A. v. Humboldt's *Kosmos* in the *Tribune* for 11 July 1845; a brief biographical notice of William Smith's *Memoir of J. G. Fichte*, for 9 July 1846; and in reviewing new editions of C. B. Brown's *Ormond and Wieland* (*Tribune*, 25 July 1846) she wrote with disarming innocence of Brown and Godwin as "born Hegelians, without the pretensions of science." Apparently she never got much beyond her earlier difficulties with Jacobi and Fichte.

15. *Memoirs*, I, 204–205.

16. Her class of beginners could read, at the end of three weeks, thirty pages at a lesson. "With more advanced pupils," she reported, "I read, in twenty-four weeks, Schiller's Don Carlos, Artists, and Song of the Bell . . . Goethe's Hermann and Dorothea, Goetz . . . Iphigenia, first part of Faust,— 3 weeks of thorough study . . . as valuable to me as to them,—and Clavigo . . . Lessing's Nathan, Minna, Emilia Galeotti [sic]; parts of Tieck's Phantasus, and nearly the whole of Richter's Titan."— *Memoirs*, I, 174.

We may be sure that this remarkable list of books was covered in twenty-four weeks only by dint of hard work and superior stimulation from the teacher. Her choice of works, especially her emphasis on Goethe, when Goethe was widely suspect, and when the teaching of German literature was in its formative stages, is testimony to her discrimination. Her choice of Tieck and Jean Paul betrays a leaning toward romanticism which is a significant portent of later developments.

17. It was observed by many who heard her Conversations later that they were based essentially on the principles and methods of the classroom.

18. Her experiences in the liberal atmosphere of Alcott's Temple School gave her decided and advanced opinions on the teaching of foreign languages to children. She was convinced that the modern European tongues, "by familiar instruction and an *intelligent method*," might be taught "with perfect ease during the years of childhood." She felt that "much of the most precious part of short human lives is now wasted from an ignorance of what might easily be done for children, and without taking from them time they need for common life, play, and bodily growth, more than at present."—*Life Without and Life Within* (Boston: Brown, Taggard and Chase, 1860), pp. 95–96, 103. It was to be several decades before the principles here enunciated got as much as recognition, much less practical introduction, in the educational system of our country.

19. For her detailed plans, see *Memoirs*, I, 168–169.

20. Higginson relates an anecdote to the effect that when Margaret's successor in Alcott's school was confronted by one of Margaret's admirers who claimed, "Miss Fuller says she *thinks* in German; do you believe it?" the reply was, "Oh, yes! I do not doubt it; I myself dream in Cherokee."— *Margaret Fuller Ossoli*, pp. 92–93.

Horace Greeley, writing after Margaret's death, seriously put forth the theory that her knowledge of German hampered her expression in English. The so-called German influence on her expression is not so much the result as the evidence of her sympathy for the writers of the German Romantic School. She admired Novalis and Jean Paul despite—or perhaps because of—their fondness for far-fetched metaphors, symbolism, dark allegory, and discursiveness. But readers who have trouble with her writing are oftener struggling with her thought than with her mode of expressing it. She was a subtle psychologist; her mind moved suddenly, sometimes brilliantly, from a central theme to tangential matters, and she had little gift for shaping her thoughts into any kind of external orderliness. She was often careless about grammatical structure and wrote too hastily to make the successive steps of her thought clear; she seldom revised and was too impatient to polish her expression. Poe, always a severe critic of expression, while calling her an "ill-tempered" and "detestable old maid," yet admitted his admiration for her style (*The Complete Works of Edgar Allan Poe*, ed. James A. Harrison [New York: Thomas Y. Crowell, 1902], XV, 79; XVII, 290, 333).

Margaret's fervent desire to visit the German scenes made vivid by her reading was frustrated first by family complications and later by her overwhelming disappointment over the sad termination of her romance with James Nathan (Gotendorf), the Hamburg merchant, whom she had met in New York. When she finally went to Europe, many things prevented her visit to Germany, among them a shift in her interests away from Germany to contemporary France, England, and Italy. So "Germanico" never set foot on German soil.

21. See her statement in the *Dial*, 2 (July 1841), 134; also *Art, Literature, and the Drama*, p. 7; *Life Without and Life Within*, p. 96; and *Memoirs*, I, 169. It is not recorded how many of her "Conversations" were on the subject of German literature. The only indication is that "Goethe" is named as one of the topics, but undoubtedly she drew largely upon her favorite reading, even when the announced topic was "Mythology" or "Nature."—*Memoirs*, I, 351.

22. *Margaret Fuller Ossoli*, p. 141. She supported the venture with characteristic generosity and idealistic enthusiasm. She received little, if any, of the promised compensation for her work as editor of the *Dial* during its first two years or for her translation of Eckermann's *Conversations with Goethe*, published in Ripley's series.

Though German literature had found champions before Margaret Fuller wrote for the *Dial*, the proportion of material on the subject was nowhere so high as in that magazine. Roughly classifying the contents of the *Dial's* literature (including literary criticisms and book reviews), philosophy, theology, social criticism, education, the arts, and the sciences, an analysis of its four volumes shows that literature absorbed 56.3 per cent of the total space, or 317 items, aggregating 1142 pages. A breakdown of the latter, according to nationalities, reveals the following percentages of space: American, 53 per cent, or 255 items totaling 607 pages; German, 18.4 per cent (21 items, 216 pages); Greek, 5 per cent (4 items, 57 pages); French, 4.3 per cent (3 items, 48 pages); Italian, 1.9 per cent (4 items, 21 pages); all others (Chinese, Latin, Indian, Egyptian, Spanish, etc.) receiving less than 1 per cent each.

23. *Art, Literature, and the Drama*, pp. 353–449. An excerpt (Act II, scenes 1–2) appeared in the *Dial*, 2 (January 1842), 399–407. In the Preface she made abundant apologies for the shortcomings of her translation: inexact metrical pattern, broken lines, slight omissions, condensations of thought, and a few misconstructions of idiomatic expressions; yet the work is rendered in clear, simple verse and, on the whole does justice to the structure and tone of the original. She took Coleridge's treatment of *Wallenstein* for her ideal of translation, preserving a tender conscience about the liberties permissible in the translator's art. See *Life Without and Life Within*, p. 96, and *Art, Literature, and the Drama*, pp. 355–356; also the Preface to her translation of *Günderode* (Boston: T. O. H. P. Burnham, 1861), p. vi: "The exact transmission of thought seems to me the one important thing in a translation; if grace and purity of style come of themselves, it is so much gained."

24. *Memoirs*, I, 287.

25. He fidgeted under her attentions, and she smarted at his rebuffs. She tried the art of pleasing, cajolery, and what she termed "shocking familiarity"; but Emerson maintained his reserve toward the woman who asked him archly, "Who would be a goody that could be a genius?" Finally they came to an understanding: Margaret recorded having "an excellent talk: we agreed that my God was love, his truth." Thereafter she was content to accept his friendship on his, not her, terms. Wistfully she wrote, "My expectations are moderate now!"—Harry R. Warfel, "Margaret Fuller and Ralph Waldo Emerson," *PMLA*, 50 (June 1935), 577–578, 581–582, 589–593.

26. *Margaret Fuller Ossoli*, p. 189.

27. As a girl, Bettina (1785–1859) had been closely associated with the Heidelberg school of romantics. In many ways she carried to an extreme the idiosyncrasies, the hyperemotionality, the pose of spiritual flirtatiousness of that group. In America she became known through her sensational, partly fictional *Goethes Briefwechsel mit einem Kinde* (1835–1837), wherein she styled herself as the admiring "child" who basked in the radiance of Goethe's company. Emerson was fond of

Bettina's "pure and poetic" nature, "her wit, humor, will, and pure aspirations," and encouraged the appearance of the first American edition of *Goethe's Correspondence with a Child* in 1841 (See *Journals of Ralph Waldo Emerson*, ed. Edward Waldo Emerson and Waldo Emerson Forbes [Boston: Houghton Mifflin, 1909–1914], V, 145, 237–238; VI, 229; IX, 212; *The Letters of Ralph Waldo Emerson*, ed. Ralph L. Rusk [New York: Columbia University Press, 1939], II, 208–209, 210n, 220, 236, 254n; III, 77); but Margaret was the first to notice Bettina, for she owned, or at least was reading, the book in May 1838 (Emerson, *Letters*, II, 135–136). There was formed quickly a little Bettina-cult among such adherents of Transcendentalism as Lydia Maria Child, Carolyn Sturgis, J. S. Dwight, G. W. Curtis, Louisa May Alcott, Mrs. Eliza Buckminster Lee, and Albert Brisbane.

28. *Die Günderode*, 2 vols. (Grünberg, 1840); published in America as *Günderode* (Boston: E. P. Peabody, 1842); reprinted as *Günderode. Correspondence of Fräulein Günderode and Bettina von Arnim* (Boston: T. O. H. P. Burnham, 1861). The first eighty-six pages are essentially the same text as that of the 1842 edition; the remainder, together with minor revisions of the first part, was translated by Mrs. Minna Wesselhoeft.

29. See Margaret's "Bettina Brentano and her Friend Günderode," *Dial*, 2 (January 1842), 351; also 316; *Memoirs*, II, 51–52, 58, 140.

30. *Günderode* (Boston: E. P. Peabody, 1842), pp. vi–x.

31. Margaret's life as a case history of pathological repression and sublimation is perhaps overemphasized in Katherine Anthony's *Margaret Fuller. A Psychological Biography* (New York: Harcourt, Brace and Howe, 1920), p. 37; but her translation of *Günderode* shows how strong was her predilection for the society of admiring young girls, and the overtones of homosexual attraction appear plainly in her description of Karoline. However, the formation of cults of friendship is so important a part of romantic *Weltanschauung* that Margaret's views must be examined for their literary and philosophical ramifications just as carefully as for their purely psychological significance.

32. *William Wetmore Story and his Friends* (Boston: Houghton, Mifflin, 1903), I, 103.

33. See *Dial*, 1 (April 1841), 494–496; *Life Without and Life Within*, pp. 21–24.

34. Many of her critics emphasized her pose of literary dictator as the mark of her work. This impression gained currency because of a mannerism of hers resulting from a strong confidence in her own powers—an evidence merely that she had the courage to speak her convictions in conformity with her principles. In a time when the sensitive feelings of a Cooper or a Longfellow were distinctly discouraging to any kind of objective criticism, and when Poe was lashing out in personal pique against the objects of his irrational animus, Margaret stoutly affirmed her determination to criticize justly and fairly in the light of universal, ideal principles which she recognized.—*Life Without and Life Within*, p. 88.

35. Helen Neill McMaster, "Margaret Fuller as a Literary Critic," *University of Buffalo Studies*, 7 (December 1928), 42.

36. *Art, Literature, and the Drama*, p. 357.

37. *Art, Literature, and the Drama*, p. 179. See also her "Short Essay on Critics," *Dial*, 1 (July 1840), 5–11, a remarkably sane yet penetrating statement of the critic's function.

38. See *Memoirs*, I, 30.

39. *Memoirs*, I, 146, 160–161. Many of her translations from Goethe were made without thought of publication, but for her pleasure or profit. They reveal much about her struggles over the fundamental questions of religion at the time when she was looking for guidance from Goethe. See Frederick Augustus Braun, *Margaret Fuller and Goethe* (New York: Henry Holt, 1910), pp. 216–241, for a full discussion of her translations from Goethe; also the bibliography in *The Writings of Margaret Fuller*, ed. Mason Wade (New York: Viking, 1941), pp. 595–600.

In her work of introducing the masters of German literature, she could contribute little to the fame of Lessing and Schiller, already relatively well known in America. She accepted both as established classics and devoted to them a large portion of the time in her classes at Alcott's school. Of Lessing she had little to say in her critical works, though Schiller is mentioned frequently as an example of the "classical" mode of dramatic composition, linked in her mind with Sophocles and Shakespeare.—*Memoirs*, I, 121; *Art, Literature, and the Drama*, pp. 111, 210. She admired Schiller's historical writings, as well as his poetry and dramas.—*Memoirs*, I, 148, 244. His high idealism and moral fervor spoke directly to the strain of New England idealism in her, and there was much less of a struggle between her nature and his than between the more complex, worldly Goethe and herself. In 1833 she said: "I don't like Goethe as well as Schiller now. I mean, I am not so happy in reading him. That perfect wisdom and *merciless* nature seems cold, after those seducing pictures of forms more beautiful than truth."—*Memoirs*, I, 117. However, in the years following, as she trained herself in the Goethean point of view, the interest in Schiller was eclipsed by admiration for the author of *Faust* and *Meister*. See *Woman in the Nineteenth Century*, pp. 30, 44–45, 232, 342: *Art, Literature, and the Drama*, p. 90; *Life Without and Life Within*, pp. 134–135.

40. Parker and Ripley both started from a supposition that they could show him to be devout, even Christian, at heart; but they censured him on the score of morality for his personal conduct toward Friederike and Lili and for bringing Christine Vulpius into his house as his unwedded wife.

41. *Memoirs*, I, 197.

42. Other pieces of Goethe criticism include a review of *Egmont*, translated anonymously (Boston: James Munroe, 1841), in *Dial*, 2 (January 1842), 394; a short notice of a new translation of *Faust*, in *Dial*, 2 (July 1841), 134; a review of George Calvert's translation of the *Correspondence between Schiller and Goethe*, in the *New-York Daily Tribune* for 14 March 1845; a review of S. G. Ward's translation of Goethe's *Essays on Art* (Boston, 1845), in the *Tribune* for 29 May 1845. The last two contain ringing answers to the attacks upon Goethe by Palmer Putnam in the 1844 Phi Beta Kappa address at Harvard.

43. In the Preface to the *Conversations* she made a brilliant attack on all classes of Goethe's critics and met the charges arranged under four heads: "(1) He is not a Christian. (2) He is not an Idealist. (3) He is not a Democrat. (4) He is not Schiller." Unlike Parker, who took recourse to the "Bekenntnisse einer schönen Seele" to argue that Goethe was a Christian, Margaret readily admitted that he was a "Greek" in spirit, and as such was not to be judged by conventional Christian standards. She pointed out that this is at the bottom of his aversion "for the worship of sorrow," and that his creed is one of self-reliance and calm acceptance—hence not moralistic at all in the usual sense of the word. He is not a spiritual writer as commonly conceived; he leaves his readers to draw the moral for themselves. As to the second charge, she pointed out that his plan was never to "alter or exalt Nature," and implied that this, too, is a justifiable way of looking at the universe. As to his being aristocratic, she was not much alarmed at the appearance of acquiescence to tradition in the old sage; she explained it on the ground that an artist needs repose to do his work, and that by nature Goethe was reflective not active, and conservative because his study was the world as it is, not as he would dream it should be. For those who wanted the other there was Schiller; but one Schiller, she felt, was enough.

Margaret pleaded for "habits of more liberal criticism" and urged Goethe's detractors to "leave this way of judging from comparison or personal prejudice." Admitting that her own tastes are "often displeased by German writers, even by Goethe," she attempted an honest assessment of his achievevents. She saw that he stood for perfection of the few, for a belief in man's continual effort, for thought rather than reformist action, for nature rather than providence. He was the best German stylist, an admirable critic of art and literature, an acute observer of human beings and of external nature. His mind saw well the individuality of character and the universality of thought. On the negative side, she admitted she was disturbed—as were many—by his aversion to pain and by the isolation of his heart. And on the point of structure, she admitted that some of his later works fell short of the masterly handling shown in the works of his classical period (pp. xviii–xxi).

44. *Dial*, 1 (January 1841), 240–274; also *Life Without and Life Within*, pp. 13–22.

45. *Life Without and Life Within*, p. 14.

46. *Life Without and Life Within*, p. 20. Though "he did not in one short life complete his circle," we cannot in this world where so few men have in any degree redeemed their inheritance, "neglect a nature so rich and so manifestly progressive" (p. 15). She admits that in the "Lili-Episode" he was "right as a genius, but wrong as a character." She disposes of the oft-repeated

charge of his Epicureanism by showing the difference between "calm self-trust" and the imputed "selfish indifference." Thus she sets the question of his importance quite apart from the question of his spiritualism. Thus she taught Emerson and the Transcendentalists (and eventually the more sensitive or squeamish moralistic critics in the ranks of the conservatives) a point of view which would take them out of their parochialism into the full current of modern life.

Her point of view is elaborated in subsequent discussions, notably the essay "Goethe" in the *Dial*, 2 (July 1841), 1-41, which is perhaps the most impressive of them all. She moved through his several periods with the assurance that results from thorough study, able to explain the significance of each work for the life of the author and his age. Werther represents a phase of his youth that he soon overcame; Faust of *Faust I* represents the highest idealistic striving that Goethe ever showed: *Meister* is a continuation of *Faust;* the *Wanderjahre* is an indispensable second part of the *Lehrjahre,* wherein the analysis of Wilhelm is completed. The portraits of Marianne, Philine, Theresa, Natalie, and Makarie are symbolical of the stages of education through which the hero must pass. Makarie emerges as the outstandingly spiritual figure, the one who touches most closely the high idealism of Margaret's nature and the one where Goethe's "simple soberness" is abandoned for a time to "glow with the central fire" (*ibid.*, p. 43). In a few paragraphs she absolves the *Wahlverwandtschaften* of charges of coldness and immortality; she reads this work as one that is "moral in its outward effect, and religious even to piety in its spirit." "Holy" Ottilie is a person of "saintly sweetness" (*ibid.*, pp. 48, 49), and the work is so carefully executed, so richly and delicately wrought, as to command the highest praise: "It is a work of art! At last I understand that world within a world, that ripest fruit of human nature, which is called art."—*Ibid.*, p. 50. Following a similar analysis of *Iphigenie auf Tauris,* she begs her reader to "enter into his higher tendency, thank him for such angels as Iphigenie, whose simple truth mocks at all his wise 'Beschränkungen.' "

In this spirit of enthusiastic enjoyment of his poetic art she presented Goethe in her "Conversations" in Boston and her essays in the *Dial*. Thus she helped Emerson to read Goethe with a less clouded vision and brought him round from an attitude of disdain to the point where he could make Goethe the writer-type in his *Representative Men*. See *The Correspondence of Thomas Carlyle and Ralph Waldo Emerson,* ed. Charles Eliot Norton (Boston: James R. Osgood, 1883), II, 114; *Memoirs,* I, 242-243.

47. She was, of course, familiar with Emerson's preachments on this score; but his self-reliance, as she interpreted what he said regarding woman's proper sphere in general and how he conducted himself with respect to her in particular, did not appear to extend equally to men and women. See Warfel, "Fuller and Emerson," pp. 592-593.

48. *Life Without and Life Within,* esp. pp. 298-299.

49. *Memoirs,* I, 149, 266.

50. See Higginson, *Margaret Fuller Ossoli,* p. 289; also p. 284; *Memoirs,* I, 167.

51. *Memoirs,* I, 160-161.

52. On the matter of her appreciation of nature, for example, she stood nearer to the romantics than to Goethe. Though Goethe taught her much in the way of careful observation of nature, and his Spinozistic pantheism had something in common with her feeling for the God immanent in nature, his *Farbenlehre* appealed to her not because it was a scientific, empirical study but because she could interpret it in its "mystical significance."—Higginson, *Margaret Fuller Ossoli,* p. 101. Like Novalis, she looked on the forms of nature symbolically and mystically, and had no sympathy with the "botanizing, geologizing, and dissecting" of the natural scientist.—*Memoirs,* I, 263.

53. The period of her greatest enthusiasm for Richter was her years at Groton. She prescribed his *Titan,* a most difficult and obscure book for school children, to be read by her advanced class in Alcott's school. The reading of Jean Paul let loose the torrents of sentiment within her, and she loved him deeply.—*Memoirs,* I, 130. *Titan,* she said, is a "noble work, and fit to raise a reader into that high serene of thought where pedants cannot enter."—*Memoirs,* I, 169-170. By 1833 she had written the poems on Richter that she published in the *Dial* in 1840. In them she celebrated him as the "Poet of Nature," a fanciful, delicate painter of scenes in the gorgeous style of Titian, a man "with Raphael's dignity" and "celestial love." Is there in Richter "a want of order," as his critics say? No, "not of *system* in its highest sense," for he has the order and plan of the universe itself, being

coequal to it and its perfect mirror. "Nature's wise temple and the azure dome/Have plan enough for the free spirit's home!" This is the effusive, girlish language with which she praised the romantic subjectivity, sublime striving, and moral earnestness of an arch-romantic.

54. See Wade, *Fuller*, pp. 215–217, and Anthony, *Fuller*, p. 155.

55. *Memoirs*, I, 118–119; also pp. 120–121, 123.

56. Note her mystical flower-fantasies, with their peculiar hints at a doctrine of the transmigration of souls: "Yuca Filamentosa," *Dial*, 2 (January 1842), 286–288; "Magnolia of Lake Pontchartrain," *Dial*, 1 (January 1841), 299–305; also her poems on the passionflower (*Memoirs*, I, 111), the "Dahlia, rose and heliotrope" (*Life Without and Life Within*, p. 367), "The flower and the Pearl" (*Life Without and Life Within*, p. 351), and "Lines" (*Life Without and Life Within*, p. 375). They are filled with symbolism derived mainly from Novalis ("die blaue Blume"), from *Faust* ("the mothers"), and from remoter neo-Platonic sources. See Higginson, *Margaret Fuller Ossoli*, pp. 96–97, 99, 305; *Memoirs*, II, 95. She was especially fond of the symbol of the carbuncle of *Heinrich von Ofterdingen*. See *Woman in the Nineteenth Century*, p. 343, and *Memoirs*, II, 95.

57. She explained these phenomena as evidences of the overdevelopment of the spiritual faculties. By no means unduly obsessed with the subject, she took the common-sense attitude that the material and spiritual parts of man's nature "should be in equipoise." She sought a rationale for the phenomena of second sight and prophecy, which, to a woman of her unusual gifts and intuitive powers, seemed an undeniable fact of her existence. In a poet with thorough training and artistic organization, she felt that these gifts of clairvoyance could be transformed into true prophetic power, but she doubted that there was much of higher meaning in the life of the seeress described by Kerner.—*Summer on the Lakes*, in *At Home and Abroad*, p. 164.

58. See her poem, "Sub Rosa Crux," *Memoirs*, II, 114.

59. She understood well what Goethe meant by "das Dämonische"; indeed, she divined that she was more under the power of the "magnetic fluid" than he—that she was better fitted than he for the role of prophet of the spiritual kingdom. "With me, for weeks and months, the daemon works his will."—*Memoirs*, I, 224–226; see also II, 218, 222, 284, and Anthony, *Fuller*, pp. 52–53.

60. "Romaic and Rhine Ballads," *Dial*, 3 (October 1842), 137–180.

61. See *Woman in the Nineteenth Century*, pp. 58–59.

62. *Dial*, 3 (October 1842), 179; *Art, Literature, and the Drama*, p. 333; Higginson, *Margaret Fuller Ossoli*, pp. 131, 294.

63. Among other Germans that occupied her attention, Theodor Körner appealed to her romantic interest in medievalism and nationalism. See her essay on Körner in the *Western Messenger*, 4 (January 1838), 306–311, 369–375, and *Memoirs*, II, 252. She admired Ferdinand Freiligrath, the exiled poet of political liberty (see *At Home and Abroad*, p. 180). Uhland and Heine figure little in her writings; her projected papers on Novalis and on Tieck never appeared in print. On the subject of Fouqué, she wrote a review of the *Undine* for the *Tribune* (4 April 1845). Klopstock, whom she studied early, is the subject of a sentimental sketch "Meta" (*Dial*, January 1841), one of her weakest performances—one in which she gave a falsely sentimental impression of Klopstock.

64. Her first response went out to Haydn and Handel, well represented in the great choral concerts of the 1830s. After 1838, when she came within easy reach of Boston, she heard many performances of classical works by Beethoven, Mozart, and others, and the realization broke upon her that a great new cultural force was opening up for her in the musical art. When, in 1841, the epoch-making Boston Academy music series presented the Beethoven symphonies, the Boston community felt that Beethoven was attuned to the currents of idealism then stirring New England. Some of the younger Transcendentalists, notably J. S. Dwight, supported the vogue vigorously and became converts to the kind of faith that seemed to speak out of Beethoven's great measures. Margaret devoted space in the *Dial* to urging public support of the concerts. The Beethoven vogue coincided with the high point of the Transcendentalist enthusiasm; after 1844 the Beethoven symphonies were dropped from the programs.

65. *Woman in the Nineteenth Century,* pp. 190–191; *Memoirs,* I, 343. In her article on Goethe (*Dial,* July 1841) she cited Beethoven as the example of the artist who succeeded where the poet failed—the one figure with whom she dared to reproach Goethe: "We pardon thee, Goethe,— but thee, Beethoven, we revere, for thou hast maintained the worship of the Manly, the Permanent, the True!"—*Life Without and Life Within,* pp. 45–47. See also *Art, Literature, and the Drama,* pp. 224–225, for her statement of how the "spiral and undulatory movements of the beautiful creation" are best expressed in music, and how the listener finds in music "thought most clearly, because most mystically, perceived." See *Memoirs,* I, 186, 309–310, and her poem "The Land of Music," *At Home and Abroad,* p. 107. Margaret came to the hearing of Beethoven with her curiosity aroused from her reading of Bettina's *Correspondence with a Child.* Even in Germany, Bettina's sympathetic appreciation did much for the recognition of Beethoven; in America there was formed something like a Beethoven cult among Margaret's friends, including Dwight, Lydia Maria Child, and the poet Cranch. In private correspondence these enthusiasts fell into the jargon of musical terminology which they playfully employed to describe emotions and feelings: the "flat seventh," "the diapason of the soul," etc., in obvious imitation of Bettina. As for Margaret, she had always been fond of such words as "harmony," "dissonance," "rhythm," "chord," and "melody." Now she yielded more and more to the temptation to write in musical metaphors and thus to becloud still further her none too clear style. For examples, see *Woman in the Nineteenth Century;* Mason Wade, *Fuller,* pp. 289–290; *Memoirs,* II, 59–60, 99–100; Emerson's *Letters,* I, 280.

66. *Memoirs,* I, 275.

67. Emerson showed a sharp perception of the way in which her partly frustrated and thwarted impulses found their "compensation" and their "solace" in art, poetry, and especially music. See her letter, written one evening on returning from the symphony, addressed to Beethoven, confiding her desperate longing—reminiscent of Bettina's adulatory letters (*Memoirs,* I, 232–234).

68. See Emerson's *Letters,* II, 239 (24 November 1839).

69. In her earlier career she had been relatively indifferent to the organized reform movements of the day, especially toward the slavery issues and the question of socialism, though she was active in the cause of women's rights from the first. It was traditional in her family to stand for democratic Jeffersonianism against Bostonian Federalism, and she was too strong an individualist to entertain the thought of residing at Brook Farm. Like Emerson, she wished the reformers well, but was not convinced that the time was ripe for building a Utopia. After 1844, she began to devote more space in her columns to articles on political developments and social experiments, here and abroad, and especially in Germany; and she welcomed the advent of the New York *Deutsche Schnellpost* as the organ of the German-Americans in this country. When she saw at first hand the turmoil of Italy and the evils there of oppression, she was stirred to take an active part in political affairs.

70. *Memoirs,* I, 213.

71. However important Goethe and the Romantic School were to her, still she recognized that the enthusiasm of regenerate Unitarianism which went by the Transcendental name was basically of New England origin, and she kept throughout her characteristic American faith in heroic, unbending idealism. But insofar as American Transcendentalism is a part of the broader movement toward romanticism that characterizes the early decades of the nineteenth century, it was inevitable that some American thinkers would become aware of the universal nature of the movement. Margaret was one of those.

72. This inheritance originated in the occasional visits that she made to Brook Farm, where the young Transcendentalists gathered to sing, read poetry, enact plays, and hold discussions. Here she often led the conversation, heard the amateur musical performances of Cranch and Dwight, and encouraged their translating the lyrics of Goethe and Schiller. In this carefree, sociable, irrepressibly joyous group of talented and congenial spirits there was engendered a new romantic approach toward life and art which in several cases dominated these men for the better part of the century and in some cases fed directly into the forces that culminated in the Genteel Tradition. In the beginning, it was the *Romantische Schule* transplanted to America, isolated and scorned for the most part by the average citizen as well as by the theological and social stalwarts of New England.

Yet it was the starting-point for an important tradition in American art and music as well as in literature and criticism. The communal character of so many of the translation projects carried out by these men is noteworthy. Ripley, John Weiss, J. E. Cabot, C. T. Brooks, and others were represented in Hedge's *Prose Writers of Germany*, while Bancroft, Margaret Fuller, Clarke, G. W. Haven, N. L. Frothingham, Hedge, C. P. Cranch, and W. H. Channing contributed to Dwight's *Select Minor Poems*. Goethe's *Autobiography* was prepared principally by Godwin, but parts were completed by Dwight and Dana. Three men collaborated in the *Memoirs* of Margaret Fuller. The *Dial*, the *Western Messenger*, and Dwight's *Journal of Music* were essentially co-operative undertakings. Collaboration continued unabated among the St. Louis Hegelians and the later school of Concord philosophers.

# "Margaret Fuller and the Abolition Movement"[1]

Francis E. Kearns°

Margaret Fuller's reputation as a feminist lies firmly established on two major contributions to the woman's rights movement—the conducting of her Conversation classes for women from 1839 to 1844 and her authorship of the tract *Woman in the Nineteenth Century*. The Conversation classes brought together some of the most intelligent women of Boston for the avowed purpose of rectifying the inadequacies resulting from the inferior education allotted to women at the time, whereas *Woman in the Nineteenth Century*, on the other hand, called for broader educational and employment opportunities for women and propounded a theory of marriage based on only the most idealistic principles. Considering her great contributions to the woman's rights movement, it is surprising that Margaret Fuller never took an active part in another equalitarian struggle which during her lifetime gripped the imagination of American reformers, the Abolition movement.

Many of the leaders in the Abolition cause were outstanding proponents of woman's rights. And it has become a commonplace observation in works dealing with the development of the woman's rights movement in America, works ranging from the early *History of Woman Suffrage* by Elizabeth Cady Stanton and Susan B. Anthony[2] to the recent *Century of Struggle* by Eleanor Flexner,[3] that the anti-slavery struggle was actually the progenitor of the woman suffrage movement. Through their efforts in behalf of the Negro slave, women first learned to organize, to hold public meetings, and to conduct petition campaigns. In the social position of the slave they saw an analogy with their own lot and soon began to evolve a philosophy of their basic rights. Indeed, it was as a direct result of the anti-slavery movement that the first woman's rights convention in America was held. In 1840 the American delegation which attended the World Anti-Slavery Convention in London included in its ranks several women, but the convention refused to seat female delegates. Two of the American delegates thus rejected, Elizabeth Cady Stanton and Lucretia Mott, both graduates of Margaret's Conversation classes, left London determined to establish an organized movement for the emancipation of women; and in 1848, at

°Francis E. Kearns, "Margaret Fuller and the Abolition Movement," *Journal of the History of Ideas*, 25 (January–March 1964), 120–127; reprinted by permission of the publisher.

Seneca Falls, New York, they convened the first Woman's Rights Convention in America. Margaret Fuller was aware of the connection between the two movements, for in *Woman in the Nineteenth Century* she declared: "Of all its [freedom's] banners, none has been more steadily upheld, and under none have more valor and willingness for real sacrifices been shown, than that of the champion of the enslaved African. And this band it is, which, partly from a natural following out of principles, partly because many women have been prominent in that cause, makes, just now, the warmest appeal in behalf of woman."[4]

The fact that she perceived this connection makes her unwillingness to join the ranks of the Abolitionists all the more puzzling. Moreover, there are other factors in Margaret Fuller's background which would seem to have impelled her toward a sympathy with the Abolition movement. Many of her friends, including James Freeman Clarke and W. H. Channing, were closely identified with this cause. Theodore Parker, whom she knew through the Transcendental Club and her editorship of the *Dial*, preached against slavery and actively assisted in the escape of fugitive slaves. Furthermore, several of the women who attended the Conversations, in particular Mrs. Ellis Gray Loring and Lydia Maria Child, the latter having assumed the editorship of the New York *Anti-Slavery Standard* in 1841, were active participants in the Abolition movement. In Margaret's own family there was a strong tradition of anti-slavery feeling. As a Representative from Massachusetts, her father opposed the Missouri Compromise in 1820; and, indeed, his first speech in Congress was made in an effort to defeat a bill designed to curb the activities of the underground railroad.[5]

Here an important distinction must be made between disdain for the Abolitionists, many of whom combined religious fanaticism with their equalitarian sentiments, and disdain for the anti-slavery movement itself. For, although Margaret Fuller steadfastly refused to join the ranks of the Abolitionists, she manifested throughout her life a thorough sympathy for the anti-slavery principle. It was only the jaundiced eyes of her more zealous contemporaries, people completely embroiled in the struggles of the Abolition group, which could view her attitude as aloof. The warmth with which she regarded the anti-slavery cause in *Woman in the Nineteenth Century* increased steadily and appears in all her works. In this respect it is interesting to note the growing intensity which she brought to her four articles on the slavery question for Greeley's *New York Tribune* during 1845, her first full year of work with the newspaper. On January 7th she greeted the appearance of *The Liberty Bell*, an annual published in Massachusetts for the benefit of the Anti-Slavery Fair, in cordial but restrained terms.[6] She complimented the Abolitionists on their clarity of argument and loyalty to principle and noted that the essays written by former slaves were incontrovertible evidence of the innate capacities of the Negro. But nowhere in the article does she indicate personal support for the Abolition movement. On March 29th she reported on a lecture given by Frederick Von Raumer before the Scientific Union in Berlin on the slavery question in the United States.[7] Von Raumer confined himself to the pro-slavery arguments and Margaret observed that: "The lecture was certainly in an anti-abolition spirit, so as to cause much distaste to the women present, and to all those who believe no improvement impossible on which the human soul is bent with earnest desire." Still Margaret's tone was impersonal, despite her evident distaste for Von Raumer's remarks. By June, however, her anti-slavery sentiment made itself felt in a more forceful manner. In a review of the autobiography of Frederick Douglass, an escaped slave, she declared: "The inconsistencies of Slaveholding professors of religion cry to Heaven. . . . Clergymen to-day command Slaves to obey a Gospel which they will not allow them to read, and call themselves Christians amid the curses of their fellow men."[8] So strong did her feeling against racial intolerance become, that by December she wrote an article attacking an instance of anti-Negro prejudice in the North. She rejected the action of the Lyceum at New Bedford, Massachusetts, in denying membership to Negroes and restricting them to segregated seating facilities. She labeled this policy "unchristian" and complimented Ralph Waldo Emerson and Charles Sumner on their decisions to cancel lecture engagements at the Lyceum.[9]

A few years later, after her experiences in the Roman revolution against Austria, she even expressed regret for her earlier hostility against the Abolitionists. In 1847, after she had settled in Rome, Margaret Fuller either secretly married or became the mistress of Marchese Giovanni Ossoli, a member of the Civic Guard and an ardent Republican. When in 1849 the Republic of Rome was declared and French forces assaulted the city in order to restore the Pope to temporal power, the Marchese took up his post on the walls of the city and Margaret assumed the rôle of director of the Hospital of *Fate Bene Fratelli*, to which the wounded were sent every day. In one of the articles she hastily wrote for the *Tribune* in an effort to arouse American support for the Republican cause, Margaret declared: "How it pleases me here to think of the Abolitionists! I could never endure to be with them at home, they were so tedious, often so narrow, always so rabid and exaggerated in their tone. But after all they had a high motive, something eternal in their desire and life; and if it was not the only thing worth thinking of, it was really something worth living and dying for to free a great nation from such a terrible blot, such a threatening plague. God strengthen them, and make them wise to achieve their purpose."[10] It was not uncommon for New England travellers in mid-nineteenth-century Italy to be drawn to sympathy for the anti-slavery movement as a result of noting the analogy between the situation of the Italians, subjected to Austrian domination and the condition of the American Negro slaves, subjected to another form of vassalage. Holmes and Lowell both reacted in this fashion. So complete was this influence on Margaret Fuller, however, that at least one scholar, Edmund G. Berry, has expressed the view that she might have emerged as a leader in the Abolition cause, had not she and her husband perished at sea while returning to American in 1850.[11]

Margaret Fuller's earlier abhorrence of the Abolitionists is not difficult to explain. Among her chief objections to the leaders of the movement was the tone of excess and exaggeration which characterized their pronouncements. Like Thoreau, she was an adherent of self-reliance and self-culture, and, like Emerson, who in "The Chardon Street Convention" had classed Abolitionists along with "Madmen, madwomen, men with beards, Dunkers, Muggletonians, Come-outers, Groaners, Agrarians, Seventh-day Baptists . . .,"[12] she found it difficult to sacrifice her hard core of New England common sense for the zeal demanded by Abolition or any other extreme reform movement. Time and again she complimented the Abolitionists on the nobility of their aims but at the same time excoriated their methods. Commenting on the preface which William Lloyd Garrison, the noted Abolitionist, had written for the *Narrative of the Life of Frederick Douglass,* she observed: "His motives and his course have been noble and generous. We look upon him with high respect, but he has indulged in violent invective and denunciation till he has spoiled the temper of his mind. Like a man who has been in the habit of screaming himself hoarse to make the deaf hear, he can no longer pitch his voice on a key agreeable to common ears."[13] Similarly, she found in Archy Moore's *The Slave,* one of the earliest, perhaps the first, anti-slavery novels, evidence of "distortion and sophistry,"[14] but she was willing to overlook these faults in view of the book's humanitarian purpose.

Margaret Fuller was by no means alone in her distrust of the Abolitionists. Many New England luminaries, including, as we have seen, Ralph Waldo Emerson, were repelled by the excesses of these anti-slavery zealots and took no active part during the early years of the struggle to free the Negro. Yet they managed to escape the charge of indifference to the anti-slavery movement. What was there then about Margaret Fuller's inaction that appeared so censurable to her contemporaries and to many later scholars? Part of the answer lies in the fact that Margaret was a life-long advocate of social action and was fond of lecturing fellow transcendentalists on the inadequacies of their more cerebral lives. Thus in a letter to W. H. Channing she declared: "Is it not nobler and truer to live than to think? . . . Really to feel the glow of action, without its weariness, what heaven it must be!"[15] And to Emerson she wrote: ". . . your excellence never shames me, nor chills my next effort, because it is of a kind wholly unattainable to me, in a walk where I shall never take a step. You are intellect, I am life."[16]

But Margaret's inconsistency in failing to apply the principle of action to the anti-slavery movement is not the major cause of her later reputation for indifference towards the movement. The chief cause of that reputation is the public attack made on her views of the slavery question by the influential English feminist, Harriet Martineau. In 1834 Miss Martineau made an extensive journey throughout the United States and three years later she published *Society in America,* a compendium of her views on life in this country. Margaret Fuller had met Miss Martineau during her visit to the United States and soon came to idolize the Englishwoman for her independence of mind and freedom from convention. Their relationship was further cemented when Miss Martineau arranged for Margaret to meet Emerson and later tried to help her fulfill a life-time dream of visiting Europe. Nevertheless, despite her discipleship, Margaret Fuller felt that she must inform her idol of her distaste for certain excesses in the latter's recently published *Society in America*. In a letter reassuring the English authoress of her continued friendship, Margaret pointed out that the heavy-handed manner in which the book espoused the anti-slavery movement obscured all other concerns in what was supposed to be a broad examination of American society: "I do not like that your book should be an 'abolition' book. You might have borne your testimony as decidedly as you pleased; but why leaven the whole book with it? It *is* a great subject, but your book had other purposes to fulfill."[17] Such plain speaking did not endear Margaret to the English reformer, eight years her senior. Some forty years later Miss Martineau apparently still smarted with resentment at the disciple's objections, for in her *Autobiography*, the English authoress rebuked Margaret with the charge that the Boston Conversations were a fanciful and shallow means of escaping real threats to American democracy and of shirking duty to the cause of Abolition:

> The difference between us was that while she was living and moving in an ideal world, talking in private and discoursing in public about the most fanciful and shallow conceits which the Transcendentalists of Boston took for philosophy, she looked down upon persons who acted instead of talking finely, and devoted their fortunes, their place, their repose, and their very lives to the preservation of the principles of the republic. While Margaret Fuller and her adult pupils 'sat gorgeously dressed,' talking about Mars and Venus, Plato and Goethe, and fancying themselves the elect of the earth in intellect and refinement, the liberties of the republic were running out as fast as they could go, at a breach which another sort of elect persons were devoting themselves to repair; and my complaint against the 'gorgeous' pedants was that they regarded their preservers as hewers of wood and drawers of water, and their work as a less vital one than the pedantic orations which were spoiling a set of well-meaning women in a pitiable way.[18]

Harriet Martineau's comment has had a significant effect upon later writers dealing with Margaret Fuller, for many of them have felt compelled to answer the English reformer's charges. In his 1884 biography of Margaret Fuller for the American Men of Letters series, Thomas Wentworth Higginson attempted to remedy the injustice with which he believed Margaret had been treated in "that singularly harsh and unfair book, the 'Autobiography of Harriet Martineau' "[19] by quoting at length from Margaret's letters and Miss Martineau's book in an attempt both to discredit the English woman's objectivity and point up the rôle played in the anti-slavery cause by women who attended Margaret's Conversations. But, as a matter of fact, Higginson only further reinforced the idea of the censurable character of Margaret's attitude toward the anti-slavery movement when he claimed in the same chapter that, "It is a point never yet wholly cleared up, either by her printed memoirs or private letters, why she entered with somewhat tardy sympathy into the anti-slavery movement" (p. 122). In her 1902 *Reminiscences*, Ednah Dow Cheney, who had attended Margaret's Boston Conversation classes, also addressed herself to Harriet Martineau's allegations. Here Mrs. Cheney explained Margaret's failure to enlist in the ranks of the anti-slavery movement on the grounds that the movement itself had not yet passed into its active phase when Margaret departed for Europe in 1846.[20] A more modern commentator, Charles A. Madison, in the *Antioch Review*, has explained the tardiness of Margaret's appreciation for the anti-slavery group as a result of her "aesthetic recoil from the 'rabid and exaggerated' behavior of the Abolitionist readers,"[21] whereas Margaret Munsterberg, in the *Boston Public Library Quarterly*, has suggested that her attitude resulted from an "impatience with platforms."[22]

All of the previously mentioned explanations of Margaret Fuller's lack of enthusiasm for the organized anti-slavery movement—her recoil at the excesses of the Abolitionist leaders, her distaste for platforms and parties, the fact that the movement had not become nearly so widely active by the time of her departure for Europe as it was later to be—are, in varying degrees, valid. But one historically significant explanation is rarely examined. This is the rivalry between the woman's rights advocates and the Abolitionists which began to manifest itself in the 1830s. The part which this rivalry played in Margaret Fuller's attitude toward the anti-slavery movement is made clear by manuscript letters contained in the Boston Public Library's Anti-Slavery Collection. Late in 1840 Maria Weston Chapman, who was Treasurer of the Massachusetts Anti-Slavery Society and was later to edit the *Autobiography* of her long-standing friend, Harriet Martineau, wrote to Margaret Fuller to request that one of the Conversations, which were now receiving wide attention in Boston, be devoted to the topic of Abolition. In her reply, written in December 1840, Margaret declined Mrs. Chapman's suggestion on the grounds that such a talk would interrupt the schedule already adopted for the Conversation class. In the same letter Margaret went on to express her respect for the ideals of the Abolition cause but added her concomitant belief that the followers of the cause demonstrated many of the faults incident to partisan zeal. She concluded:

> The late movements in your party have interested me more than those which had for their object the enfranchisement of the African only. Yet I presume I should still feel sympathy with your aims only not with your measures. Yet I should like to be more fully acquainted with both. The late convention I attended hoping to hear some clear account of your wishes as to religious institutions and the social position of woman. But not only I heard nothing that pleased me, but no clear statement from any one. . . . As far as I know you seem to me quite wrong as to what is to be done for woman! She needs new helps I think, but not such as you propose. But I should like to know your view and your grounds more clearly than I do.[23]

Thus Margaret Fuller felt disappointed that the Anti-Slavery Fair organized by Mrs. Chapman did not clearly insist on the rights of woman as well as those of the Negro. She regarded herself as having a prior commitment to the woman's rights cause and did not wish to dissipate her efforts on behalf of woman by spending time on movements "which had for their object the enfranchisement of the African only."

The question of just how closely they would ally themselves with the woman's rights movement deeply perplexed Abolitionists in 1840. In that year, as has been pointed out, the World Anti-Slavery Convention in London refused to seat female delegates; and in this country, in the same year, when the Anti-Slavery Association passed a resolution permitting women to become committee members, the action was met with a series of resignations by less radical members, thus resulting in a crippling split within the Association. Moreover, there was much opposition to the fact that the Grimké sisters frequently lectured before mixed audiences on the slavery question, and in 1836 a Pastoral Letter denouncing such unfeminine and dangerous conduct had been issued by the Council of Congregationalist Ministers of Massachusetts. Abolition leaders realized that the willingness of women to participate in their cause was a mixed blessing and many wished to sever their association with woman's rights agitation. It is not difficult to understand how in this climate Margaret Fuller could feel that she must choose between two movements, one to liberate women and the other to liberate slaves. The note with which Anne Watson, Mrs. Chapman's sister, answered Margaret Fuller's letter underlines the uneasiness which many Abolitionists felt at this time when confronted with the woman's rights question. Miss Watson wrote:

> Permit me, as a matter of fact to correct one error in your letter. In speaking of the recent Convention you seem to think it a movement of the Anti-Slavery party— The only object of that party *as such* is the promulgation of the principle that all men are created with a right to personal liberty and as in this country the Slave is the only being to whom the right is denied, the assertion of his claims is the scope to which Abolitionists *as such* are limited. . . .
> . . . The fact that the A. S. Reform is calculated to lead the minds of a community to still further reform is one that we have no disposition to deny—Great changes, religiously & socially must undoubtedly be produced but these results are collateral & not direct & must be modified by circumstances over which the Anti Slavery community have no control.[24]

It would appear then that Margaret Fuller's aloofness towards the anti-slavery movement has been thoroughly exaggerated. Her cautious attitude towards partisans of that movement was caused not by her refusal to come to grips with the problems facing American democracy, as Harriet Martineau would have her readers believe, but resulted from the fact that her equalitarian principles, embracing the desire to liberate not only the Negro but also woman, were far more radical than those embraced by the more conservative reformers constituting the Abolition group.

## Notes

1. This study has been made possible by a grant from the Penrose Fund of the American Philosophical Society.

2. (New York: Fowler and Wells, 1881), I, 52.

3. (Cambridge: Harvard University Press, 1959), p. 4.

4. (New York: Greeley and McElrath, 1845), pp. 17–18.

5. See Leona Rostenberg, "Diary of Thomas Fuller in Congress," *New England Quarterly*, 12 (September 1939), 523–524: see also *Debates and Proceedings in the Congress of the United States*, Fifteenth Congress, First Session (Washington, 1854), p. 825.

6. "*The Liberty Bell* for 1845."

7. "Frederick Von Raumer upon the Slavery Question."
8. *"Narrative of the Life of Frederick Douglass,"* 10 June 1845.
9. "Lyceum of New-Bedford, Mass.," 9 December 1845.
10. Quoted in Margaret Fuller, *At Home and Abroad,* ed. Arthur B. Fuller (Boston: Crosby, Nichols, 1856), p. 255.
11. "Margaret Fuller Ossoli, 1810–1850," *Dalhousie Review,* 30 (January 1951), 376.
12. *The Complete Works of Ralph Waldo Emerson* (Boston: Houghton, Mifflin, 1903–1904), X (*Lectures and Biographical Sketches*), 374.
13. *"Narrative of the Life of Frederick Douglass."*
14. *"The Slave; or Memoirs of Archy Moore," New York Daily Tribune,* 4 February 1845.
15. Quoted in Frederick Augustus Braun, *Margaret Fuller and Goethe* (New York: Henry Holt, 1910), p. 137.
16. Letter, n.d., n.p., Houghton Library, Harvard University, "Fuller Manuscripts," IX, 118b.
17. Quoted in [Ralph Waldo Emerson, William Henry Channing, and James Freeman Clarke,] *Memoirs of Margaret Fuller Ossoli* (Boston: Phillips, Sampson, 1852), I, 194.
18. *Harriet Martineau's Autobiography,* ed. Maria Weston Chapman (Boston: James R. Osgood, 1877), II, 71.
19. Higginson, *Margaret Fuller Ossoli* (Boston: Houghton, Mifflin, 1884), p. 123.
20. *Reminiscences of Ednah Dow Cheney* (Boston: Lee and Shepard, 1902), p. 211.
21. "Margaret Fuller: Transcendental Rebel," *Antioch Review,* 2 (September 1942), 431.
22. "Margaret Fuller Centenary," *Boston Public Library Quarterly,* 2 (July 1950), 258.
23. "Weston Papers," MS.A.3.14, 82.
24. "Weston Papers," MS.A.3.14, 83.

# [Fuller and Lowell's *A Fable for Critics*]

## Martin Duberman

The "Miranda" portrait was the most serious lapse of taste and judgment in the poem, and its only wholly negative characterization. One need not admire Margaret Fuller in order to recognize that in drawing her portrait Lowell was needlessly—and uncharacteristically—cruel. Two years before, Miss Fuller had baldly asserted, in an essay on American literature, that "Lowell . . . is absolutely wanting in the true spirit and tone of poesy . . . his verse is stereotyped, his thought sounds no depth; and posterity will not remember him." Given Lowell's output to that point, it would be hard to fault this judgment, yet remembering, too, that he was still in his mid-twenties, her pronouncement was unnecessarily sweeping—especially since she had herself earlier expressed at least limited admiration for some of the poems. At the time, Lowell had professed not to mind the attack, even while admitting that he was tempted to do "a little retaliatory satire." Momentarily he had resisted the temptation, deciding to let time settle accounts, but the *Fable* seemed too good an opportunity to let pass. Even then he hesitated, wondering whether he might not best revenge himself simply by writing better, but when Maria suggested that perhaps after all he ought to give Miss Fuller "a line or two," he gave up the gentlemanly ghost.[1]

Once unleashed, his accumulated sense of grievance overwhelmed his judgment. Even in a day when literary back-biting was acceptable fare, the portrait of "Miranda" could be considered savage:

> . . . a woman must surely see well, if she try,
> The whole of whose being's a capital I:
> She will take an old notion, and make it her own,
> By saying it o'er in her Sibylline tone . . .
> There is one thing she owns in her own single right,
> It is native and genuine—namely, her spite;
> Though, when acting as censor, she privately blows
> A censer of vanity 'neath her own nose.

---

*Martin Duberman, [Fuller and Lowell's *A Fable for Critics*], *James Russell Lowell* (Boston: Houghton Mifflin, 1966), pp. 98–101, 414; copyright 1966 by Martin Duberman. Reprinted by permission of the Houghton Mifflin Company.

Lowell tried to strike the lines about "spite" just before the *Fable* went to press, but it was too late; Miranda was published "spite" and all, and brought down a fair-sized storm.²

Lowell believed the general verdict was "served her right," and perhaps it was—Oliver Wendell Holmes, for one, thought the portrait "too good." Yet there were many delighted by the rest of the *Fable* who found the Miranda section distasteful. Thomas Wentworth Higginson expressed warm indignation to Lowell in a private letter: Margaret Fuller, he wrote, had dared, though a woman, "to study, think, talk & write," and though none of this ought to shield her from comment, it should shield her "from undiscriminating solely contemptuous criticism." From Italy, where Margaret Fuller then was living, W. W. Story also sent a protest: "because Fate has really been unkind to her, & because she depends on her pen for her bread & water (& that is nearly all she has to eat), & because she is her own worst enemy, & because through her disappointment & disease, which embitter every one, she has struggled most womanfully & stoutly, I could have wished you had let her pass scot-free." All this upset Lowell. He had not known that Margaret Fuller was poor and ill, only that she had been harsh and dogmatic. "You may be sure," he replied to Story, "I have felt more sorry about it than any one: only I always reflect *after* the thing is done." But Lowell's repentance may not have been genuine, for he retained the offending lines in later editions of the *Fable*, even after Margaret Fuller's tragic death by drowning.³

Notes

1. Margaret Fuller, *Papers on Literature and Art* (New York: Wiley and Putnam, 1846), II, 132; Lowell to E. Davis, 26 September 1846, Davis Letters, Houghton Library, Harvard University ("a little retaliatory satire"); Lowell to C. F. Briggs, 26 March 1848, Berg Collection, New York Public Library (revenge by writing better).

2. Lowell to C. F. Briggs, 4 October 1848, *Letters of James Russell Lowell*, ed. Charles Eliot Norton (New York: Harpers, 1894), I, 194 (effort to strike lines).

3. O. W. Holmes to Lowell, 1 November 1848, Norton Collection, Houghton Library, Harvard University; T. W. Higginson to Lowell, 5 December 1848, Norton Collection, Houghton Library, Harvard University; W. W. Story to Lowell, 21 March 1849, University of Texas; Lowell to W. W. Story, 23 September 1849, as quoted in Henry James, *William Wetmore Story and His Friends* (Boston: Houghton, Mifflin, 1903), I, 181. Other adverse comments on the Miranda section can be found in Francis Bowen to Lowell, 2 November 1848, Norton Collection, Houghton Library, Harvard University; C. E. Norton Journal, 15 May 1873, *Letters of Charles Eliot Norton*, ed. Sara Norton and M. A. DeWolfe Howe (Boston: Houghton Mifflin, 1913), I, 510.

## " 'This Impassioned Yankee': Margaret Fuller's Writing Revisited"

Margaret V. Allen*

It has been the fate of Margaret Fuller, since her tragic death in 1850, to be remembered more for the romantic legend of her life than for the enduring value of her writings. A tempestuous and protean personality, she was nourished in the soil of New England transcendentalism, became an energetic social and literary critic in New York, mingled in Europe with the greatest writers and artists of the age, played an active role in the Italian revolution, and shortly thereafter, with her new husband and infant son, died in a shipwreck at the age of forty. Henry James was fascinated with her legend, and in *William Wetmore Story and His Friends* wrote of her that "this impassioned Yankee, who occupied so large a place in the thoughts, the lives, the affections, of an intelligent and appreciative society . . . left behind her nothing but the memory of a memory." The fact is, however, that Margaret Fuller left behind her many essays, critical pieces, letters, and poems, and so she is a great deal less shadowy than James fancied.

The last few years have seen a marked resurgence of interest in Margaret Fuller, and there are now plans underway for complete editions of her letters and her writings, some of which still remain in manuscript form. These writings have never been very readily available, though many libraries have an anthology edited by Mason Wade in 1941. Another collection, more fragmentary, appeared in 1963 in a paperbound anthology edited by Perry Miller. More recently, there has been a reissue of her *Woman in the Nineteenth Century*, the feminist tract which was one of her most talked-about writings when it first appeared in 1843 in the *Dial*, the transcendentalist journal. But Margaret Fuller was not only a feminist; in fact, she was not primarily a feminist. She wrote shrewd comments on American life and society in her *Summer on the Lakes*, and much valuable literary criticism for the *Dial* and for Horace Greeley's *New York Daily Tribune*. As a journalist and the first woman foreign correspondent, she sent back to the *Tribune* lively and perceptive accounts of a Europe in the throes of social convulsion in the 1840s. Her last and, as she thought, best work, a

---

*Margaret V. Allen, " 'This Impassioned Yankee': Margaret Fuller's Writing Revisited," *Southwest Review*, 58 (Spring 1973), 162–171; reprinted by permission of the *Southwest Review* and the author.

history of the Italian revolution from which she had just emerged, was still in manuscript form on her last fatal voyage home, and was forever lost to the sea.

Why have the writings of such an extraordinary and gifted woman remained virtually forgotten for more than a hundred years? There are several reasons. The first of these is the judgment of some of her contemporaries that they had little merit. Elizabeth Barrett Browning, who knew Margaret Fuller briefly in Florence and was attracted to her as a friend, thought her an interesting person who far outshone her writings. She said of Margaret Fuller in a letter,

> Her written works are just *naught*. She said herself that they were sketches, thrown out in haste and for the means of subsistence, and that the sole production of hers which was likely to represent her at all would be the history of the Italian Revolution. In fact, her reputation, such as it was in America, seemed to stand mainly on her conversation and oral lectures. If I wished anyone to do her justice, I should say, as I have indeed said, "Never read what she has written." The letters, however, are individual, and full, I should fancy, of that magnetic personal influence which was so strong in her.

Mrs. Browning's disparagement of Margaret Fuller's writing was undoubtedly affected by two factors: one was political disagreement, the more conservative Mrs. Browning being alarmed by her friend's left-leaning views; and the other was the fact that Mrs. Browning had found traditional forms, such as the sonnet, within which she could comfortably work, whereas Margaret Fuller all her life was searching for the best form to express and perfect her thought. The Englishwoman, finding the work of the American rough and unfinished, could not perceive its forcefulness and vitality.

Henry James repeated Mrs. Browning's words: "She left nothing behind her, her written utterance being naught." (Yet earlier James said, in his biography *Hawthorne*, that "some of her writing has extreme beauty, almost all of it has a real interest." What are we to make of two such contradictory opinions as to the value of her writing?) James, who used such terms as "haunting," "apparition," and "ghost" in speaking of Margaret Fuller, was quite capable of making a cult of elusiveness. He was too young to have known Margaret Fuller personally, and he, like Mrs. Browning, seems to have completely overlooked the vitality, the intelligence, and the ardent social commitment that characterized Margaret Fuller's writings, especially in the last decade of her life. One could easily guess that the real Margaret Fuller would probably have been too tempestuous and too egotistic for James's taste, and he was more comfortable thinking of her as a dim insubstantial legend.

Emerson, for many years one of Margaret Fuller's closest friends, edited her *Memoirs* after her death, and in those volumes he too belittled her writing ability. He said, for example, that she was unsuccessful as a nature writer, that she had poor powers of observation, and that most of her descriptions of nature were only a superficial kind of rapturizing. Such judgments have stood unquestioned for over a century, echoed and reechoed by Margaret Fuller's biographers and anthologizers. This weighty body of opinion as to the relative worthlessness of her writings has prevented any serious examination of their intrinsic merits by modern readers or scholars. The fairness, generosity, and levelheadedness that characterized her own literary criticism have not been preeminent qualities of her critics.

A second reason for the neglect of her writings is that her reputation as a conversationalist far outweighed her reputation as a writer. James Freeman Clarke, another friend and coeditor of her memoirs, said in his tribute, "Those who know Margaret only by her published writings know her least; her notes and letters contain more of her mind; but it was only in conversation that she was perfectly free and at home." Margaret Fuller was much loved by her friends. Another of them, Rev. F. H. Hedge, said that all who knew her concurred that her genius was in talk, not in her writings, which did her very imperfect justice. Though Henry James never heard her conversation, he too thought that her value and influence was from her person, not her written words. "Her function, her reputation, were singular, and not altogether reassuring: she was a talker; she was *the* talker; she was the genius of talk. . . . She has left the same sort of reputation as a great actress."

All this is faintly irritating to us, for we cannot hear this brilliant conversation that amused, delighted, and inspired her contemporaries. Unlike Dr. Johnson, Margaret Fuller had no Boswell, and if we prefer a more substantial knowledge of her than that offered by James's enchanting apparition, we have nothing but her writings to consult. Poe, who knew her personally, thought that her conversation and literary style were not different but much the same. In his essay "The Literati of New York City," Poe wrote, "Her personal character and her printed book are merely one and the same thing. We get access to her soul as directly from the one as from the other—no more readily from this than from that—easily from either. . . . Her literary and her conversational manner are identical." Quoting a passage from her *Summer on the Lakes,* Poe remarked, "Now all this is precisely as Miss Fuller would speak it. She is perpetually saying just such things in just such words. To get the conversational woman in the mind's eye, all that is needed is to imagine her reciting the paragraph just quoted." While Poe scolded her for slovenliness with grammar and hasty disregard for the details of writing, he praised her style as one of the best he knew. "In general effect, I know no style which surpasses it. It is singularly piquant, vivid, terse, bold, luminous—leaving details out of sight, it is everything that a style need be." Despite Poe's favorable judgment, received opinion for a century has exalted what is irrevocably gone—her life and conversation, and undervalued what remains—her writing.

The final reason why Margaret Fuller's works have not been seriously evaluated is that she was her own severest critic. Present-day feminists have said that the lack of personal confidence is a blight on the efforts of many women who aspire, as did Margaret Fuller, to success in any sphere of achievement other than the traditionally female ones. Unfortunately, her reputation as a writer has suffered from this absence of self-confidence. She had no high opinion of herself as a writer, as is seen in Mrs. Browning's comment quoted earlier. Passages from her *Memoirs* confirm that she believed her talents were of a different order: "These gentlemen [the New England literati] are surprised that I write no better, because I talk so well. But I have served a long apprenticeship to the one, none to the other. I shall write better, but never, I think, so well as I talk; for then I feel inspired. . . . My voice excites me, my pen never." In part because she had been so moved by Emerson's eloquence, in part because she longed for a life of action and leadership (in the debate on women's "proper" sphere in life, she said imperiously, "Let them be sea captains!"), she wrote:

> If I were a man, the gift I would choose should be that of eloquence. That power of forcing the vital currents of thousands of human hearts into ONE current, by the constraining power of that most delicate instrument, the voice, is so intense,—yes, I would prefer it to a more extensive fame, a more permanent influence.

Yet she was perpetually drawn back to efforts to create in words. A journal entry expressed this yearning: "Who, that has a soul for beauty, does not feel the need of creating, and that the power of creation alone can satisfy the spirit? When I thus reflect, the Artist seems the only fortunate man. Had I but as much creative genius as I have apprehensiveness!"

Margaret Fuller never felt that she had solved the problem of form, of the best vehicle for self-expression. Like Thoreau and Emerson, she felt compelled to write poetry, she wanted to write poetry, but her poems are not usually her best work. Florid or excessive sentiment, a stiff awkwardness in the use of meter and rhyme, and artificially forced inversions are frequent defects of her poems. "All rhetorical and impassioned," was her disparaging comment on her own verses. Poe thought her poetry "tainted with the affectation of the transcendentalists." She seemed hampered by traditional poetic forms, yet able to find no others suitable to her purposes. She was well aware of this. "For all the tides of life that flow within me, I am dumb and ineffectual, when it comes to casting my thought into a form. No old one suits me. If I could invent one, it seems to me the pleasure of creation would make it possible for me to write."

Popular essays satisfied her no better as a form. "What a vulgarity there seems in this writing for the multitude," she once exclaimed. "We know not yet, have not made ourselves known to a single soul, and shall we address those still more unknown?" However, from 1844 to 1846, when she was a columnist and literary critic in New York, she came to reverse her ideas about writing for the multitude, thinking that form became less significant than helping others by disseminating her ideas. She said of her *New York Daily Tribune* pieces that her old friends in New England did not regard them highly.

> They think I ought to produce something excellent, while I am satisfied to aid in the great work of popular education. I never regarded literature merely as a collection of exquisite products, but rather as a means of mutual interpretation. Feeling that many are reached and in some degree helped, the thoughts of every day seem worth noting, though in a form that does not inspire me.

When those words were written, Margaret Fuller had left New England in search of a broader experience of life than that allowed there by her role as a high priestess of culture. In New York she became actively concerned with problems like poverty, prostitution, mental illness, and industrial exploitation.

New York acquainted her with hard social realities that she was only dimly aware of in literary Boston. With her pen, she tried to awaken in *Tribune* readers this same concern. She did not know how these problems should or would be solved, but she believed it was wrong to ignore them. Thus, while she remained unsatisfied with the form of the journalistic essay, and while she continued to regard inspiration as necessary for producing works of enduring merit, the fact is that these *Tribune* essays have much more maturity, breadth of viewpoint, and incisiveness of language than she realized. At the time she left New England, Margaret Fuller had criticized Emerson for being aloof, remote, otherworldly, and her own writing in the New York years was reflecting a deepened understanding of the world and a compassionate involvement in it. Yet she still evaluated it by narrowly aesthetic standards that she had personally outgrown. Her self-criticism was far too severe, for her work was indeed the "something excellent" her New England friends had been urging her to produce. Most of what she said in the 1840s about American society has just as much truth and immediacy today. Still, her own disparagement of her writing has been taken at face value and her work regarded as an inferior footnote to the colorful annals of her life.

An examination of these writings reveals not only compassion and commitment, but also a rare and remarkable poetic imagination. This quality is, paradoxically, more apparent in her essays than in her poems. What Emerson said of Thoreau, that he "had the source of poetry in his spiritual perception," is equally true of Margaret Fuller. Her essays are rich in the image-making faculty, the ability to see analogies. Emerson, in his essay "Poetry and the Imagination," called poetry the perception of the symbolic character of things, and imagination "a perception and affirming of a real relation between a thought and some material fact." Margaret Fuller seemed to fall naturally into metaphor to express her thought, and vivid images abound in her essays. For example, writing at a time when revolution was brewing in Europe and the United States was convulsed with tensions rising out of slavery and the Mexican war, she wrote in a *Tribune* New Year's editorial:

> Altogether, it looks as if a great time was coming, and that time one of democracy. Our country will play a ruling part. Her eagle will lead the van; but whether to soar upward to the sun or to stoop for helpless prey, who now dares promise? At present she has scarce achieved a Roman nobleness, a Roman liberty; and whether her eagle is less like the vulture, and more like the Phoenix, than was the fierce Roman bird, we dare not say. May the new year give hopes of the latter, even if the bird need first to be purified by fire.

The bird image changes from eagle to vulture to phoenix: because each of these birds is strong, dominating, and impressive, inspiring awe or respect, the image points up America's importance and leadership position among nations. In its metamorphosis, the image evokes national pride (the noble aspiring eagle), anger and disgust (the predatory vulture), and hope for the future after purification by fire, a prophecy of the Civil War.

In a lighter mood, Margaret Fuller wrote of the opinion of European nations about America, using a metaphor of family life:

> America cares for shallow blame, just or unjust, because she wants not only self-respect but faith. She has, as the foreigner thinks, the unmannerly tricks and disagreeable obtrusions of an over-grown child. Like children of a rich and energetic nature, prematurely brought forward, she is peculiarly likely to offend the decorum and even the good feelings of uncles and aunts. She makes dirt-pies, kills flies, and oversets the tea-pot. Still she is learning all the while.

The image of the unmannerly precocious child carries criticism for America's misdeeds and crudities, but simultaneously an affectionate conviction that this yet undisciplined youngster among the family of nations shows great promise.

The images and the subjects they illuminate are varied. Discussing the settling of the western frontier, she wrote, in a passage reminiscent of Thoreau, of "the love of ravage which distinguishes the American settler and which makes the marks of his first passage over this land, like those of a corrosive acid upon the cheek of beauty, rather than that smile of intelligence which would ensue from the touch of an intelligent spirit." Commenting on Swedenborg and his many disciples and imitators, Margaret Fuller criticized slavish dependence on another mind. "Plants dwindle in perpetual shadow, even from the stateliest tree." When, in Europe, she visited the Chamber of Deputies library in Paris to see the manuscripts of Rousseau, she wrote of his importance as a prophet of the modern age: "Such is the method of genius,—to ripen fruit for the crowd by those rays of whose heat they complain." Examples of such apt and vivid images can be multiplied, of course, but to take them abruptly out of context in this manner hardly does them justice.

The metaphors Margaret Fuller most frequently used were those from nature. In "Poetry and Imagination" Emerson wrote, "Whilst common sense looks at things or visible Nature as real and final facts, poetry, or the imagination which dictates it, is a second sight, looking through these and using them as types or words for thoughts which they signify." Emerson made light of Margaret Fuller as a nature writer, but he ignored the fact that nature entered her writing in another and more essential way, in just the manner he explains above. Nature was a constant source of metaphor on which she drew to illuminate even the most abstract of subjects, such as the fine distinctions between types of literary criticism.

Every thoughtful reader of Margaret Fuller's writings will see how her images and metaphors give point and immediacy to her thought. Yet so persistently wrongheaded has been the criticism of her writing that in a 1964 study by Arthur W. Brown she is accused of being "guilty of figurative language that obscures rather than clarifies her thought," and her writing is pronounced decidedly improved "once she grew out of this habit of coloring her prose with obscure ... metaphors and murky images." Margaret Fuller's writing did change and improve with the growth of her experience, but metaphor characterized her work to the end: it was a habit of her mind, not an ornamentation to be hung on or taken off at will.

Occasionally in her style there is a mixing of metaphors, as in the following passage on Carlyle, whom Margaret Fuller often visited during her stay in England in 1846:

> I approached him with more reverence after a little experience of England and Scotland had taught me to appreciate the strength and height of that wall of shams and conventions which he more than any man, or thousand men,—indeed, he almost alone,—has begun to throw down. Wherever there was fresh thought, generous hope, the thought of Carlyle has begun the work. He has torn off the veils from hideous facts; he has burnt away foolish illusions; he has awakened thousands to know what it is to be a man,—that we must live, and not merely pretend to others that we live. He has touched the rocks and they have given forth musical answer; little more was wanting to begin to construct the city.

Despite the conflation of tearing veils, making music, and constructing cities, there is no incongruity in the thought or ludicrousness in the effect, but rather a powerful perception of what Carlyle had done for his age. This passage captures not only the energetic spirit of Carlyle but also his very language with its juxtaposition of forceful verbs that convey the acts of tearing down, exposing, cutting through and so on. And because Carlyle thought of himself as a latter-day prophet, there is a startling appropriateness in the image of Carlyle as Moses striking the rocks.

Emerson thought that the true poet strove toward the essences of things. In "Poetry and Imagination" he explained:

> The poet contemplates the central identity.... Poetry is the perpetual endeavor to express the spirit of the thing, to pass the brute body and search the life and reason which causes it to exist;—to see that the object is always flowing away, whilst the spirit or necessity which causes it subsists. Its essential mark is that it betrays in every word instant activity of mind, shown in new uses of every fact and image, in preternatural quickness or perception of relations. All its words are poems.

The reader of Margaret Fuller's work discovers these qualities continually. Admittedly she wrote hastily, with little time or patience for revision. It would be an exaggeration to claim that "all her words are poems," and yet the poetic sensibility is here, undeniably. Her interests, and the subjects on which she wrote, were as broad as life itself. She brought to these subjects a highly developed intelligence and highly developed feeling, a unique vision of existence that has lost none of its cogency and interest from her age to our own.

When she was alive, Margaret Fuller aroused in others a passionate admiration or a passionate aversion. This seems to be true still, long after her death. Perhaps the detractors of her writings were so captivated—or repelled—by the woman or her legend that their literary judgment was somehow blurred. Perhaps Margaret Fuller measured her own work by more stringent standards than she used to measure the work of others. At times she thought of her life as a work of art, to be consciously created and shaped, continually renewed. But to insist that because there was so much poetry in her life there can be none in her work, does both an injustice. "High genius she unquestionably possesses," said Poe. It is lamentable that for twelve decades the writings of one of America's most gifted women have remained in dusty obscurity. But in our own time, with their promised publication, Margaret Fuller may at last receive the recognition and the readership she deserves.

# "A Biographer's View of Margaret Fuller"

Madeleine B. Stern*

Thirty-odd years ago, when I began research for my *Life of Margaret Fuller*, my principal purpose was to reanimate a personality and her time and fulfill Carlyle's demand: "Margaret was a great creature, but we have no full biography of her yet. We want to know what time she got up in the morning, and what sort of shoes and stockings she wore."

It was my belief that the wealth of details found in Fuller journals and letters at Houghton and the Boston Public Library could be assembled in such a way—without lengthy quotations or the biographer's intrusive comments—that the past could be made to live again. And so, having steeped myself in the events and appurtenances of her life, I sat before a typewriter in a screen porch in Maine and, surrounded by pictures of Margaret Fuller, her homes and her friends, I tried to shake the dust from yesterday's bandbox.

In the writing of that biography I consciously employed a method which I believed would, by the assembling of details into a kind of mosaic, evoke Margaret Fuller's personality and integrate it with her times.

The method was hailed by some and castigated by others, and the biography itself was allocated more critical space than would be thought possible today. As a matter of fact, I was asked to discuss my biographical method before the American Literature Group of the Modern Language Association at the December 1942 meeting concerned with "The Place of the Critical Estimate in Literary Biography." That meeting was canceled because of the war. However I did prepare a paper—"Approaches to Biography"—published in *The South Atlantic Quarterly*, in which I elaborated upon the "chronological method" and the techniques I had used to reanimate the past.

I have mentioned the extensive review space accorded my biography and this of course was a tribute not to me but to my subject. There was in the early 1940's a strong interest in Margaret Fuller. Actually, when I handed in my completed manuscript my publisher informed me that another biography of Margaret Fuller was at that moment on the press of another house. This was, as you know, Mason Wade's fine book, *Margaret Fuller: Whetstone of Genius* which appeared in 1940. It was felt by Van Wyck Brooks and others at the time

---

*Madeleine B. Stern, "A Biographer's View of Margaret Fuller," *AB Bookman's Weekly*, 53 (4 February 1974), 427–428, 430; reprinted by permission of the publisher.

that my book was sufficiently different from Wade's to merit publication, and so, close upon the heels of the Wade biography, my *Life of Margaret Fuller* was published by Dutton in January 1942. Van Wyck Brooks had written, "There is still a large public for such authentic pictures of our way of life," and in January 1942 there was indeed a large public who responded to lengthy first-page reviews.

Both the public and the response were shortlived, owing in large measure to the Second World War, and it is only in recent years, I think, that a comparable interest in Margaret Fuller has been aroused.

The reason for this reawakened interest is not the sudden availability of a mass of manuscripts and related materials, although some materials unavailable to me have, in the interim, become available. The Tappan Papers at Harvard include 53 Margaret Fuller letters to Caroline Sturgis Tappan covering the years 1837 to 1847, in addition to an undated notebook of miscellanea and five autograph poems. There are also 10 letters from Caroline to Margaret. In 1959, two years after John Wesley Thomas edited James Freeman Clarke's *Letters to Margaret Fuller* (Hamburg 1957), James Freeman Clarke gave to Harvard 12 Fuller letters to Clarke and one to Sarah Freeman Clarke. As for the Emerson letters, although scholars have worked on the Fuller side of that correspondence, the letters not published in the Rusk edition are restricted until Prof. Eleanor Tilton of Barnard College completes the supplement to Rusk. As for the extensive Channing Family Papers at the Massachusetts Historical Society, these are still, unfortunately, uncatalogued.

A heightened interest in Margaret Fuller became evident during the 1960's, perhaps as a result of her role in the Women's Liberation movement. Perry Miller's *Selection from Her Writings and Correspondence* (1963) revealed Margaret Fuller as "one of the most thoroughly alive of the Transcendentalists" although the editor unfortunately made no mention of his very able predecessor in the field, Mason Wade, who in 1941 had published a similar compilation. In 1964 Margaret Fuller was the only minor Transcendentalist studied, notably by Arthur W. Brown, whose *Margaret Fuller* is a brief, balanced and precise biography. Previous portraits were supplemented during the 60's by Russell Durning, whose *Margaret Fuller, Citizen of the World: An Intermediary Between European and American Literature* was full of well documented insights, and by Joseph Jay Deiss, whose *The Roman Years of Margaret Fuller* stressed the Italian life of a liberated New England woman.

The recurrent themes of Margaret Fuller's emotional relationship with Emerson and the members of her circle and Margaret Fuller's work as literary critic have preoccupied latter-day scholars. Reprints with new introductions have done the service of restoring out-of-print works to circulation and these include *Woman in the Nineteenth Century*, reprinted from the 1855 edition in 1971 with an introduction by Bernard Rosenthal: *Summer on the Lakes* reprinted last year from the original Boston-New York 1844 edition with my own lengthy introduction; and the recent *Feminist Papers* edited by Alice S. Rossi and published by Columbia University Press. In this connection I may also be permitted to mention that my 1942 *Life of Margaret Fuller* was reprinted by Haskell House in 1968.

The most extensive—and intensive—Fuller scholarship today, however, is in the field of definitive editions whether they be of a brief and fragmentary journal such as Joel Myerson's edition of "Margaret Fuller's 1842 Journal" (*Harvard Library Bulletin*, July 1973) or of the whole corpus of Margaret Fuller correspondence which Prof. Hudspeth is editing. The annotators are or will be at work and by the time their textual studies are completed we shall certainly have the materials for a new biography based upon and designed for the scholarship of another age.

That other age is of course the future. What specific studies can I recommend to you whose work in progress will shape the future of Margaret Fuller scholarship? Margaret Fuller's importance in comparative literature had been broached by Russell Durning but the last word has not been said. Here the scholar must be steeped in the books Margaret Fuller read, in Proclus and Plotinus, in Swedenborg and Goethe. My own recent publication of the catalogue of Elizabeth Peabody's Foreign Library (1840) may be of some help here, for the foreign library of 13 West Street was also assuredly the library of Margaret Fuller's mind. It never rains but it pours. Goodspeed's Catalogue 577, recently issued, lists as item 762 Elizabeth P. Peabody's Catalogue of the American and Foreign Circulating Library, ca. 1841, at $50. This has gone to an institution and now it must be studied in relation to Margaret Fuller and her importance in comparative literature. In this connection too, not only her foreign readings but her foreign readership might be traced.

While textual studies of Margaret Fuller's writings are engrossing scholars today, they have not given as much attention as they might to bibliographical and bibliophilic pursuits. I think, for example, of Margaret Fuller's publishers both before and after her death. What was her relationship to them? Why and how did they publish her? Specifically, the interest of the firm of phrenologist-publishers—Fowler & Wells—in Margaret Fuller after her death would make a productive investigation that could throw light upon publisher, published and the taste of the times. Margaret Fuller's attempts at writing fiction might also prove a fruitful subject to explore. Some years ago Alexander E. Jones discussed her missing story, "Lost and Won," in an article in the *Boston Public Library Quarterly* (April 1954) and elsewhere there are hints of her interest in fiction, notably the "Mariana" episode in *Summer on the Lakes*. A survey of this interest might further elucidate her mind and her literary technique.

Along broader lines, I need not repeat that our subject must be re-evaluated for a new generation. What is it that gives Margaret Fuller stature today? Is it her role in comparative literature or her work as a critic; is it her stand in women's liberation or in the liberation of all mankind; is it her personality and the reaction of that personality to her times?

And so we are left with the preoccupations of thirty years ago. It is still essential to integrate our subject with the time in which she lived. It is still essential to know the universe she accepted and to understand how she was interrelated with that universe. To go a step farther, it may be essential to know whether or not she would have accepted the universe today. What kind of universe, in other words, did she accept and what kind would she have refused to accept?

In all these endeavors we must of course depend upon the definitive texts that are now being scrupulously edited for us. But we must not in that dependence lose sight of the forest for the trees, nor become so involved with points and variants that we forget the text itself. She is our text and to read her wisely is a most exhilarating pursuit. A wise reading is beholden not only to the definitive annotated edition but to the imagination of the reader. If the scholar is without that imagination he should not involve himself in biography. Without it, current scholarship will produce only the so-called monumental biography so popular today containing a mass of multitudinous detail offered up in gray-flannel style. Without it, current scholarship will be dry as dust, more arid by far than much of 19th-century biography. And a wilderness of annotations will obscure instead of illuminate one of the most radiant personalities of the 19th century.

# "The Genesis, Form, Tone, and Rhetorical Devices of *Woman in the Nineteenth Century*"

Marie Olesen Urbanski*

The first impression a reader may get from a hasty perusal of Margaret Fuller's *Woman in the Nineteenth Century* is one of effusiveness and formlessness. Containing a display of erudition that is impressive, it is prolix,[1] as was the work of many transcendentalists as well as of other writers of the past century. In the April, 1845 issue of his *Brownson's Quarterly Review*, Orestes Brownson observed that *Woman* has "neither beginning, middle, nor end, and may be read backwards as well as forwards." In his satire, Brownson has expressed aspects of the organic living quality of the work, but he does not discern its form. In the midst of its verbosity, it is still possible to see more of a pattern in *Woman* than has been maintained. Its basic structure is that of the sermon, which is appropriate, because *Woman*'s message is hortatory. Its complexity and apparent lack of form are due to its dual nature. Within the sermon framework, *Woman* partakes of the major characteristic of transcendental literary art.

But before analyzing *Woman* as a literary work from the standpoint of form, tone, and use of rhetorical devices, it is necessary to examine its genesis. If a study can be made of its genesis from an early draft, then some insight may be obtained as to the way in which Fuller's ideas were developing and thus a clearer perception of her composition of *Woman* is possible.

*Woman* developed from "The Great Lawsuit.—Man *versus* Men; Woman *versus* Women," which was published in the July, 1843, issue of *The Dial*, a year after Fuller had relinquished its editorship to Emerson. In her preface to *Woman* she explains she has prepared her expanded version for publication in compliance with wishes expressed from many quarters. Then she discusses her change of title. She concedes that the meaning of the original title is puzzling— "it requires some thought to see what it means." Fuller's preference, she tells her readers, was to retain the first title in her enlargement, but she was dissuaded from doing so by friends. Although awkward, her early biographer

---

*Marie Olesen Urbanski, "The Genesis, Form, Tone, and Rhetorical Devices of *Woman in the Nineteenth Century*"; revised from "Margaret Fuller's *Woman in the Nineteenth Century*" (Ph.D. dissertation, University of Kentucky, 1973), copyright 1973 by Marie Olesen Urbanski. Printed by permission of the author.

Higginson explains the original title was intended "to avert even the suspicion of awakening antagonism between the sexes."[2] Nevertheless, this title does sound "antagonistic" because it suggests court action. But why is the title worded "man versus men" instead of "man versus woman," or *vice versa*, which is the usual order in the battle of the sexes? Her intention was not to write a long history of woman's grievances against the tyranny of the male sex. Instead she keynoted the grievance of the individual man or woman whose aspirations were thwarted by the multitude, or by himself or herself, from becoming the developed soul he or she might become. She explains:

> I meant by that title to intimate the fact that, while it is the destiny of Man, in the course of the ages, to ascertain and fulfil the law of his being, so that his life shall be seen, as a whole, to be that of an angel or messenger, the action of prejudices and passions which attend, in the day, the growth of the individual, is continually obstructing the holy work that is to make the earth a part of heaven. By Man I mean both man and woman; these are the two halves of one thought. I lay no special stress on the welfare of either. I believe that the development of the one cannot be effected without that of the other.

She develops this concept in *Woman* by adding to "Lawsuit" her dual epigraphs. Then by rephrasing them, she makes them applicable to men as well. Her intention in the work is that what she has to say applies to both men and women; her message is not ambivalent but hortatory, and its significance, again referring to her original title, is "great."

When comparing both works, it appears at first glance that *Woman*, published in New York by Greeley & McElrath in 1845, is much longer than "Lawsuit," but a line by line examination of the content indicates that the number of words per page in "Lawsuit" is much greater than that in *Woman*. Comparison of the two texts reveals that the first 130 pages of the 179 page text of *Woman* are a close adaptation of the 47 pages of "Lawsuit." In most instances, Fuller uses a verbatim transcription of "The Great Lawsuit" in *Woman*. Occasionally she changes a few words to clarify or modify the meaning of a sentence, but she does very little polishing of her original text. For example, in the original essay she writes: "Is it not enough, cries the sorrowful trader," and in her second version she changes *sorrowful* to *irritated* (p. 28). In the original version she writes: "But our doubt is whether the heart does consent with the head, or only acquiesces its decrees." In the second version, she changes *acquiesces* to *obeys*, and then adds to her sentence: "With a passiveness that precludes the exercise of its natural powers, or a repugnance that turns sweet qualities to bitter, or a doubt that lays waste the fair occasions of life" (pp. 29–30). Another word changed to clarify meaning is *incessant* which in *Woman* becomes *frequent*: "Shrink not from frequent error in this gradual, fragmentary state" (p. 19). She deletes a phrase or a sentence a few times, but mostly she develops and elaborates on points she had already made. In her discussion of property rights for widows she says the wife "inherits only a part of his fortune" and then inserts in her second version the phrase "often brought him by herself" after "fortune" (p. 31). Again in her treatment of illustrious old maids: "No one thinks of Michael Angelo's Persican Sibyl, or St. Theresa, or Tasso's Leonora, or the Greek Electra, as an old maid," she adds: "more than of Michael Angelo or Canova as old bachelors" (p. 99), in order to give her sentence and idea balance. Sometimes she adds discussions of writers, such as Charles Fourier or Walter Savage Landor, whom she had not included before. Furthermore, she tends to add capital letters and italics for emphasis, and occasionally corrects punctuation.

There are, however, forty-nine pages of new material. The portion she adds contains the most daring subject matter in the book because much of it is contemporary application of her thesis. Her new material contains some frank discussions of sex, an example of an incompatible marriage: "I have known this man come to install himself in the chamber of a woman who loathed him, and say she should never take food without his company" (p. 32); the double standard of morality: "Let Sir Charles Grandison preach to his own sex" (p. 151); the notorious trial of Amelia Norman; a mother's sadness when she gives birth to a daughter; the father's kidnapping of his own children as a means of coercing his wife; problems of older women—a well-preserved woman at forty who is spoken of "upholstery-wise" (p. 99); property rights for married women; and her idea that "ladies" are responsible for rehabilitating prostitutes. More trenchant social criticism is used to supplement her earlier points: "Those who think the physical circumstances of Woman would make a part in the affairs of national government unsuitable, are by no means those who think it impossible for negresses to endure field-work, even during pregnancy, or for sempstresses to go through their killing labors" (p. 35). Also included in her enlargement is her remark about letting women be sea-captains. Although she adds the ancient belief that a baby's body was inherited from his mother, and his soul from his father, in general her new material contains less spiritual transcendentalism until the peroration. Therefore, the most controversial writing in *Woman* was that which she added to "The Great Lawsuit."[3] The importance of the earlier draft is that it gave Fuller the courage to treat inflammatory subject matter. Because the reception of "The Great Lawsuit" was on the whole favorable among the *Dial*'s small coterie of readers, she became more outspoken. One criticism she did receive about her earlier draft, as she herself explains, is that she did not make her "meaning sufficiently clear" (p. 168). Consequently, she may have been guilty of repetition. And in order to make her meaning unmistakable, less of it is veiled in metaphor.

The residue of a trial from "The Great Lawsuit" remains. The thinking man or woman, who has not yet become the enlarged soul he would become, is admonished to perfect himself despite all obstructions. Once this extraordinary person frees himself from ordinary frailty, then this individual could become the king or queen she seeks to lead and to inspire his waiting adversaries.

The broadest structural framework of *Woman*, reflects the sermon, which she mentions both in her introduction—"sermons preached from the text" (p. 19)—and in her statement in the conclusion that she would retrace her design "as was done in old-fashioned sermons" (p. 168). Closely akin to the sermon is the oration, and *Woman* contains elements of both forms. Fuller begins her work with the classic *exordium* in a vague way so that her thesis is not clear for several pages. Using caution, Latin and German quotations, and preliminary conciliation, she does not introduce her *propositio* until the tenth page. It is that woman needs her turn, and that improvement of her lot would aid in the reformation of men, too. Then she states her sermon topic—"Be ye perfect." Having established her thesis at last, she proceeds with *partitio* or analysis of her subject. She does her analysis in a debate style by raising the popular arguments men use with which to oppose women's rights, and then rebutting them. She begins her conversational method of questions and answers characteristic of the speaker who wishes to dramatize his point. She has a husband ask a question:

> "Is it not enough," cries the irritated trader, "that you have done all you could to break up the national union, and thus destroy the prosperity of family union, to take my wife away from the cradle and the kitchen-hearth, to vote at polls, and preach from a pulpit? Of course, if she does such things, she cannot attend to those of her own sphere. She is happy enough as she is. She has more leisure than I have,—every means of improvement, every indulgence."
> "Have you asked her whether she was satisfied with these indulgences?"
> "No, but I know she is." (pp. 28–29)

She ends this dialogue by saying that liberating measures are proposed to ascertain truth. Objectively, she continues: "Without enrolling ourselves at once on either side, let us look upon the subject from the best point of view which to-day offers" (p. 31). She debates the issue with rebuttals accelerating in strength until she concludes with "We would have every arbitrary barrier thrown down" (p. 37).

Then in a long *digressio* composed of sermon-style exemplar, she considers all that is known of Woman, delineating her story in myth, folklore, the Bible, poetry, fiction, history and in her own time. She examines the life cycle of a woman, beginning with an extensive analysis of the institution of marriage. She seeks women whose lives she finds inspiring such as Queen Isabella of Castile, or Marina, the Indian girl who accompanied Cortez, but she evaluates the lives of other women, such as Queen Elizabeth and Mary Stuart, lauding their strengths and castigating their weaknesses. Interwoven in her examples is an attempt to buttress her argument with authority, as she gives the views of recognized authors to support her position. She concedes that women have always had some power, but they want freedom from men to learn the secrets of the universe alone. Within her narrative in a form suggestive of the *reprehensio*, is admonition to men who refuse to grant women freedom and who call strong women "manly," and to women who misuse what power they have. Scornfully she recognizes that a coquette, a shrew, or a good cook can have life-long sway.

She inculcates within her discussion a realistic assessment of the options open to women in various societies, ancient and modern. Reasonably enough, since most women marry, she spends a lot of time examining the institution of marriage. She contrasts idealized concepts of courtly love in which the lady serves as inspiration with the reality of arranged marriages of convenience. It is no surprise that she advocates not only a marriage of love but a spiritual union of two souls on a common pilgrimage. Other options women have she discusses, such as, women who write, women as mothers, women as old maids, and women in middle and old age. She praises women abolitionists brave enough to speak on the platform but warns they must work for measures not only favoring the slave but also for themselves. In her all-inclusive discussion of a woman's life cycle, she discusses the child towards the end of this section, lamenting the father who stunts his daughter's education for fear she would not find a husband. Again pointing out a woman must work alone and use her special gifts of intuition, she mentions the crisis at hand, and prophecies a New Jerusalem which the prophets Swedenborg, Fourier, and Goethe foretell. Then her sermon becomes more direct as she preaches about the problems of prostitutes, polygamy, and warns that men must be as pure as women. In an accelerating evocative vision of the future in which both men and women would rule their passions by reason she places her hope with the young—"harbingers and leaders of a new era" (p. 155). Triumphantly she concludes her long narrative by proclaiming her expectation that a young "Exaltada" would serve as an "example and instruction for the rest" (p. 156).

The structural pattern of *Woman* next takes the sermon form of an *applicatio* in a departure from the main thrust of the argument, and moves from the visionary future to the prosaic present. Fuller sighs over books recently published in which she finds the chief point is to fit a wife "to please, or, at least, not to disturb a husband" (p. 158). She recognizes the dilemmas women face, and completes this section by admonishing American women to use their moral power and not to let themselves be intimidated by aspersions on their modesty. Her application of her sermon, therefore, is that women must act to save themselves (p. 168).

From practical application of the sermon, the form of *Woman* soars back to the sublime world of the spirit. In a peroration, Fuller outlines the major points of her argument and of her vision of the harmonious world that an ideal relationship between men and women would bring. Then, like a minister ending his sermon, she addresses a prayer to God—"Thou, Lord of Day!" After a cold winter, she prophesies a distant day of glory. With a final hortatory admonition to cherish hope and act, she concludes with poetry which echoes the Bible: "Persist to ask, and it will come." With an allusion to her epigraphs, she envisions—"So shalt thou see, what few have seen,/ The palace home of King and Queen"—and thus gives structural and thematic wholeness to her work.

The structure of *Woman* does seem to fit loosely the sermon-oration form. What tends to obscure its pattern is Fuller's use of writing techniques derived from transcendentalism. According to precepts generally accepted by the transcendentalists, a work of literature grows out of experience and hence is organic. As the Romantic Coleridge wrote: "The organic form is innate; it shapes, as it develops itself from within," or as Keats using a nature metaphor explained it grew as naturally as the leaves on a tree. Emerson later used this concept, saying a poem is "a thought so passionate and alive that like the spirit of a plant or an animal it has an architecture of its own." The basic assumption of transcendental art is of the "superiority of the spirit to the letter." "Art" as inspiration meant that the word became one with the thing. Ultimately, the "transcendental theory of art is a theory of knowledge and religion as well." Hence transcendental expression must coalesce, the seer and spectacle into one, an organic whole.[4] Margaret Fuller, the observer, unites the spectacle—her experience—with that of all women into the final fusion of *Woman in the Nineteenth Century*.

As early as 1826 Sampson Reed published his "Observations on the Growth of the Mind," setting forth transcendental literary theory. In this work, Reed writes: "Syllogistic reasoning is passing away," leaving nothing behind but a demonstration "of its own worthlessness." Both Julia Ward Howe and Arthur W. Brown point out that there is no systematic parallelism in *Woman*; however, Fuller does not intend that there should be.[5] Because she does not follow a rigidly organized pattern of syllogistic reasoning, she is merely demonstrating that she has accepted the transcendentalist aesthetic theory that as a member of the group she had helped to shape. The movement of her treatise is not parallel but soaring and circular. Its dominant mode of composition is an unfolding from the subconscious, in a form of spiraling thought patterns. One of her recurrent themes is an optimistic refrain that appears in a mood of confidence and then disappears in a burst of admonition, and later reappears in a form of wave-like undulation characteristic of transcendental writing. Moreover, the polarities of optimistic expectation (symbolized by the epigraph: "The Earth waits for her Queen") and impatient anger (symbolized by: "Frailty, thy name is Woman") have an ebb-and-flow rhythm to them. She may begin in a lull with a mundane matter such as the problem of a poor widow whose husband has died leaving no will and accelerate in intensity to the sublime "ravishing harmony of the spheres," or start at the crest of the wave as it flows back to the sea. From practical application of her sermon, the thought patterns of *Woman* soar back to the world of the spirit. Instead of syllogistic reasoning, order comes from the authority which the certitude of intuition brings.

A characteristic of transcendental literature, which *Woman* reflects, is subjectivity—the individual as the center of the world. At times this method suggests a free association of ideas—one authority requires that another be included; one mythological figure suggests another. Ultimately the thought patterns lead from the conscious to the subconscious mind, to the transcendental wellspring of truth, the divine intuition. Fuller uses her own experience as representative of the experience of all women, that indeed the lot of woman is sad, that all women need, and in fact, should aspire to the same self-culture and fulfillment that she herself had desired. She begins *Woman* by using the conventional "we" but she changes to "I" after only fifteen pages. Later she reverts back and forth between "we" and "I." She gives an account of her youthful education by her father under the guise of the persona, "Miranda," as an example of an independent girl who was respected for being self-reliant. Fuller tells this story by means of an imaginary conversation in which the "I" takes the role of the foil to Miranda's explanation of her youthful training in self-reliance, so unusual for a girl of that day (pp. 38–41). In her subjectivity there are times when she almost links herself with the queen that the earth awaits. If not the queen directly, she associates herself in her description of Miranda with the woman of genius, possessor of the magnetic electrical element (intuition), who has a contribution to make to the world—" a strong electric nature, which repelled those who did not belong to her, and attracted those who did" (p. 39). At another time in the discussion of woman's power of intuition, she writes: "Women who combine this organization with creative genius are very commonly unhappy at present. They see too much to act in conformity with those around them, and their quick impulses seem folly to those who do not discern the motives" (p. 103). By looking into her own soul, she saw reflected there the problems and the frustrated aspirations of other women: "but what concerns me now is, that my life be a beautiful, powerful, in a word, a complete life in its kind. Had I but one more moment to live I must wish the same" (p. 177). Starting from her own angle of vision, she unfolded her hopes to the world, and she concludes her treatise as a prophet:

> I stand in the sunny noon of life. Objects no longer glitter in the dews of morning, neither are yet softened by the shadows of evening. Every spot is seen, every chasm revealed. Climbing the dusty hill, some fair effigies that once stood for symbols of human destiny have been broken; those I still have with me show defects in this broad light. Yet enough is left, even by experience, to point distinctly to the glories of that destiny; faint, but not to be mistaken streaks of the future day. (p. 178)

Thus her subjectivity becomes universal as she links her own experience to that of the experience of all women, and prophesies that in the future life would be better for them.

The tone of *Woman* reinforces the idea that Fuller is writing a didactic work. At times the voice admonishes the audience to act; at other times it is declamatory, but its dominant tone is conversational. Since many people who knew Fuller said that her chief talent was as a speaker, it is not surprising that instead of syllogisms, many phrases contain the emotive power of a conversation of which Fuller would have been the star. Her writing technique includes both questions and answers in a debate form, but it also reveals the hallmark of the accomplished conversationalist—a flair for the dramatic. At best her conversational technique suggests breathless ejaculations rather than sentences. In a kind of accelerating excitement she uses the hortatory style: "Let us be wise, and not impede the soul. Let her work as she will. Let us have one creative energy, one incessant revelation. Let it take what form it will, and let us not bind it by the past to man or woman, black or white. Jove sprang from Rhea, Pallas from Jove. So let it be" (p. 117). Then her tone changes to one of intimacy. Her writing sounds as if she were talking to a small group and studying the reaction of her audience.

In the following passage, she reveals that she is a perceptive performer who could quickly adapt an argument to match the mood of her imaginary audience, by modifying, explaining, and then hammering home at the proper psychological moment the point she intended to make in the first place: "If it has been the tendency of these remarks to call Woman rather to the Minerva side,—if I, unlike the more generous writer, have spoken from society no less than the soul,—let it be pardoned! It is love that has caused this,—love for many incarcerated souls, that might be freed, could the idea of religious self-dependence be established in them, could the weakening habit of dependence on others be broken up" (p. 118). Her excuse for her stand is love. In effect, what she seems to be doing is to anticipate objections. Her most famous suggestion combines a speaking conversational style with her flair for dramatization: "But if you ask me what offices they may fill, I reply—any. I do not care what case you put; let them be sea-captains, if you will" (p. 174). Her frequent use of dashes suggest the pause used by the accomplished speaker.

There are other passages in *Woman* that combine the dramatic method of composition with an aphoristic technique, "Tremble not before the free man, but before the slave who has chains to break" (p. 63). "Whatever abuses are seen, the timid will suffer; the bold will protest" (p. 77). In her dramatization of her thesis, she uses an aphoristic method of attracting attention by reversing sex roles, beginning with her suggestion that the time has come for "Eurydice to call for an Orpheus, rather than Orpheus for Eurydice" (p. 23).[6] Again she writes: "Presently she [Nature] will make a female Newton, and a male Syren" (p. 116). "But Penelope is no more meant for a baker or weaver solely, than Ulysses for a cattle-herd" (p. 44). Later she makes a suggestion, not unlike semantic changes in vogue today, that the title given to a party abroad, "Los Exaltados," be changed to "Los Exaltados, Las Exaltadas" (p. 156). This stylistic device of sex role reversal is used to advocate one of her central ideas, that there is no "wholly masculine man, no purely feminine woman" (p. 116), which culminates in the "sea-captain" passage.

Whether that of a preacher, orator, or confidant, the tone of *Woman* expresses the spoken word. Hence it is no wonder that many of her images relate to sound. Perhaps here she echoes Shelley, whom she admired: "And, if men are deaf, the angels hear. But men cannot be deaf" (p. 26). She uses music as a means of expressing the divine: "Then their sweet singing shall not be from passionate impulse but the lyrical overflow of a diving rapture, and a new music shall be evolved from this many-chorded world" (p. 121). Or she sees woman as a bird with clipped wings that desires to fly and sing: "no need to clip the wings of any bird that wants to soar and sing" (p. 175). That she frequently preferred sound imagery to that of sight is again indicated by her final poem:

> For the Power to whom we bow
> Has given its pledge that, if not now,
> They of pure and steadfast mind,
> By faith exalted, truth refined,
> *Shall* hear all music loud and clear,
> Whose first notes they ventured here.   (pp. 178–79)

Another type of rhetorical device that Fuller often uses is imagery derived from organicism that implies movement, growth, expansion, or fruition. Her argument rests on the "law of growth." She uses phrases such as "ampler fruition," "Fruitful summer," or "plants of great vigor will always struggle into blossom." She likes movement related to the life force symbolized by the heart—"I must beat my own pulse true in the heart of the world; for *that* is virtue, excellence, health" (p. 178). Or the cycles of nature—the flowing of streams, the waxing moon, and noon-morning-dawn imagery—are favorites.

Yet despite her frequent choice of auditory and organic imagery, her work's salient characteristic is its great use of references to literature, history, religion, and mythology. These references are used primarily as an exemplar for her readers to emulate, as recognized authority to support her topic, or as allusions to Holy Writ.

Since the structure of *Women* is sermon-like, it is no surprise that Fuller uses Biblical allusions as the major support for her near rhapsodic religious vision of the great potentialities of men and women. She derives her thematic exhortation—"Be ye perfect"—from Matthew 5:48, from which she deletes "therefore." On occasion she quotes directly from the Bible: "This is the Law and the Prophets. Knock and it shall be opened; seek and ye shall find" (p. 19). Another way that she uses Biblical sources is to reshape a scriptural passage. Matthew 5:13 reads:

> Ye are the light of the world. A city that is set on a hill cannot be hid.
> Neither do men light a candle, and put it under a bushel, but on a candlestick;
> and it giveth light unto all that are in the house.

Fuller changes the meaning: "The candlestick set in a low place has given light as faithfully, where it was needed, as that upon the hill" (p. 17). In this passage she incorporates Biblical allusions and Christian concepts: "Love has already been expressed, that made all things new, that gave the worm its place and ministry as well as the eagle; a love to which it was alike to descend into the depths of hell, or to sit at the right hand of the Father" (p. 20). She uses a clause such as "a love that cannot be crucified," or commonly used Biblical terms as future Eden, Lamb, green pastures, Prince of Peace, and Holy Child to symbolize hope and renewal. From traditional Christian theology she derives a reference to the deadly sin of sloth. Phrases that connote Calvinism, such as "doomed in future stages of his own being to deadly penance," can be found in *Woman*. Elements of the Providential doctrine appear: "Yet, by men in this country, as by the Jews, when Moses was leading them to the promised land, everything has been done that inherited depravity could do, to hinder the promise of Heaven from its fulfillment" (p. 25).

She finds inspiration in the figure of the Madonna, whom she mentions several times: "No figure that has ever arisen to greet our eyes has been received with more fervent reverence then that of the Madonna" (p. 56). She refers to the Virgin Mary's powerful influence to reinforce her idea that women are born not only to nurture and alleviate the loneliness of men but also are possessors of immortal souls.

But it is to the Old Testament, to which she turns for the woman who would redeem mankind. Adam, she writes somewhat ironically, "is not ashamed to write that he could be drawn from heaven by one beneath him,—

one made, he says, from but a small part of himself" (p. 56). Adam "accuses" Woman—through her "Man was lost, so through Woman must Man be redeemed" by "Immortal Eve" (p. 156).

Fuller employs Biblical and religious allusions in the usual way, that is, to clarify meaning, and as the wellsprings of her treatise. In addition, she cites contemporary writers, feminists, socialists, and transcendentalists to buttress her argument that women can play a broader role in society. Her use of allusions to outstanding women from all recorded time, however, is complex. Despite the vast number she chose, their use is not an affectation but an intrinsic part of her way of thinking, and the rhetorical method she adopts in order to make her point. Her allusions not only clarify her meaning, but also serve as models of conduct to inspire or instruct women. These examples used as affirmations, are taken from poetry, such as Britomart; from history, such as Aspasia; from mythology, such as Isis and Iduna or Sita in the *Ramayana*; from folklore, such as Cinderella; or from more contemporary life, such as the Polish Countess Emily Plater. Instead of cataloguing lists of words as Emerson suggested and Whitman did, her technique is to catalogue women. She barely escapes creating an encyclopaedic effect, because she appears not to have wanted to leave anyone out. She admits she "may have been guilty of much repetition" (p. 168). It could be argued, that Fuller should have been more selective,[7] but on the other hand,[8] through sheer weight of numbers, the women cited from the ages become a catalogue that is an evocation, a challenge to men to remove "arbitrary barriers" through proof that women can succeed. Thus she explains her use of her numerous examples: "I have aimed to show that no age was left entirely without a witness of the equality of the sexes in function, duty, and hope" (p. 172). As Fuller says, the function of her examples is to serve as a witness. Her citation of women from history and women from fiction finally blends into women from mythology. Her search leads her to delve beyond patriarchal Hebrew-Christian society to the prototype mythic woman—an earth-mother who was recognized as a powerful figure, a priestess with powers of intuition who served as a medium to the divine. Fuller's figures become in themselves the incarnation of concepts. Cassandra and Iphigenia serve as witnesses to her argument that not only are women enslaved in western civilization, but that they are not allowed to use their special gifts of "electric or magnetic powers" with which they could be enriching the world. She cites the Seeress of Prevorst and "a friend" as examples of contemporary women whose gift of psychic power was wasted. Summarizing this concept, she asks: "Grant her, then, for a while, the armor and the javelin. Let her put from the press of other minds, and meditate in virgin loneliness. The same idea shall reappear in due time as Muse, or Ceres, the all-kindly, patient Earth-Spirit" (p. 121). It was then to classical mythology that Fuller turned in order to find models to illustrate her ideas of the possibilities of the feminine principle.

In her search for an ideal of feminine virtue, she considers many of Shakespeare's heroines. Of all of his heroines, she prefers his portrait of Cordelia whose virtue she greatly admires. She also discusses the quality of the marriages he portrays, and finds the marriage of Portia and Brutus superior to those in

*Cymbeline* and *Othello*. Nevertheless, she uses the relationship between Portia and Brutus as an example of the way women were neglected in ancient Rome. She thinks Shakespeare is a genius with greater poetic power than Ford and Massinger whom she also cites, but believes he does not portray as heroic women as they did, or as did Spenser:

> Shakespeare's range is also great; but he has left out the heroic characters, such as the Macaria of Greece, the Britomart of Spenser. Ford and Massinger have, in this respect, soared to a higher flight of feeling than he. It was the holy and heroic Woman they most love, and if they could not paint an Imogen, a Desdemona, a Rosalind, yet, in those of a stronger mould, they showed a higher ideal, though with so much less poetic power to embody it, than we see in Portia or Isabella. (pp. 66–7)

Her main interest in her evaluation of Shakespeare's female characters is whether or not their images are heroic.

It is not surprising, then, that of all of the authors in British literature, Fuller chooses Edmund Spenser as the one who gives the best portraits of female characters: "The range of female character in Spenser alone might content us for one period" (p. 66). Britomart is her choice for an ideal woman, not only because she is virtuous, but also because she is strong and independent. Mentioning Britomart several times, Fuller eventually begins to compare her with contemporary women. She believes Madame Roland was as valiant as Britomart, that Mary Wollstonecraft and George Sand would not have become outlaws had there been "as much room in the world for such, as in Spenser's poem for Britomart" (p. 75). When a character like Britomart satisfies her expectations, Fuller sounds as if she is speaking of a real person, and begins to mix fictional women with historical women.

According to Fuller, having a woman monarch (whatever Elizabeth's quality as a ruler) had its value in inspiring Spenser's creation of epic women characters: "Unlike as was the English queen to a fairy queen, we may yet conceive that it was the image of *a* queen before the poet's mind that called up this splendid court of women" (p. 66). If Queen Elizabeth helped to inspire Spenser, *any* strong woman inspired Fuller. She uses her outstanding women—dead or alive, literary or historical or mythical—to witness the capabilities within women when they rely on themselves. Figures as disparate as Lady Godiva, Cinderella, George Sand, Mrs. Hutchinson, Cassandra, Eve, Hagar, and Venus serve as testimonials in her sermons on the power within women.

Such plethora of examples represents a remarkable amount of scholarship, and Fuller delved into countless sources in her search for answers. Although written in nineteenth-century language with some words as outmoded as *purity* and *delicacy*, her work is surprisingly modern in its concepts. Her brilliant treatise presents and prefigures such "modern" ideas as the need for role models. Fuller searches beyond Judeo-Christian patriarchy for the feminine principle and the earth mother. She posits an androgenic quality in all people, a need to do away with sexual stereotyping. In essence, Fuller's creation becomes the archetype of Woman, of "The Woman in the Nineteenth Century," and of any woman who has aspired, who has wondered and been thwarted—but who has still refused to compromise. Fuller's archetypal woman knows that in any compromise she compromises not only herself, but everyone else as well; and that men who become exploiters, suffer and lose their humanity themselves.

As with all scholarly and complex literature, reading *Woman* calls for active participation from the reader. Also, since *Woman* is a highly suggestive work, the reader must be receptive to its message. Both Edgar Allan Poe and Henry David Thoreau have said that Fuller's writing and speaking voice were one. A careful scrutiny of *Woman* reveals the dynamism and insights which Fuller's conversation praised, and readers who are willing to become engaged in the profundity of her thought processes will be amply rewarded.

Essentially *Woman* is an affirmation, a witness to the possibilities within women and men who discover within themselves their spirituality and permit it to grow. It is a call for excellence. The first obstruction, the self, is on trial. Beginning with the individual, who must take responsibility for her or his own life, *Woman* envisions a world that would correspondingly reflect this changed self. Ultimately, *Woman* transcends the issue of woman's rights. Paradoxically, after preaching self-reliance for women, it becomes a philosophic message on the interdependence of all people.

*Woman in the Nineteenth Century*'s philosophic framework is predicated on universals: principles of right and wrong do indeed exist. Margaret Fuller was not ashamed to preach because she believed an individual could reshape her or his life—in fact, could approach perfection. And her sermon had effect: early feminists were inspired to action by *Woman in the Nineteenth Century*. Three years after its publication, they called the first Woman's Rights Convention in Seneca Falls, New York.

Notes

1. See Vivian C. Hopkins, "Margaret Fuller: Pioneer Women's Liberationist," *American Transcendental Quarterly*, No. 18 (Spring, 1973), 29–35. She writes: "Profusely illustrated and somewhat over-written, the book nevertheless has the effect of bringing the real closer to the ideal."

2. Thomas Wentworth Higginson, *Margaret Fuller Ossoli* (Boston: Houghton, Mifflin, 1884), p. 200.

3. Another factor to consider in this discussion is that she wrote *Summer on the Lakes* between the publication of the earlier and later work. It served as a journey of self-discovery for Fuller, a means of crystalizing her thinking. Observing Indian and pioneer women in the West enlarged Fuller's perspective as to the hardships women had to endure.

4. F. O. Matthiessen, *American Renaissance* (New York: Oxford University Press, 1941), pp. 24–31.

5. Julia Ward Howe, *Margaret Fuller* (Boston: Roberts, 1883), p. 151; Arthur W. Brown, *Margaret Fuller* (New York: Twayne, 1964), p. 127.

6. In a letter of 1841, Alexander H. Everett writes to Orestes Brownson and refers to her as "Eurydice Fuller" (George Willis Cooke, *An Historical and Biographical Introduction to THE DIAL* [Cleveland: Rowfant Club, 1902], I, 79).

7. "As Edmund Berry has pointed out, 'some of the extracts from her reading look suspiciously like padding . . .' Moreover, one detects a faint aroma of pedantry about these long extracts. Frequently they appear to be totally out of context and to be dragged in merely to illustrate Margaret's erudition. And not only is the style inflated, but it is annoyingly repetitious" (Francis

Edward Kearns, "Margaret Fuller's Social Criticism," Ph.D. dissertation, University of North Carolina, 1960, p. 148).

8. Poe points out the flaws in her style but concludes: "the style of Miss Fuller is one of the very best with which I am acquainted. In general effect, I know no style which surpasses it. It is singularly piquant, vivid, terse, bold, luminous; leaving details out of sight, it is everything a style need be" ("The Literati of New York City.—No. IV. Sarah Margaret Fuller," *Godey's Magazine*, 33 [August 1846], 73).

# INDEX

Abolitionism, 146–147, 247–254
Alcott, A. Bronson, viii, xiii, 110–111, 143, 166, 169, 173; *see also* Temple School
Alcott, Louisa May, 241n27
Aldrich, Thomas Bailey, 236
Allen, Joseph, 134
Allen, Margaret V., viii, xv, 257–263
Allen, Mary, 134–140 *passim*
Allston, Washington, 211, 213; *see also* "A Record of Impressions produced by the Exhibition of Mr. Allston's Pictures in the summer of 1839" (M. Fuller)
"American Literature" (M. Fuller), 42, 53–55, 62, 108, 216, 255
*American Notebooks* (N. Hawthorne), xiii, 126, 182
Anthony, Katherine, xi, 144, 147, 241n31
Arnim, Bettine von. *See* Bettina Brentano *and* Günderode (M. Fuller)
Arnold, Matthew, viii, 96
*Art, Literature, and the Drama* (M. Fuller), ix; review of, 107–108
Athenæum, review of *Papers on Literature and Art*, 57–61
*At Home and Abroad* (M. Fuller), ix

Bacon, Francis, 162
Baer, Helen G., xiii
Bailey, Philip James, 236; *see also* "Festus" (M. Fuller)
Balzac, Honoré de, 226
Bancroft, Elizabeth Davis (Mrs. George), 152, 158
Bancroft, George, 45, 179, 193
Barbour, Frances M., xvi
Barker, Anna. *See* Anna Barker Ward
Barlow, Almira, 153–154, 156
Barlow, David, 153–154
Barlow, Joel, 44
Barrett, Elizabeth. *See* Elizabeth Barrett Browning
Beck, Charles, 237n1
Beecher, Henry Ward, 236
Beethoven, Ludwig van, 212–213, 233–235, 244n64, 245n65

Bell, Margaret, xi
Berger, Patrick Frederick, xv
Berry, Edmund G., 249
"A Biographer's View of Margaret Fuller" (M. B. Stern), 264–267
Blackburn, Charles E., xiii
Blanchard, Paula, xi
Bliss, Alexander, 158
*The Blithedale Romance* (N. Hawthorne), xiii, 126–127, 132, 156, 185–187, 193–194, 206n24
Bode, Carl, xiii
Bolster, Arthur S., xiii
Boston Athenæum, 213
*Boston Daily Advertiser*, 179
Boston Public Library, ix–x, 216, 227n2, 252
Bowen, Francis, 256n3
Braun, Frederick Augustus, xv, 206n30, 207n42
Brentano, Bettina, 5, 93, 229, 233, 240n27; *see also Correspondence with a Child* (Goethe) *and Günderode* (M. Fuller)
Brickett, Elsie Furbush, xv
Briggs, Charles F., review of *Woman in the Nineteenth Century*, viii, 8–15
Brigham, Loriman S., xii
Brisbane, Albert, 241n27
*Broadway Journal*, review of *Woman in the Nineteenth Century*, 8–15
Brook Farm, xii, 118, 147, 151, 166, 173, 181, 185, 192, 245n72
Brooks, Charles Timothy, 204, 235, 237
Brooks, Van Wyck, 264–265
Brown, Arthur W., xi, 262, 265, 273
Brown, Charles Brockden, 44, 239n14
Browning, Elizabeth Barrett (Mrs. Robert), 56, 132, 225–226, 258–259; *see also* "Miss Barrett's Poems" (M. Fuller)
Browning, Robert, 56
Brownson, Orestes A., 150, 169, 268; review of *Summer on the Lakes*, viii, 5–6; review of *Woman in the Nineteenth Century*, viii, 19–25
*Brownson's Quarterly Review*, 169; review of *Summer on the Lakes*, 5–6;

281

*Brownson's Quarterly Review (cont'd)*
   review of *Woman in the Nineteenth Century*, 19–25
Brutus, 179
Bryant, William Cullen, 44–45
Buell, Lawrence, xv
Burley, Susan, 152
Burton, Roland Crozier, viii, xv, 209–215
Byron, George Gordon, Lord, 5, 51, 94, 223

Cabot, James Elliot, 142
Campbell, Thomas, 46–48
Cargill, Oscar, viii, xiii, 178–194
Carlyle, Thomas, xiii–xiv, 37, 56, 58, 71–72, 85–86, 98–99, 104, 164, 195–196, 204, 262–264
Carpenter, Richard V., xvi
Chamisso, Adelbert von, 206n30
Channing, Ellen Fuller, 118, 181–182
Channing, Mary, 152, 156
Channing, Walter, 181
Channing, William Ellery, 45, 150, 165, 180, 229
Channing, William Ellery II, xiii–xiv, 45, 54, 181–184, 192–193, 235
Channing, William Henry, 145, 235, 237n1, 248; helps edit *Memoirs of Margaret Fuller Ossoli*, viii, x, 68, 73, 84, 89, 94
Channing Family Papers, 265
Chapman, Maria Weston, 112–113, 252
"Chardon Street and Bible Conventions" (R. W. Emerson), 250
*Charleston Courier*, 14
*Charleston Mercury*, 14
Cheney, Ednah Dow Littlehale (Mrs. Seth), 158–159, 251
Cheney, Seth, 159
Chevigny, Bell Gale, xi
Child, Lydia Maria, xiii, 33, 152, 157, 159, 241n27, 245n65, 248; review of *Woman in the Nineteenth Century*, viii, 7
Chipperfield, Faith, xi
*Christian Examiner*, review of *Memoirs of Margaret Fuller Ossoli*, 68–69; review of *Papers on Literature and Art*, 62; review of *Summer on the Lakes*, 3–4; review of *Woman in the Nineteenth Century*, 26–27
*Christian World*, review of *Summer on the Lakes*, 2

Clarke, James Freeman, xiii–xiv, 99, 124, 195, 235, 237n1, 248, 259; helps edit *Memoirs of Margaret Fuller Ossoli*, viii, x, 68, 73, 94, 103, 105; review of *Summer on the Lakes*, viii, 2
Clarke, Sarah Freeman, 107–108, 124, 126, 153
Clough, Arthur Hugh, 96
Coleridge, Samuel Taylor, 4, 37, 51, 204, 238n4, 238n13, 240n23
*Concord Days* (A. B. Alcott), 110–111
Conrad, Susan P., xv
"A Conversation in Boston" (G. Hicks), 150–160
*Conversations with Goethe* (M. Fuller), ix, 32, 84, 169, 199–200, 220, 230, 232
Conway, Moncure Daniel, 236
Cooke, George Willis, xii–xiv
Cooper, James Fenimore, 42, 45
*Correspondence with a Child* (Goethe), 5, 231, 245n65
"Count Julian" (W. E. Channing II), 182
Crabbe, George, 49, 222
Cranch, Christopher Pearse, 235, 245n65, 245n72
Crowe, Charles R., xi, xiv
Curtis, George William, 124, 241n27

Dall, Caroline Healey, viii, xii, xiv, 124; review of Fuller's *Works*, 102–109
Dana, Richard Henry, Sr., 44
Dana, Richard Henry, Jr., 33
Dante, Alighieri, 176n47, 226
Davidson, Jane Ball, xiv
Davis, Elizabeth. *See* Elizabeth Davis Bancroft
Deiss, Joseph Jay, xi, 265
Detti, Emma, x
De Wette, Wilhelm M. L., 238n2
*Dial*, ix, xii, 32, 35–36, 40, 84, 146, 150–151, 153, 155, 157, 166, 169–171, 173, 180, 198, 240n22, 244n64; review of, 1
"A Dialogue. Poet. Critic." (M. Fuller), 59–61, 219, 226
Douglas, Ann, xv–xvi
Douglass, Frederick. *See* "Frederick Douglass" (M. Fuller)
Duberman, Martin, viii, xiv, 255–256
Durning, Russell, xiv–xv, 265–266
Dwight, John Sullivan, xiv, 204, 241n27, 244n64, 245n65, 245n72
Dwight, Timothy, 44

Eakin, Paul John, xiii
"Earth's Holocaust" (N. Hawthorne), 183
Ebbitt, Wilma R., viii, xv, 216–227
Eckermann, Johann Peter. *See Conversations with Goethe* (M. Fuller)
*Eclectic Review*, review of *Memoirs of Margaret Fuller Ossoli*, 81–88
Eichhorn, Johann Gottfried, 238n2
Eliot, George, 141
Eliot, Samuel A., x
*Elizabeth* [ship], 186, 193
Ellis, Charles Mayo, review of *Memoirs of Margaret Fuller Ossoli*, 68–69
Eloisa, 10–11
*Elsie Venner* (O. W. Holmes), xiii
Emerson, Lidian (Mrs. Ralph Waldo), 113, 152, 158, 163
Emerson, Mary Moody, 172
Emerson, Ralph Waldo, vii–viii, xii–xiii, 45, 52–54, 56, 88, 99, 101, 106, 113, 119, 124, 133, 141–142, 145, 147–148, 150, 161–177, 196, 233, 235, 240n25, 243n46, 245n67, 249, 258–261, 265; helps edit *Memoirs of Margaret Fuller Ossoli*, viii, x, 68, 73, 82, 84, 89–91, 94, 105, 258
"English Writers Little Known Here" (M. Fuller), 223–224
Eustis, Frederick, 156
Everett, Edward, 237n1

*A Fable for Critics* (J. R. Lowell), viii, xiv, 64–65, 156, 206n24, 255–256
Farrar, Eliza Rotch, 154, 157, 159–160
Farrar, John, 160
Fay, Josephine J., xv
*The Female Poets of America* (R. W. Griswold), 63
Fenelon, François, 100
"Festus" (M. Fuller), 219
Fichte, Johann Gottlieb, 100, 237n2, 239n14
Firkins, O. W., viii, 141–142
Flaxman, John, 213, 229
Follen, Karl, 237n1
Ford, John, 278
Fouqué, Friedrich H. K., 244n63
Fourier, Charles, 23, 270
Fourierism, 147
Fowler & Wells, 266
"Frederick Douglass" (M. Fuller), 146, 249

Freilgrath, Ferdinand, 204, 208n57, 244n63
"Friendship" (R. W. Emerson), xiii
Fuller, Arthur B., ix–x, 103
Fuller, Ellen. *See* Ellen Fuller Channing
Fuller, Frederick T., viii, 117–128
Fuller, Hiram, 137, 140n1
Fuller, Margaret. *See* Sarah Margaret Fuller
Fuller, Margaret Crane (Mrs. Timothy), 74–75
Fuller, Richard F., x–xi, 103
Fuller, Sarah Margaret: biography, xi–xiv, 32, 264–267, *and see Memoirs of Margaret Fuller Ossoli, passim*; Conversations, xii, 96, 100, 112–113, 147, 150–160, 169, 173, 180, 198, 238n13, 239n17, 240n21, 242n43, 243n46, 247–248, 251–252, 274, *and see Memoirs of Margaret Fuller Ossoli, passim*; fiction by, ix, 226; life in Italy, xi–xii, 115–116, 122–124, *and see Memoirs of Margaret Fuller Ossoli, passim*; life in Providence, xi–xii, 134–140, 167–168, *and see Memoirs of Margaret Fuller Ossoli, passim*; musical interests, xvi, 234–235, 244n64, *and see* "The Lives of the Great Composers" (M. Fuller); poetry, 63, 174
Fuller, Timothy, x, 32, 71, 74–75, 83, 93, 97, 103, 113, 122, 144, 248
Fuller Family Papers, xi

Gall, Franz Joseph, 23
Garrison, William Lloyd, 146, 250
"The Genesis, Form, Tone, and Rhetorical Devices of *Woman in the Nineteenth Century*" (M. Urbanski), 268–280
George, Sharon Kaye, xv
*German Culture in America* (H. Pochmann), 228–246
German literature, vii–viii, xiv–xv, 5, 13, 19, 23, 58, 93, 98, 148, 165, 194–208, 228–246
Gilman, William H., xiii
Gittleman, Edwin, xiv
*Godey's Magazine and Lady's Book*, 35
Godwin, William 239n14
Goethe, Johann Wolfgang von, xv, 98, 105, 108, 146, 148, 169, 195–204 *passim*, 206n30, 210–211, 226, 228–

Goethe (*continued*)
  233, 237n1, 239n16, 241n39, 242n43, 243n46, 243n52, 244n59, 245n65, 245n72, 266; *see also Correspondence with a Child* and *Tasso*
"Goethe" (M. Fuller), 200, 220–221, 232, 243n46
Gohdes, Clarence L. F., xii
Golemba, Henry Lawrence, xv
Gräter, Friedrich, 237n1
Graham, George R., 41
*Graham's Magazine*, review of *Papers on Literature and Art*, 53–55
"The Great Lawsuit" (M. Fuller), 268–270
Greeley, Horace, vii, xii, xiv, 124, 148, 197, 239n20
Green, Henry L., xi–xii
Green, William Batchelder, 155
Green Street School [Providence], xi–xii, 134–140, 165
Gregory, Lucy, xiv
Griswold, Rufus Wilmot, viii, 32–34, 36, 42, 63
*Günderode* (M. Fuller), ix, 84, 173, 199, 206n29, 230–231
Guerin, Kathleen Deidre, xvi

Haliburton, Mary Ann, 158
Hale, William Harlan, xiv
Halleck, Fitz-Greene, 48
Handel, Georg Frederic, 244n64
Harding, Walter, xi, xiii
Hare, Julius, 223–224
*Harriet Martineau's Autobiography*, 112–113, 251
Harring, Harro, 35
Harris, William T., xiii
Harvard University Library, ix–xi, 265
Hawthorne, Elizabeth, 126
Hawthorne, Julian, viii, 114–130 *passim*
Hawthorne, Louisa, 187, 193
Hawthorne, Nathaniel, vii–viii, xiii, 33, 44, 114–130 *passim*, 132, 156, 166, 178–191 *passim*
Hawthorne, Sophia Peabody (Mrs. Nathaniel), 114–130 *passim*, 150–151, 156, 160, 166, 179–182, 184–185, 193
Hawthorne, Una, 118
"Hawthorne and Margaret Fuller" (F. T. Fuller), 117–128
"Hawthorne in the Old Manse" (W. E. Channing II), 182

"Hawthorne, Margaret Fuller, and 'Nemesis,'" (A. Warren), 192–194
Haydn, Franz Joseph, 244n64
Hazlitt, William, 225
Hedge, Frederic Henry, 124, 146, 161, 166, 169–170, 173, 195–196, 237n1, 259; review of *Papers on Literature and Art*, 62
Hegel, Georg Wilhelm Friedrich, 239n14
Heine, Heinrich, 196, 237n1
Hennessy, Helen, xii
Henningsen, Charles F. See *The White Slave*
*Herald of Freedom*, review of *Woman in the Nineteenth Century*, 28–31
Heraud, John A., 169
Herbert, George, 41; *see also* "The Two Herberts" (M. Fuller)
Herbert, Lord Edward, 41; *see also* "The Two Herberts" (M. Fuller)
Herder, Johann Gottfried von, 238n2
"Heroism" (R. W. Emerson), 168
Herrnstadt, Richard L., xiii
Hicks, Granville, viii, xii, 150–160
Hicks, Thomas, portrait of Fuller, 109
Higginson, Thomas Wentworth, vii, x–xi, 181, 185, 192, 197, 199, 230, 237, 251, 256, 269
Hillard, George, 194
*Historical Pictures Retouched* (C. Dall), 102–109
"History of the Roman Revolution" (M. Fuller), 116, 257–258
Hoar, Elizabeth, 152, 158
Hoffman, Charles Fenno, 33
"Holiness" (R. W. Emerson), 168
Holmes, Oliver Wendell, 256; *see also Elsie Venner*
Hooper, Mrs. Anne Sturgis, 158
Hooper, Ellen Sturgis (Mrs. Robert), 157–158
Hooper, Robert, 158
Hooper, Samuel, 158
Hopkins, Vivian C., xv–xvi
Hosmer, William. See *Yonnondio*
Houghton Library. See Harvard University Library
Howard, Leon, xiv
Howe, Julia Ward, xi, 273
Hoyt, Edward A., xii
Hudspeth, Robert N., ix, xiv, 266
Huntington, Frederic Dan, review of

*Woman in the Nineteenth Century,* viii, 26–27

"In Defense of Brutus" (M. Fuller), 179, 193
Irving, Washington, 33, 42, 45
*Italian Notebooks* (N. Hawthorne), 187

Jackson, Charles T., 152
Jackson, Marianne, 152
Jacobi, Friedrich Heinrich, 237n2, 239n14
Jahn, Johann, 238n2
James, Henry, viii, xiii, xvi, 131–132, 194, 231, 257–258
*James Russell Lowell* (M. Duberman), 255–256
Johnson, Harriet Hall, viii, xii, 134–140
Johnson, Judith Kennedy, xiv
Jones, Alexander E., ix, 266
Judd, Sylvester. *See Margaret*

Kant, Immanuel, 228–229
"Karl Theodor Korner" (M. Fuller), 203
Kean family, 213
Kearns, Francis E., viii, xiii, xvi, 247–254
Kearns, Ursula, xiv
Kemble family, 213
Kerner, Justinus Andreas. *See "The Seeress of Prevorst"*
Kirby, Goergiana Bruce, xiv
Kirkland, Caroline, 33
Klopstock, Friedrich Gottlieb, 196, 237n1, 244n63
Knapp, Samuel L., 42
*Knickerbocker Magazine,* review of *Memoirs of Margaret Fuller Ossoli,* 97–101
Knortz, Karl, xii
Körner, Karl Theodor, 197, 202, 204, 206n30, 233, 237n1, 244n63

*Ladies' National Magazine,* review of *Woman in the Nineteenth Century,* viii, 16–18
Lamennais, Hugues Félicité Robert De, 204
Landor, Walter Savage, 4, 223–224, 270
Lane, Charles, review of *Woman in the Nineteenth Century,* viii, 28–31
Lee, Mrs. Eliza Buckminster, 241n27
Lee, Nathaniel, 50
Lee, Mrs. Thomas, 157

Lessing, Gotthold Ephraim, 196–197, 207n33, 210–211, 228, 237n1, 241n39
*Letters of James Freeman Clarke to Margaret Fuller,* x, 265
*The Liberty Bell,* 248
"The Life of Sir James Mackintosh" (M. Fuller), 41
*The Life of Margaret Fuller* (M. B. Stern), x–xi, 264–265
*Life Without and Life Within* (M. Fuller), ix
"The Literati of New York City.—No. IV. Sarah Margaret Fuller" (E. A. Poe), 35–39, 259
Littlehale, Ednah. *See* Ednah Dow Littlehale Cheney
"The Lives of the Great Composers" (M. Fuller), 41, 108
Locke, John, 228
Longfellow, Henry Wadsworth, 35, 44, 54, 224–225
Lord, William W., 36
Loring, Louisa (Mrs. Ellis Gray), 152, 159, 248
"Lost and Won" (M. Fuller), 266
*Love-Letters of Margaret Fuller,* x, 133
Lowell, James Russell, xiv, 54, 132, 156, 255–256
Lowell, Maria White (Mrs. James Russell), 156

McGill, Frederick T., Jr., xiv
McMaster, Helen Neill, xv
McNulty, John Bard, xiii
Macready, George, 213
Madison, Charles A., 252
*Main Currents in American Thought* (V. L. Parrington), 143–149
Mann, Mary Peabody (Mrs. Horace), 150, 156, 160
*The Marble Faun* (N. Hawthorne), 178–179, 193
*Margaret* (S. Judd), 45
*Margaret Fuller: American Romantic* (P. Miller), ix, 257, 265
"Margaret Fuller and Ralph Waldo Emerson" (H. Warfel), 161–177
"Margaret Fuller and the Abolition Movement" (F. E. Kearns), 247–254
"Margaret Fuller as Known by her Scholars" (H. H. Johnson), 134–140
*Margaret Fuller: Essays on American Life and Letters* (J. Myerson), ix

"Margaret Fuller, Rebel" (V. L. Parrington), 143–149
"Margaret Fuller—Transcendentalist Interpreter of German Literature" (Schultz), 195–208
"Margaret Fuller's Criticism of the Fine Arts" (Burton), 207–215
"Margaret Fuller's Ideas on Criticism" (W.R. Ebbitt), 216–227
Martin, John, 211
Martineau, Harriet, viii, 99, 112–113, 161–162, 250–252
Massachusetts Historical Society, 265
Massinger, Philip, 278
Mather, Cotton, 144
Mathews, Cornelius, 44–45, 52
Maxine, Mary, xvi
Mazzini, Giuseppi ("Joseph"), 72, 80, 86, 145, 148, 204
*Memoirs of Margaret Fuller Ossoli* (R. W. Emerson, W. H. Channing, J. F. Clarke), vii, x–xi, 112, 141; reviews of, viii, 68–95, 97–107, 118
"Memorial of Mrs. Margaret Fuller" (A. B. Fuller), 103
"Menzel's View of Goethe" (M. Fuller), 199–200, 220, 232
"Meta" (M. Fuller), 244n63
"Methodism at the Fountain" (M. Fuller), 41
Mexican War, 261
Meyer, Annie Nathan, 133
Michelangelo, 211, 213
Mickiewicz, Adam, x
Miller, Mary Ruth, xiv
Miller, Perry, ix, 257, 265
Milnes, Richard Monckton, 223–224
Milton, John, 204, 226; see also "The Prose Works of Milton" (M. Fuller)
"Miranda" (M. Fuller), 273–274
"Miranda" (J. R. Lowell's *A Fable for Critics*), 64–65, 206n24, 255–256
"Miss Barrett's Poems" (M. Fuller), 41, 225–226
"Miss Fuller and Reformers" (O. A. Brownson), 19–25
"Mr. Hawthorne and His Critics" (J. Hawthorne), 129–120
"Modern British Poets" (M. Fuller), 46–52, 62, 222–223
"Modern Drama" (M. Fuller), 41
Montégut, Émile, review of *Memoirs of Margaret Fuller Ossoli*, 92–95

Moore, Archy. *See The Slave*
Moore, Thomas, 48
*Mosses from an Old Manse* (N. Hawthorne), 183
Motley, John Lothrop, 236
Mott, Lucretia, 247
Mozart, Wolfgang Amadeus, 244n64
Mozier, Joseph, 115–116, 123
Munsterberg, Margaret, x, 252
Myerson, Joel, ix–xiv, xvi, 266

Nathan, James, x, 133, 145, 185–186, 240n20
*Nathaniel Hawthorne and His wife* (J. Hawthorne), 114–117
*National Magazine*, review of *Memoirs of Margaret Fuller Ossoli*, 92–95
*Nature* (R. W. Emerson), 163
Neal, John, 42
"Nemesis and Nathaniel Hawthorne" (O. Cargill), 178–194
Newcomb, Charles King, xiv
*New Monthly Magazine*, 169
*New Quarterly Review*, review of *Memoirs of Margaret Fuller Ossoli*, 70–72
*New York Illustrated Magazine of Literature and Art*, review of *Papers on Literature and Art*, 56
*New York Tribune*, ix, xv, 32, 35, 40, 63 84, 156, 170, 223, 257
Nichols, Arthur B., x
*North American Review*, review of Fuller's *Works*, 102–109
Norton, Charles Eliot, xiv, 256n3
Novalis, 94, 98, 197, 202–204, 206n19, 228–229, 233, 237n1, 244n56, 244n63

"Orphic Sayings" (A. B. Alcott), 23
Ossoli, Giovanni, 79, 86–87, 115–116, 122–124, 145, 178

Pabodie, William J., vii–viii, 1
*Papers on Literature and Art* (M. Fuller), 34, 63, 84; reviews of, viii, 40–62; see also Art, Literature, and the Drama
Parker, Lydia Cabot (Mrs. Theodore), 154–155
Parker, Theodore, 19, 99, 146, 148, 155, 166, 173, 180, 192, 195, 198–199, 206n25, 235, 248
Parrington, Vernon Louis, viii, xvi, 143–149

Peabody, Elizabeth Palmer, 150–151, 154, 159–160, 179–182, 185, 192, 231, 266
Peabody, Elizabeth Palmer (Mrs. Nathaniel), 115
Peabody, Mary. *See* Mary Peabody Mann
Peabody, Nathaniel, 150–151, 160
Peabody, Sophia. *See* Sophia Peabody Hawthorne
Penta, Constance, xii
Petrarch, 98
"Philip Van Artevelde" (M. Fuller), 36, 221–222
Phillips, Ann Terry, 159
Phillips, Wendell, 157, 159
Pippin, Kathryn A., xvi
Plater, Emily, 10
Plumbe daguerreotype of Fuller, 109
Pochmann, Henry A., viii, xiv, 228–246
Poe, Edgar Allan, viii, xiv, 33, 42, 175, 205n19, 240n20, 259-260, 263, 279, 280n8
"Poetry and Imagination" (R. W. Emerson), 261–263
"Poets of the People" (M. Fuller), 41
"The Poor Man—An Ideal Sketch" (M. Fuller), 213
Prescott, William Hickling, 44, 54
Prince, John Critchley, 212
Proclus, 266
"Prometheus" (Goethe), Fuller's translation of, xv
"The Prose Works of Milton" (M. Fuller), 41
*The Prose Writers of America* (R. W. Griswold), 32–34
*Prospective Review*, review of *Memoirs of Margaret Fuller Ossoli*, 73–80
*Providence Daily Journal*, review of *Dial*, 1
Prynne, Hester, xiii
"P.'s Correspondence" (N. Hawthorne), 183
Putnam, George, 43, 169
Putnam, Palmer, 242n42
Putnam, Mrs. Samuel, 157

Quayle, Maud Cannell, xiv
Quincy, Mrs., 152

Racine, Jean, 98
*Ralph Waldo Emerson* (O. W. Firkins), 141–142

Randall, Belinda, 158
Randel, William Peirce, xiii
Raphael, 211
"The Real Margaret Fuller," viii, 133
"A Record of Impressions produced by the Exhibition of Mr. Allston's Pictures in the summer of 1839" (M. Fuller), 41, 61
Reed, Sampson, 273
Retszch, Friedrich August Moritz, 213, 229
*Revue des Deux Mondes*, review of *Memoirs of Margaret Fuller Ossoli*, 92–95
Reynolds, Sir Joshua, 210–211
"The Rich Man—An Ideal Sketch" (M. Fuller), 213
Richter, Jean Paul Friedrich, 98, 100, 196–197, 202–204, 206n19, 233, 237n1, 239n16, 243n53
"Richter" (M. Fuller), 203
Rider, Daniel Edgar, xvi
Ripley, George, xiv, 99, 151, 166, 169, 173, 199
Ripley, Sarah Alden (Mrs. Samuel), 156–157
Ripley, Sophia (Mrs. George), 151,166
Roland, Madame, 11, 93, 278
"Romaic and Rhine Ballads" (M. Fuller), 203–204, 234
*The Romantic Revolution in America 1800–1860* (V. L. Parrington), 143–149
Rosenthal, Bernard, 265
Rossi, Alice S., 265
Rostenberg, Leona, x
Rousseau, Jean-Jacques, 72, 98, 148, 204, 210, 262
Rusk, Ralph L., x, xiii
Russell, George, 155
Russell, Mrs. George R., 154–155
Russell, Ida, 154

Saint-Simon, Claude Henri, Comte de, 23
Sanborn, Franklin Benjamin, xiii–xiv
Sand, George, xiv, 10, 71, 80, 93, 141, 145, 204, 226, 278
"Scenes and Thoughts in Europe" (M. Fuller), 34, 257
Schelling, Friedrich Wilhelm Joseph von, 229, 238n13
Schiller, Johann Christoph Friedrich von, 98, 197, 204, 206n30, 207n33,

Schiller *(continued)*
   210, 228, 230–233, 237n1, 241n39, 245n72
Schlegel, August Wilhelm von, 210, 231
Schoolcraft, Henry R., 33
Schultz, Arthur R., viii, xv, 195–208
Scott, Walter, 12, 49
Seatsfield, Charles. *See* Tokeah
"The Seeress of Prevorst" (J. Kerner), 4, 186, 203, 234, 244n57, 277
"Self-Reliance" (R. W. Emerson), 167
Shakespeare, William, 204, 277–278
Shaw, Anna, 154
Shaw, Francis George, 155
Shaw, Mrs. Francis George, 154–155
Shelley, Percy Bysshe, 17–18, 49–50, 100, 222–223
Shepard, Odell, xiii
Shore, Elizabeth F., xv
"A Short Essay on Critics" (M. Fuller), 209–210, 217–219
Siddons, Sarah, 14
Sigourney, Lydia H., 14, 236
Simms, William Gilmore, 33, 42
Simpson, Claude M., xiii
Slater, Joseph, xiii
*The Slave* (A. Moore), 250
"Slavery in Rome" (G. Bancroft), 179
Slochower, Harry, xv
Southey, Robert, 51
*Specimens of Foreign Standard Literature*, 198–199
Spenser, Edmund, 278
Spurzheim, Kaspar, 23
Staël, Madame de, 98, 228
Stanhope, Lady Hester Lucy, 93
Stanton, Elizabeth Cady, 247
Stern, Madeleine B., viii, x–xi, xiv, 264–267
Stetson, Caleb, review of *Summer on the Lakes*, viii, 3–4
Stoddard, Richard Henry, 236
Story, Emelyn (Mrs. William Wetmore), 122, 124
Story, William Wetmore, 256
Stowe, Harriet Beecher, 145
Strauss, David Friedrich, 236
"Studies for Two Heads. I." (J. R. Lowell), 66–67
Sturgis, Anne. *See* Anne Sturgis Hooper
Sturgis, Caroline. *See* Caroline Sturgis Tappan
Sturgis, Ellen. *See* Ellen Sturgis Hooper
Sturgis, William, 157

Sue, Eugéne, 226
*Summer on the Lakes* (M. Fuller), xvi, 32–33, 36, 63, 107, 186, 203, 234, 259, 266, 279n3; reviews of, viii, 1–6
Sumner, Charles, 249
Swedenborg, Emanuel, 262, 266
"Swedenborgianism" (M. Fuller), 41

Tappan, Caroline Sturgis, 158, 241n27, 265
Tappan, William, 158
Tappan Papers, 265
*Tasso* (Goethe), Fuller's translation of, ix, xv, 161, 164, 198–199, 230
Taylor, Bayard, 235
Taylor, Henry. *See* "Philip Van Artevelde" (M. Fuller)
Temple School, 150, 164–165, 179, 197–197, 205n14, 207n33, 229, 239n18, 239n20, 241n39, 243n53
"'This Impassioned Yankee': Margaret Fuller's Writing Revisited" (M. V. Allen), 257–263
Thom, William, 212, 224
Thomas, John Wesley, x, xii–xiv, 265
"Thomas Fuller and His Descendants" (A. B. Fuller), 103
Thoreau, Henry David, vii, xiii, 148, 166, 182, 250, 260–262, 279
Thurman, Kelly, xiii
Ticknor, George, 237n1
Tieck, Johann Ludwig, 197, 203, 231, 237n1, 239n16, 244n63
Tilton, Eleanor M., 265
"To a Priestess of the Temple not Made with Hands" (S. P. Hawthorne), 180
*Tokeah* (C. Seatsfield), 225
"To R. W. Emerson, July 1844" (M. Fuller), 174
"To S. C." (M. Fuller), 108
"The Tragedy of Witchcraft" (M. Fuller), 34, 44–45
Transcendental Club, 164, 166, 169, 173
Transcendentalism, viii, xiv, 5, 19, 23, 37, 50, 58–59, 68, 70, 97–99, 143, 146–148, 156, 192, 204, 207n42, 235–237, 243n46, 244n64, 245n71, 260, 268, 272–273
Tree, Maria, 213
Tuckerman, Sarah, 152
Tull, Martha Ann, xii
'The Two Herberts" (M. Fuller), 41, 108

Uhland, Johann Ludwig, 196, 203, 206n30, 237n1
"Unfaithful Friendship" (W. E. Channing II), 184
*United States Magazine and Democratic Review*, review of *Memoirs of Margaret Fuller Ossoli*, 89–91; review of *Papers on Literature and Art*, 40–52
Urbanski, Marie Olesen, viii, xiii, xvi, 268–280

Vainhagan, Rachel de, 93
Vance, William Silas, xiv
Vandenhoff, George, 213
"Vanity *versus* Philosophy. Margaret Fuller Ossoli," 89–91
Very, Jones, xiv
Vigny, Alfred Victor, Comte de, 226
Vogel, Stanley M., xv
Von Raumer, Frederick, 248–249

Wade, Mason, ix, xi, 257, 264–265
Wallace, Margaret, xv
Waller, Charles Thomas, xiii
Walton, Izaak, 41
Ward, Anna Barker (Mrs. Samuel Gray), 154
Ward, Samuel Gray, 155–156, 186
Warders, Donald F., xii
Ware, Harriet, 134
Warfel, Harry R., viii, xiii, 161–177
Warren, Austin, viii, xiii, 192–194
Watson, Anne, 253
Weiss, John, 235
Welter, Barbara, xvi

Wendell, Barrett, 144
Wesselhoeft, Minna, 206n29, 241n28
*Western Messenger*, ix
Westervelt, Henry, 186, 193
White, Maria. *See* Maria White Lowell
*The White Slave* (C. F. Henningsen), 225
*William Wetmore Story and His Friends* (H. James), 131–132
Willis, Nathaniel Parker, 33
Willisz, Leopold, x
Wesley, John. *See* "Methodism at the Fountain" (M. Fuller)
Wilson, David Alec, xiv
Wollstonecraft, Mary, 147, 278
*Woman in the Nineteenth Century* (M. Fuller), ix, xvi, 32, 35–36, 40, 46, 63, 84, 110–111, 147, 158, 201, 207n41, 208n56, 232–233, 248, 257, 265, 268–280; reviews of, viii, 7–31, 107, 114–115
*Woman in the Nineteenth Century, and Kindred Papers* (M. Fuller), ix
Wordsworth, William, 51, 72, 204, 222–223
*Works* [of Fuller, published by Brown, Taggard, and Chase], 230; review of 102–109
*Works* [of Fuller, published by the Tribune Association], 110
*The Writings of Margaret Fuller* (M. Wade), ix, 257, 265

*Yonnondio* (W. Hosmer), 225

'Zenobia." *See The Blithedale Romance*